I CHOSE CHINA

The Metamorphosis of a Country and a Man

I CHOSE CHINA

The Metamorphosis of a Country and a Man

SIDNEY SHAPIRO

HIPPOCRENE BOOKS, INC.

NEW YORK

Originally published in 1997 as *My China*
by New World Press, Beijing, China.

ISBN 0-7818-0759-X

For information, address:
HIPPOCRENE BOOKS, INC.
171 Madison Avenue
New York, NY 10016

Cataloging-in-Publication Data available from the Library of Congress

Printed in the United States of America.

Contents

Growing Up in Brooklyn, the Scholar
1915-1938

We lived on the third floor of a five-story walk-up in the Borough Park section of Brooklyn in 1919, from which I date my first fairly clear childhood recollections. The building, on the corner of 47th Street and 8th Avenue, had hot water and steam heat, but no elevator—no problem for an energetic four year old. Across the street stood a modest synagogue enclosed in an iron picket fence. I was thin and supple enough to be able to slip through the bars, accompanied by a couple of daring pals, and explore the yard and peek into the exotic interior of the temple until we were shooed out by the *shames* (caretaker).

That was just about the extent of my Jewish activities then, except for my admiration of a wonderful man, our neighbor on the second floor, Dr. George Bacarat. He came from Lyons, and had been the Jewish chaplain of the French scientific investigation of the ruins of Pompeii. He said that when they opened a vacuum-sealed room they found a family gathered around a table as if they had just sat down to dinner. The figures quickly crumbled to dust when exposed to the fresh air.

After coming to America, Dr. Bacarat was invited to serve as the Chief Rabbi of Memphis, Tennessee. There he married Minni, a sweet Jewish girl from Paterson, New Jersey, who acquired a molasses-thick southern drawl, still strong when they moved to Borough Park. They and my parents became good friends, and I felt free to wander into their apartment unannounced. On Sunday mornings I would stand beside Dr. Bacarat, holding on to the fringes of his prayer shawl as he intoned his devotions in a rich baritone. Our two families remained close for many years.

Dr. Bacarat was a learned man who could speak half a dozen languages and understand and read half a dozen more. He told us that "Shapiro" was of Aramaic origin. My father explained that our family name was actually Kaliarski, but that when his parents first came to New York, they lived on the top floor of a cold-water tenement. Unfortunately, nearly all the other occupants were Russian and Polish immigrants, and their names also ended in "ski." When the mailman delivered letters he would stand at the bottom of the stairwell, blow his whistle and shout out the names. By the time the sounds floated up to the top floor only the "ski" could be heard clearly.

My grandparents grew tired of running down six flights of stairs in vain, and then having to climb up again. They therefore changed Kaliarski to Shapiro, which they considered a "good American name." My father was always joking, so I'm inclined to take that tale with a grain of salt.

To me, my mother and father were Mom and Pop, the usual titles for parents in our neighborhood. Softly pretty Mom had a spine of iron. She was the tough integument which held us together. Mom had to be strong. While I managed to escape the influenza epidemic which killed half a million Americans at the end of World War I, I caught most of the prevalent childhood diseases and endured two mastoid operations before I was six. Mom nursed me at home and took me to doctors on subways and buses.

In addition she had to watch over my father's health. He had only recently finished convalescing from a bout of pulmonary tuberculosis, the "poor man's disease" so common among immigrant families raised on New York's Lower East Side. A struggling young lawyer, he traveled by subway to his office in lower Manhattan every day, and was in no condition to be of much help around the house by the time he returned.

I was born on December 23, 1915. Many years later, in 1960, when I was already a long-term resident of China, Mom sent me a touching letter on the occasion of my birthday. I treasure it because it graphically reflects her courage and love. It reads:

> Forty-five years ago this afternoon you first saw the light of a blizzard, for that is what happened that day. Should you have forgotten, the night before you were born the hospital on East Broadway, New York, telephoned me at midnight to come to the hospital at once. The Culver Line was running very infrequently from Boro Park in Brooklyn, where we lived.
>
> When Pop and I finally got to the Manhattan side of the old Brooklyn Bridge, we were told that the horse cars which ran along East Broadway had stopped at midnight. We had to walk in that snowstorm all the way to Montgomery Street and stop in doorways where I could catch my breath, and then continue on. (Cabs were not in use then.) We finally reached the hospital at 5 a.m., half dead, and found no beds available. I had to sit in the supply room with other women on stacks of linen until the following noon.
>
> You decided not to appear until 5 o'clock that afternoon. As I am telling you this, it all seems as though it happened just yesterday. You were a red lobster infant with long dark hair which eventually became very fair. You certainly were some baby!

Mom was not amused when her brother Jerry Samuelson came to visit her in the hospital. Jerry was then a student at Cornell, in the Ag School. He jestingly said I had the fine rosy skin of a pig, the bright eyes of a Rhesus monkey, and went on to note my resemblances to various other animals incarcerated in Cornell's experimental laboratory. Mom was so indignant she wouldn't speak to Jerry for the next ten years.

He became the most successful financially of her five brothers and sisters. Jerry later ran a feed and grain mill in Toms River, New Jersey, and employed younger brother Max. Jim was studying law. Vivacious Ida went through a series of romances before marrying and settling down. Anna, the eldest, a dark-haired beauty, acquired her second husband, Uncle Julius, a wealthy realtor who killed himself when he went bankrupt. The Samuelsons were a handsome, colorful bunch.

Pop had two brothers but no sister. Jack was a post office clerk, Sam was an optician. They were quiet, pleasant enough, but we didn't see them very much.

Knowledge of my antecedents went back only as far as my grandparents. Both paternal and maternal grandparents arrived in America in the 1890s with the tide of refugees from the pogroms of czarist Russia. My father's people were Ukrainians from Kiev, former serfs. Grandma Shapiro was a milkmaid as a girl. Grandpa Shapiro was a tailor. They lived above his shop on Brighton Beach Avenue, less than a mile from the Atlantic Ocean shore. Though rather short, Grandpa skillfully operated the big pressing machine. I liked watching the steam hissing out.

Grandma ran a "candy store" next door. When we visited, once or twice a month, she would make me the most delicious chocolate malteds, thick, with ice cream mixed in. She also baked superb potato knishes, not the light sissy stuff you get today, but bedded in chicken fat, and blended with grits and fried onions. They rested in your stomach with a cannon-ball solidity which provided nourishment for hours.

She never lost her peasant practicality, even after years in America. Their bathtub was used mainly as a pool for big black carp, waiting to fulfill their role as gefulte fish for Friday night dinners, or to be served cold to Sunday visitors like us. The meals would be topped off by home-brewed "vishnik" brandy. Grandma Shapiro's formula was to put cherries, water, and a little sugar in bottles which she corked tightly and buried in their small backyard. Two or three years later, she filled our glasses with—ambrosia.

The only impediment to our complete enjoyment was the elevated railway outside the windows of the second floor flat in which they lived. Each time the Brighton Express went roaring past it shook the walls and rattled the dishes. All conversation stopped for at least a minute. Perhaps nostalgia has smoothed out the rough inconvenience, but I sometimes think how useful it would be to have hurtling iron cars come clattering by to provide even a temporary respite to some of the turgid silly chatter to which we are often exposed!

Mom's parents were "Litvaks" from Vilna, Lithuania, typically fair, blond, northern Europeans. Grandpa was Samuel Samuelson, and this had been the name of his father, and his father before him—and of every first-born son back into family history—Samuel, son of Samuel. I was told that in Lithuania the Samuelsons had been "scholars," which meant, I suppose, that they had been literate and didn't have to work with their hands.

I was only mildly curious about my European background. What little I heard of it sounded fusty and dreary. My grandparents had left Russia voluntarily, gladly, and had come to America with a dream of a new and better life. To a certain extent they found it. From the lower East Side of New York City, where they and many of their fellow refugees had settled, they worked their way up into the ranks of the lower middle-class. It was the vibrant present that counted, not the past.

My own parents were not only disinterested in their European origins, they hated them, disowned them. They took pride in being Americans, they were fiercely patriotic, they laughed at neighbors who still hadn't shed their foreign ways, foreign accents.

It was this kind of environment in which I was raised. My pretty mother by the time I was born was able to give up her job as a typist and devote herself entirely to household chores, and to my father and to me. Pop had satisfied the ideal of his immigrant parents, who at great financial sacrifice had put him through college, and had become a "professional man," a lawyer. His dream was for a constantly rising income, a happy home, success in his career as an attorney, and to be a respected member of the community.

I was then only a child, and as yet had no lofty dreams. But as I grew older I could see that Pop's dream wasn't mine. While I agreed with his aims, and even embraced them, I sensed that for me they were not enough. There was a vague desire gnawing within me which I couldn't identify. I knew only that I wanted more, that I should do more. But what, and how, and where? I had to travel thousands of miles, all the way to China, to find the answer.

Our next step up the ladder was when I was six, and we moved to the upper floor of a two-family house on the corner of 12th Avenue and 54th Street, also in Borough Park. I started primary school, about four long blocks away, where I would walk every morning. I liked school, and developed confidence bordering on aggression.

In third grade I had a fight with another boy. We arranged to meet in a nearby lot after class, and flailed away with more enthusiasm than technique, cheered and jeered by an audience of surrounding schoolmates. I went proudly home that day sporting a black eye. Uncle Julius, who happened to be visiting, was delighted. He rushed to a neighborhood sporting goods store, bought an expensive punching bag set, and attached it to a beam in the basement. Though I never became, as he hoped, the National Flyweight Champion, I enjoyed pummeling the bag. My mother was less pleased, since the exercise sent shivers through our jerry-built house.

4

I learned to roller-skate, and played hockey on the smoothly paved street in games between pick-up teams. The skates, swung in the hand, were used as weapons in battles between the Jewish kids and raiding Italian boys from a neighborhood nearby. I stayed far away from those clashes. By a miracle no one was killed, but some of the wounds were severe.

In winter, when snow covered the sloping road, we went "belly-whopping" on our Flexible Flyers. Translation: we ran with our sleds, threw them down with ourselves flat on top, and steered the swift slide to the bottom of the hill. If we could persuade a friendly driver of a car, we tied our sleds in trains to the rear bumper of his car, and he pulled us around the block in what to us was breathless speed.

Mom gave up her struggle to maintain a kosher kitchen and keep the "milk" dishes separate from the "meat" dishes, but she did occasionally prepare delicious traditional North European Jewish treats. *Taiglach*—little dough balls baked together with honey, almonds and ginger; potato pancakes; and two kinds of borscht—the cabbage variety, with its meat and potatoes, which my Russian paternal ancestors preferred; or the beet type, served with sour cream and boiled potato, the favorite of my Litvak maternal grandparents. . . . We kept bottles of the beet soup in the ice box, along with bottles of pasturized milk, and I would drink glasses of one or the other to quench my thirst when hot and sweaty.

In line with further catering to my voracious boyhood appetite, I would walk a block to a store where for a nickel, five cents, you could buy half a chunk of Nestlé chocolate. A dime, ten cents, would give you half an Eskimo pie, chocolate covered ice cream. A slightly less honest method was applied on Saturday afternoons, when we had no school. With a few classmates I would repair to the local Loew's movie theater and watch the "double feature," to which a newsreel and a serial were usually added. We enjoyed feats of dangerous derring-do, and groaned loudly and hissed the scenes of tender kisses.

Attached to the back of each seat was a gadget which dispensed a roll of chocolate lozenges if you deposited a five-cent coin. The delicacy was called Eatmores, and it bore the slogan "the more you eat the more you want." We did full honor to this assertion, having found a way to induce the machine to disgorge the product without being fed the nickel.

My childhood literary tastes were not of the highest. I liked the series called "The Rover Boys." Though fond of Tom, "the fun-loving Rover," I found Dick, the priggish, virtuous hero, hard to take. An early favorite was the Dick Merriwell paperbacks, breathless adventure tales staged in a mainly city environment. Mom forbade me to read them because they were badly printed on terrible paper. I would read them anyhow in bed at night, using a flashlight under the blanket. This hastened my rapidly developing myopia. I had to keep getting thicker glasses. Mom burned the Merriwells whenever she got her hands on them.

5

From these I moved progressively to Tarzan and stories about Martian monsters, and other science fiction, and then graduated to Pinnocchio and the Three Musketeers.

A real estate boom was spreading in the mid-1920s. Pop's law practice flourished. Every small business man bought property, storefronts, second, and even third, mortgages. Pop was kept busy searching titles, drawing contracts, closing deals. At last we had some money to spend. We went on short vacations; I went to summer camps; Pop bought a Buick.

Having wheels broadened our horizons. Every few months we drove to Lakewood, New Jersey, and spent the weekend with Mom's parents. They lived in a small frame house on the outskirts of town. It had been farmland not many years before. There were trees all around, and the fragrance of honeysuckle was everywhere. Grandma Samuelson raised chickens in the backyard. About ten yards beyond the rear gate was a large pine forest which grew well in the sandy soil.

They spoke proudly of their neighbor John D. Rockefeller. He had a summer home in the former Gould estate, in a pine forest a mile or so down the road. J.D. carried a bag full of dimes which he handed out to little boys he met in the course of his walks in public. In the Depression years he cut these down to a nickel.

We would start for home early on Sunday afternoon. It was a five-hour drive back to Brooklyn. We had to go through the Amboys to reach the ferry that would take us across Staten Island Bay. Sometimes we would see fiery crosses burning in the dark on nearby hillsides. The Ku Klux Klan were active in violence in the North, South and Midwestern United States, on the heels of a general rise of vicious repression against Blacks.

I must have been a precocious little devil. Pop thought it necessary to speak to me seriously a month or so after we got home. We had called on a client of his in Lakewood who ran a hotel and had a nine-year-old daughter. I was six or seven. She was a cute blond child. The client phoned Pop to say I had written her a romantic letter which had considerably upset her, and would Pop please ask me to quit. Though I generously consented, I have never lost my appreciation of beauty.

By the time I was 12, in 1927, we reached new heights in our imagined affluence. The market continued in its upward trend. You could buy stock on very small margins. Optimism reigned supreme. We reached the Nirvana of middle class Brooklyn Jews—a home of our own in Flatbush.

Covered by a Spanish-style tile roof and a substantial mortgage, it was a wooden frame one-family house, two stories high, resting on a large terraced plot. We had gardens front and back, and a two-car garage in the rear. All the houses on the block were of the same general structure, but were painted in different colors. A few were of brick, rather than wood. Newly planted saplings lined the unpaved road.

We were on East 28th Street between Avenues P and Q. The street ended at Q also called Quentin Road. Beyond that was open farmland. In the middle of a huge field was a complex of houses occupied by a large Italian family, reputed to be prosperous bootleggers. I was taken there by a classmate, one of the many progeny. They were warm, effusive people, and plied me with rich food of delightful aroma.

The fathers of some of my best friends were bootleggers, or high-jackers, or members of the other dangerous professions engendered by the Volstead amendment, better known as Prohibition. Genuine liquors were very costly. A boy on our block took me to his family's finished basement and showed me a closet full of expensive choice imports. His Italian father, a successful bootlegger, could scarcely speak English. His younger, smartly dressed, mother drove an open red roadster.

Arty Coogan and I were classmates in James Madison High School. His family were strictly moral Irish Catholics. The sons were forbidden to say a single improper word in their mother's presence. They had to go to early mass every Sunday morning, no matter until what hour they were up drinking and carousing the night before. Arty's dad and his associates earned their living persuading gentlemen driving trucks laden with bottles of booze smuggled in from ships off the shores of Long Island Sound to transfer their cargoes to them. Weight was added to their arguments by the presence of heavy wrenches and long crowbars in their hands. Usually a few taps were all that was necessary. Not too many persons were killed. Slaughter was more widespread in the shoot-outs between rival gangs fighting for control of the illegal liquor business.

Also lethal was bathtub gin, as the home-made brew concocted by unskillful and unscrupulous amateurs was generally called. It was popular, cheap, and readily available. It caused the untimely end of thousands. Many of those who survived went blind.

I don't mean to give the impression that the Italians and the Irish had a monopoly on rum-running. Jewish gangs, originating in the Brownsville section of Brooklyn and spreading city-wide, were among the most powerful of the racketeers in liquor, prostitution, gambling, and extortion. On the flip side, Jews produced significant figures in science, business, entertainment, and the arts. That both of these aspects should exist side by side was not surprising in a city hosting the world's largest Jewish population.

Sometimes the two overlapped. My father was offered a hefty annual retainer to act as lawyer for the Shirtmakers Association of Allentown, Pennsylvania. He was tempted until he learned they were controlled by Mr. Joe Adonis and his friends. When the Mob moved in, Pop moved out. His honesty and decency always prevented my father from becoming a financial success.

He had vision and courage. Pop organized a theatrical company to stage a revival of an old musical comedy, *No, No, Nannette*. He promoted a soccer match between leading European players in Madison Square Garden using a slightly deflated ball. Somehow none of his ventures panned out. Yet while his failures temporarily depressed him, like that slightly deflated ball he kept bouncing back.

Our street was new and raw, equipped with only temporary sewers. Heavy rains would flood our finished basement and create a small lake stretching from the top of the terraces on our side of the road to terraces on the other. We slim young lads were able to heighten the Venetian atmosphere by poling around on two-by-six boards, singing like happy gondoliers.

That part of Flatbush, though it would be considered virtually contemporary from the Chinese historical viewpoint, was very old by American standards. Running through the center was the old Kings Highway, built in the days of George III. A number of Dutch buildings predated British rule. One carefully preserved farmhouse, only five blocks from where we lived, retained its large yard, a stable, and big trees. A Hessian mercenary soldier had carved his initials on one of the farmhouse windowsills.

The primary school I attended, P.S. 197, fronted on Kings Highway, and was brand new. It had just been built the year before, replacing the old dilapidated structure known as the "chicken coop." We boys would try to get there early each morning to have time for a quick game of handball against the high building wall before the daily music appreciation session began.

This meant lining up in the big paved yard according to class, and listening to "good" classical music played on a large phonograph. The purpose was to teach us to recognize and name the selection and the composer. We were aided in attaining that purpose by memorizing suitable catchy jingles. Gems like "This is the symphony which Schubert wrote and never finished," and "Listen to the Song of Spring by Mendelssohn" certainly did the trick. To this day I never fail to identify such pieces every time I hear them. Unfortunately, those cursed jingles immediately squawk in my ears and utterly ruin my appreciation. Nevertheless, despite the advanced pedagogical methods of P.S. 197, I did develop a real love of music over the years.

Our classes in "civics" seemed to tell me little about national and world affairs, either because I was apathetic or because they were poorly taught. One of the few events I remember was the solo flight across the Atlantic in the "Spirit of St. Louis" by Charles Lindbergh in 1927. The whole school turned out and stood on the side of Kings Highway to watch "Lucky Lindy" and his cavalcade roll by. He was the picture of a true hero, young and handsome. He married a fine girl, the daughter of an American ambassador. They suffered a shocking tragedy five years later when their infant son was kidnaped and murdered.

I graduated from P.S. 197 in the summer of 1928, and started in James Madison High School that autumn. It was much bigger than my primary school, and seemed

8

to me to be filled with brilliant and beautiful students. Perhaps this was because I was just entering my teens, but Madison did indeed produce many attractive graduates.

I would be 13 in December, which meant I had to begin preparing for my Bar Mitzvah. Jewish boys, on becoming adolescents, go through a confirmation ceremony in a synagogue. They thank their parents for having raised them, and vow to fulfill the duties of adulthood. First, they must read some verses from the Torah, in Hebrew.

In order to learn enough of the ancient script to be able to read without stumbling, I joined a special training class with a few other boys the same age, and struggled to recognize and recite some of the words. It was difficult, but rather fascinating, trying to make sense of a language people had been conversing in thousands of years before. Our tutor was our old friend and learned scholar, Dr. George Bacarat.

He was excellent in inculcating us with a smattering of Hebrew. But it was much harder for him to explain the passages of Genesis, which he used as a text. I thought the story of creation unscientific and unconvincing. And God was, in turn, quick to anger, petulant, remorseless, and very prejudiced. It was nice for us Jews to be His favorite people, but what about the other races and religions? Didn't they count at all? God seemed to be sadly lacking in godlike qualities.

Obviously the Babylonian scribes who edited the first edition of the Old Testament imbued the Almighty with their very limited personal understanding and semi-civilized emotions. Although according to the Bible "God created man in His own image," it might be more accurate to say "the Babylonian scribes created God in *their* own image." They were absolutely the worst PR men God could have had. If He exists, I am sure he is infinitely superior to the faulted figure they depicted.

I was told I gave a creditable performance my day on the synagogue platform, closing with the traditional words, "Today I am a man." Hair on my upper lip, a breaking voice, and interesting developments in the pubic region had already led me to that suspicion. This confirmed it, but it also marked my last encounter with the religion of my ancestors. For my parents' sake I would go to synagogue services on high holidays, and I retained my love for Jewish jokes, culture, and culinary fare. But I became and remained a strictly secular Jew.

Mom and Pop gave a catered meal in a restaurant in my honor. Guests bestowed not only the usual cufflinks and fountain pens but also, no doubt stirred by the prevailing bullish optimism on Wall Street, stocks and bonds. In those days every small shopkeeper and pushcart peddler was speculating in the market.

In 1929, the bubble burst, stocks plummeted. According to a joke then going the rounds, whenever a well-dressed, harried-looking man requested a room on an upper floor of a hotel, he was asked: "For sleeping or for jumping?" Although I had the doubtful distinction of being wiped out in the market at the age of 14, I never was driven to such desperate measures. While I had not heard of Marx or Lenin at that time, I wouldn't be surprised if that blow had not planted the first seed of doubt in my faith in the capitalist system.

Our family fortunes began moving down again, and I supplemented our income slightly by taking a paper route for the Brooklyn Eagle, which I delivered daily, flinging copies from my bicycle to customers' doorsteps. I also sold fresh eggs shipped to me by Uncle Jerry from his farm in New Jersey. Not terribly profitable, but it did give a taste of the joys of free enterprise.

The Depression didn't depress us much. Our house was large and roomy. We had a full-time maid. There were many immigrant European girls looking for work. I watered the lawn and cut the grass and polished the car, and walked the dog. We had a large affectionate German shepherd named Blitz who would put his front paws on the shoulders of my kid sister, Ruthy, who was then about eight, and knock her to the ground. It was no use explaining he only wanted to lick her face. We had to change him for a female Boston Bull, ugly as sin and soft as butter. Ruthy adored her. I called her Roxanne, after the heroine of surpassing beauty in *Cyrano de Bergerac*, a then very popular and excessively romantic play.

Our neighbors came from a variety of ethnic origins, typical of most Brooklyn communities. Next door, to our right, was an Italian mortician, whose business office was on Manhattan's East Side. He spoke New Yorkese with an Irish accent, no doubt due to the influence of his Irish wife, a large bosomy woman. She was devoutly Catholic. In times of heavy thunderstorms she would get under the bed with all three kids and intone urgent prayers to "the Father, the Son, and the Holy Ghost!" I had a fight with their boy Vinnie the day we arrived, by way of my initiation ceremony as the new kid on the block, and we were fast friends ever after.

Further down the block was an Irish husband-Jewish wife couple, who were always in debt, but who produced three daughters of surpassing beauty. Ruthy and one of them were classmates.

We also had the head of a well-known electrical appliance company, the owner of a laundry servicing babies' nappies, the busy bootlegger, and a leading fashion tailor of men's clothing. His two sons were my special buddies. With them, and a few others, I engaged in running and standing broad-jump contests, "stoop ball," and punch-ball and touch-football games. These were sports ingeniously created by city youngsters to be played on the streets in front of their homes. You had to stop once in a while to let automobiles go by. There were not so many of them in those days.

Besides displaying a certain skill on the school's gymnasium equipment, I joined the track team and ran in indoor meets in both the 440 m and 880 m events. My energy was endless. I would get up at five in the morning, put on my heavy socks and sneakers, and trot through the sleeping streets with two or three other pals. My parents thought I was crazy, but they didn't try to stop me.

Horseback riding was another of my passions. I had learned to ride in summer camp, where we knew nothing of breeches and boots. Our apparel was shorts and moccasins. In the city I usually cantered, more properly attired, through Prospect Park on Sunday mornings. My rented steed cost only a dollar an hour. That much I could afford. In later life I rode whenever I could, on a diversity of mounts in a variety of places.

Music obsessed me. I listened to the weekly broadcasts of symphony and opera with absolute concentration, refusing to be distracted by even a single question. I was a trial to my parents and to kid sister Ruthy, who always had a great number of questions to ask. I disdained Verdi's *Aida* with its live elephants and the booming cannon of Tschaikovsky's *1812 Overture*, embracing composers like Ravel and César Franck.

But it was Bach who held me in his thrall. One night at an open-air performance under the stars in Lewissohn Stadium in upper Manhattan I sat listening entranced to Bach's *Art of the Fugue*, played by two pianos. It is a scientific exposition on the fugue, starting with a simple theme for one hand, and working its way up with deliberate and almost mathematical clarity through more and more convolutions to a soaring reverse triple-mirror fugue. I ended emotionally exhausted and dripping wet.

Not all music had that effect on me, nor was I snobbishly limited in my tastes. I swooned with the rest of the audience watching Alfred Lunt and Lynn Fontanne doing their love-struck waltz in Franz Lehar's *Merry Widow*, enjoyed the *Mikado*, Fats Waller, and Eddie Duchin. Films I liked ranged from *All Quiet on the Western Front*, *Dr. Jekyll and Mr. Hyde*, *The Private life of Henry VIII*, to *It Happened One Night*, and the Marx Brothers.

I loved Groucho, Chico and Harpo long before I ever heard of Karl. Groucho, explaining to Chico the provisions of commercial contract, says: "This is the sanity clause." To which Chico replies: "You can't fool me, boss. There ain't no Sanity Claus."

And Jimmy Duranty breathes deeply through his king-size proboscis like a kind of poor-man's Thoreau and murmurs: "I want to commute with nature."

And Dorothy Parker quips: "If all the girls at the Yale prom were laid end to end I wouldn't be a bit surprised."

And the Mrs. Malapropish Gracie Allen solemnly affirms: "Time wounds all heels. . . ."

The humor of comedians like these convulsed me. On the surface zany, it held an underlying vein of satire. Jokes and puns and wisecracks are an integral part of the American psyche. When friends got together, or someone made a speech, or

11

even gave a formal address, it was virtually compulsory to start off with a joke, hopefully a new one. Many of them were wry, and self-spoofing, particularly among ethnics, the Jews included, though it was considered bad form for members of one ethnic circle to make cracks about members of another. Every time I visit the States today I find jocularity still a prevailing social attribute.

Back in the 1930s I was impressed by two young men in the house opposite us on East 28th Street. They went to Dartmouth, and used to complain about the size of the allowance their father gave them. But then they stopped, and the story they told explained why. One of their classmates was a son of John D. Rockefeller. Most of the other boys drove to school in their own roadsters. Young Rockefeller had to come by trolley. His father only gave him ten dollars a week. Parents on our block widely circulated this parable among their sons as an object lesson on how to become a millionaire, and stay that way.

Girls didn't appeal to me much, at first. I was at a party one evening contentedly munching a hot dog with mustard and relish. We were playing "spin the bottle." I was irritated when the bottle pointed at me and a shapely girl came over and enthusiastically kissed me with my mouth full of delicatessen.

But before long I developed a friendlier attitude toward the fair sex. Girls who went to Madison High and lived in the neighborhood took turns in inviting a dozen or so young couples to their homes on Saturday nights. They served snacks and soft drinks and rolled up the parlor rug. We danced to the broadcast music of the top bands—Benny Goodman, Ben Bernie, Guy Lombardo. . . . The lights were turned lower after our hostess's parents went to bed. There was a certain amount of necking and petting, but it rarely went beyond that.

Many of us had a regular girlfriend, or boyfriend, as the case might be. Not to have one was damaging to prestige. We went out on "dates" together, to dances, to parties, to the movies. My girl was a lovely child named Beatrice. We met when we were about 16. She was merry and very pretty, with long dark hair and a fair creamy complexion. We got on wonderfully, and laughed a lot, and talked for hours about serious philosophic questions neither of us really understood.

Beatrice was soft and gentle and kindly, everything I was not. After high school we drifted apart. I had no money and was just starting on a quest for a career. Inevitably she married young. We ran into each other once or twice, but our meetings were awkward and painful. I don't know what she saw in the teenage me, but I'm grateful for the few years we had together.

I was learning about personal problems and, perhaps for that reason, becoming more sensitively aware of the dangers growing all around us. In Spain, Franco and his fascist hordes were taking over, aided by Germany and Italy, honing their tanks and bombers for the coming World War II. Washington declared "neutrality," leaving the democrats to their fate. The Nazis were rounding up German Jews, robbing them of their possessions, and sending them to concentration camps.

Unemployment in America was high. Men peddled apples and pencils on the streets. Homeless people lived in shanties they built on empty lots in communities called "Hoovervilles." There were strikes and hunger marches. Fanatics boldly preached racial and religious hatred in radio broadcasts and on street corners. A gang of home-grown Nazis set up a platform in front of the East 17th Street library in Flatbush and harangued the crowd, trying to convince them that the butchers in Germany were being maligned. Several off-duty Jewish policemen in plainclothes who happened to be in the audience beat them to a pulp.

My father enjoyed a brief flurry representing clients going down in bankruptcy and mortgage foreclosures. Pop said there was a place for me in his office if I later decided to join him. After graduating from high school, I had put in two years in a pre-law course at New York's St. John's University, mainly because I didn't see prospects of any other jobs available.

I didn't want to be a lawyer particularly. The stories I heard Pop and his colleagues tell about the vagaries of their profession held little interest for me. The problem was I didn't know what I wanted. I was healthy, fairly good-looking, and reasonably intelligent. I played ball with the boys, romanced the girls, and had no difficulty in getting good marks in school. Mothers held me up as an example for their sons to emulate, causing private snickers among my cronies. Things came to me easily, too easily, fanning the normal jauntiness of youth. Surely I could do better than sit in an office drawing legal documents?

But do what? Jobs were scarce and I had no special skills. It was at this point that I did something I was to do again when confronted by an apparently insoluble dilemma—I pulled up stakes and struck out for parts unknown.

While in college I had become friends with a classmate named Jerry Mann. Jerry also lived in Flatbush, and we knew people in common. What brought us together, however, was long and frequent theoretical discussions. Jerry was more advanced than I and had a rudimentary concept of class struggle. I saw it simplistically as a division between the haves and the have-nots, with the first callously trampling upon the second. My aim was to get into a position where no one could ever trample on me. I had no higher aspirations than that.

Jerry, whose father was a cutter in the garment industry, was also restless. A tough boy, handy with his fists, he too was seeking a more exciting future than life as a lawyer. We decided to go out together and look, to hitchhike across the country to California during our summer vacation. A friend of my father had settled there and ran the Twin Palms Hotel in Palm Springs. On a visit to New York some years previous he had told us glowing tales of the wonders of the West. Jerry and I agreed if we could find better prospects there, we'd take them. If not, we'd return to law school in New York.

13

We set out one morning in late June, 1934, heading for Chicago. We arrived four days later, feeling ourselves already veterans in thumbing rides and cadging meals. Pop had bet me ten dollars we never would get there. I immediately sent him a telegram asking him to promptly remit. He did.

In Chicago a world's fair was welcoming visitors from all over the globe. On a strict economy budget, we paid our calls after closing time, skirting around the fence where it met Lake Michigan, having persuaded the Georgia red-neck guard that we weren't out to steal anything, only to sleep on the long well-upholstered seats of the excursion buses parked inside. When the fair opened the next morning we breakfasted at the stand of the Beechnut Company, whose slogan was "Every-thing Beechnut but the coffee." We lined up a dozen times for each sample— tomato juice, toast, and bacon and eggs—until our appetites were sated.

We spent the next two days leisurely viewing the Fair, while dining on food samples and sleeping in the exhibition buses at night. What I remember most clearly was a pretty Swiss girl and the huge Saint Bernard dog she was looking after.

Reaching our next stop, Kansas City, proved more difficult. People seemed reluctant to give us rides. Was it our sprouting beards, and increasingly unkempt appearance? We found the reason one afternoon when, after waiting hours in vain for a lift on the outskirts of a city, we glanced at the telephone pole behind us. On it was a poster that said: WANTED, DEAD OR ALIVE, JOHN DILLINGER . . . and went on to give a detailed description of the killer for whom the police of seven states were searching. No wonder drivers wouldn't pick up rough-looking charac-ters like us!

Because we had only about 50 dollars apiece we tried to stretch our money by sleeping out in the open, weather permitting, and working for our meals. The well-to-do home owners and restaurant keepers we approached usually made us sweat for our suppers. But in the run-down dwellings our host or hostess would say: "Eat first, then we'll see." And when we'd finished, they'd laugh and say: "Forget it. We don't have enough to do around here ourselves."

Early one day we were on US Route One, the Lincoln Highway, an asphalt swath over rolling plains which should have been covered with corn and wheat. Instead, only parched shoots stubbled the cracked soil, for there was a terrible drought. Homesteads were few and far between.

We walked to the nearest one and found the family at breakfast. The mother, the father, and three or four hulking sons or farm hands. We explained who we were, that we had come from the East and were heading for California.

"Have you written to your family lately?" the woman asked.

We admitted that we hadn't. She fetched paper and envelopes and pens and said: "Before you do anything else, sit right down and write letters to your mothers."

We meekly obeyed. She gave us stamps and made us seal the envelopes.

"Now," she said, "you look as if you could stand a bite to eat." She motioned to the table. "Sit here."

She plied us with eggs, milk, butter, homemade bread, and deep-dish cherry pie. The father told us they were having a disastrous year, even as they kept urging us to eat more. We were young and healthy and hungry, but we couldn't match their appetites.

"What's the matter with you boys. Are you sick?" the mother asked concernedly.

So strong is the tradition of American farm hospitality that it never occurred to them to let their hardships influence the treatment of guests at their table. We were very moved. Throughout our trip we found that generally the poorer the people we approached were, the more generously they behaved.

It was a refreshing change from what we big city dwellers were accustomed to. You could live next door to people for years in an apartment house and rarely exchange a word. It wasn't that they were misanthropic or cold. They were just so tied up with tensions and worries that they had to form a callus over their natural warmth and emotions, and wrap themselves in a protective isolation.

The rural areas were different. When you walked down the street in a village or small town, people would smile and say "Howdy." Or if you bought something in a store the girl at the counter would say, "Have a nice day." It was only common courtesy, but it made you feel good when you were a stranger, hundreds of miles from home.

As the population thinned out, and with Dillinger on the loose, rides grew scarcer. At last we reached Kansas City, then a poverty-stricken town half in

Kansas and half in Missouri. We decided to do what we had sworn to our families we never would—take to the freights.

We had thought originally that freight trains were used mainly by hoboes. We met some of them, as well as gamblers, pimps, hustlers and con men. But in the summer of 1934, a year of depression and drought, the bulk of the non-paying passengers on the railroads of America were migratory workers, men traveling from state to state harvesting crops, picking fruit.

Freight trains hauled few empty cars, and they rode on top, sitting on the long three-plank catwalk, as the cars jerked and rattled along. Sometimes they were so thick up there it was hard to find a place to sit down. These men were very different from the slovenly hoboes. Lean but dignified, most of them carried a small cheap suitcase. On arriving at their destination they would remove their smoke-grimed traveling clothes, wash thoroughly at a water pump, shave, change into clean overalls, put their dirty garments in the case, and set out for their prospective jobs.

There was an art to catching freights. While most towns didn't care, some were patrolled by nasty "yard bulls" who enjoyed arresting and beating up men they caught. You had to hide in the outskirts, and wait until the freight was already picking up speed, then race for it, grab a ladder and climb to the top. It had to be a ladder at the front of the car. If you lost your footing the momentum would swing you against the side, and your feet could still regain the rungs. If you were on the short rear ladder you might be flung between your car and the one behind it. Many a man lost a limb, or perhaps his life, that way.

You also had to avoid open gondola cars carrying pipes or other loose freight. These could shift suddenly with the rocking of the train and cause serious injuries if you were resting on them.

We picked up all this lore from the more experienced travelers, and were wise enough to take it seriously.

Jerry and I hit a "red ball" express freight out of Kansas City that brought us into Colorado Springs almost non-stop. We traveled right through the night and were riding, as usual, on top. We could rest only by turns in short naps, the one staying awake holding on to the sleeper with one hand and clutching the catwalk with the other. Not especially relaxing for either of us.

A nice elderly couple gave us food and shelter for tending the garden and doing odd jobs around the house. They were from another state, but had been living in Colorado Springs for years "because of our lungs." The high altitude and the pure fresh air attracted TB convalescents from many parts of the country.

The famous Pike's Peak, a few miles from town, has an elevation of 14,000 feet. I insanely set out one night to climb it. It was too hot in summer to attempt it during the day. I went alone, since Jerry's shoes had worn through completely and he was housebound while having them repaired. Mercifully, I was dissuaded at the foot of the slope by local villagers. The temperature dropped precipitously after midnight, they said. A party of mountaineers only the week before had been compelled to stop and build fires every half hour to keep from freezing to death. I was wearing only a thin sweater.

A dozen square miles of the lower slope were preserved as a unique natural park called the Garden of the Gods. I walked half a mile and came upon a livery stable, awakened a sleeping groom, who grumbled about the lateness of the hour, and hired a horse. There was no moon, but the stars, thickly studding the blue-black sky, faintly lighted the road as I slowly wound my way amid grotesquely shaped boulders which appeared to have been cast there by some giant hand. Little animals stopped and stared at me with gleaming eyes before scurrying across the path and vanishing into the darkness.

Rocking slowly in the deep, high-pommeled Western saddle, I felt soothed and sleepy, timeless, absolutely alone. Suddenly an open car filled with singing and shouting revelers roared up the road, and the spell was broken. I trotted the horse back to the stable and returned to Colorado Springs, still bemused by that moment of rare enchantment.

When Jerry and I resumed our journey a few days later we once again were guests of the Atcheson, Topeka and Sante Fe Railway. We rolled uneventfully southwest and climbed down to rest and stretch our legs in a small town named Belen, New Mexico. We felt sufficient veterans by then to be sure of catching another freight to continue our trip when we were ready to go.

The majority of the population were Mexicans, descendants of the original inhabitants of the area when it was part of old Mexico in the 19th century. They were poor and lived in adobe shacks, but there was enough prosperity among the white sheep and cattle raisers to support a general store in the middle of town. It was there we rambled, and were greeted by Mr. Sam Kaufman, owner of the emporium. He was more than cordial on learning that we were member of the same tribe, and insisted on taking us to his home to dinner. Mrs. Kaufman whipped up a divine traditional meal, starting with fragrant chicken soup and ending with a fruit compote dessert.

We were pleased of course by this hospitality, but a little puzzled by its effusiveness. Sam explained. Their only son was something of a playboy, spoiled by his over-indulgent upbringing. He had no interest in the business, and was off in their large Packard, touring California. Sam needed help from people he could trust to help him run the general store. Would one, or both of us, like the job? He would pay well.

He was very kind, we said, but no, thank you. We had to get to California where, we thought privately, a much more exciting, if less financially rewarding, career was awaiting us.

It was one of those moments when you have to make a choice that can determine your entire future. I seem to have gone through a whole series of them. Often my decision was almost haphazard, not at all well thought-out. Yet either thanks to a benevolent fate, or just dumb luck, my choices eventually brought me to China, something I would never have dreamed of at the time.

We resumed our freight car travel. The line ran south. Another few hundred miles, and it would turn west, cross Arizona, and take us to California.

But for me that was not to be. Familiar with the rules by then, we hopped off as the train slowed to enter San Antonio, Texas. We walked through to the southern outskirts and waited for it to emerge. About two hours later, after having discharged some cargo and taken on other, and adding more coal and water, the freight came puffing along the gleaming rails.

Jerry and I dashed out of our hiding place and ran alongside. He grasped a front ladder of a car and climbed to the top. I stumbled over a switch, breaking my stride.

17

I recovered only in time to grab the rear ladder of the car behind. The train gathered speed. We were rolling across flat desert land. Rear ladders had only four rungs on the lower ends of the cars, where brakemen could signal with swinging lanterns. These ladders were not intended to reach any higher. I couldn't climb up and I couldn't get off.

The sun burned my neck and my bare arms and legs. I was wearing a short-sleeved polo shirt and a heavy knapsack. The straps were eating into my shoulders with each jolt of the train. I could feel the grip of my hands on the rough rungs of the iron ladder weakening. "Well, good-bye Shapiro," I said to myself. "This is a stupid way to die."

Fortunately, the rails rose in a slight incline, and the train slowed. I made up my mind and jumped in the same forward direction the train was going, a method we had been taught for leaving moving freights by fellow travelers. I landed on my feet, and then my hands, lacerating them on the roadbed cinders. The train quickly picked up speed again. Jerry was waving his arms and yelling something I couldn't hear. With bleeding palms, I watched the freight roll across the desert and disappear into the distance.

Now what? There was no chance I could find Jerry again, even assuming I could catch another freight, a feat I was not likely to accomplish with my torn hands. I wasn't very keen on going to California any more. By the time I walked for two hours under the burning desert sun and got back to San Antonio, Texas, I was sure about it. With my remaining few dollars I bought a ticket on a Greyhound bus. Two days later I was back in Brooklyn.

Jerry went on and reached the West Coast. A few weeks later, he also returned, and entered St. John's Law School with me. This brings me a little ahead of my story. We graduated and passed the Bar together but he was so enchanted with California that he persuaded his whole family to move to Los Angeles. They went into business for themselves, and Jerry became one of the wealthiest manufacturers of women's sportswear.

Would I also be in California, sitting beside my swimming pool, if I hadn't missed that freight? Perhaps. But I certainly wouldn't have had a more exciting, fulfilling life than the one I have found here in China. Of that I am positive!

Lawyer, Soldier, and the Trip to China
1939-1947

St. John's Law School was in an office building in the Borough Hall section of Brooklyn, near the courts and the county departments, and not far from the old Brooklyn Bridge spanning the East River into Manhattan. We had no campus and no ivy-covered walls, only a Bursar's Office which insisted on prompt payments, in advance. There was good reason for their caution. America was in a deep depression in the mid-1930s, and money was hard to come by.

I was able to afford tuition because of a job in the Payroll Division of the US Treasury Department in Manhattan which Pop obtained for me through a connection with the Democratic Party organization. They owed him a favor for something or other. To provide sustenance for part of the millions of unemployed, the federal government created a Works Project Administration (WPA) embracing a wide variety of activities from construction to the arts. The US Treasury Department, swamped by the vast numbers of new employees, had to set up special Payroll Divisions in various parts of the country. I was in the New York City branch.

We worked from nine in the morning to five in the afternoon, with a long break for lunch. At the end of the day I took the subway to Boro Hall, reading my homework assignment from the text in one hand while holding on to a strap with the other. The flickering light and the swaying car did not improve my concentration. Then a quick bite at the counter of a cafeteria, and classes from seven to nine, five nights a week.

It was an education in law on the run, catch as catch can. But it aroused and held my interest. Torts, contracts, justice, freedom, pleading and practice, rules of evidence . . . I hadn't expected to like law, but I was intrigued. There were parameters, but no absolutes. You had freedom of speech, but you couldn't get up in a crowded theater and yell "Fire!" . . . A person might tell you his word was his bond, but it was better to get it down in writing, especially if you were dealing with a relative or a close friend. . . .

Direct evidence was ideal in either civil or criminal proceedings, but most of the time you had to rely on the circumstantial. One case report engraved itself on the students' memory. A wife suing her husband for divorce put a detective on the stand who testified he followed the man and another woman to a hotel, saw them go upstairs and waited two hours in the lobby until they returned. New York at that

19

time required evidence of adultery. The husband's lawyer contended there was no proof of any wrong-doing. The judge held against the husband. Under such circumstances, said the judge, "It is presumed he saith not a paternoster." These little touches showed me the law could not only be human, but amusing as well.

I was impressed by the apparent stress on the sanctity of the individual, of his or her person, of his or her property. Violations by others required that they pay compensation. Or be imprisoned, or executed—if their crimes were committed with deliberate intent. Later I was to learn that in many countries, such as China, while heed is paid to the rights of the individual, first priority is given to society as a whole. It is true that in America we talk of measuring rights by "the greatest good to the greatest number," but in many instances it gives way to the "greatest good to those with the greatest number of megabucks."

Admittedly, in China today, coinciding with an increase of freedom and democracy, that tendency is also beginning to rear its ugly head. The difference is that here the greatest good is starting to go not so much to those with the greatest number of megabucks but to those with the greatest power. This is even more convenient, since with sufficient power you can get all the money you want, and many things money can't buy. Of course, new social blemishes in China cannot be blamed on freedom and democracy, any more than these can be held responsible for America's rising crime rate. The underlying cause in both countries lies in the failure to implement genuine freedom and democracy, based on genuine equality.

Anatole France, talking about the problem in his own country, said sarcastically, "We have complete freedom and democracy here in France. All persons, be they rich or poor, are absolutely forbidden to sleep under bridges or steal a loaf of bread!"

Lip service and good laws on the statute books are not enough. When I became a lawyer I found that all too often it was a case of "money talks." Laws, as a practical matter, in criminal cases were interpreted differently for the rich than for the poor. In civil litigation you could seldom win against a big corporation—they could appeal you to death. Theory and practice were not the same.

Jerry Mann had come back from California, warm in its praise. He joined me in St. John's, and for three years we studied law and crammed for the New York State Bar examination together. Jerry spent many hours at our house. One of his fondest memories was of Mom's breaded veal cutlets. He mentioned them to me nostalgically when I saw him in California for the last time 50 years later.

In New York young lawyers had to serve a year's apprenticeship before they could practice on their own. I found employment with Moses & Singer, so-called Wall Street lawyers because they represented the same kind of corporate clients. Their offices were actually on Pine Street.

20

The going rate for law clerks at that time was 12 dollars a week. But since the prestige of working for a large famous firm was so high, I was persuaded to take eight. The partners were mainly descendants of German Jews who had come to America in the mid-19th century. Some had become quite rich, and looked down on the poor Russian Jewish immigrants who arrived 50 years later.

There were others with considerably less money who also harbored delusions of grandeur. Young men in the Wall Street area—lesser employees of the New York Stock Exchange and various brokerage houses—barely had two nickels to rub together. We would lunch at a small Chock Full of Nuts store where you could buy a sandwich called a nutted cheeseburger for ten cents, or two for a quarter if you were really hungry, including a five-cent glass of grape juice.

We would then stroll over to the Sub-Treasury Building, and sit on the steps and absorb the sunshine, which didn't cost anything. The young men, in imitation of the senior members of their firms, wore rolled-brim homburg hats, suits of charcoal gray, well-laundered shirts, and conservative ties. They were all cheap imitations, costing a fraction of the price of the vestments of their idols. Poorly paid, they were generally laid off shortly before Christmas, on the pretext that the market was slack, so that their employers wouldn't have to pay them the regular Yuletide bonus.

Yet these gentlemen starvelings were positive they would rise if only they convinced their bosses of their devotion and dedication. When an organizer got up on the pedestal of the statue of George Washington gracing the steps of the Sub-Treasury building and urged them to join a white collar union of office workers they hooted with superior laughter.

I was forming a different picture of the world. It seemed to me that neither diligence nor ability was any guarantee of success. I knew many people who worked hard all their lives, and were quite skilled at their jobs, who eked out only a marginal existence.

On the other hand, most of the senior partners in my Wall Street law firm were men of not more than average intelligence. One or two were rather stupid. Yet they drew enormous salaries. Why? They had wealthy clients. What mattered was not so much what you knew but who you knew. You could always hire bright young people to do the actual spade work.

Corporate law seemed so dull, and people involved in high finance so narrow. Whatever was good for business they approved. Among the clients of Moses & Singer were companies with large turpentine pine forests in the South, and Goldman Sachs, the firm whose decline in share prices had caused my bar mitzvah stock market losses. I didn't hold that against their attorneys, but what did sour my attitude was the lawyers' appraisal of Adolf Hitler. One afternoon several of them sat around our luxurious office listening to Hitler ranting over the radio. They understood German.

"A great man. What a pity he has that one little flaw about the Jews," they said, shaking their heads regretfully. "He's been excellent for the German economy."

Hobnobbing with gentry such as these for the rest of my life seemed too great a price to pay for possible affluence and ease. I transferred my allegiance to another firm of attorneys.

Not so lofty, they also pulled down big fees, though more rarely, for they were negligence lawyers, better known as "ambulance chasers." They didn't do the chasing in person, but had a network of interns, policemen, safety inspectors, etc., who informed them promptly of promising accidents, while praising them highly to the victim until they could rush down and get his or her signature on a retainer. They worked on a contingency basis—one third of whatever damages they recovered for the client. Occasionally they demanded and got half.

Witnesses would be found, or created, and taught how to render the most damning kind of evidence against the defendant. Doctors or psychiatrists were hired for the medical testimony. Proceedings were instituted and preliminary hearings held. Then negotiations would start with the insurance company. Only insured defendants were sued, since few individuals had sufficient assets to pay the judgments my law firm hoped to get. And since they had a record of whopping recoveries in court, the insurance company adjusters were usually willing to reach a pre-trial settlement. Sometimes they were encouraged by means of a kickback.

If the case actually went to trial, every gun in the arsenal was brought to bear. There was jubilation in the office whenever we won a big one, and open crowing over the smart tricks we had got away with.

I couldn't see this type of practice as my career. The firm was forever skating on the edge of, if not a breach of the law, then a violation of the legal profession's canon of ethics. Indeed, shortly after I left them, the senior partner was suspended from practice for several years for professional misconduct.

In spite of myself, therefore, I ended up doing what I had been trying to avoid—joining my father. Why had I been so set against it? Pop was a good lawyer, had a varied practice, was located right off Times Square, and was unencumbered with partners. He had told me a number of times I would be welcome. I suppose I had wanted to show that, after all the years of being raised and supported by my parents, I could make it on my own.

My political ideas were only beginning to form. I was a registered Democrat and voted in every election, but I could see many flaws in American democracy. We had a few criminal cases, which brought me into the precinct police stations, the courts and the prisons. There was a marked difference between the treatment of those with money and connections and those without. I discovered, too, that people were maimed or killed in accidents because landlords had been able to bribe municipal inspectors to overlook fire and safety hazards on their premises. I learned that the two major political parties which dominated the elections were machine-run, patronage-dispensing organizations, more responsive to their backers and free-spending lobbyists than to the interests of the average citizen.

On the international scene the US government was permitting the sale of scrap steel from the dismantled New York City elevated railways to the Japanese who were slaughtering Chinese civilians, steel which would later return in the form of bullets in American boys' bodies.

I was generally dissatisfied with my own life, with what was happening in America and the world. Reading more, discussing more, I was groping for understanding, but not attaining much. Young Communists I knew tried to proselytize me, but I couldn't go along with their views. They uncritically praised anything that came out of the Soviet Union, including obviously poor films and inferior fiction. I had nothing against the Russians, in fact I admired the way they were building up their country, and the position they took against the Nazis. What I couldn't stomach was the mindless weather-vane spinning of the American Communist Party with every change in the Soviet wind.

Neither the Democrat nor Communist type of party appealed to me, yet I wasn't content to sit around bemoaning the state of affairs. I wanted to do something positive. An opportunity presented itself when I was approached by young composers and sketch writers who needed an organization where their creations could be made available to nightclubs, unions, and resort hotels patronized by liberal audiences. These places were enlightened politically, but they were a little careless about paying for the theatrical material they used. Their agents could come to my office and look at a variety of the latest songs and scripts, without having to seek them out all over the city. I saw to it that the artists were properly compensated.

I established the Review Writers Guild in 1941. The Japanese attacked Pearl Harbor in December of the same year, and America entered the war. It was a time of national unity, with nearly everyone rallying behind the war effort. Our Guild members wrote songs and skits in its support, as well as strongly pro-labor, pro-union pieces. It was even possible to say a kind word about Our Soviet Ally. With the rabid Right temporarily muted, there was a flowering of progressive creations. A few of our writers became famous. Alex North composed music for motion pictures. Earl Robinson's "Ballad for Americans" is an established classic. Lewis Allan's "Strange Fruit" is perhaps the most harrowing indictment in song against lynching of Blacks in the southern part of the United States.

Though stimulating, my piloting of the Review Writers Guild was not very remunerative. I took only a small fraction of our members' modest royalties. Our law firm earned its fees in more mundane ways—deeds and contracts, wills and probates, commercial suits.

Once in awhile we had something more glamorous. In the early 1940s we had two mental incompetency proceedings in a row. Our clients in both instances were elderly men who had inherited life estates from extremely wealthy families which had founded railroads and the like. Because they were merry old rogues with expensive tastes in women and wine, the alarmed holders of the residual estates—the relatives who would get what was left when the old boys died—brought actions to have them committed to mental institutions as manic depressives, and to have themselves appointed guardians of their financial affairs. Manic depression is difficult to prove. We all have our ups and downs, it's mainly a question of degree. We managed to win both cases.

While they were pending, as the junior partner I had to do the running around, interviewing our clients, their mistresses and hangers-on, getting their signatures on legal documents. They were a peculiar lot, and I thought privately the aged lotharios were indeed abnormal. They made me uncomfortable, and I always came away feeling pretty depressive myself.

Nor was I exactly enchanted by the other people who sought our services. Just as doctors' patients are usually ill, people don't come to lawyers unless they are involved in some sort of unpleasantness. They want to draw a will in anticipation of death, or squabble over somebody else's will; they are being sued, or they want to sue, or keep out of jail. In nearly every instance they are motivated by fear or greed. I knew that was the way of the world, or at least of as much of the world as I had encountered thus far. But I hated to think I would be spending my days in so grubby an atmosphere.

And so, when my draft number came up in November of 1941, I went off to the army with almost a feeling of relief. I was glad to get away from a dull life and uninspiring career. The army would be new, different, I thought, it held promise of adventure. Besides, I hated the enemy for what they were doing in Europe and Asia, and considered them savage maniacs who had to be stopped. I was quite willing to help in stopping them.

In 1942 I was one of a crew of nursemaids to a 40 mm Bofors anti-aircraft gun. We were stationed in a swamp euphemistically known as the Jersey Meadows, guarding Westinghouse and General Electric plants from attack by German bombers. There were about a dozen of us. We served in shifts—two hours on, four hours off, around the clock—waiting for the raids which fortunately, considering our marksmanship, never came.

It was a lonely job, though we had plenty of rats and mosquitoes for company. When the smog wasn't too thick we could see the Empire State Building and the New York City skyline. Another reminder of civilization was the fragrance of Secaucus, famed pig slaughtering center, wafted to us by the breeze.

Then word spread that an Army Specialized Training Program had been established. Men were being sent to the universities, in uniform, to learn foreign languages for possible future assignment abroad.

Why not? I had had a few years of French in high school and college. At least it would get me out of the swamp. I applied.

Some weeks later, I was sent to the City College of New York, ASTP testing center for the military region.

I had forgotten a lot of French but managed to scrape through the written exams. Next came the oral. Although my spoken French was virtually nonexistent, the army grapevine was operating with its usual efficiency, and we all were quickly informed of the pattern of the oral tests. "What is your name? Where are you from? What did you do before the war? . . ." I prepared accordingly.

My inquisitor was an old City College professor, a Frenchman. Sure enough, he put forward the routine questions. I answered promptly, my Flatbush accent impeccable.

"What were you before the war?"

"*Un avocat, monsieur.*"

He looked at me with interest. Switching to English, he confided that he too had been *un avocat* when a young man in France. And what was my opinion of *Les Frères Coudert*?

Coudert Brothers, one of the largest French law firms in New York? I had just been reading about them in the papers. They were the attorneys for the Vichy French government. Though somewhat mystified I gave a candid reply.

"I think they stink."

The old professor's eyes glowed. It turned out that we were in complete accord. Not for political reasons, but because *Les Frères Coudert* had ruined his life. Forty years ago he had landed in New York with dreams of making his fortune as a French lawyer and applied to Coudert Brothers for a job. Since he was not from a rich family and couldn't introduce any wealthy clients, they turned him down. He was forced to take up the teaching of French, a profession he loathed. For this, Coudert Brothers were responsible. He had never forgiven them.

I had uttered sentiments very close to his heart. He smiled amiably, and passed me on the oral.

There seemed to be little doubt I would be studying French again. I relaxed.

But it wasn't that simple. The last step was to appear before a board of army brass and college professors who formally announced your assignment. A few days later, spruce and polished, I stood smartly at attention before the board.

They informed me I had passed the French tests. However, they said, they had more French students than they could use. How would I like to study Chinese?

I stood goggle-eyed, gaping like a cod.

A major oiled in smoothly with a soft sell.

"You live in New York City, don't you?"

"Yes sir."

"Well, while I'm not at liberty to divulge the details, I can tell you this—the college we are planning to send you to is in New York State. You'll be able to get home fairly often."

I still hesitated. Chinese? I'd never given it a thought. The major threw in the clincher.

"It's co-ed."

"I'll take it!"

Little did I know, as they say in the Victorian novels, that the decision I had made was the first step along the road to a life and a career in China.

The next week I was at Cornell, ensconced in a fraternity house with a well-equipped bar in the basement. It was wartime, and most of the male student population was gone. The girls seemed glad to see us. Their sororities took turns inviting us to tea dances. Cornell, amid wooded hills "high above Cayuga's waters," is beautiful. Quite a change from the "Jersey Meadows."

Our language course was intensive. We were divided into groups of five or six, conducted by Chinese tutors who drilled us daily on conversational material written in the English alphabet, with diacritical marks indicating the tones. We picked it up fairly quickly, though the tones were a headache. Every Chinese syllable has one of four possible inflections. You may, for example, get a positive "down" tone at the end of a question, or a rising inquisitive one at the end of a statement. This is in the standard "Mandarin," spoken by the majority of the population. Cantonese, the dialect of most of the Chinese who emigrated to the United States, is favored with eight tones!

Nine months later we finished our course. We could carry on simple conversations, read a bit, write practically not at all. We were given a few orientation lectures by businessmen and missionaries who had spent many years in China, as well as by famous warlord Feng Yuxiang, much to the consternation of the pro-Nationalist Chinese students at Cornell. General Feng was on good terms with the Communists and despised Chiang Kai-shek. He died in a mysterious fire aboard a ship while returning to China.

We had a smattering of Chinese language, history, geography and current affairs. By US Army standards that made us experts. We went to Chinese restaurants whenever possible and practiced using chopsticks. We were, we thought, ready to go.

Again, forces mightier than ourselves were at work. The rumored landing in China, if it had ever been seriously contemplated, was called off, and with it the need for Chinese interpreters.

What to do with us? The army had spent thousands of dollars training high IQ men in Chinese at half a dozen different universities. With typical genius, some brain in the Pentagon made a brilliant decision—we would translate Japanese, not just the ordinary kind, but Japanese in code. The fact that there is hardly any resemblance between the two languages bothered no one.

A few weeks quickie course at a school for cryptanalysts, with a perfuntory nod at Japanese grammar, and we were whisked off to MIDPAC—Middle Pacific Headquarters—in Honolulu.

We spent the next six months till the end of the war deciphering low priority intercepted messages, mostly between Japanese pilots and their control towers regarding the state of the weather. It was just another army boondoggle and everyone was bored stiff.

Off duty no one was bored. Honolulu was idyllic in the 1940s. Semitropical, drenched in fragrance, beaches of fine white sand, no tourists, and old-fashioneds at the Royal Hawaiian made with fresh pineapple. The islands were almost completely controlled by the Four Big Families, wealthy descendants of 19th century missionaries who, as the locals put it, "Came to do good, and did very well indeed."

To keep ourselves busy and because we were interested, a few of us sat in on Chinese language courses at the University of Hawaii in our spare time. Two of my fellow ASTP trainees also audited the courses—Jack Steinberg, the future owner of Twayne, which did poetry publishing, and Julian Schuman, who later joined me in China. They had studied Chinese in the ASTP at Harvard and, like me, had also been made Japanese cryptanalysts. Julian, a New Yorker, was still in his early twenties, while I was already past 30. We studied and practiced on chow lines and during our work shifts whenever the officer on duty goofed off, which he did very frequently. By that time I was really hooked on Chinese.

The end of 1946 found me back in New York, a civilian again. My father had died during the war. I couldn't afford to keep up our office in the Paramount Building and I didn't want to work for any of the big law firms.

Under the GI Bill a veteran was entitled to paid tuition in a university plus subsistence allowance for roughly as many years as he had served in the armed forces. I decided to use some of that time studying more Chinese, until I could make up my mind what I wanted to do with my life. I enrolled at Columbia, taking nothing but Chinese language courses. I did two terms there, then transferred to Yale where I did a third.

At Yale I roomed with Julian Schuman, whom I had met in Hawaii. Wandering amid Yale's ivy-clad towers was pleasant enough, but I couldn't go on being a schoolboy indefinitely. To what use could I put the Chinese which so intrigued me? A few of the Chinese students I had met at Columbia and Yale suggested that I go to China. They said an American lawyer who spoke Chinese would certainly do well.

I wasn't so sure, but the idea appealed to me. I was unmarried. My mother had a job which could sustain her. I was fed up with the rat race, the money grubbing, the wheeling and dealing which was the milieu of the average lawyer. Commercial law was the only field I knew, but I hoped that in the glamorous East business might somehow be different. Although a certain amount of risk was involved, it didn't worry me. After hitchhiking and riding freight across America during the depression, why not a trip across the Pacific? I still had a craving for adventure.

My total finances consisted of US$500—my army discharge bonus. I spent US$300 of it for a ticket on a small freighter which had passenger accommodations for four, traveling from New York to Shanghai via the Panama Canal. The only commercial possibilities I could line up before leaving were a couple of small exporters who gave me samples of army surplus clothing and a promise of commissions if I sold anything, and a stringer arrangement with *Variety* for coverage of China stage and screen events. I never wrote a line for *Variety*, but the clothing came in handy when my own suits began wearing out.

Julian Schuman said he might join me later, depending on what I found. I promised my mother I would come back soon if I couldn't make a go of things.

I was not to see New York again for 25 years.

We set sail one dreary day early in March, 1947. My cabin mate was a French Canadian Catholic priest on his way to one of his order's numerous missions in north China. He spoke no English, but was generous with bottles of excellent brandy he had brought along for *le mal de mer*, and we soon were on good drinking, if not speaking, terms.

The passengers sharing the other cabin were a young husband and wife; she very pregnant. He had been with the US Marines in south China during the war and discovered that the Chinese had no milk to drink. He was going to set up a dairy farm somewhere in Fujian Province and make his fortune. He didn't know, nor for that matter did I, that cow's milk was never part of China's diet. They had got along without it for centuries, using a "milk" of dried powdered soybean mixed with hot water, which was a lot simpler to make and had nearly the same nourishment. Though his scheme was highly impractical, he had obviously been smitten by the charm of China, and his enthusiastic descriptions of lush southern scenery was good for my morale.

I needed all the morale boosting I could get, for I was sick as a dog from the time we passed Cape Hatteras, off the Carolinas. What is it they say about sea-sickness? "First you're afraid you'll die, then you're afraid you won't!"

Miraculously, from the Panama Canal on, I was cured. I began to enjoy the beauty of the sea, its changing shades of blue and gray and green. We saw porpoises and whales. We came quite close to one great cow of a mother whale and her baby. They lay meditating, placidly unconcerned.

We stopped for a day in Honolulu, and I wandered around. The colors were so bright, the flowers so fragrant. It looked cleaner and more spacious without the thousands of men in uniform who had filled the streets only two years before.

We started the last lap of our journey. Chinese stations were coming in loudly on my radio. I could understand quite a lot. I was thrilled.

What would I do when we actually got there? My mind was vague. I had about US$200 in my pocket, a duffel bag full of army surplus clothing samples, a few letters and gifts from Chinese students in America to their families in Shanghai, some things of my own, and that was all.

I suppose what I wanted most was to improve my Chinese until I was really fluent, then see what the job opportunities were. It seemed to me I would have to go to Beijing for language training, since Shanghai dialect is very different from the "national language" used north of the Yangtze River. But first I would spend some time in Shanghai and get the feel of things.

The ocean began turning yellow when we were still three days from land. We were approaching the estuary of the Yangtze running from the far west across China's middle, past Chongqing, Wuhan and Nanjing to the bustling eastern port of Shanghai, which means literally "on the sea."

The yellow tinge deepened to brown. A hazy blur grew on the horizon. China! I slept like a log that night, worn out by the excitement.

When I awakened the following morning we were already steaming slowly up the Huangpu, which leads from the Yangtze to the center of the city. A man was running along the shore, his long black gown flapping in the wind. I stared from the rail of the freighter. A medieval monk? It was my first view of the *chang pao*, the long gown then worn by Chinese men, if they could afford one. He was no monk, but the medieval impression was prophetic. China in April 1947, was something very much out of the Dark Ages.

Soon he was joined by another man, similarly clad. They both kept trotting along in the direction from which we had come until they were out of sight. I could see squat houses with thatched roofs and walls of daubed wattle. Cars and trucks tooled along the dirt roads, trailing clouds of dust. Tall modern buildings appeared. Wharves and docks lined the river. Beside them ferries and ocean-going passenger ships were berthed. Foreign warships rode at anchor.

A launch pulled alongside, and we were boarded by the Customs and Immigration officers. They made a perfunctory examination of our luggage. One of them, a smartly dressed fellow who spoke good English, took me aside and asked if I wanted to exchange any US dollars.

"I'll give you top rate," he said.

It seemed there were two rates for foreign exchange. One was official, a prestige form of wishful thinking and an opportunity for manipulation of public funds by crooked bureaucrats. The other was the black market rate, which was quite open, and changed from day to day in keeping with supply and demand. Chinese yuan, rolling off the printing presses of the "Nationalist" government, ruled by Chiang Kai-shek's Kuomintang (KMT) party, was worth very little, and inflation was rapid.

I handed the gentleman US$50 and he counted out what looked to me like a large sum of yuan in crisp new bills. I discovered later, when I became familiar with the rates, that he cheated me handsomely.

On landing I was met by the family of Nancy Yang, a girl with whom I had exchanged English lessons for Chinese at Yale. I brought them gifts—mostly men's clothing, which I was able to bring through the Customs as my personal belongings. The Yangs insisted I stay with them temporarily, and I gladly agreed, for I hadn't the slightest idea where I was going to live or what I was going to do, and Shanghai was like no place I had ever seen.

Everyone was in a great hurry, and there were tall buildings and buses and trolleys. That, at least, was like New York.

But there the resemblance ended. Many people rode in pedicabs or rickshaws. The first was a tricycle with the driver pedaling in front while a passenger, or two in the larger types, sat in the rear. Rickshaws were two-wheeled carts with long shafts gripped by the runner, usually thin to the point of emaciation, who pulled the vehicle. They ran or plodded, depending on their age and physical condition, and were very dexterous at weaving in and out of traffic. Later, I often rode in pedicabs, but after one ride in a rickshaw I could never bring myself to do it again. Being hauled along by a sweating, panting fellow man was too repugnant.

The buses and trolleys seemed to be in a perpetual rush-hour state. They were packed with people who, for the most part, managed to maintain their good humor in spite of their obvious discomfort.

Hawkers and peddlers of every variety thronged the streets, crying their wares. A lot of the merchandise bore US Army or UNRRA labels, evidence that "free trade" was being conducted by enterprising individuals of both countries who had discovered a simple way of getting American taxpayers to finance their business.

Beggars were everywhere, people in patched and tattered clothes, old folks, women with babes in arms, wide-eyed older children clutching the edges of their mothers' tunics. Most of them came from the impoverished countryside, and swarmed after the more smartly dressed, who occasionally tossed them a few coppers, or simply ignored them.

Affluence was also visible among the chosen few. Sleek limousines, horns insolently blaring, nosed relentlessly through the narrow streets choked with pedestrians, cars, rickshaws, pedicabs, and vehicles of every description. The refugees, not used to big city traffic, scattered when automobiles bore down. But the blasé Shanghai natives stolidly proceeded at their own pace until the creeping vehicles virtually pushed them out of the way.

Clothes were a mixture of East and West. Some of the men wore European-style business suits, but most were dressed in tunic and trousers, over which was a long cotton, or quilted gown in the cold weather.

For the country women it was mainly tunics and slacks. Their city sisters tended more to the *qi pao*, a kind of sheath dress slit up the sides. These, for the richer ladies, were made of flowered silk or satin and tailored to hug the contours of the body.

The noise was incredible. Loudspeakers roared Chinese opera or whined saccharine love songs from innumerable store fronts in a feverish effort to attract customers. Drivers used their horns instead of their brakes. People had to shout to be heard above the din. Others had to yell still louder to be heard above them. The endless, hopeless competition went on and on.

And of course there were the smells, so characteristic of the exotic colonial Orient. Intermingled with the fumes of cars and buses was the odor of thousands of sweat-stained bodies, the fragrance of tidbits cooking in the many street stalls for consumption on the spot, and over all, when the wind was right, the smell of the "honey boats"—barges laden with human excrement being hauled to outlying farms for use as fertilizer.

The sudden combination of these assaults on the senses was overwhelming. I tottered dizzily to the car which the Yangs had provided and drove off with them to their home.

They lived in the Bubbling Well section of the city, not the poshest area in Shanghai, but definitely upper middle class. The house was a slightly run-down three-story building, identical with dozens of others arranged in rows along paved lanes, and all enclosed within a high wall to form an estate.

The house was dimly lit and had creaky wooden floors. There was no steam heat or even coal stoves, Shanghai people being under the illusion that they are southerners, and that it doesn't get really cold until you go north a few miles across the Yangtze River. As a sop to the elderly and infirm they may light a charcoal brazier, which provides some warmth to whichever part of your anatomy is facing it, while your opposite area freezes.

As a result, you're compelled to wear the same clothes indoors as out, either padded or fur-lined. In this way the winters are fairly tolerable. Even in north China where homes and offices are heated the warmth is so slight you must wear long woolen underwear from autumn to spring, plus as much padded clothing as you can navigate in.

It took me about three years to get this principle through my skull, during which I suffered perpetual colds every winter, plus an occasional bout of flu. Finally I climbed out of my fashionable threads into more practical Chinese garb, and I was alright.

31

The Yangs ushered me to my room. It was large, high-ceilinged and had a big four-poster bed, canopied over with thick mosquito netting, an indispensable piece of equipment. While not as large as the New Jersey variety, Shanghai mosquitoes moved in fast and hit hard, like dive bombers.

My bed was a wooden platform on which a thin mattress was laid. Most Chinese prefer a hard bed. After I got used to it, I liked it too.

I slept well that first night in China. The next morning a servant led me to the bathroom. It had the usual Western style equipment, but there was no hot water. This was supplied in thermos flasks, freshly filled.

Breakfast was "foreign" in my honor and consisted of toast, butter, jam, and a cocomalt drink mixed from powder out of an American can and hot water. Later, I was to eat more conventional Shanghai breakfasts—rice gruel, bits of pickled vegetable, and tasty little steamed dumplings stuffed with meat or fish or shrimp.

I spent the next few days delivering gifts to relatives of Chinese students I had met at Yale. Each time the recipients expressed their thanks with an invitation to lunch or dinner. The food was fabulous and had little resemblance to the Chinese fare I had eaten in New York.

That's a delightful thing about the Chinese. Any occasion is an excuse for a feast. When you visit someone they always try to get you to stay for a meal. Holidays, send-offs, welcome-backs, birthdays, anniversaries—they're not considered properly celebrated without a banquet. Even what they throw together on short notice seems sumptuous to a foreigner. When you see their simple kitchens—sans refrigerators, master mix blenders, and electric ovens—you wonder how they do it.

I also called on a few people I had been asked to look up by mutual friends in the States. The first was Fengzi, a pal of Nancy Yang. Fengzi was actually her stage and pen name, but that was how she was known. It means "phoenix." That is the name I use in this book, since most foreign readers would have difficulty in pronouncing "Fengzi" correctly. Nancy had said that Phoenix was also studying English and probably would be interested in exchanging English lessons for Chinese. I telephoned and arranged to drop by in the afternoon.

It was a sunny day and I walked down the Bund toward Garden Bridge. The Bund, a broad thoroughfare along the Huangpu River, was lined on one side by old-fashioned granite edifices which then housed many of the foreign companies extracting huge profits from modest investments. The Japanese, having lost the war, had been driven out. But the French still controlled the electricity supply and trolley lines, the British ran most of the shipping and banking, and American interests were expanding fast.

I crossed Garden Bridge into the Hongkou section where Phoenix lived. Most of Shanghai had been divided into foreign concessions before World War II—Japanese, French and British. In these concessions the foreigners levied taxes, had their own courts, their own police and owned the public utilities. The Chinese had sovereignty in only one part of Shanghai—the section known as the "Chinese City," and even this was actually run by the Shanghai Municipal Council, on which the foreign representatives outnumbered the Chinese. There were similar foreign concessions in other major cities such as Tianjin and Hankou. After World War II the concessions were "surrendered" to China but foreign interests continued to dominate.

Hongkou, formerly part of the Japanese concession, had been the scene of heavy fighting during the war. Now the Japanese were out, their holdings confiscated by the ruling Kuomintang (KMT) party of Chiang Kai-shek, an inefficient gang of crooked politicians. The area was very run-down. Whole streets were lined with bars. There were many prostitutes, catering mainly to foreign sailors and merchant seamen.

Phoenix lived on the top floor of a dilapidated five-story apartment building. The elevator hadn't worked for years. As I trudged up the stairs I was enveloped in smoke. The flats had no kitchens, and everyone cooked in the hallways on stoves burning coalballs—a mixture of coal dust, lime and mud.

I knocked on the door. It was opened by a very pretty woman in her thirties. She was wearing a simple *qi pao* sheath dress, high heels, and very little makeup. I had noticed this lack of cosmetics on Chinese girls. They used only powder and a faint touch of lipstick. That was alright with me. Since Chinese women have about the best skin in the world—smooth, hairless, small-pored—the application of cosmetics was only gilding the lily.

With a rather worried expression, Phoenix ushered me in. I was wearing a raglan sleeve topcoat. Years later she told me she was relieved when I took it off and revealed that I had shoulders, after all.

Phoenix wrote a memoir in 1993 recalling a great deal about our lives together and the momentous developments in which we were involved. Since she understood China better, and knew me better than I did myself, I will include several of her versions as well as my own.

Regarding our first meeting she says:

> In April 1947 I was living in a small flat in the Hongkou section of Shanghai. Suddenly I heard "knock, knock, knock" on the door. It was about ten in the morning. "Come in," I shouted. Nobody entered, though I called several times, so I got up and opened the door. Standing there was a "blue-eyed, golden-haired" young man. [A common aphorism. To many Chinese foreigners looked outlandish.]
>
> "I'm looking for Miss Phoenix," he said, in heavily accented Chinese.
>
> He was Sha Boli, the man I have been living with as husband and wife for the past 45 years!

My friend Nancy Yang had written that an American who had been a student with her at Yale was coming and wanted to continue studying Chinese. She knew I was planning to go to America and suggested that I teach him, in exchange for him helping me learn some English.

"Are you Mr. Shapiro?" I asked.

"I am Sha Boli." He didn't use English, but insisted on speaking his broken Chinese as he strode into my flat.

I was surprised. Why should this young American from the opposite side of the Pacific choose to come to China at this time? It was with American support that the Kuomintang had plundered Shanghai after the Japanese surrendered. American military transport planes had flown arms and supplies to the northeast to help the Kuomintang continue the civil war in its dream of "exterminating the Communists."

Shanghai was short of everything, the national treasury was empty, prices were soaring, the newly issued "gold yuan" could not save the collapsing economy. The people were protesting, they could barely survive. There were corpses on every corner, crime was rampant. Shanghai had become a paradise for Chinese and foreign speculators, it was indeed a world of devils.

Because of the language barrier, it was a long time before I could gradually get the answers to my questions from the young American.

She asked me to be seated and immediately poured the inevitable cup of tea. There is a large variety of teas, and different regions have different favorites. People in north China prefer jasmine, but south of the Yangtze River they go in mostly for green teas which are "heat removing," particularly the Dragon Well kind. There are about a dozen grades of this, ranging in price accordingly. It comes from the tea plantations on the hills outside of Hangzhou, whose beauties Marco Polo extolled seven centuries before. The most expensive kind is made from buds picked at dawn in early spring with the dew still on them. In the old days it was thought best if the girls who did the picking were virgins, but this is now generally considered an exploded theory.

I looked around the apartment. There was a small room to the left as you came in, piled high with copies of a magazine she was editing. A short hall led directly into a large combination parlor and bedroom, with a small sofa and a couple of big chairs grouped around a low glass-topped table. Four large windows faced a view of the river and, beyond that, lowlands running down to the sea. It gave the impression of being on the bridge of a ship. On stormy days, when gales lashed rain against the glass, the building swayed slightly, and you almost expected to see spume-capped billows breaking against the wall. There was also a small bathroom with the usual plumbing, but no heat or hot water.

Phoenix says:

I had never entertained a foreigner before. It was nearly lunch time. I couldn't ask him to share my simple fare in my cramped little flat, so I invited him to a nearby foreign restaurant. I ordered two orders of soup, cold cuts, steak, coffee and dessert. I assumed this was a typical Western meal. But he ate very little. Some things he didn't even touch. I was surprised.

"Have you already eaten?" I asked.

"No," he replied.

It was a question that puzzled me for a long time—for more than 30 years, to be exact. I went with him to America and visited his sister in New York. That was when I finally began to realize a bit about the differences in racial and national customs, particularly about the way Americans lived.

I was as much a source of fascination to Phoenix as she was to me. She goes on in some detail in her memoir about American versus Chinese eating habits, and their effects on this remarkable creature, her husband, Sha Boli.

Meat are the main courses at American meals, either cooked or grilled, either pork, or beef, or lamb chops, with a few vegetables on the side. They don't necessarily have soup at the end of their meals, but finish with coffee or fruit.

For lunch they may have only a sandwich, or leftovers from the night before. They don't take midday naps. Since office workers have only an hour for lunch, they may eat just a hot dog. Only at night, when the whole family is home for dinner, do they have a substantial meal, perhaps with soup, or fruit.

Foreign friends are always amazed when they eat in Chinese homes at the tables laden with half a dozen dishes. "Do you eat like this all the time?" they ask. They don't understand that lavish hospitality is considered a virtue in China.

The rule now is that official banquets must be limited to four dishes and a soup. Actually, that doesn't include the cold cuts and the dessert. There are always a lot of expensive, rare viands left at the end of the meal.

Especially wasteful are the official banquets given in honor of some famous expert or scholar. The cost runs into thousands of yuan. The host is sure to be accompanied by his entourage, who frequently fill several tables.

Culinary culture has a long tradition in China. In Yunnan, Guizhou and Sichuan, people like their food spicy. In Guangdong and Fujian, they eat snakes and roast suckling pigs. The favorite in Beijing is, of course, roast duck. China is a multiracial country, and each ethnic minority has its own specialties. Sha Boli, while doing research along the Old Silk Road, was surprised to find when he got to Xinjiang that the mutton you eat with your hands was not greasy, and the taste not a bit gamy. He particularly enjoyed the crisp oil fritters of the Uygur people.

In a different land, follow the local customs. Over the decades Sha Boli certainly has done that where food is concerned. And he became Sinicised in other ways as well. He prefers cloth shoes and silk-padded jackets because they are comfortable and practical. He has an excellent ear for languages. Many of my friends are actors and actresses, who speak the purest Chinese, and from them he picked up the proper intonations. After over 40 years in Beijing his pronunciation is better than that of many friends from the southern part of the country. He laughs at me because as someone born and raised on the banks of the Yangtze I can't distinguish between the L and N sounds. I twit him with his errors in cadence.

To get back to Shanghai in 1947: I told Phoenix of my earlier life. She was interested in the fact that I had represented young theater people when I was a lawyer in New York. She herself had been an actress for over ten years, on the stage and on the screen. Though she had become a newspaper reporter during the Japanese invasion—China's first woman war correspondent—and was now an editor of a magazine, she was still devoted to the theater. She promised to introduce me to her friends, most of whom were connected with the arts.

Phoenix and I began hacking our way through our first attempt at conversation. I knew a bit of Chinese sentence structure, but hadn't nearly enough vocabulary. She, to my surprise, had a fairly large vocabulary, but her approach to English tenses and grammar was highly original and creative.

We arranged to meet at her place three afternoons a week and exchange an hour of English for an hour of Chinese, starting the following week. When we parted later that evening I felt pleased and comforted. I had met someone intelligent, attractive and concerned with my welfare. A friend—that was how I thought of her then. I rode back to the Yangs in a pedicab and watched the moon through the clouds above the roofs of Shanghai. Already, China was beginning to lose some of its strangeness.

The weeks slipped by, and with them what remained of my US$200. No one wanted my army surplus clothing. Shanghai warehouses were full of merchandise, part of the billions worth of goods and equipment left over in the Pacific by the US armed forces after the war and "sold" to Chiang Kai-shek's "Nationalist" government—in exchange for more rights and concessions. It was supposed to be used in the "fight against communism," but most of it wound up as the private property of the high officials running the country.

Chiang Kai-shek, T.V. Soong, H.H. Kung, and the Chen brothers—the "Big Four"—were the top dogs. Through various government banks and organizations they owned or controlled the best land, skimmed the cream off the rural usury network, and had a tight grip on all industry and commerce. At the same time, for suitable cuts and bribes, they gave away rich plums to foreign investors. They fronted for dummy Chinese corporations actually owned by Europeans or Americans, or received large blocs of stock in foreign corporations which were then legally permitted to operate on Chinese soil. On behalf of the government they entered into treaties of the most servile nature with the imperialist powers.

In 1946 they had signed an agreement with the United States called "Treaty of Friendship, Commerce and Navigation" which allowed both countries to export their products without limit to their opposite number, tax free. An "equality" between David and Goliath. (A harbinger of China's entry into GATT today?) Since Chinese industry was still in its infancy, it was promptly crushed by a deluge of technologically superior American goods. The United States could sell cars and trucks and tractors in China. All the Chinese were capable of manufacturing were bicycles and pedicabs. Not much market for that in America.

The "Big Four" didn't mind. They bathed in the stream of gold, from whichever direction it flowed. The only problem was that real business was practically dead. There were few ultimate consumers. The handful who could afford cars already had several. Ninety percent of the population considered themselves lucky if they had enough to eat. I saw piles of trucks and tractors rusting on islands in the river. Brand new automobiles gathered dust in warehouses. A great deal of commerce consisted of paper speculations in warehouse receipts and bills of lading. That was about all that moved for domestic consumption by way of foreign trade.

Exports were a different matter. Silks, cotton goods, soybeans, tobacco, coal, tin, bristles and hog casings were siphoned out of bleeding China smoothly and efficiently, at rock-bottom prices. Wages paid by foreign enterprises were delightfully low. "After all, the Chinese aren't like us. They can live on a bowl of rice a day."

Unemployment was very high. There were no statistics. Many of the "employed" received such pitiful stipends they were barely able to feed themselves.

Among the foreigners there was also some unemployment. Jewish refugees from Hitler's Germany, many of them distinguished scientists, doctors and professors, were living in fetid slums in Hongkou, waiting endlessly for visas to America. One man offered me US$20,000 to enter into a marriage of convenience with his daughter so that she could go to America as my wife, and therefore automatically an American citizen, after which we would be divorced. I politely thanked him, and said no.

37

Later, at the request of the US Consulate, I visited the community and explained that the streets of New York were not really paved with gold, and urged the Jewish refugees, if they could get visas to other countries, to take them. Eventually, that is what most of them did, migrating mainly to Latin America.

White Russians, who had fled the Bolshevik Revolution and ended up in the big cities of China—Harbin, Tianjin and Shanghai, had long since reached the end of their financial tether, but had difficulty in finding work suitable to their gentlemanly background. Some of their ladies did better and were among the highest paid in their chosen professions.

Jobs for Anglo-Americans were no problem at all. Any idiot could pull down US$50 a week for doing next to nothing. At that salary he could have a nice flat, keep a servant who also cooked delicious Chinese meals, and drive his own car. After all it wouldn't do to have one of the supporters of the White Man's Burden panhandling in public.

But I had rather special requirements. I wanted to work for an American company in Beijing, where I could combine business with perfecting my Chinese. I decided to make the rounds of the American law firms in Shanghai (there were only three or four), and see whether they had any clients in Beijing who could use a young American attorney.

At that stage an ambivalence was creeping into my feelings about China. I had little doubt that I could find a job, and perhaps a career, in China, and learn more of the language and the culture. But I began to sense that the country was poised on the brink of a volcano. Corpses every day on the streets of people who had starved to death, the casual cruelty and callousness of the rich and the ruling machine, the plunging economy. . . . Obviously it couldn't last much longer. What form would the eruption take when the volcano exploded? Should I remain in China or leave?

I was fascinated and burning with curiosity. Cataclysmic changes were obviously brewing. What would happen next? I decided I would stay a while longer, just to see. I had no thought of playing any part in these changes. I certainly never dreamed that I would become deeply involved, as a devoted and active participant, in the Chinese revolution. But that was later.

The first lawyer I visited was H.D. Rodgers. He was then about 50, ruddy complexioned, with a gray clipped mustache. Rodgers had got his American law degree through a correspondence course. By a stroke of luck he won a sweepstakes at the Shanghai Racecourse, which brought him enough money to open a law office. He found himself a smart partner, who did most of the research and paper work. Rodgers was the business getter, the back-slapping, hail-fellow-well-met who threw dice for drinks on mahogany-topped bars with leading members of the commercial community.

38

Rodgers explained that very little business was conducted in Beijing, and that any American companies operating there had their main offices in Shanghai. But, he said, he'd like to make me a proposition. His partner had gone to America when the war broke out and had not returned. He needed someone badly. If I would become his partner he would pay me a third of the profits or US$500 a month, whichever was greater.

A very attractive offer, I thought, particularly since I had only about US$20 left in my pocket. On US$10 a day a single man could live in comfort. Still, it wouldn't get me to Beijing, which was my main objective. I told H.D. I'd think it over and let him know.

I discussed the matter with my Chinese friends. They said it was a marvelous opportunity and that I should grab it. After I accumulated a decent reserve I could always quit and head north. I accepted their advice and closed a deal with Rodgers.

Perhaps it sounds a little wild for a lawyer to take on a partner he'd never seen before. But for foreigners Shanghai was a wide-open, free-swinging city. It wasn't known as the paradise of adventurers for nothing. Quick fortunes were made and lost. Shanghai had the casual atmosphere of an old frontier town in the American West.

Phoenix, Marriage, and the
Decision to Stay
1947-1949

Rodgers' office was on the 11th floor of the 15-story Development Building, then the tallest in Shanghai. Many of his clients were Chinese companies who wanted to be registered as American corporations. A US federal statute called the China Trade Act permitted firms doing business in China to obtain this status by filing simple forms annually and paying a nominal fee. The treasurer and the president had to be US citizens. Chinese companies paid lawyers like Rodgers for assuming these roles and putting them through the necessary formalities. It gave the Chinese businesses prestige to be known as China Trade Act corporations, and lowered their taxes to the Chinese government to a minimum. Not that they ever paid any—they kept special loss-showing books for the government tax officers, whom they always sweetened with suitable gifts. There was no tax requirement by the United States.

Rodgers had a number of interesting clients. One was a certain Spanish religious order which had sold real estate to the Japanese during the occupation for a substantial sum. Now, along with all other Japanese-held property, this parcel of land and buildings—tenanted by brothels, gambling dens and warehouses—had been taken over by the Alien Property Custodian of the Kuomintang. The gentle fathers had suddenly come up with a claim that they had been forced to deliver title to the Japanese, that they hadn't been paid a cent, and they wanted the property back.

No one was particularly deceived by this, but business was business. Rodgers went to Nanjing several times a month to negotiate with the KMT officials, each time upping a bit the size of the proposed bribe.

I was left to handle the more prosaic matters of wills, contracts and assignments. Still, it was a far cry from the Paramount Building in New York. One of the duties of the clerks was to keep you supplied with tea and, in summer, hot towels. Chinese businessmen, while every bit as sharp as their American counterparts, had to be treated more ceremoniously. Tea had to be poured, polite small talk had to be made. Only then could you come to grips with the matter at hand.

One of Shanghai's more imaginative con men honored me with a visit. Mr. Ionin was a White Russian who dressed neatly in a quiet business suit and whose eyes were slightly out of alignment. He told a fascinating story about kegs of gold napoleons which had been retrieved from a sunken freighter and were stored in an abbey under the label of nails. He had the papers for them and needed only a buyer who could take delivery. He showed me the documents and entrusted me with a few of the coins, but cautioned that under no circumstances was I to mention his name to the customer. I was to be paid a large commission, Ionin a small one.

Madder things had happened in Shanghai. I said I would see what I could do. I discussed the matter with some European gentlemen who dealt in currency. They examined the coins and said they were genuine enough. But when, at their urgent persuasion, I told them who my client was, they laughed. They said because I was new to Shanghai and had not yet heard of Mr. Ionin's reputation, he no doubt was trying to work me for a few dollars. The touch would come soon, they predicted.

Sure enough, a few days later Ionin dropped in again. He said he needed 25 dollars to pay the monk who was keeping an eye on the nails. It was to be a loan, of course, which I could deduct from his commission. I said I was sorry, that I had no ready cash on hand. He said ten might do. I shook my head.

That was the last I saw of Mr. Ionin.

Phoenix took me to a dinner given by famous archaeologist Zheng Zhenduo for some of Shanghai's intellectuals. Most of them were writers and newspaper people. All, including the archaeologist, were having a hard time making ends meet. Publishers didn't pay much, there was only a small reading public since the majority of the population was illiterate, and the cost of living kept increasing in a vain struggle to keep pace with the soaring inflation.

The Kuomintang, Chiang Kai-shek's ruling party, offered sinecures and well-paying jobs to anyone who would write for their periodicals or do public relations work for them. Only a tiny fraction responded. China's literati scorned and hated the Kuomintang, which had run when the Japanese invaded. Corrupt and venal, it was creating new spheres of influence for foreign capital, and was content to see the country slide into ruin while it lined its own pockets.

Few of China's writers were members of the Communist Party, but most were patriots who were infuriated by what the KMT was doing in China. They spoke out against it as best they could, using indirection and historical analogy. Everything had to pass the ferret eyes of the Kuomintang censors. Writers' manuscripts were always being sent back with deletions and demands for revision, or simply rejected. But the literati I met were seldom depressed. In addition to their own pleasant charm, they were possessed of a wit and gaiety which warmed my American heart.

That night we were drinking Shaoxing wine, a honey-colored liquor which tastes something like sherry when cold and something like ambrosia when heated, which is the customary way to serve it. At banquets, you start drinking before the

41

meal is served, and continue right through to the end, when anyone who still hasn't had enough food is brought bowls of rice to fill in the remaining crevices. As the toasts go round the hilarity grows, with wisecracks and puns. I'm afraid I missed most of them, since my limping Chinese couldn't possibly keep up with the racing humor.

Thanks to my language inadequacies I provided a bit of humor myself. During the course of the meal I observed various people getting up and going out, obviously to answer calls of nature. I too rose and strolled unsteadily from the banquet room.

"Where is the bathroom?" I asked a passing waiter in my best Yale Chinese.

"Bathroom?" He looked puzzled.

"I want to wash my hands."

"Ah, wash your hands. This way, please." He led me to a room where there was a basin and water, and nothing else.

I made my way dejectedly back to the table. Phoenix noted my expression.

"What's the matter?"

I explained.

"This gentleman wants to go to the toilet," she called to a waiter on the far side of the room.

"Big convenience or small convenience?"

All eyes turned to me expectantly.

"Small," I said bravely.

"Come along," said the waiter.

Everyone went on with their conversation, smiling a bit at my obvious embarrassment as I left the room.

I was to be frequently reminded that Chinese customs are free in many ways of the prudery and cant which pervade the West. The facts of life are discussed freely in front of children, women nurse their infants in public, toddlers wear split pants until they are toilet-trained. It is thought better for them to wet the floor than wet their clothes.

At the same time, China in the forties had a special prudery of its own. Boys and girls never dared to show any interest in each other. To be seen even speaking to a girl usually let the boy in for a lot of snide ribbing, which I always found irritatingly puerile and mawkish. As a result, they could never get to know one another, and had to rely on the old feudal matchmakers.

Yet if they did meet on their own and live together there was never any particular onus attached to them. In the old days people were pretty casual about registering their marriage, anyway. You lived together, so you were married. If you had children you had to support them, with or without a marriage license. You simply registered as a *fait accompli*, usually in the county magistrate's office, that your marriage had occurred.

Everyone was still talking about the war, which had only recently ended, and whose ravages were still felt. When the Japanese had invaded China, Chiang Kai-shek's armies gave ground, mostly without a fight. The capital moved from Nanjing to Chongqing, deep in Sichuan. The rich, the bureaucrats, the big operators, devoted themselves to money-making and high life while the rest of the country staggered under the blows of the virtually unopposed foe. Only the Communist forces fought back, but they were constantly harassed by the Chiang Kai-shek gang, who showed more ardor against them than against the Japanese, in spite of the fact that they were supposed to be joined in a "united front."

Americans in China had nothing but contempt for the Kuomintang. "Peanut!" was the epithet for Chiang Kai-shek of "Vinegar Joe" Stillwell, Commanding General of the US Armed Forces in the China-Burma-India Theater. State Department advisers like John S. Service recommended close cooperation with the Communists, who were leading the fight against the Japanese. This was never done. In fact men like Service were subsequently hounded for their honesty by the McCarthy Committee.

When the Japanese surrendered, the Kuomintang moved into the cities like a swarm of locusts, seizing the best apartment houses, the best office buildings, handing out spoils to their friends, imposing the same dirty regime they had before. Whoever harbored any hopes the government would improve was quickly disillusioned.

In many parts of the country only Communist-led armed forces were present to accept surrender from the defeated Japanese. Chiang Kai-shek had pulled his armies far back from the battlefronts. They were hundreds of miles away. This was a source of deep disturbance to reactionaries on both sides of the Pacific, who were terrified lest the Communists consolidate the excellent relations they had established with the local populations and strengthen themselves militarily with surrendered Japanese arms.

An "Armistice Commission" was hastily whipped together, composed of American, Kuomintang and Communist representatives, with an "Executive Headquarters" in Beijing. Teams of one of each were sent to restore peace wherever clashes broke out between Communist and Kuomintang troops. In the meantime, US ships and planes were secretly rushing Chiang Kai-shek armies back from the hinterlands. They shifted 41 KMT divisions and eight military police regiments—half a million men—into the Communist-controlled Liberated Areas. The moment these were in position, they attacked. Ninety thousand US Marines were landed in Shanghai, Tianjin, Beijing and Qinhuangtao to guard Kuomintang lines of communication.

People were sick of the Chiang Kai-shek gang, and resistance grew. Fighting spread in the Liberated Areas. A revolutionary movement also developed in the cities, in which workers, students and intellectuals joined.

I began meeting members of the American community. The business and diplomatic crowd led a closed ingrown social life, remote from the ordinary Chinese. What mixing they did was more with the rich merchants and the government officials, which categories frequently overlapped.

There were other kinds of Americans, as well. Gerry Tannenbaum, for example, had been a captain stationed in Shanghai in charge of US Armed Forces Radio during the war. He secretly used these facilities to help the Communist underground communicate with their headquarters in the interior. After the Japanese surrendered he went to work for the China Welfare Fund (CWF), a society devoted to giving educational opportunities to poor and underprivileged children. Headed by Madame Soong Ching Ling, widow of Sun Yat-sen, the hero of the bourgeois Revolution of 1911, the organization enjoyed the undying hatred of the wealthy ruling class and the officialdom, who had always monopolized education as their private prerogative. The KMT suspected her (in this case, with complete justification) of having close links with the Communist underground. But Madame Soong was too prominent to be attacked openly, even more so since the CWF was known and supported by prominent personages abroad. Moreover, her sister Soong Mei Ling was married to Chiang Kai-shek!

Then there was Bill Powell Jr., editor of *China Weekly Review*, a magazine founded by his father. Powell Sr. had been one of those old-fashioned American newsmen who told the truth as he saw it and let the chips fall where they may. He adhered to this policy even after the Japanese occupied Shanghai, and he wound up in a Japanese-run prison where ill-treatment caused injuries which led to his death. Not only was the magazine widely circulated abroad but, as one of the few reliable sources of information, it was avidly read by Chinese who knew English. Since many of the articles flatly contradicted the lies of the Chiang Kai-shek gang and exposed their scandals, the magazine aroused the fury of the KMT. But it would have been awkward for them to interfere with an American enterprise at a time when they were using American arms to slaughter Chinese of alleged Communist sympathies, so they let Bill Powell alone.

Julian Schuman had come out, at my suggestion, and he joined *China Weekly Review*. He stayed on until 1955 as Bill's assistant editor. Julian roomed with me at the American Club. He took to Shanghai like a duck to water, wandering around, eating local delicacies in little hole-in-the-wall restaurants, chatting with Chinese and American friends far into the night. He became a first-rate newspaper man, and broadcast live the last days of the Kuomintang for ABC. His book *Assignment China* is the best thing written by an American about the end of old Shanghai.

By then, Phoenix and I knew each other pretty well. She was the last child of a large family, born when her father was already 40. They lived in Hankou, a bustling river port on the Yangtze, though their ancestral home was in the Guangxi Zhuang Autonomous Region, far to the south, bordering on Vietnam. Father was a well-known classical poet, and later became Guangxi's provincial historian. He was very fond of the baby of the family and taught her to read and appreciate the classics, an indispensable attribute in a truly educated Chinese. It was mainly on the strength of this knowledge—since her acquaintance with subjects like chemistry and math was remote—that she was able to gain entrance to Fudan University in Shanghai while still in her teens.

Well-brought-up girls from proper feudal families were rarely permitted to leave home to attend universities, but times were changing. People were looking for new attitudes, new solutions, to save China from its rapidly accelerating decay. Education of the younger generation, even girls, in the methods of the West, was one approach.

At Fudan, Phoenix became quickly involved in student unrest and protests against the persecution of liberals by the Chiang Kai-shek government and its supineness in the face of exploitation by foreign imperialist powers. She also discovered an aptitude for acting and took part in student performances of some of the new plays. These were so successful that they were tried out in a Shanghai theater. Audience response was enthusiastic. Fearing that word would get back to her feudal father, she adopted the name "Fengzi" (Phoenix). Nice girls didn't go on the stage. After graduation she became a professional actress.

She starred in the dramas of Cao Yu, a young writer strongly influenced by Eugene O'Neill. His vehicles, like those of his mentor, exposed the corruption and decadence of his country's society. Phoenix played also in a few films. Drama consisting solely of spoken dialogue, without singing and musical accompaniment, was a new art form in China, as were motion pictures, and both dealt with contemporary themes. Traditional theater was mainly historical costume opera.

After the Japanese invasion in 1937 Phoenix worked as an editor and war correspondent. In 1945 when the Japanese surrendered, she returned to Shanghai, where she became the editor of a left-wing magazine. At the same time she performed in several plays.

Though she had never known any foreigners personally, they were not as strange to her as they would be, say, to a peasant. She had seen many in Hankou, Guilin, and Chongqing. Shanghai, a big seaport, was full of them. She had read extensively about foreign lands in novels and plays translated from the English, French, Russian and German. She saw the best and worst Hollywood had to offer in Shanghai cinemas named *The Palace*, *The Granada* and *The Roxy*. Among the educated classes Western dress was popular, as were restaurants which cooked Western style. Western music could be heard at concerts, on the radio, on phonograph records.

Phoenix, like many of her contemporaries, was influenced by the romantic aspects of Western culture. In some ways they were comfortably similar to feudal chivalry and sentimentality, and yet seemed to be a step forward in that they called for the emancipation of women and such shining goals as liberty and democracy.

By the time I met her in 1947 she had come under much stronger influences. During the war she had encountered leaders of the Communist Party, and they had helped and guided her in her work. Though not herself a member, she felt that what they advocated and practiced was more suited to the realities of China than the political approaches of the West. In fact the magazine she was editing was being directed by the Communist underground in Shanghai. Chiang Kai-shek's Kuomintang party and government were hopelessly venal and corrupt. They hadn't fought the Japanese invaders; they attacked the Communist forces who did; they oppressed the people. As a patriot, she could only support the Communists.

These aspects of her personality I came to know gradually over the coming months. What struck me first were the outward things, her animation and expressiveness. I couldn't tell whether this was something she was born with, or whether the projection of emotion which she had learned as an actress had become second nature. When indignant her eyes would flash fire, when happy she would laugh unrestrainedly like a child. I quickly changed my preconceived notions about the "inscrutableness" of Orientals.

She had few questions about life in America. Perhaps she thought the films she saw presented the true picture. She did, in typical Chinese fashion, want to know all about my family, what my sister did, how many children she had, who looked after my widowed mother. . . .

About herself she spoke freely. She was a rebel in an age of rebellion. China was still very feudal. In Hankou she had nearly been arrested for walking arm in arm with a schoolmate along the riverbank in broad daylight, until it was discovered that "he" was actually another girl with a boyish bob.

Educated young Chinese were fed up with outmoded strictures. Phoenix had been deeply impressed by two literary creations, one Chinese, one foreign—the novel *The Family* by Ba Jin, and Ibsen's play *Nora (A Doll's House)*. The first is the story of a young man who runs away from his wealthy feudal family after a hopeless affair with a pretty servant girl that ends in her suicide. In the second, Nora leaves her pompous husband because he treats her more like a cherished plaything than a person.

Phoenix herself had broken many of the rules. She had gone to college, she had become an actress, she had traveled around, alone, as a newspaper correspondent. She had also divorced a young professor when she discovered that he expected her role in their marriage to be primarily that of a housewife and hostess to his guests. "I wasn't going to be a Chinese Nora," Phoenix said firmly. She had not remarried because she had not found anyone for whom she could care enough and who would respect her independence.

Not, at least, till I came along. Our physical attraction was immediate and mutual. But more than that, we shared an identity of interests and found pleasure in each other's company. We went to the theater together and saw new Chinese plays and old Chinese operas. Explaining these to me meant interpreting not only plot, but also the thinking, motivation, customs and cultural background. I, in turn, tried to make sense of the American films we saw and the translated fiction she read. On the way home after an evening out we walked through the streets and stopped at one of the all-night stands for a few crisp oil fritters, or a bowl of fragrant *huntun*—Chinese dumplings in soup. We might ride the rest of the way in a pedicab—a big tricycle pedaled by the driver in front and two seats in the rear, with a folding awning, like a baby carriage cover, for shelter against the rain.

We sat in tea gardens amid flowering shrubs and fanciful pavilions and sipped green "Dragon Well" tea and cracked watermelon seeds. We wended through the City God Temple, with its many shops of marvelous handicrafts connected by a zigzag bridge around a lotus pond.

And we met in Phoenix's flat with a few other Chinese friends and talked in low voices, with the radio turned on loud against possible eavesdroppers, about who had just been arrested, or what bookstores had been raided, or whether more revolutionaries had been executed, and what the news from the Liberated Areas was. Sometimes we could pick up Yanan on my short wave set.

I asked her to marry me. The word that first struck me as I got to know her was "gallant." It took guts and daring to run a Communist-backed magazine under the nose of a fascist government, and this lady had plenty of both. I admired her even before I came to love her. Here she was, a girl from a genteel background, risking imprisonment, or worse, in a city of sharks. I wanted her to be my wife. After some hesitation, she consented. As she explained in her memoir:

> It was difficult for a single woman. People talked if she spent time with any man. I was busy writing—novels, short stories, essays. I was preparing a collection of pieces about the War of Resistance Against Japan period for publication. And I was hoping to go abroad, find a different environment. Yet I wanted to wait for the day of liberation, when I could plunge into a new life.
>
> Sha Boli's sudden appearance was like a stone cast into a placid pool, spreading circles of ripples. How hard it was for me to change! Still, combining and separating my ways of life during our years of marriage and love seemed natural enough.
>
> The young man certainly attracted me. Most Americans gave me the impression of being crude. But he was very handsome and intelligent, very

47

relaxed, generous, courteous. Everything about China aroused his curiosity. He was very fond of things Chinese. He wasn't a bit like the Americans we saw in the movies. Through him I came to understand Americans and America much better.

Phoenix had no doubts about our compatibility. If our future was unsure, she said, so was the future of everyone in China. Nor did my "foreignness" seem to present any problems. She had got used to my appearance, in fact she had become bemused to such an extent that she thought I was good-looking. No one stared when we appeared in public together, nor did I, for some reason, attract the crowds which usually trailed other foreigners, awe-struck by their outlandish garb and, by Chinese standards, huge noses. Her family offered no objections whatever.

Absence of racial or religious prejudice is traditional in China. For 2,000 years foreigners had been encouraged to settle in the Middle Kingdom and practice their religions and retain their customs. There was some talk among the rustics that all foreigners had red hair and blue eyes and walked without bending their knees. But those who had actually seen them knew better. None of Phoenix's compatriots was shocked by our affinity, though some perhaps wondered why she chose a foreigner when there were so many Chinese around.

As for me, I was finally ready for marriage. In 1948 I was 33, earning a good living and confident I could fend for myself as a lawyer. China intrigued me, and China was where I wanted to remain. Though I had no anticipation that Chiang Kai-shek would be overthrown so quickly, I thought that even with a change of government there surely would be use for an American lawyer with a knowledge of Chinese. I wanted only to live in modest comfort and be able to pursue my studies of Chinese language and culture.

For that, Phoenix would be an ideal wife. Charming, with a host of intellectual friends, she was a guarantee that I would never lack for an interesting life. She knew a great deal about Chinese classics and history, and was an invaluable interpreter of current politics. And she mixed well with my foreign acquaintances, who were clearly enchanted by her.

I was a little concerned about what my mother's reaction might be but, as she often did, Mom surprised me. Whether it was the absence of any historical conflict between Chinese and Jews, or seeing them in America as another discriminated-against minority that won her favor, I don't know. In any event, she fully approved the match, and that made it unanimous.

Phoenix and I were married on May 16, 1948. We signed a simple statement of marriage in Chinese, to which a Master of Ceremonies, an Introducer and a Witness also affixed their signatures. That was it, simple, quiet and dignified. I also registered the fact of marriage with the US Consulate in Shanghai.

We found a small apartment at a reasonable rent at the far end of the old French concession. But we had to pay a stiff fee, known as "key money," in US dollars to the departing tenant. This was the custom, and the only way you could get an apartment at that time. We were much better off than the bulk of the population, who lived in crowded, run-down tenements, and the thousands whose only shelters from the elements were flimsy mat sheds.

Phoenix liked the place. In her memoir she wrote:

> I don't know how much money he spent fixing up our new flat. He was very meticulous. Aside from the kitchen and the bathroom, the so-called two-room flat was actually only one large room, with a curtain in the middle separating the bedroom from the parlor. He had the walls painted a pale blue, giving the flat an air of elegance and quiet. I didn't care much about such things, but I was moved to see the care and feeling he devoted to building our home.

By current standards I was a success. I had left Rodgers and opened my own law office. I was earning more money than I could use, sending half of it back to my mother. I had a wife, an apartment, a fluid-drive Chrysler, good clothes, a law practice. What else could I want?

For one thing, I wanted life to have more meaning. I had traveled 12,000 miles because I had the romantic illusion that physical distance would enable me to escape the environment of the market place. But Shanghai was just another market, if anything more sordid and openly corrupt than the one I had left. I spent most of my waking hours with people who were trying to think up improved means of screwing their fellow man, and I was supposed to help them make it legal. Not a very inspiring existence.

Also I felt uncomfortable living it up surrounded by utter poverty and degradation. You couldn't walk along Tibet Road near the racecourse without being mobbed by hundreds of prostitutes, many pitifully young, whose hard-faced "mothers" would grab your arm and hang on with a grip of iron.

If my Chrysler had to stop for a red light at Nanjing Road, beggars would swarm all over it, climbing on the running board, thrusting grimy hands in through the open window, pleading for pennies. In winter these poor people died like flies. Garbage trucks went around every morning to collect the frozen corpses off the sidewalks.

The whole regime was dying, but it struggled desperately, striking out hysterically, viciously, at the mounting opposition. People were arrested in the middle of the night, tortured, murdered. Sirens howled incessantly on police wagons racing through the streets.

One night a young woman, a friend of Phoenix, asked us to hide her in our apartment. She was a newspaper reporter. The Kuomintang was after her. Arrangements were being made for her to escape to Hong Kong. A few days later she left.

Not long after, we gave shelter to a boy who rushed in, pale and sweating. He was active in the student movement in one of the universities, and had been tipped off that the police were looking for him. His father finally managed to buy them off with a substantial bribe.

A roundup of noncooperative intellectuals had also begun. Friends in the underground said that the Kuomintang was taking an unhealthy interest in Phoenix and the magazine she was running. They suggested this might be a good time for her to go.

Go where? For some time we had been closely following the Communist-led revolution, listening to shortwave broadcasts from the Liberated Areas, secretly reading articles that had been made available to us, and talking with men in the underground.

I too had become involved to a certain extent. I had helped a student group edit a magazine in English that favored land reform. The Kuomintang, representing the big landlords, didn't like that at all, and the magazine had been forced to close down. My fancy office in the Development Building had been used as a meeting place for discussions with emissaries from the Liberated Areas seeking to get medicines through the Kuomintang blockade. Everything we heard about these areas sounded positive, exciting. Why not go there?

Phoenix was all for immediately agreeing on a permanent change. I was more cautious. I didn't want to commit myself finally, but was willing to have a look, and then decide.

A message was sent to the Liberated Areas asking whether it was alright for me, a foreigner, to go. Two weeks later word came back: Yes.

We started making preparations. I told everyone we were going to Tianjin on a business trip. Taking Gerry Tannenbaum into my confidence, I gave him the keys to my law office, and asked him to return all my files to the people concerned as soon as he heard we had got across. I left him enough money to refund the annual retainers I had received from certain clients, pay off my secretary and close down the office. I also requested him to sell my car, home and office furniture, and dispose of my apartment.

Phoenix put her affairs in order.

Gerry asked if we could take Joan Hinton, an American girl, who wanted to join her fiancé, Sid Engst, a Vermont agronomist already in the Liberated Areas. We checked with the Chinese: Agreed.

We packed only absolute essentials, having been advised that we might have to do a lot of walking and carry our belongings ourselves.

50

Then, on November 11, 1948—I remember because it was Armistice Day—we boarded a plane and flew to Beijing. It had snowed the night before, and when we landed we could see nothing but an expanse of white. We took a taxi to the city, where we had reservations at the Beijing Hotel.

It was comfortable and old fashioned, with large high-ceilinged rooms. I had a rotten cold, but the radiators were sizzling. I sweated buckets, and felt much better in the morning. We had a big breakfast and waited for the contact we knew would call.

At about ten o'clock a courteous Chinese man dressed in Western clothes knocked at our door. He greeted us warmly, like old friends, until the floor attendant who had escorted him to our room was gone. Then he entered, shut the door and strolled around, his eyes taking in every detail. We invited him to be seated, and served tea. He asked whether our journey had been pleasant, inquired after our health. He said a friend of his, a prominent movie director, had a large house and garden on the north shore of Rear Lake. Since we were interested in the arts, we might find staying there more enjoyable than living in a hotel. Other guests, some of whom we knew, were also visiting there. He was sure it would be a convivial gathering.

Protesting politely that we would be putting our host to too much trouble, we let ourselves be persuaded. Late that afternoon, Phoenix, Joan and I moved over.

The house was large, with well over a dozen rooms, but had a homey atmosphere. There were gardens front and back. A high retaining wall closed out any curious eyes. Our host was indeed a film director, but he and his wife, an actress, plus their permanent house guest, a composer, were all working for the Communist underground, and the house was a way station for persons headed for the Liberated Areas. Several other "visitors" were already there, waiting like ourselves to be escorted through the Kuomintang lines.

We were delighted to see a few old friends from Shanghai. They too had kept their plans secret, but now we all relaxed, and there was much banter and laughter.

Every few nights someone would drop in, garbed as a peasant, or merchant, or peddler. This would be the escort, and he would discuss plans and routes and disguises with the next to go. The following day, or night, they would slip off together. New guests would arrive, and the same type of routine would follow.

Our problem was considered more complicated, since Joan and I were undisguisable foreigners—at least nobody would ever mistake us for Chinese. We were told to wait while the details were being worked out.

"You're rich American tourists," the film director reminded us. "Get around. Go sightseeing, take pictures, go shopping, eat in the big restaurants. Then you won't be noticed."

We followed instructions, wining and dining and doing the town. A week passed, two. We were growing impatient. Why the delay?

At last late one night our escort arrived. He was a young man wearing a long dark gown and a snap-brim felt hat. A Beijing University student, he had been doing these jobs for about two years. He said the plan was this: Joan and I would pose as husband and wife, using our own names and identifications. I was to claim that I was an American lawyer going to Jinan, in Shandong Province, to help American clients still there wind up their business interests, and bring them back. Jinan was already in Communist hands; in fact, once you crossed a small river about 50 miles north of the Yellow River you were in a Liberated Area.

Phoenix would play the role of a widow from the northeast whose husband had just died and who was joining relatives in Jinan. We would pretend not to know each other. The guide would be a traveling merchant who, naturally, didn't know us either. He ostensibly would pay no attention to us, but we were to follow him wherever he went. We would go via Tianjin.

Two possible routes had been considered. The first was to take a train south from Tianjin, which was quick and would get us all the way to the Shandong border. But this method had been rejected because on the train papers were checked very carefully. The second alternative, which was the one adopted, was to go by bus. This was slower and not so comfortable, but in the heavy traffic which flowed regularly along this route check-ups were inclined to be more hasty, and sometimes skipped altogether.

In any event, said our guide, the Kuomintang treated Americans very gingerly. If questions arose, we were to pretend not to understand Chinese, and browbeat our way through with foreign arrogance. It was highly unlikely that any petty functionary would dare to stop us.

Phoenix's case might be more awkward. Being small and slim, she didn't look much like a typical strapping woman from the northeast, and her accent was all wrong. But if she didn't say much and remained as inconspicuous as possible, she would probably get by in a crowd.

If, for some reason, we should be separated during the journey, we were to go back to Tianjin and meet at the underground way station from which we would start.

We left Beijing for Tianjin by train the next day. Joan and I were checked at both ends of the line by Kuomintang security men and our passport numbers noted. Tianjin seemed drab after Beijing. It was more like Shanghai, nothing particularly Chinese about its architecture, most of the better buildings standing in what had been the various foreign concessions. There were long rows of gray three-story houses, their front yards separated by high stone walls.

It was to one of these that our guide led us. We mounted the creaking stairs to the second floor and were greeted by our host. He was a thin ascetic-looking man of about 40, with wild unkempt hair and dressed in a long quilted gown. Dusk was falling and he lit a few oil lamps. The electricity had been turned off because he had refused to pay his bill. I gathered this was part of some long feud he was waging with the municipal authorities.

Or maybe he was just poor and too proud to admit it. Obviously he hadn't always been in this condition. The house was full of beautiful mahogany furniture in classic Ming style, scrolls of calligraphy, old traditional paintings, bowls, vases, bronzes—remnants of a treasured family collection. He had been selling them off, reluctantly, piece by piece, and living on the proceeds. In ordinary times, he could have gone on doing this for years. But a revolution was raging, and the type of Chinese who went in for antiques was cutting down on his collection rather than adding to it, while the foreign connoisseurs were leaving China. I was to encounter quite a few decaying scholar-gentry families in later times. Some of them owned fine works of art.

There wasn't any heat in the house either, and this was the coldest late November in living memory. Or so it seemed to us, sitting around in our overcoats, hatted and gloved, barely able to see each other through our icy breaths, which spread in clouds whenever we could rouse ourselves sufficiently from our torpor to speak.

The greatest nuisance was going to the john. It was on the second floor of a rear building which you got to by crossing a kind of flying bridge, as the gale tried to knock you off into the yard below. Wind whistled through every crack in the well-ventilated walls of the chamber itself, so that by the time you finally returned to the chill living room you were thoroughly frozen.

Strangely enough, we had an excellent dinner, which our host somehow managed to prepare in another dim recess of the house. He even served wine, warmed well above room temperature. The place seemed a bit brighter after the meal, and we chatted with him for a while. He talked mostly of his battle against the electricity company, and of antiques, about which he was clearly very knowledgeable. But why he was running this underground station and what his connection with the Communist Party was he said not a word, and we didn't feel it diplomatic to ask.

We slept that night in our army surplus sleeping bags, weighted down with whatever clothing we could muster from our luggage. It was still bitterly cold, and that, plus the fact that we were excited wondering what tomorrow would bring, kept any of us from getting much rest. We staggered wearily to our feet when our guide called us shortly before dawn.

Without pausing for breakfast, we got our gear together. Joan and I had a duffel bag each. I also had a portable typewriter. Phoenix, as befitted a peasant woman, carried a kerchief-wrapped bundle. I, the big lawyer, wore a large overcoat to cover my padded clothes, and was topped off with a smart fur hat. Joan, never very fashion-conscious, dressed in sensible padded slacks and tunic. Phoenix wore a long padded *qi pao* over tunic and trousers.

The sky was just brightening and there wasn't a pedicab in sight. We had to tote our heavy luggage to the nearest trolley stop, which seemed miles away. We were all in a sweat by the time we got there, in spite of the north wind screaming around our ears. We boarded a trolley full of morning-shift factory workers, who gazed at us curiously.

Arriving at the station, we examined our "bus." It was an old two-and-a-half-ton army truck, completely open, without even a canvass cover. Passengers, mostly peasants, were already throwing their bundles into the back and climbing in after them. I persuaded the driver to let Joan ride up front in the cab with him. Then I too clambered into the back to watch our luggage. Phoenix and our guide were seated on their respective bundles. We studiously ignored each other.

The "bus" started. Ten minutes later, it stopped. We had reached a Kuomintang military police inspection post in the outskirts of the city. Everyone out. All papers had to be checked, all luggage examined.

We were in trouble the moment a soldier began going through Joan's duffel bag. Half of its contents were bottles of medicine. Joan was recovering from sprue and the doctor had prescribed an assortment of pills and liquids. She had taken enough to last for several months. Although we didn't know it, there was a thriving business going on of smuggling medications into the Liberated Areas. The smaller Kuomintang officials cooperated readily enough, given suitable bribes.

The soldier examining my bag found nothing exceptionable, but my portable typewriter worried him.

"What's that?" he asked with a puzzled frown.

"A *da zi ji*, a word writing machine," I explained.

"Can you send telegraph messages on it?"

I laughed. "No, of course not."

He wasn't convinced. He walked off, and five minutes later came back with his superior, a military police officer.

"May I see your papers?" the officer asked politely.

I showed him my American passport and a letter I had written on that same portable typewriter, at the suggestion of our guide, only two nights before.

"What does it say?"

"The United States Embassy requests that every courtesy be extended to Mr. Sidney Shapiro, American attorney, and his wife, who are going to Jinan on temporary business."

"And is it signed?"

"Oh, yes." I pointed to the flourishing scrawl at the end. "Leighton Stuart."

"Ah." He smiled skeptically. "Why doesn't it have a red seal?"

"The US Embassy doesn't go in for that sort of thing," I said haughtily.

"I see. Will you wait, please?" He was gone for about 20 minutes, telephoning, no doubt. When he returned, he said: "Why don't you go back to the city and come tomorrow with a note from the US Consulate in Tianjin? Then you won't have to ride in this old bus. We'll send you through in a car."

I argued that it would be too much of a nuisance. Since we had already come this far, we insisted on going through.

"Those wretched foreigners are delaying us too long," Phoenix grumbled aloud. She was trying to signal me to drop the whole thing. Clearly our little device had failed. An important American lawyer, with a letter of introduction from the embassy, certainly wouldn't be riding in a local peasant bus. We had been naively optimistic.

But a peasant woman didn't voice dissatisfaction before a high and mighty Kuomintang officer. He strode toward Phoenix menacingly.

"What's that you said?"

The other passengers closed around her quickly in a protective phalanx.

"Don't pay any attention to her. She's upset because she just lost her husband."

The officer glared at Phoenix, then turned back to us. "See you tomorrow," he said, with a tinge of sarcasm.

There was nothing we could do. I got two pedicabs, and Joan and I started back for town, our bulky duffel bags between our knees. Phoenix watched us as we left the MP check point, her face expressionless. I knew she was worried.

"What are you going to do?" said Joan. "We can't return to the house in broad daylight." It was only nine in the morning.

"Let's go to a hotel and rest until dark. I'll slip back quietly this evening. You stay at the hotel till someone calls for you."

It had been agreed that if any of us couldn't get through, the others would leave the bus at the nearest railway station and return by train to Tianjin. We all would meet that night in the house of our underground friend.

Our pedicabs jolted along the pitted road, past hovels and grimy factory buildings. Gradually these gave way to the pompous Victorian structures of the old foreign concessions.

"Where to?" demanded one of our pedicab drivers.

"The Astor House," I replied, after a moment's thought.

It was the best hotel in town. If we were going to bluff, we'd do it in style. The Chiang Kai-shek gang worshipped wealth and position. They were jumpy now, as the fortunes of the revolution improved, and made frequent raids, usually late at night, to check the identity of visitors in homes and hotels. But they stayed away from the posh places, afraid of offending someone important.

We rolled up to the entrance of the Astor House. I paid off the pedicabs, hailed a hotel porter in a lordly manner for our bags, and walked up to the desk.

"A double room for my wife and myself." I pulled out my passport and a wallet of greenbacks.

"Certainly, sir. For how long?" the registration clerk asked obsequiously, eyeing my money. He barely glanced at my passport.

"One day. I'm not sure of my plans yet."

We were ushered into a large double room. Joan and I looked at each other. She grinned.

"You should see yourself."

I laughed. "You wouldn't win any beauty prizes either."

Our ears and noses were still red from the cold, and both of us were covered with dust.

"I don't know about you," said Joan, "but I'm going to take a bath and go to bed."

"After you, madame."

Half an hour later, we were both much cleaner and fast asleep, I on the floor in my sleeping bag, having gallantly relinquished the large double bed to Joan.

We awakened at about four in the afternoon and had a substantial meal served in the room. By five it was already dusk. I waited another hour, then went back to our agreed rendezvous. I had some difficulty locating the house in the dark, they all looked so much alike. Both the gate and the front door were unlocked.

I went in and climbed the stairs. Not a glimmer of light showed anywhere, and there was no sign of our host. As before, the rooms were very cold. I groped my way to a chair and sat down, my mind in a whirl. I would just have to wait.

Not long after, I heard footsteps on the stairs. Phoenix and the guide must have returned.

"Who's there?" I called softly, so as not to startle them.

"Me," a voice replied. A man entered. It was our host, with bags of food in his hand. "What are you doing, sitting in the dark?" He lit a lamp. "Have you eaten?" His manner was casual.

I told him what had happened. He merely nodded.

"Why aren't they back yet?" I fretted.

"Don't worry," he said. "They'll be back. They're just being careful."

But I was worried. I had seen the brutality of Kuomintang police. They thought nothing of punching or kicking anyone of the poorer classes who displeased them. Suppose they began pushing someone around at the next check point? Suppose they got rough with Phoenix? She was hot-tempered, impetuous. She didn't behave like a peasant woman. There would be real trouble if she blew up. She might be questioned, tortured.

Time dragged on. Eight o'clock, nine. I kept looking at my watch, my anxiety growing. Then, more footsteps on the stairs, and Phoenix and the guide were in the room. I rushed up and threw my arms around her, speechless with relief. Phoenix was a bit embarrassed. Chinese don't indulge much in public demonstrations of their emotions. But there were tears in her eyes.

Shortly after Joan and I left them, she and the guide had climbed back on the truck and gone on. At the next town the railroad and the highway met. Many people went off in various directions to relieve themselves. The guide ambled into a grove of trees. Phoenix followed slowly at a distance. The guide continued through the grove and kept walking for about half a mile till he came to small village. He went into the only restaurant, sat down and ordered a bowl of noodles. He was calmly eating when Phoenix joined him. He urged her to have something, too. Food was the last thing she wanted, but she forced herself to consume half a bowl.

Then they returned to the town. The bus was gone. They had to wait nearly an hour for a train. It brought them to Tianjin fairly quickly, so they wandered around for a few more hours, stopping in little restaurants from time to time to warm up. When it was good and dark they came back to the house.

I told my story. The guide went to pick up Joan. Soon we were all sitting around the lamp-lit table again, cold and tired and depressed. But our guide's spirits were unflagging.

"Get some rest," he urged. "I may have news for you tomorrow." He said good night and left.

We didn't see him until the following evening, and when he returned another man was with him. He introduced us to "Comrade Li." Li said the underground group had talked over our problem. They had considered sending us by small boat along the network of waterways that connected with our destination. But this was rejected as too dangerous. The boats were often checked as they neared the Liberated Areas. Another alternative was to go via the Western Hills outside Beijing. But this region was the scene of clashes between the guerrillas and the Kuomintang forces, and was already under Communist artillery bombardment. Therefore, the best thing for us to do was return to Beijing and wait for "liberation."

Comrade Li must have seen the disappointment on our faces, for he added with a smile, "It's coming very soon."

We thought he was only consoling us, but we were to learn that he wasn't exaggerating in the least. Two months later the Kuomintang was gone from the ancient city for good.

Late the next afternoon we arrived in Beijing. We decided against going back to the hotel and put up for the night in the house of a Chinese friend. We couldn't remain long. By now the Kuomintang was alerted to what we had been up to, and

57

while they couldn't do much to Joan and me, they probably would be very nasty to any Chinese caught giving us shelter.

An underground contact recommended that we find some prominent American residents and move in with them. This would keep the Kuomintang off our tails.

Whom did I know? I remembered that a couple of the teachers in the College of Chinese Studies had been my professors at Yale, in the Chinese department—George Kennedy, Gardiner Tewksbury. I dropped in at the college. My friends were gone, as were all of the teachers and students. Only Henry Fenn, the dean, remained, in the process of closing down.

I said I would like to rent one of the foreign-style houses. He said I could have the whole place, campus and all, if I would keep an eye on it for them. I said I couldn't do that, since I wasn't sure of my plans, but that I would find a custodian and keep an eye on the custodian.

And so it was arranged. I found a certain Hungarian gentleman, who took over the actual maintenance but lived off the grounds, while Phoenix and Joan and I moved into a rather old-fashioned, steam-heated three-story house. Fenn left for the States.

We were fairly safe. From time to time officers of General Fu Zuoyi's Kuomintang army would appear at the compound entrance and demand that they be allowed to quarter troops inside. The gatekeeper would stall them off with a tale that this was the residence of a high American dignitary, and advise them to take the matter up with the US Consulate. They never did, of course. To make sure that we could maintain our privacy, we usually kept the front gate bolted with a foot-thick beam.

We weren't exactly alone, however. Several hundred students and teachers from the high school in Baoding, where a battle was raging, were living in the college dorms. They were well-behaved and kept pretty much to themselves.

Our life was quiet, peaceful. On the recommendation of one of the local Americans we hired a "Western style" cook who had experience working for foreigners. He must have been a magician in his spare time. For while he provided us with excellent apple pies he managed to make enough flour and sugar disappear to feed ten times our number.

The boom of artillery grew louder and more frequent. Tianjin had been taken in a brief but bloody fight. The People's Liberation Army was closing in on Beijing. Soon they were lobbing shells just outside the crenellated city walls. There was a growing undercurrent of excited anticipation. Groups of Chinese literati began dropping in "for tea"—actually to discuss how they should coordinate with the impending takeover.

Kuomintang frenzy mounted to a fever pitch. They murdered political prisoners and arrested hundreds of innocuous people in a paranoiac hysteria. One

58

girl—a devout Christian and member of the YWCA—we had to conceal in our house for several weeks until liberation because someone or other had said something or other to some idiot in the police.

Fu Zuoyi, the general holding the city, was stubbornly refusing to capitulate. The Communists didn't want to take Beijing by storm, though their strength was overwhelming, out of consideration for the lives of its citizenry and to save the city's priceless art treasures from damage. They sent emissaries to negotiate with Fu—including, according to one account, his daughter, a revolutionary who was a correspondent for the Tianjin newspaper *Ta Kung Pao*. They said if he surrendered he and his men would be treated honorably, and Fu would be given a post in the new government commensurate with his rank.

After hesitating for several days, he agreed. On January 31, 1949, the artillery barrages ceased. A hush fell on the city. I rode my bike to Xizhimen, Beijing's northwest gate. The People's Liberation Army began marching in, clean, smartly stepping, smiling young men. Contingents of jeeps, trucks, artillery caissons—made in the United States—rolled through the streets. No wonder the Communists referred to Chiang Kai-shek ironically as their "Quartermaster General." As his troops went over to the Communists in droves, most of the equipment which Washington gave him ended up in PLA hands.

The people cheered and applauded. Parents held their kids higher on their shoulders for a better view. Pleasure and relief were universal. No doubt there were some who wondered whether to give any credence to the horror stories the Kuomintang had spread about the newcomers. But good news travels fast, and many had also heard how correctly this army had behaved in other, already liberated, parts of the province. In any event the fighting was over, and this was something welcomed by all. The streets were gay with flags and bunting.

New Beginnings
Early 1950s

In the next few days representatives of several organizations called on me to request that we lease them the college premises. I put them in touch with an American who was on the college board, an administrator of PUMC, the Peking Union Medical College, a Rockefeller foundation. He entered into a contract with the unit which later became the Ministry of Culture. The ministry paid rent, plus the wages of the old staff, who were kept on. Only when the United States pulled their diplomatic personnel out of China and sent the Seventh Fleet into the Taiwan Straits were rent payments suspended. Eventually, the Chinese government took over the property and paid what I heard was a very good price to the title holders, the North American Council of Churches. That was some years later.

Administrative organizations were set up, a government was functioning—though it was characteristic of the new regime that it wasn't formally proclaimed until October 1, 1949, when most of China had been liberated and more experience had been gained in governing a huge country.

We stood that day with hundreds of thousands in the square before Tiananmen—the Gate of Heavenly Peace—massive entrance to what foreigners had called the Forbidden City, the place where for 500 years China's emperors had ruled. Now, on the magnificent gate house, topped with tiles of imperial yellow, Mao Zedong and his staunchest colleagues had gathered. Mao, the philosopher, poet and scholar, was surely profoundly conscious of the significance of that day as he ringingly proclaimed the establishment of the People's Republic of China.

Phoenix was in tears, and I was deeply moved. It wasn't my country—I was a foreigner. But in that sea of humanity I could feel the emotions sweeping through like an electric current. People in shabby, patched clothes. Army men and women, sprucer, but whose uniforms showed signs of hard wear. The crowd had been silent at first, recalling years of suffering and fierce fighting. But now, at last, victory. A roar welled from thousands of throats, a heart-cry of triumph and resolve.

We began to see changes almost immediately. Hills of uncollected refuse were removed—in Beijing, 200,000 tons in 90 days. Courtyards were swept, houswives organized to keep the lanes clean. Streets had their foreign names converted to Chinese.

On Wangfujing, formerly Morrison Street, the main shopping thoroughfare, for a time the black market currency dealers continued to stand openly on street corners, jingling piles of silver dollars. Security police informed them that this was no longer allowed. A few days later, those still at it had their money confiscated. If, after another week, they persisted, they were arrested.

A new currency was issued, pegged to the value of a few essential commodities like grain, edible oil and cotton goods, whose prices were kept strictly controlled. Gradually, the inflation subsided and prices stabilized.

There was a crackdown on crime. Phoenix took part in the closing of the brothels. Beijing's houses of joy were anything but. The girls were mostly peasant children who had been sold, often for a pittance, by their desperately poor parents to professional collectors who, in turn, resold them to the brothels. Theoretically, if a girl earned enough, she could pay off her purchase price and regain her freedom. This, in fact, rarely happened. The girls told the raiders some shocking stories. They had been beaten, ill-fed, and treated with callous brutality by the owners of the establishments. A dying girl was nailed into a coffin even before she drew her last breath because she was "no longer of any use. . . ."

The worst of the monsters were arrested and tried, with the girls giving testimony. A few, after the details of their crimes had received full publicity, were shot, in the presence of their victims and the local citizenry.

Rehabilitation was not easy, at first. The girls couldn't conceive of anyone being genuinely interested in their welfare. But after several days of good food, rest, and medical treatment—nearly all had venereal disease—they relaxed and started talking openly with the women, including Phoenix, who had been sent to look after them. Then they aired their suffering at "Speak Bitterness" Meetings.

The Women's Association and political workers told them that the root of their troubles, like the troubles of all of China's poor, was "class oppression," meaning exploitation by the rich and powerful and their hangers-on. While the terminology was new to the girls, the explanation in practical terms they could understand. The arrest and punishment of the brothel keepers impressed them. They were finally convinced that the old days were not going to return.

Training programs were created. The girls were taught to operate sewing machines and other useful skills. Those who wished to were sent home, all expenses paid. Those who preferred to start a new life were found jobs in other parts of the country, and their pasts were kept secret from the general public. Many of them subsequently married and had children.

Phoenix went to work as an editor of *Beijing Literature and Art*—a monthly magazine. She also wrote film and drama articles for newspapers and periodicals.

A thinnish foreigner in his forties, dressed in an army padded uniform, dropped in at the house. Big liquid brown eyes shone behind horn-rimmed glasses. He introduced himself as "Dr. Ma" in an American accent you could cut with a knife. Originally George Hatem, a doctor from North Carolina, he had gone to the Red

Areas with Edgar Snow in 1937 and remained on with the Chinese revolution, dispensing medical treatment to everyone, from the lowest to the high.

He told Joan to pack her things, that she could leave tomorrow to join her fiancé, Sid Engst, on a dairy farm in Inner Mongolia. George chatted pleasantly for a few minutes, then said good-bye and left. We were to become close friends. Joan departed the next day. I didn't see her again for nearly ten years, when I visited her in a commune on the outskirts of Xian, where she and her husband, plus a couple of kids, were tending milk cows.

No one seemed to know what to do with me. There wasn't much use in socialist China for an American lawyer at that time. While waiting, I found a new novel which appealed to me called *Daughters and Sons*, and began translating it, hopefully for the American market. The story of guerrilla warfare against the Japanese amid the reedy marshes of southern Hebei Province, it was fast-moving, hard-hitting, and full of peasant colloquialisms, which I'm afraid I rendered into rather Damon Runyonesque prose. Still, it was published in New York by the Liberty Book Club, and had the distinction of being the first novel out of "Red" China to appear in the States.

If I could translate, why not make me a translator? I was taken on by the Bureau of Cultural Relations with Foreign Countries, where I worked on turning into English diverse books and pamphlets. We operated in a charming setting—a large traditional compound of one-story tile-roofed buildings in a hollow square around a garden. The head was Hong Shen, a well-known dramatist who had once startled a movie audience in Shanghai by leaping onto the stage and denouncing the film for its imperialist content. He was a colorful, emotional fellow, another living refutation of the canard about the "inscrutable Oriental."

Only in 1994 when Phoenix's memoir was published did I learn how I got the job. Phoenix had written to Zhou Enlai requesting that I be given something to do. He had assigned me to the bureau. Hong Shen dropped by to tell us the news. As Phoenix's former drama professor at Fudan University and an old friend he was a frequent caller. Only this time he came in his official capacity of director of the Bureau of Cultural Relations with Foreign Countries.

Apparently Zhou had been keeping a watchful eye on Phoenix and me. Tian Han, composer of the lyrics of "Arise!," China's national anthem, had gone through the same underground station with us in Beijing. He told us that when he got to Shijiazhuang in the Liberated Areas, Zhou Enlai had asked him what had happened to us, and why we still hadn't arrived.

A year or two after I started work in the Bureau of Cultural Relations with Foreign Countries an assistant head was appointed, a short mild-mannered man with glasses, Chen Zhongjing. It turned out that this innocent-looking fellow had done extremely dangerous work in the Communist underground during World

War II, posing as a Kuomintang army officer. He managed to get himself a position as staff officer to Hu Zongnan, warlord of Shaanxi Province. One day he was tipped off that he was under suspicion, and had to leave quickly. The Communist Party sent him out of the country. He spent the next few years as a student—at Columbia University.

I once asked him about the risks he took in the old days. "They weren't much," he said with a smile. I had the feeling he really thought that, too. I met quite a few Chinese who had shown incredible courage at one time or another in their lives. But you only embarrassed them if you tried to discuss it.

Phoenix, sent to interview several women who had been called to Beijing for a National Conference of Outstanding Workers, ran into this same modesty. It was difficult to get a story out of them. One woman she spoke to was puzzled. She said she didn't understand why she had been invited—she hadn't done anything special.

A modest attitude was part of the Chinese way of life in the 1950s. Braggarts and blowhards were viewed with pitying scorn. And the modesty was not just superficial. When you lived in a country where the prevailing motto was "Serve the People," one was not likely to get too big for one's britches. Today, in the 1990s, the call to "Serve the People" is somewhat muted by the clamor of the money nexus, but modesty is still regarded as the only acceptable demeanor.

In January 1950 our daughter was born. We called her "Yamei," the "Ya" standing for "Asia," the "Mei" representing "America." Yamei had also been Phoenix's baby name, but the meaning had been different. Her father, a feudal poet-scholar, was enormously fond of the little girl, the last in a long series of progeny. He wanted to express his adoration, but at the same time he had to be appropriately reticent and modest. He settled at last on "Yamei," since while "Mei" means "beauty," "Ya" can also mean "inferior." So Phoenix spent her early years hailed as a "Second-Rate Beauty."

Fortunately—Phoenix and I were very new at being parents—Yamei was aggressively healthy right from the start. We hired a nursemaid, or *bao mu*, who picked up the baby every time she cried. Yamei quickly caught on and developed an excellent pair of lungs, bawling at all hours of the day and night. That was practically the only suffering we had to endure, for the *bao mu* took care of all the messy details which infancy entails, besides cooking, washing, and cleaning the house.

Adulation for the West was still very strong. China, perhaps the most culturally and scientifically advanced country in the world 400 or 500 years before, had fallen behind by the turn of the 20th century. There was an eagerness to learn—from Japan, from the Soviet Union and, more recently, from America. The rich sent their sons to universities in these countries, books were translated by the thousands and avidly read.

With America's growth as a world power, interest in the United States had grown. Many city-bred Chinese intellectuals before liberation were attracted by the "absolute freedom," the "art for art's sake" philosophy which promised to free them from social commitment and responsibility to the downtrodden majority. America's scientific and technological skills were undeniably of the highest order. American affluence, as seen on the streets of China's big cities in flashy cars piloted by well-tailored drivers, had certainly been impressive. There was a tendency to equate everything American with "desirable" and "good." As one Chinese writer sarcastically put it, the worshipers thought "the American moon is brighter than the Chinese."

There was a sizable hangover of this mentality after liberation. Of course people were angry that the United States had helped Chiang Kai-shek with billions of dollars in arms and equipment, and thus delayed the collapse of his hated regime. But there had been little direct confrontation, and a reservoir of goodwill remained toward Americans for helping defeat the Japanese.

But Washington's hostility to China remained unrelenting. In October of 1950 South Korean and US troops had pierced the 38th Parallel, driving north, and American planes bombed Andong, an industrial city in China's northeast. In December of 1950, Harry Truman imposed a ban on all shipments to China and to any Asiatic port which did business with China. He sent the Seventh Fleet to patrol the Taiwan Straits and cut Taiwan off from the mainland. Douglas MacArthur, commanding general, boasted that his men would cross the Yalu River—China's border with Korea—by Christmas. After repeated warnings from Beijing were ignored, the Chinese People's Volunteers joined the fight.

They were indeed volunteers, men from villages only just recovering from the ravages of war—imposed first by the Japanese, then by the Chiang Kai-shek hordes. Now the Americans were threatening another invasion. This the Chinese could not tolerate. They flocked to the colors and marched off to battle, in tennis sneakers, meagerly equipped, with no planes and not much in the way of anti-aircraft guns, but grimly determined.

The whole country rose to back the war effort. This was the first of the Chinese "movements" I was to see—masterpieces of nationwide education and organization which mobilize the entire population in support of major policies.

The US soldiers were shooting at Chinese boys in Korea; US planes were striking Chinese cities with conventional and bacteriological bombs. We saw newsreels of atrocities and devastation in Korea committed by American troops. Children in the lanes of Beijing, too young to have a concept of nations, formerly had used the word "American" synonymously with "foreigner" in an interested and friendly sense. They now shouted it at each other in swearing matches as the worst imprecation.

People in the arts also played an active role. The dramatist Cao Yu wrote a play about doctors in the PUMC Hospital, funded by the Rockefeller Medical Foundation. A team is being formed to go to the front to treat the wounded and cope with germ warfare. One or two of the doctors cannot believe that the civilized Americans would actually indulge in such obscenities. Facts are uncovered which prove that some years previous in that same hospital a number of American philanthropists had been experimenting on impoverished Chinese patients to discover which strains could make the most deadly bacteriological weapons. Their doubts resolved, the doctors join the team. As the play ends they depart for Korea.

All through the Korean war I was treated with complete amity and naturalness. I carried on with my job as usual; I visited and was visited by Chinese friends as usual. If my relationship to the war was mentioned at all, it was only to assure me that China makes a clear distinction between the American people and their government.

In spite of the kindly attitude of the Chinese, I was ashamed, probably because I wasn't much of a Marxist. What America was doing in Korea was disgraceful, indefensible. I had a lot of pride in and affection for my country of origin. I felt personally responsible. And I was responsible, to the extent that every man is responsible who silently watches his government performing reprehensible acts and takes no measures to prevent them. But the ultimate blame lay with the policy makers, whom Eisenhower labeled the "military-industrial complex," the men who called the tune. The American people were only the suckers who did the dying.

Phoenix left for the front with a group of writers and artists to convey greetings from the folks back home. There was quite a bit of this by delegates representing different segments of Chinese society. She returned seething with fury. The story in her memoir of her visit was very moving:

> The American imperialists invaded Korea, and our Volunteers went to the front to defend our country and our homes. I joined one of the Visitors From Home Groups the Chinese people organized in 1951. Liao Chengzhi was the leader. He was seconded by Tian Han.
>
> Though I had never been on a battlefield, I had nearly been killed several times in Chongqing by Japanese bombing. Japanese bombs had blasted me from my dreams in Hong Kong, and I risked enemy strafing to go by small boat from Kowloon to Hong Kong, and then back from Kowloon to flee, disguised as a peasant woman, to the guerrilla areas.
>
> I had a bellyful of the war and misery the Japanese had inflicted on innocent civilians. August was a particularly trying time during the foggy season in Chongqing. The moment we heard, "The warning lantern is up!" we prepared to go into the cave shelters. "Two lanterns!" was the emergency

signal, and everyone ran to the caves. They were crowded and stuffy and not really very safe. If a bomb landed near the entrance, the whole front might collapse and seal everyone inside to suffocate to death. I can't forget those big bombings of 1941, to say nothing of the eight-year War of Resistance Against Japan. No pen can adequately describe the calamities cascading down on the heads of the destitute refugees!

China had long been on the defensive, on the receiving end. I hated myself for not being able to go to the front with a gun in my hands. As a member of a Visitors From Home Group I could at least see some of our Volunteers. They had been through four campaigns. When I got to Korea the fifth had already started. I could go forward and meet them. They were resisting America and aiding Korea, they were defending our country and our homes. I would be able to realize the dream of my youth to fight back against the invaders.

All 3,000 *li* of Korea's rivers and mountains were a battlefield. There was no front and no rear. The moment we crossed the Yalu River we were put on full alert. We had been given physical examinations before coming to Korea. I had brought two pairs of glasses because I was nearsighted and had astigmatism. But I was not allowed to wear them because their reflections might be seen by enemy planes.

Pyongyang was a burnt-out husk when we arrived. Government officials welcomed us with a sumptuous dinner. We could hear the clump of explosions not far away. It was a new kind of baptism.

We were to travel around 100 *li* to visit our Volunteers. Trucks would be our means of transportation. We would move only at night. Our vehicles were camouflaged by pine boughs.

Our trucks rolled through the misty night to a nameless mountain valley. All of the traffic directors were women, and so were the persons who received us in a small village. They had prepared tea. We saw very few men. The people at work were mainly women, old folks and children.

After we had rested a while two Chinese Volunteers led us off in two separate squads of about a dozen each. We walked along a stream that wove through a ravine for what seemed like a long time. I soon was dripping sweat— a perfect cure for my cold! We passed through several groves of trees and finally came to a siding at the foot of a mountain. This was where my squad was to stay.

I looked at my watch. It was only five o'clock in the morning. Bumping along on the truck, I had dozed off fitfully in spite of myself. Early sunlight was seeping through the clouds, puffy and white against a water-color blue sky. All around us were mountains. A few thatch-roofed homes were scattered in the valley. Green wheat sprouts, pushing up through the red soil, were just beginning to bud. A few old peasants and women in white tunics and trousers, after a night of ploughing, were leading their oxen to places of concealment.

Birds flitted among the pine trees. Sunbeams, gilding the pine needles, laughed and danced. They drew me toward them. Leaning to pick a flower in the field I saw two little Korean girls in colorfully patterned skirts coming down the slope. Each was carrying a large bunch of red azaleas. When they got to the stream they washed the soil off the long stems and tied the flowers into small bunches. What were they going to do with them? I was too far away to hear their laughter or see their faces. I could see only that they were very happy, very young, very adorable!

Wang, a Chinese Volunteer, led us to a building for breakfast. He was about seventeen or eighteen, with a wholesome smile. A bugler, he had been put in charge of our squad temporarily. I asked him why he had joined the Volunteers. The smile left his face.

"I'm from the northeast," he said. "When my brother was my age the Japanese devils occupied our land and made him a slave laborer. Only after they were defeated was he able to get a real job and provide our family with enough to eat. I even went to school! The American devils are worse than the Japanese. They're attacking Korea so that they can invade China. We can't let them in. I'm Chinese. I don't want to live in a country of slaves. That's why I joined."

I looked at him. This teenage boy knew what to love, what to hate. His generation had been tempered by the eight-year War of Resistance Against Japan (the Japanese had occupied the northeast for 13 years). They knew the meaning of living, the value of dying. That is why they fought to defend our country and win world peace, and confronted the enemy so bravely.

Just as we picked up our bowls, enemy planes flew over. We were hurried into nearby air-raid trenches. After the planes left, we were able to snatch a bite to eat. Wang took us to a forest. There, in a clearing, sat a company of Volunteers. I stepped forward.

"Long live Chairman Mao!" they cried. "Long live our motherland!"

"*Xingkule*, comrades!" I responded. [Meaning literally, "You're having a tough time," an expression of sympathetic admiration.]

I began to sob, but controlled myself with effort. I told them about the construction going on in China and the many new developments. They punctuated my talk with cheers. A *Guangming Daily* photographer took a picture of that memorable scene. I still have it.

The plan was that our visit would last three days. On the second day enemy planes flew over in more than 100 sorties. It was believed that spies had reported our presence to the Americans, and they had instructed their planes to smash us and flatten the small valley. We were led into a bomb shelter and told not to come out again without a direct order.

We had nothing to eat or drink all day, but I felt neither hungry nor thirsty. Near dusk we were allowed to emerge and were told to return to our quarters for a meal. It was not yet dark, and I walked back to the farmhouse where my squad was staying. The place was empty, except for Wang, our young Volunteer guide. He had a few simple dishes laid out on a small low table. Hunger returned at the sight of them.

But before I could eat, we heard the drone of approaching planes. Korean farmhouses are squat structures of earthen walls and thatched roofs. In the hamlets they are separated by narrow lanes. Because of the bombings, only a few buildings were left in our lane.

Suddenly, heavy blasts shook the earth. Wang shoved me down in a corner and threw himself on top of me. A chattering machine gun stitched a line of bullets five inches from my hand. I looked up. A plane was circling so low I could see the face of the pilot. He was strafing and dropping incendiary bombs. The roof of the building opposite was ablaze.

After the planes left, Wang helped me to my feet. I hadn't been hit. I didn't offer the boy a word of thanks for saving my life. Nothing I could say could express my gratitude.

I hadn't been frightened. I felt only numb. Didn't that young American pilot have parents of his own? Why did he fly 10,000 *li* to Korea to murder and burn? Only because the wind was blowing in the opposite direction did the flames across the lane fail to consume our building as well.

Volunteers came running, and soon put out the fire.

Later we were told a famous vaudeville comedian, another member of our group, had been eating when the planes attacked, and refused to take shelter. He was killed by machine-gun bullets.

Another score to settle with the American imperialists!

It was a devastating experience for Phoenix. It nearly broke up our marriage. She tells about this too in her memoir:

Among those waiting to welcome us when we got back to Beijing was Sha Boli. He seemed like a stranger. My coldness wounded him. We couldn't communicate. I moved into a hostel where our Visitors From Home Group was summing up our visit and preparing to go on a speaking tour. I busied myself with my speech. The hardships of the Volunteers, their courage in battle, the support the Korean people gave them, the savagery of the US armed forces . . . were still fresh before my eyes.

Members of the speaking tour said: "Phoenix has changed. She's a different person."

Had I changed? I asked myself bitterly. Sha Boli was an American. American bombers and the image of that American pilot were burned into my brain. He was much younger than Sha Boli, but he was an American! Their bombs and bullets nearly killed me. I hated the American imperialists, I hated the Americans!

And my husband was an American! I was utterly miserable.

When we returned from our speaking tour, I told my office's Communist Party organization about my mental turmoil. They patiently explained the difference between the American imperialists and the American people.

I went to see our best friend, Ma Haide (George Hatem). He had gone to the Liberated Areas in the northwest in the 1930s with Edgar Snow. In Yanan during the War of Resistance Against Japan he became a member of the Chinese Communist Party, and was the first American to obtain Chinese citizenship after liberation. He had joined the revolution. As a doctor he had treated and cured thousands of Chinese.

He asked me what I intended to do. I had no answer. After a silence he said: "He loves you!"

Ma Haide didn't ask me whether I loved Sha Boli. I hadn't thought of that. I was like a small injured animal desperately seeking protection. My mind was in a whirl.

Sha Boli was also very unhappy. He loved me, loved our home, and loved new China even more. He had seen it built on the wreckage of the old society. He had personally experienced one of the greatest revolutions in Chinese history. He had shared the fruits of the life and work of a people who had risen to their feet. He was a member of a committee defending Julian Schuman and the Powells whose *China Weekly Review* had exposed American germ warfare in Korea. Sha Boli stood firmly on the side of China and Korea. He unquestionably was a staunch friend of the Chinese people.

American planes were dropping canisters of insects which carried deadly infectious bacteria. We saw the newsreels of germ warfare raids on Chinese cities in the northeast, saw how white-gowned figures rushed to the areas where the canisters had broken open on contact with the ground and sprayed the crawling lethal hosts, saw how thousands of people built walls of burning brush and flailed the insects with brooms. We read the reports of the distinguished team of international scientists who had made investigations on the spot, both in Korea and China. Everyone understood that it was vital to destroy potential disease spreaders and eliminate the kind of environment in which they thrived.

The whole population turned out in a huge campaign, disposing of garbage, improving sanitary facilities, killing flies, mosquitoes, lice, fleas, bedbugs and rats. They nullified the germ raids in northeast China, and the nationwide clean-up resulted in a marked drop in the incidence of contagious disease.

One of the few accidental goods to come out of the war was the increased stress on environmental hygiene. China had been a filthy place for decades. Before liberation toilet facilities were primitive. Collectors who sold excrement to outlying farms came around and ladled it out of the privies every week or so. They were fairly regular because human manure had value as a fertilizer. But garbage was something else. It would accumulate for months, until the underpaid, haphazard sanitation department men of the Kuomintang felt inclined to scrape a little off the top. The stink and flies and mosquitoes were a menace, and in the hot weather they were unbearable.

I remember visiting a small village not far from Shanghai in 1948. We had been walking for hours, and we were tired and hungry. We went into a local restaurant and ordered bowls of noodles. The swarms of flies that joined us the moment the noodles were served presented an intriguing problem. You had to hold the bowl in one hand and the chopsticks in the other while shoveling the noodles. But how could you shoo off the flies and avoid pushing them down your gullet? The more experienced members of our party had a simple solution, which I quickly emulated. They put their bowls on the table, leaned close and plied their chopsticks with their right hand, and kept the flies off with energetic waves of their left.

Meanwhile the war raged on. The North Koreans forced the Americans back across the 38th Parallel, chased them all the way down to the southern tip of the peninsula, nearly drove them into the sea. The US forces made a landing at Inchon on the west coast and counterattacked almost to the border with China. The Chinese volunteers had entered the war. Battles seesawed furiously. Saturation bombing leveled every city and town in North Korea. The Chinese learned to dig deep caves in the mountainsides. They studied or entertained themselves while blockbusters ineffectually churned up the earth outside.

In July of 1951 armistice talks began at Panmunjom. They were not to be concluded for another two years. The fighting continued. Each time the Americans made a little military progress, they broke off the negotiations. Then the defenders would give them another drubbing, and they would rush back to the conference table crying: "Let's talk this over!"

We heard quite a bit about Panmunjom from a Western newsman who lived in Beijing and attended the conference. The foreign correspondents were dissatisfied with the handouts they were receiving from the US press officer on the progress of the battles. These usually proved to be glowingly triumphant fabrications, or were

70

so vague as to be useless. Our friend got the real news from the Chinese and passed it on to his brother gentlemen of the press, who incorporated it in their dispatches.

This included, at a time when the Pentagon was baldly claiming that there were no GIs in enemy hands, photos of thousands of US soldiers disporting themselves at baseball and other pleasant activities in Chinese camps for POWs.

Within China major developments were taking place. Land reform had reached almost every corner of the country. It was the most important economic measure to date, since 80 to 90 percent of the population lived on the land. What they wanted most was to possess their own plot of ground, free and clear, and to break the economic strangle-hold of the landlords. It was estimated that 90 percent of the tillers—the peasants—owned only 30 percent of the land. Seventy percent was owned by the landlords and rich peasants, who constituted only ten percent of the rural population.

In December 1951, Phoenix went to Jiangxi Province as a member of a land reform team. It was one of many dispatched to various parts of the country. The teams were composed of personnel from government organizations, and worked with local cadres and PLA men stationed in the vicinity.

The first thing they did was calling on and holding meetings with the poor tenant farmers and hired hands. They would get them to speak up and tell what the situation had been before liberation. The story generally followed a simple dreadful pattern: A peasant leased a few fields from a landlord, paying rent in kind ranging from 50 to 80 percent of the harvest. He would need money for seed or food grain to tide his family over till harvest time. The only place he could get it was from the village landlord. (Larger communities might have two or three, but ordinarily one big landlord controlled the entire village.) He would make the loan to the tenant at a usurious rate of interest. At harvest time he would weigh the rent grain in his own measure boxes, which invariably were rigged to cheat the tenant. The amount the tenant would be "short" would be added to his debt, also at compound interest. It was only a question of time until the tenant was so crushed that he couldn't make payment. The landlord would then confiscate his property and kick him and his family off, or keep them on as semi-serfs. The tenants' wives and daughters were, of course, always fair game.

In some places a few peasants at first were reluctant to talk. They had been oppressed by centuries of feudal rule. The landlords had been very powerful, the backbone of the Kuomintang government. They were the magistrates and local officials, they collected the taxes, they ran the police, had private gangs of their own thugs. Their sons officered the army. It was commonplace for them to have people brutally beaten or murdered. Their military power had been broken, but they were still around, as were their families and their cronies. What would happen after the land reform teams left? The gentry spread rumors that Chiang Kai-shek was going to make a landing very soon, and uttered dire threats against anyone who dared touch their property.

But the timid ones were definitely in the minority. There were plenty of people who spoke out. At the mass meetings they exposed in detail, from personal experience, the landlord's cruelty and oppression. Men and women wept as they testified. The audience yelled angrily, shouted political slogans, until the haughty or hypocritical landlord cringed abjectly. If he had committed shocking crimes, such as murder or rape, and the people demanded it, he was turned over to the judicial authorities for trial. A few of the particularly vicious types were executed, but only a very few.

The land reform teams helped in the formation of Poor Peasant Unions, Women's Associations and militias. The members of these were the most militant and most politically aware, and became the nucleus of government, security and education in the village. People were taught that the enemy was not so much this or that individual landlord, but the entire landlord class. They heard about landlords in other counties, in the provinces, and began to understand the meaning of "class struggle."

In a village in Guangdong Province a landlord slaughtered three members of a land reform team in their sleep with a knife. Some years later there was a famous case of an ex-landlord who got a job as a cook at a construction site and nearly killed half a hundred workers by poisoning their food. Luckily, they were treated in time. In the late 1960s I heard accounts from people in a village not far from Beijing of mysterious figures in white who howled like banshees night after night outside the homes of the more enthusiastic commune members. The "ghosts" when caught turned out to be ex-landlords who were still seeking revenge on the poor peasants who had received shares of their land.

The average person felt such actions proved that Mao Zedong was justified in his warning about the persistence of class struggle. And if it slipped his mind for a time, there were always class enemies to forcibly remind him.

Land reform, because it was in the people's interest and had their support, succeeded. The majority of the landlords accepted it, however reluctantly, because they had to. Only their excess land, draft animals, farm implements and surplus grain were divided, but they were left with an equal share of land with everyone else. None of their industrial or commercial interests were touched. Landlords lost their civil rights, but if they behaved themselves the villagers could restore them at the end of five years. The status of their children was not affected.

Naturally, the situation did not remain static. In the countryside, where the bulk of the Chinese population lives, many involved struggles were yet to come.

At this time, we were still living in the former College of Chinese Studies (now Ministry of Culture) compound, occupying an entire three-story house. I had the minister, in a similar house, on my right, and another high official on my left. Everyone was very polite, but I felt awkward living there. I wanted something homier and more relaxed, a place where visitors didn't have to sign in at the gate. I asked the Ministry of Culture to find me other quarters. Phoenix hadn't come back from the Land Reform yet, and I thought it would be a nice surprise to be all set up in a new house before she returned.

I looked at a few prospects and finally settled on a traditional hollow-square compound, also belonging to the Ministry of Culture, to be shared with three other families, Chinese, who occupied the wings. The rooms were smaller than what we'd had in the college, and the floors were stone flagging instead of wood, but we had our own little garden in the rear of the large one. I liked the privacy, the tile roofs, the paper windows, and having less exalted Chinese cadres for neighbors. The only concession to modernity was electric lights and flush toilets. Gone was our steam heat and gas range. We cooked with the popular coalballs and kept warm with old-fashioned pot-bellied stoves. But all the housekeeping was done by our *bao mu*, who ate and slept in.

My new neighbors were very friendly. They helped us get settled. From various parts of the country, they had different characteristics. What they had in common was that they all, the men, that is, worked for a department under the Ministry of Culture, which collected and published folk songs. The wives stayed home and looked after the kids. Later, as more opportunities opened up and literacy spread, most of the younger women were absorbed into full or part-time jobs.

Our neighbor Ho was short, stocky, round-headed, with a shaven pate, and had a short, stocky, roly-poly wife who laughed a lot. They had two kids, a little girl about a year old, very cute and cuddly, and a boy of about five, a holy terror who was always getting into scrapes. They seemed to be perpetually cooking and eating, and they looked it.

Wang, on the other hand, was a thin ascetic type, of peasant origin, but intellectual and bookish. While still in the Liberated Areas he married a village girl, a doe-eyed beauty, slim and graceful. For some reason she was very jealous, and she often wept and raged over suspected infidelities. I'm sure they were imagined, for Wang was quiet and reserved and a little cross-eyed. Afterwards, they had a baby, which fortunately took after the mother, and she lavished on it all of her sensitive emotion.

Our third neighbor, the Tangs, were from Sichuan, which meant they liked hot spicy food and were great yarn spinners. She was small, but nicely rounded. He was big and fleshy, and talked in a slow, easygoing manner, in spite of the fact that he was really high-strung and suffered from high blood pressure. Of course they both spoke with a Sichuan accent, which evokes the same kind of pleasurable amusement among other Chinese as a southern drawl produces in New York. They had a daughter of two or three when we moved in, and were expecting another baby soon.

Phoenix returned from her land reform work, very healthy and full of stories. She had seen at close hand the differences between ordinary people and class enemies, and that brought our relationship back to normal. Since she had been in Sichuan during World War II, she and the Tangs had a lot to talk about, and we became quite friendly. Our daughter Yamei greeted her mother politely as "aunty." Phoenix was stricken. The kid didn't know her.

She bemoaned the fact in her memoir:

> The baby, by then nearly two years old, didn't recognize me, I had been away from home so long. I could have wept. It was my own fault. Immersed in battles and struggles, I hadn't given our family a shred of warmth. It was Sha Boli who had provided the child with love and care. They were very devoted. Sometimes she sat on his shoulders while he worked at his typewriter. I was envious and ashamed. I hadn't done my duty as a mother. I had only myself to blame!

> Sha Boli was on excellent terms with our neighbors, men and women, young and old. There were many people from the USSR in China in the 1950s. The kids on the block called him "Soviet Elder Brother," as they fondly hailed any "green-eyed, golden-haired" foreigner. He played with them, and his Beijing accent improved.

I had been both father and mother to Yamei. In the evening she would climb into my lap and demand stories. Having exhausted what little I remembered of Grimm and Andersen, I was forced to resort to science fiction of my own creation. This placed a strain on my Chinese vocabulary. But evidently I got my meaning over pretty well, for Yamei would correct me if I told it any differently on the fifteenth or sixteenth rendition. I think I placed first in her affection, followed as a close second by her kitten, which she clutched to her a good part of the day, when she wasn't dressing it in doll's clothes and trying to induce it to sleep in her crib.

What would it have been like if I had become a father in the States with both my wife and myself working? I certainly couldn't have afforded to pay a full-time nursemaid, or put the baby in a nursery. Neither could most Chinese parents, for that matter. But usually there was a widowed grandma who was glad to take over the running of the household. Phoenix's mother was dead, and mine was 12,000 miles away. Fortunately, our relatively high salaries enabled us to hire a *bao mu*.

Ten years before, I would never in my wildest dreams have imagined that my offspring would be Chinese. Yet now that she had come, she didn't look any different to me than any other baby—except that she was more beautiful, of course. Yamei was in turn capricious, sweet, ornery, inconsolable, sunny, pensive, and completely adorable. No Flatbush infant could have captivated me more.

One of our friends and frequent visitors was Dr. Lin, a Chinese woman obstetrician from Southeast Asia. Lin Ling had been born in a wealthy overseas Chinese family, and had studied piano as a girl. She must have been good at it, for she won some kind of British Empire scholarship to a music academy in London. A brilliant erratic person, she didn't actually care much for piano, and switched to medical school. She finished the course with honors, qualified, and returned home. There she quickly became bored with a social life alternating between sets of tennis and bouts of drinking.

New China captured her imagination. She came and was given a post in one of the big hospitals. She was an excellent obstetric surgeon, but she was too individualistic and temperamental to get along with her steadier, self-disciplined colleagues. For that same reason, although she was strikingly attractive, she scared off anyone who might have considered her as a marriage partner. When we met her, she was frustrated in her job and in her private life, and had taken to drinking again. A few years later, she returned to her own country where I hear that, professionally at any rate, she's doing well.

Lin Ling came to dinner one spring night. At about nine o'clock we were chatting over our teacups when we heard wild shouts from the courtyard. Our neighbor Tang, his head bound in an aromatic compress to lower blood pressure, was milling about, uttering incomprehensible cries. When we calmed him down sufficiently, he sobbed that his wife had just given birth to a baby—in the house.

We left him, half fainting on a chair in the yard, and ran inside. Sure enough, his panting wife was lying on the bed, a tiny infant, the umbilical cord still attached, there beside her. Lin Ling swiftly took charge, sent me for a razor blade and matches, a basin of hot water, towels. . . . Feeling a bit faint myself, I did what I was told, and before long mother and child were in fine shape. It took somewhat more time to bring the father around.

Gradually, we pieced together the story. The mother had been taking one of those breathing and painless childbirth courses. A reservation had been made for her at a maternity hospital; the telephone number of the taxi company had been written down. Perhaps the course hadn't been taught very well, or maybe she just didn't understand it correctly, but when the labor pains started she told herself firmly that it was all psychological, and relaxed.

The Tangs decided that everything had turned out for the best. The baby, another girl, had indeed been born painlessly. She was pretty and healthy, and had been tended by one of the best obstetricians in Beijing. They hadn't even had to pay for the taxi. What more could you ask?

75

They thanked Lin Ling again and again. I was honored with the position of the child's godfather. For several years after, until they returned to Sichuan, they brought the little girl to pay her respects to Godfather at every Spring Festival, the Chinese lunar New Year holiday.

This painless childbirth routine was something new to China, and was part of a spate of medical reforms. In the past there had been two kinds of medicine—traditional, for the vast majority, and Western, for a handful of rich in the cities. Even in the cities many of the well-to-do preferred the Chinese form of treatment. The Western-trained doctor tended to be scornful of the traditionalists, and considered them quacks, while many of the patients were cautious of the former's "new-fangled" ways. With the coming of liberation, Mao called on both kinds of practitioners to learn from each other, especially for the Western-type doctor to learn from China's vast store of ancient medical lore. Of course it was only the complete change in the social fabric that enabled the average Chinese to receive any medical treatment at all.

Western medicine advanced from being acceptable and available to a sort of panacea in the minds of some. There was a tendency to give children penicillin freely for the slightest touch of fever, until it was found they were building up a resistance against the drug, rendering it ineffective at times when it was really needed. Geriatric injections according to a Romanian formula were popular, as was "tissue therapy" from the Soviet Union. These methods may be valid under certain conditions, but for a period they seemed to be used indiscriminately in China.

People were inclined to accept on faith almost anything coming out of the Soviet Union. This was the honeymoon period. America had boycotted New China, rejected all friendly overtures, threatened military invasion from Korea, air-dropped CIA agents and KMT saboteurs, and kept up a vicious stream of hate-China propaganda. Washington could have found no more effective means of thrusting the Chinese into the arms of Moscow.

The Soviet Union helped the Chinese build industrial and engineering projects, and sent experts and advisers. While the Chinese had to pay stiff prices and high salaries, they were pleased, for the most part, with what they got. Soviet prestige was never higher.

There were some reservations. A few of the big engineering projects did not come up to standard, or failed completely, because Soviet engineers insisted on mechanically transposing copies of their own projects in disregard of Chinese materials and conditions. While many of the experts were sincere, hardworking people, some were not. You used to see them rolling up to the Friendship Shop that caters to foreigners in big Zis and Zim limousines, and walking in with large suitcases, which they would cram with purchases of Chinese furs and silks. They could get several times the price back in Moscow. People began to suspect they were not all "selfless proletarian internationalists." Even the kids in the lanes had a jingle they used to recite while skipping rope:

> *Soviet big brother in a big car goes to town,*
> *Soviet big sister wears a fancy gown.*

Still, recognition of the nature of Soviet backsliding into capitalism did not come in a day, nor was it as virulent in the beginning as it grew later, and a lot of the Soviet achievements were genuinely admirable. The Chinese wanted to learn from them. Russian was taught in the schools, lessons were broadcast over the radio. Soviet movies and dramas played in the Chinese theaters; Soviet directors showed how to put them on, and taught the Stanislavsky method of acting.

A few Soviet films stressed the horrors and sufferings of war, and said all wars are bad. Did that mean the Russians were not supposed to fight back when invaded by the Nazi legions? Were people ground down under the heel of a foreign imperialist or a domestic dictator simply to bow their heads and take it? Was it immoral to fight a defensive war or a war of liberation?

We saw a Chinese version of *Twelfth Night*, not exactly one of Shakespeare's most immortal dramas, put on with the aid of a Soviet *régisseur*. All I remember is large putty noses on the Chinese actors, yards of lace at the cuffs, and splendid plumed hats. I don't think the audiences took this opus too seriously. For weeks after it hit the boards, irreverent Chinese teenagers were greeting each other on the street with deep courtsies on the part of the girls and hat-flourishing bows by the boys.

What devastated Beijing audiences was *La Traviata*, done by a Chinese opera company schooled by a Soviet impresario. They must have spent a fortune getting the costumes and scenery rigidly correct. Everything was sung, including the recitative. That tickled the Chinese. The night Phoenix and I went, when rich papa came to plead with Violetta, a high-priced courtesan, to release his darling son Alfredo from her wiles, even before he had time to enter the parlor, the maid began to warble:

"A gentleman here to see you."

"Who is it?" trilled Violetta.

"Monsieur Germont," in dainty staccato.

"Ask him to come in," Violetta chimed.

The audience collapsed in tears of helpless laughter. It was several minutes before the show could go on.

Yet much of the Soviet art that came to China was excellent—Oistrakh, Richter, Ulanova, the Bolshoi . . . Several new novels, translated into Chinese, reached millions of readers. The Soviet impact on Chinese culture was large.

If some of it was negative, ideologically wrong, the Chinese weren't worried. Mao's attitude to foreign arts, and to China's own cultural heritage, had always been one of critical appraisal. He felt it was good for the public to be exposed to a wide variety of fare. A certain amount of ugly or hostile material wouldn't hurt, in fact it would serve to immunize people and sharpen their political perceptions.

Consumer demand increased. In a country of hundreds of millions even a modest rise of consumer purchasing power takes an awful lot of satisfying. Suddenly there weren't enough thermos bottles, bicycles, sewing machines . . . all the things poor Chinese families previously could never afford.

Industrial production—heavy and light—had to be stepped up.

When the Communists came to power in 1949, industry and commerce were in a sorry state. What heavy industry there was had been in the hands of the Four Families—the bureaucrat-capitalists. This, along with their holdings in fields like banking, the new government confiscated. But the rest of trade and manufacturing was conducted by relatively small and medium-sized companies. Many were on the verge of bankruptcy, because the big boys had scraped off all the cream, plus the disruption caused by years of fighting.

To get the wheels rolling again, the government entered into contracts with the manufacturers whereby it supplied the raw materials or semi-finished goods, bought their entire output, and handled all sales and distribution. It also intervened in labor relations to ensure that the workers got a fair wage without putting too high a demand on the enterprises. In addition, the government began building industrial projects of its own.

This worked well. Machines were soon humming all over the country. The number of industrial workers increased. More goods appeared on the market, though they still couldn't meet the growing consumer demand.

Businessmen prospered. They redecorated their homes, took their cars out of storage, dressed well, and resumed their social life. For the new government they had nothing but praise. The more influential people joined the Chinese People's Political Consultative Council which, while it had no power, cooperated with the elected National People's Congress, and served as a forum for discussion and study.

But the leopard hadn't changed its spots. The tricks began again, assuming they had ever stopped. Entrepreneurs bribed government officers, cheated on their taxes, swiped goods and materials they were working on under government contract, substituted cheaper stuff and turned out shoddy merchandise, and stole economic information from government sources. On the government side, graft, waste, and bureaucracy helped provide a conducive environment for crooked machinations.

A double-barreled nationwide campaign was launched against these "peccadilloes," starting at the end of 1952, known in typical Chinese shorthand as the "Five Anti's" and the "Three Anti's." It was conducted in a style people had learned to recognize—throw everything open to the public, get everyone involved.

This is how the Chinese Communist Party operates, an aspect of what they call their "mass line." In every drive for or against something, up to and including the present day, they follow this pattern.

It didn't take long before the people working in the various enterprises, public and private, produced enough evidence to expose the gentlemen involved. Most of them cried *mea culpa*, or muttered that they had only been engaging in what had been honorable business practice for centuries. Which brought the discussions to the crux of the matter. While cheating your competitors, and your customers, and your government, may not only be good form but even admirable in a predatory, dog-eat-dog society, should such habits enjoy the same moral sanction in a socialist society?

"Absolutely not," cried wife Phoenix indignantly. "The situation is fundamentally different. In a feudal or capitalist society, a minority rules the majority. It's a jungle type of existence, where ruthlessness and cunning are indispensable, where only the most ruthless and most cunning make any headway. But socialism isn't like that. Here the majority rules, and every new development is designed to better their well-being. People don't have to worry so much about food or clothing or shelter any more, and taking advantage of others is discouraged. If a person is dishonest, we only shake our heads and say: 'How crude. Just a pig!'"

This may sound impossibly idealistic today, but that is how the majority of the Chinese, and I, felt in the 1950s. The moral regeneration to me was one of the most stimulating aspects of New China. People were changing. As the tension and pressure eased, they became more affable, more kind. Perhaps that's how most people in "democratic" societies also are, before the struggle for survival erodes their instinct for decent behavior.

There were still tensions in China; people had to work hard. The struggle between the haves and the have-nots continued. All of the problems and petty annoyances of daily life went on. The Chinese people are not saints. But the degree of selfishness was noticeably diminishing. You didn't feel the need to make pre-emptive strikes. The world, in New China at any rate, was not out to get you.

Today we have a new problem. How much of what we have professed to be a socialist morality can be retained in a "socialism with Chinese characteristics," in a socialist market economy? This is a question profoundly exercising the Chinese people as we near the end of the 20th century. We will discuss it further later on.

But if, in the early 1950s I, like everyone else, was moved by the new social atmosphere, I was simply staggered by the beauty of Beijing. It was a very different China, after preliberation Shanghai.

Shanghai was a mixture of East and West. For a mile along the Huangpu River ran the Bund with its row of foreign banks and offices, mostly in heavy 19th century European style, their majesty somewhat marred by the rickety old trolleys, French owned, rattling before them. The entrance to the Hong Kong and Shanghai Bank was flanked by two pedestaled bronze imperial lions. Millions of passing hands, rubbing their front paws for luck, had burnished them to a shiny gold.

At one end of the Bund lay the Chinese City—the oldest part of the original Shanghai—a jumble of handicraft shops, restaurants, and crowded dwellings. The other end was graced by the British Consulate and spacious lawns. There the road crossed the steel-girdered Garden Bridge where, during the occupation, Japanese soldiers slapped foreigners who failed to come out of their vehicles and bow to sentries.

On the other side of Suzhou Creek, which the bridge spanned, was Hongkou, an area of docks, bars and brothels. Its most visible landmark was the tall apartment hotel called, appropriately enough, Broadway Mansions. Before liberation it housed American and other newspaper correspondents, as well as some of the highly paid personnel of various foreign commercial enterprises, and its interior life was much closer to Broadway than to the Bund.

The city was populated by a large poverty-stricken class, a fair-sized middle class, and a small but powerful group of the very wealthy. The poor were every-where—stevedores, rickshaw pullers, shipyard and textile workers, itinerant drifters, famine refugees—their clothes often little more than rags and patches—weary men, emaciated women, large-eyed spindly children. The lucky ones occupied crowded warrens resembling tenement houses. Many lived in shacks and shanties made of whatever material came to hand. Thousands slept in doorways and on the streets.

I was shocked and heartsore at the sight of such misery when I first arrived in Shanghai in 1947. But the sheer numbers of suffering humanity had a numbing effect. Though each sick and dying individual you encountered was a sharp prick to your conscience, your mind boggled at being immersed in hundreds of thousands. In self-defense it reduced them to statistics. I found, to my horror, that I was coming to accept them as part of the local scene.

This was because I myself was living, though modestly by American standards, much closer to the opposite end of the spectrum. I was comfortably married. We had a car, an apartment, a maid. I ran a law office, listened to big talk at the bar of the American Club, partook of the French cuisine at the Hotel Metropole for lunch. When the fancy struck me, I could stroll over to Jimmy's on Nanjing Road and have the best American apple pie and chocolate ice cream in the Orient. Feelings of guilt could always be put down by the rationalization that depriving myself could in no way help to solve the inequities of Chinese society.

And I was only on the fringes of the real money. Foreign financial giants—the foundations of whose fortunes had been laid on opium running and real estate speculation . . . big absentee landlords from the provinces . . . Chinese merchant kings . . . heads of Chiang Kai-shek's Kuomintang and their coterie who simply used government funds and property for their own private purposes. . . . All these gentry lived in sumptuous manors or in smart new high-rise apartments and rode about in chauffeur-driven limousines.

I met them at parties, luncheons, banquets, receptions. Whether Chinese or foreign, they talked nothing but business or politics. A few of the Chinese had studied abroad—in America, England, Germany, Japan—and had pretensions to Western culture. In general they were a cynical lot. Many of them knew the end of their day was approaching. It was only a question of time. Discussion tended to center around how to squeeze the last possible dollar out of China and get it, and themselves, abroad before the final curtain fell.

The middle class, though smaller proportionately than its counterpart in the West, also hoped to climb to a higher bracket, and also was whipsawed between low incomes and rising prices, but much more severely. They included office employees, store sales personnel, civil servants, students and teachers. Except for the last two, they knew little and cared less about political affairs, their previous experience having taught them that politicians and officials, of whatever stripe, were greedy and corrupt. They longed only for peace and stability, and an opportunity to earn a basic living.

But try as people might to stay away from it, politics influenced every aspect of their existence. Bribes to government flunkies could keep their sons out of the army, or diminish or exempt the taxes they had to pay. Racketeers—musclemen of the politicos—also required financial assuaging for the "protection" they afforded. The great value of the "Old China Hands" was that they could advise foreign concerns exactly who and in what manner, should be paid how much. Many arrangements had to be made with local political figures to ensure the smooth operation of the black money market, where 90 percent of the city's foreign trade was conducted. Politics was as inevitable as death in Shanghai, and much more inevitable than taxes.

It was essentially a foreign city in flavor. The buildings were in the shoddy European style of the century before, except for a few new elegant apartment houses in what had been the French Concession. Street signs were both in English and Chinese—"Bubbling Well Road" and "Avenue Joffre" were known to the local residents by the way their ear heard the foreign pronunciation. (Bus conductors announced Petain Road as "Pei Tang Lu.") My office was in the "Development Building." "St. John's University," an American institution, bordered on "Jessfield Park" established by the British. Turbaned Sikh policemen controlled traffic. European food and dress were popular. Movies were mainly Hollywood creations. Western products flooded the markets. There were even dance halls where charming partners were available for a set fee per dance. On the outskirts of the city riding stables and a large golf course offered healthful relaxation for the tired executive.

But Beijing was something else. In the early 1950s no city could have been more traditionally Chinese. It breathed antiquity, power and refinement. It first became the capital when the Mongol emperor Kublai Khan took the throne in 1280, and was built to its present magnificence in the 15th century by the emperors of the Ming Dynasty.

Situated in the exact center of Beijing is the Imperial Palace, a huge complex of courts, compounds, terraces and tiers, all paved with stone and surrounded by ornately carved marble balustrades. A series of great halls rises gradually to a height overlooking the city, each with massive pillars supporting gleaming tile roofs of imperial yellow.

From here the city extends in the four directions of the compass with geometric precision. Ancient places of worship—Buddhist, Taoist, Confucian, Tibetan, Muslim and Catholic, temples, cathedrals, nunneries and monasteries—attest to Beijing's diversified religious and cultural influences. The whole city is neatly laid out in regular lines of streets and lanes. And in these lanes, mostly earthen and unpaved when we first arrived, the bulk of the population lives in hollow square compounds of tiled-roof one-story structures, enclosed by high, plastered brick walls.

There was a serenity, a solidness, about Beijing in the 1950s. Northern Chinese tend to be tall, large-boned, their movements and speech more deliberate than those of the volatile southerners, their courtesy unfailing. They are a people who have beaten back endless incursions of foreign marauders. Even when over-run, as by the Mongols in the 13th century and the Manchus in the 17th, they absorbed them into their rich culture and vast multitudes until the invaders were completely assimilated.

Though Shanghai had been interesting in appearance, its European architecture and office buildings, its cars and business suits provided familiar footholds to a person climbing slowly into a new and alien culture. But practically everything about Beijing was different. It was a storybook world, filled with colors and shapes the like of which I had never seen. Princely residences guarded by stone lions, arches of stone and wood painted in beautiful and intricate designs at street intersections, the whole city encased in a thick crenellated wall punctuated at regular intervals by gates—massive brass-studded doors topped by tiled-roof forts. . . . I was enchanted and overwhelmed.

Now, in ancient medieval cities like Beijing, throughout the land, new concepts were taking hold, and the new regime was strengthening.

Settling In
The Mid-1950s

Conditions were fairly stable in 1953. Peasants were forming agricultural co-ops. Business, too, was moving forward. In July, the Korean armistice was signed, and the Chinese Volunteers started for home. China's First Five-Year Plan commenced.

It was also the year I joined the Foreign Languages Press. In 1951, when I was still with the Bureau of Cultural Relations with Foreign Countries, we had begun, experimentally, a magazine called *Chinese Literature*. With our main stress on current creations, we chose the best of the latest fiction and literary articles we could find, as well as classics and early 20th century writings, and translated them into English. But it was felt that a broader organization was needed to introduce New China to the world through the medium of books, magazines and pamphlets, and in 1953 the Foreign Languages Press was formed. Our magazine, along with others, was amalgamated under its aegis.

Our office was a delight, housed in the usual one-story tiled-roof buildings in a large hollow square around a lovely garden, formerly the home of a Manchu aristocrat. Two of our staff, an English woman, Gladys Yang, and her Chinese husband, Yang Xianyi, also lived there, and they usually served tea or coffee during the breaks. She was the daughter of a British missionary and had been raised in China. Her command of Chinese was very good. She had met Xianyi while they were both studying at Oxford. They married and came back to China after the Japanese surrender. His English was fluent, and his knowledge of literary, including classical, Chinese was excellent. They made an ideal team of translators. In later years they produced a fine English rendition of the classic novel *A Dream of Red Mansions*.

All told, we had only about a dozen people, but we managed to put out quite a decent quarterly. This eventually became a bimonthly, then a monthly.

My job tended mainly toward the translation of contemporary works, especially those with war themes, fighting, and rough and tumble. Having been raised on the diet of violent fiction which is the privilege of every red-blooded American boy, I seemed to have the vocabulary and imagery required.

Actually, I enjoyed doing them, and felt a rapport with many of the characters. Whether fighting an enemy on the battlefield or a natural calamity in a commune field, Chinese heroes and heroines have a courage and dash strongly reminiscent of the American pioneer spirit. They do what has to be done, come hell or high water, or as the Chinese would say, "Fearing neither heaven nor earth." I've often wondered whether the instinctive friendliness between the Chinese and the American peoples might not be due in part to this common trait they sense in each other.

I liked the work, too, because it gave me an opportunity to read a great deal more in Chinese than I ordinarily would have had occasion to. China is a huge country with a long and involved history. No one, certainly not a foreigner, can thoroughly cover all that time and space. A lot can be learned from a country's stories and poems and plays. They give more of the "feel" of the thoughts and emotions, the people are more vivid, more real, than in purely factual accounts.

As the society changed we saw the style of writing also changing. A few hundred years before, form was all. It didn't matter what you said, but you had to say it elegantly, and within the framework of a rigid formula. Vagueness and circumlocution were the order of the day. Less than half a dozen noteworthy novels were produced in half a dozen centuries. These were mainly in the vernacular, and for this innovation their authors were heaped with the same abuse their European counterparts had met when they tried to break the grip of Latin on the written language in the Middle Ages.

After World War I there arose a general revolt against the old ways. Writing in the vernacular became more popular. From the early 1920s, the Communists encouraged the movement. But it wasn't until the Party came to power that it could push for writing "in the language of the people" on a nationwide scale.

The writers had to feel their way. Many classical phrases had long been current in common speech, even among the illiterate, and they enriched and beautified the language. The idea was to retain these while fostering a gradual colloquializing of the written word. The addition of new terms and expressions reflecting changing ethical concepts and a developing technology, created a prose that was very different from what you found, say, in a Taiwan or Hong Kong newspaper.

China has many fine traditions which very rightly are continuing to be cherished. I became enamored of one of them early in the 1950s. *Tai ji quan* is an ancient form of body conditioning. I began learning it while our *Chinese Literature* office was still in the big compound. My English colleague and her husband started taking lessons from an old gentleman who came after hours at the end of the day. I watched them practicing the elementary movements in the garden and became so intrigued I joined the class. Our teacher, Yang Yanting, was a man in his sixties. He had spent his life giving instruction in what the Chinese call "the military arts," as had his father and grandfather before him. These included exercises with lance (single) and sword (single or a pair), and his own particular version of *tai ji quan*.

Quite a bit has been written about *tai ji*, and its popularity is spreading well beyond the confines of China. It started in Han times, some 2,000 years ago, as a

84

karate for soldiers in the imperial army. It remained a combat drill until the Ming (14th to 17th centuries), when an offshoot developed as a solo exercise. This was increasingly refined until it reached its present form as a kind of therapeutic dance. Often prescribed by doctors and taught in sanatoriums, it is effective in helping sufferers from ailments connected with disturbances of the nervous system—ulcers, high blood pressure, insomnia, and the like.

I certainly have found it a good dispeller of tension. The movements are slow, almost dreamy, in coordination with long deep breathing, not deliberate—yet sufficiently complex to keep you concentrating on them, and them alone. There is a procession of rise and fall, advance and retreat, rhythmically flowing. You go along with it, yet you exert your will at the same time, in a floating dialectic. As you expel your breath and sink downward or draw back, you can feel the pressure going out. Over a period of months you build up a habit pattern until even when you are sitting at your desk or walking along the street, you can consciously relax. The whole routine takes about half an hour. You end up perspiring freely, but your breathing is even, your heartbeat normal.

In China in the old days *tai ji quan* used to be larded over with mysticism. Today, that's out. What used to be "lightness and dark," "male and female," are now simply positive and negative, stress and relaxation. Very straightforward. Amusingly enough, it was in the scientific West, though perhaps that's not exactly the term for Hollywood, that I recently found people learning *tai ji quan* with a good dose of abracadabra thrown in, linking it with the *Yi Jing*—Confucius' *Book of Change*—to which they managed to give an astrological interpretation.

Tai ji is not a panacea. It does not work for everyone and does not succeed every time. For me, most of the time, it does.

Phoenix had been transferred to the Beijing Art Players, a legitimate drama company. Her job was to find plays for them to stage, and to help the writers lick their opuses into shape. I saw dozens of performances, usually at dress rehearsals. Directors and actors were always dropping in at the house. They were a lively, intelligent bunch, reminding me of left-wing theater people I knew on Broadway in the 1940s. We had long, animated discussions on the relationship between form and content, what should and should not be learned from foreign theater experience. . . .

Our daughter Yamei had started going to a kindergarten run by the wife of Shao Lize, a high Kuomintang official who had come over to the Communists. It was several blocks from where we lived, and every morning a pedicab with a little enclosed van in the back with seats for eight kids rolled up to our door to call for the eager pupil. The first two mornings Yamei howled as if she was being sent to the North Pole. But when the tiny bus brought her home at the end of the third day, she was completely adjusted and already boasting of her new accomplishments.

85

"Teacher said I was the best today," she announced with quiet pride.

"The best what?"

"The best eater. I finished first at lunch."

It just shows what good home training will do for a child.

The kids learn that it is bad form to grab things from or slug your little play-mates, that people have to be reasoned with. They get into the habit of discussing things in groups, with every tyke encouraged to speak out freely. Bad conduct is criticized lightly, usually in a private chat with teacher, who does more explaining than scolding. The main stress is placed on praising the good. They have the usual kindergarten fun and games and, when they become five or six, begin learning to read and write.

Chinese children don't start primary school until the age of seven, though they are obviously capable of doing so at six or even younger. I have never been able to discover whether this late commencement is due to some backward pedagogical concept about the children's learning ability, or a shortage of teachers and class-rooms. Anyhow, the kids are raring to go by the time they hit senior kindergarten, and you simply have to give them a crack at the books.

I am talking here only about China's few large cities in the 1950s. For children in the rural areas, where 80 to 90 percent of the population lives, there was little formal education. Primary school was ordinarily about three years—for the boys. Girls generally did not go to school at all. City children were more fortunate. Their parents were in a better position to pay for their education and tended to be more enlightened.

Yamei was one of a privileged minority. She knew I was a "foreigner," though she was rather vague about what that implied. It certainly didn't bother her. Among the children it was not a disparaging term, in fact it gave a certain amount of pres-tige, for it meant that, in her case, her parents were invited to the reviewing stands to see the parade on National Day, and that she was taken to watch the fireworks from the Tiananmen Rostrum in the evening.

When I first came to China, the small tots tended to hail all foreigners as "Americans." It was a good word then, but it grew tarnished with US involvement in Korea, military bases on Taiwan, and persistent US government hostility. The new operative term became "Soviet," that is, people from the USSR. This too grad-ually lost its gloss. Today "foreigners" are simply "foreigners" or, among the more ceremonious, "international friends" or, among the more friendly, *lao wai*, that is "folks from abroad."

In the early 1950s there were not many foreigners in Beijing, other than Soviet "experts" and the diplomatic corps. The business people, the missionaries, the idle lovers of the "exotic," had almost all gone home. They didn't fit into the new society. Foreign trade, shipping, manufacturing, were now under government control. Religion was dying in China. There was no market for Buddhist monks and Taoist priests. What interest was there in foreign preachers?

Even before liberation, religion had always been a pragmatic affair. The main organized faith was Buddhism, with Taoism second, and the various forms of Christianity running a poor third. But it was not unusual for a man to pay lip service to two, or three, parleying his bets not so much to gain an ultimate paradise as to make sure he would get whatever good fortune was being divinely dispensed in his lifetime.

In a land of strong family ties, China's peasants had an intimate and democratic relationship with their gods. In some villages it was the practice at spring planting time to parade their idol through the streets with exhortations that he provide them with plenty of rain. If in the months that followed he failed to oblige they took him out again—and beat the living daylights out of him with sticks and clubs.

As for foreign religions there were certainly some true and sincere believers. But many more were what were known as "rice Christians." On Sunday mornings certain foreign pastors rewarded their flocks with handouts of free rice after services. As long as the rice kept flowing, the turnouts were good. But if ever it stopped, the congregations mysteriously vanished.

After the People's Republic was formed in 1949, organized religion began fading away. Not that it was restricted. On the contrary, religious freedom was guaranteed in the Constitution. The government exempted houses of worship from taxation, and provided funds for the restoration of run-down temples and churches and the maintenance of clergy.

But most folk couldn't see the point any longer. The little niches in walls of village homes where idols had stood or squatted were now empty. I asked an old peasant the reason. He shook his head.

"Those gods never brought us any luck. We had drought and floods and famines. The landlords and usurers squeezed us. The Kuomintang taxed us and dragged our sons off for their armies. We had nothing but misery. Chairman Mao and the Communists have put an end to that. Things are getting better all the time. Who needs religion?"

The young people wouldn't be caught dead in a church or temple. Old stuff, "square," was their reaction. They were learning Marxism, the teachings of Mao. Religion was "metaphysical idealism." What they wanted was "dialectical materialism."

So the foreign missionaries went home, except for a few who remained to grace Chinese prisons for activities of a definitely nonecclesiastical nature.

The last to go were the exoticists, the orientalists, the lads who had found in Beijing a home away from home. They usually, but not always, had money of their own, and collected jade, or paintings, or delved into ancient poets, and lived in

87

"quaint" little homes, wore old-fashioned Chinese clothes, and had servants to shield them from the crass intrusions of an everyday world. Generally harmless, woolly, a few good in their particular field, they were a living anachronism of a bygone day. They gradually drifted off to find another quiet backwater in another old impoverished land.

That left among the foreigners a handful of left-wing journalists and people working in government organizations or teaching school. Social life was pleasant, relaxed. Everyone knew everyone else.

I was a member of a small amorphous group which met every week or two at a bar and grill we rudely christened "The Dump." It was rickety, the walls tilting slightly inward beneath the weight of years, and had sawdust on the floor. But it had beer on tap and served steak and french-fried potatoes that could have held their own in any high-class Flatbush emporium.

Most of the time the quorum consisted of George, Rewi, "Yap" and me, a select, if varied, gathering.

George was Dr. George Hatem, of Lebanese extraction, American born, raised in upstate New York and courtly North Carolina, who had studied medicine in Beirut and Geneva.

Not long after his arrival in Shanghai in 1933, where he set up a practice, he met Rewi Alley, a New Zealand engineer, who was a factory inspector for the Shanghai Municipal Council. This body, composed mainly of foreigners representing big Western business interests in China and a few wealthy Chinese, had meant Rewi's job to be a sinecure, eyewash for the public, part of the humanitarian facade. Rewi, however, took it seriously, and asked George to check the health and sanitary conditions in chromium-plating factories.

George was shaken by what he found—children working long hours in filthy, appalling, dangerous surroundings, often beaten, some chained to their machines. Pity and indignation at the outrages he witnessed daily moved him to a determination to stand with the oppressed. Rewi and Agnes Smedley, one of the best American writers on the early stages of the Chinese revolution, then also in Shanghai, helped him to analyze and understand the fundamental causes and point the way to a solution.

When, in 1936, word came down from the Liberated Areas that Mao wanted an American doctor and an American journalist, George was ready. He arrived at the revolutionary base in the northwest hinterlands in the company of Edgar Snow after a series of wild adventures and immediately began an arduous medical career under very difficult conditions. He was given the Chinese name "Ma Haide." He married a lovely Chinese girl, Sufei, who later bore him a sturdy son. Snow was to write *Red Star Over China*, the long-lasting classic on the new revolution astonishing the world.

Still the American prankster, George appeared on a Yanan stage in a Chinese opera performance in full ancient costume regalia and elaborate painted facial mask. At the same time he was a hard-working, conscientious doctor in a region where medical men were scarce. He treated literally thousands of patients, from impoverished peasants to Zhou Enlai and Mao Zedong, the highest ranking Communist leaders. When Norman Bethune, the famous Canadian surgeon arrived, George was there to greet him. It was during the Yanan period that George and Edgar Snow grew especially close, in a friendship that was to last until Ed's death in Geneva in February 1972, with George at his bedside.

After the People's Republic as formed in 1949, George, who had been an internist, switched to venereology and dermatology because, he said, "That was what was needed." He went tramping all over China with teams eliminating venereal diseases which had been endemic for years, thanks to foreign incursions, among ethnic minority people in China's border regions. Similar teams halted schistosomiasis, scourge of the Nile and the large watery regions of south China where the tiny snail hosts breed.

In Beijing George worked in the Dermatology and Venereology Institute and seemed to spend the rest of his time solving other people's problems. He was everybody's friend, everybody came to him with their troubles. If there hadn't been the phrase "Let George Do It," we would have had to invent it. He would listen carefully, thoughtfully, to what you had to say, then offer some suggestion that suddenly made the whole thing obvious and simple, and usually conclude with a quip that tickled you into a grin. My blood pressure was up a bit, a few years back, but every time George took it, I was normal. He was the world's greatest calmer-downer.

Rewi Alley was another fabulous personality. Arriving from New Zealand in 1927 for a "look around," Rewi remained to devote his life to China. He founded China's industrial cooperatives during World War II when Kuomintang corruption and supineness in the face of Japanese invasion had brought a dangerous disruption of manufacture and transport. He set up a school in a remote village in Gansu Province in the far west, and taught hundreds of local kids and famine refugee orphans from other provinces—children of "ignorant" peasants—to become first-rate technicians and designers in preparation for the new day he was sure was coming. This enraged the ruling authorities who limited educational opportunities to privileged members of their own clique.

Rewi wrote over a dozen books on China, and published collections of verse—his own—about China, as well as translations of Chinese poetry, both ancient and modern. There wasn't a place in China Rewi hadn't been, there was hardly a facet of Chinese life and culture, past and present, he couldn't discuss knowledgeably, fascinatingly.

Rewi and George were "old-timers," but we kept getting infusions of new blood. Yap Zhupei was a Chinese friend recently arrived from the United States, where he was born and raised. He spoke no Chinese, except a little of the dialect of his Fukienese parents, who pronounced "Ye," their family name as "Yap." A wiz at steel making, he left us dizzily behind when he soared off into the realms of higher steel theory, but he was a delightful companion, and in some ways more American than the Americans. Yap could quote the batting average of every important baseball player in the major leagues, and tell you which shortstop stole the most bases in 1935. He was married to an American girl he met in the States and brought back with him. She taught English at Beijing University. They had three kids—a boy and two younger girls.

Men like George and Rewi and Yap did much to broaden my cultural and political base in those enlightening evenings at The Dump, while the beer and steak and french-fried potatoes did the same for my waistline.

They were more my friends than Phoenix's, for when we were together we talked, naturally, in our native tongue, and Phoenix's English was limited, a sad commentary on my abilities as a teacher. She had a fairly extensive vocabulary, but no noticeable grammar. This was entirely my fault, for I got in the habit of not immediately correcting her when she made a mistake, so as not to break in on her train of thought. Soon I got used to her brand of English. I could understand her perfectly. I rather liked her reorganization of English sentence structure. Hers was much more logical, and closer to the Chinese. By concentrating hard, her quick intelligence enabled her to follow, and even take part in, our conversation. But anything more that ten or 15 minutes was too much of a strain.

Then those of us, like George and me who knew the language, would switch to Chinese, which we spoke to a greater or lesser extent. But we were by no means fluent in the vocabulary of the artistic fields which were Phoenix's special interest. Over the years we got better at it, and eventually developed an ability to communicate in depth.

One of the things that brought foreigners together as foreigners—I'm speaking of those working in government organizations—was political study. It was something the Chinese took very seriously. They were always engaged in some course of formal study, some drive, some movement. This invariably involved them in reading Marxist classics, in reading Mao, in discussing Chinese and world affairs, analyzing, arguing, applying theory to practice. It was constantly around us, and very infectious. Foreigners who had the necessary language ability were permitted, if they wished, to participate in some of the sessions of their Chinese colleagues. Usually, the foreigners set up their own groups and conducted their own discussions of whatever was currently being mooted.

To me it opened new vistas. Before I came to China the Marx I knew best was Groucho. Like most Americans I was quick to recognize and resent injustice. I didn't like seeing big guys pushing little guys around. But though I bitched loudly I didn't do much about it. I was cynical. I considered myself a sophisticated New Yorker. Everyone was out to get his. That's the way the world was and always would be.

Then, in China, I discovered I wasn't quite so clear as I thought. I had been ignorant, naive. People were not born bad, tainted with Original Sin. Nor do they come into the world with a clean copybook that they have to defend frantically from being blotted. It isn't primarily a question of the individual, but of haves and have-nots, of classes and class struggle. A small powerful minority, aided by a culture, a way of life assiduously peddled, keeps the majority toeing the line, brainwashing them into thinking they like it.

This had not only been the Chinese experience, as I learned from reading Mao and talking with my Chinese friends: the same thing was happening in every corner of the globe. The foreigners in my study group came from several different lands, and everything they related of the history and struggles in their own countries bore this concept out.

For that matter in America, too, as a lawyer I frequently enough had seen marked class distinctions in attitude and behavior. I had no illusion by the time I came to China that equality or freedom could exist in the abstract, separate from people's class status. The fat purses always prevailed. In America the situation had seemed just bad and hopeless. But my Chinese friends were telling me it was by no means necessarily so.

What can be done about it? I demanded. The only answer, said the Chinese, is revolution, nonexportable revolution, by each people in their own land. But why revolution? Why couldn't you vote the villains out of office? Why couldn't you vote in a new form of government, an entirely new social system?

They referred me to Mao's *On Contradiction*. I found it easy to understand. Mao says the physical world is composed of an infinite number of entities within which are two mutually contradictory aspects, and that these entities are at the same time in mutual contradiction with other entities, and so on endlessly up and down the scale through time and space. Unrelenting battle goes on—between positive and negative, between the new and the dying—until one dominates and conquers the other and changes the very quality of the object or state involved. With this, I believe, most physical scientists agree.

But, says Mao—and here he parts company with the bourgeois philosophers— what is true in the physical sciences is comparably true in the social sciences. Technologies become outmoded, social relationships—master and slave, feudal lord and serf, capitalist boss and worker, are no longer efficient, the concepts which sanctified them—in law, religion, philosophy—are no longer germane. No thing, no condition, is immutable.

"Are you trying to tell me it's impossible to change a social order of minority control by peaceful transition?" I demanded of an office colleague with whom I was arguing.

"No, not theoretically impossible, under certain conditions," he said. "Environment—the domestic and international economic and political environment—has a great influence on local change. If all the world were 'Red,' with the exception of the Principality of Monaco, for example, it is quite likely that country could complete its revolution without a shot being fired. But only because the pressure, internal and external, would be so overwhelming that resistance against change would be obviously futile.

"In the world today," he continued, "the ruling cliques, shaky though some may be, still have plenty of power. They don't take their defeats lying down, and they have outside forces helping. Vote them out of office tomorrow, and you have a military junta staging a coup within a week, a month, a year. They don't like removing their snouts from the gravy trough, and have no objections to a blood bath if it will get them back in again. They are the negative aspect of the contradiction, and they keep wriggling and kicking and squirming until, as a class and as an ideology, they are completely supplanted."

That was how Chinese intellectuals saw the situation in the 1950s, and I could find no flaw in their logic. While aware of the difficulties, they were essentially optimistic. Many were delightful characters, good friends in the arts, similar in many ways to counterparts in the West who also made scathing comments on the social scene. The difference was the Chinese were not only demanding change, they were confident they had a program to bring it about.

One of my favorites was Seto Waiman. A Cantonese, he left Guangzhou (Canton) rather hurriedly and "joined the revolution" at 17 by diving into the Pearl River and swimming underwater, except for intermittent gulps of air, because the Kuomintang police were popping at him with rifles. He had been delivering messages for the Communist underground. Later in his career he became a film director, a good one, and a motion picture technician. Phoenix played in one of his movies, made in Chongqing during the anti-Japanese war.

In the period of Kuomintang-Communist cooperation, he went to New York in a mixed group to buy movie equipment. They took rooms in an old brownstone in the east sixties. Seto formed an instant and hearty loathing for one of the Kuomintang film people—a fat greasy type who was very superstitious.

One afternoon, while the gentleman was out, Seto ran a wire ending in a small speaker under his bed. Around midnight, Seto, from his room above, began muttering curses and groans into a microphone, punctuated with eerie gibbering. Fatty was pale and haggard at breakfast the next morning. His hand shook as he reached for the butter. After two or three days of ghostly visitations, he moved to other quarters.

Seto was a frequent caller at our stone-flagged home in Beijing. By then he was working in the Film Bureau. Like many Chinese men he was a marvelous cook. He would arrive with a couple of his kids on a Sunday morning, carrying a live chicken or a still faintly moving fish. Commandeering the kitchen, he would line up his condiments and get to work. It's the preparations that take the most time in making Chinese dishes. The actual cooking is fast, because they like fresh natural flavor.

After a delicious meal, which Seto consumed with more gusto than anyone (it improved your appetite just to see him enjoying his food), we would sit around talking movies, or theater, or world affairs. His job was on the technical end, and he was working on the manufacture and printing of color film, and three-dimensional movies, and a cycloramic theater. . . . We talked and argued, smoked and drank tea, until the children were dozing in their chairs and had to be taken home, grumbling sleepily.

Chinese men not only like to cook, they have no compunction against holding babies in public. You often see them outside the front door with an infant in their arms, chatting with neighbors. The love of children is universal. It's one of the things by which all visitors are struck. People take their kids everywhere. Babes in arms sleep, nestled against one or another parent in movies and through the loudest clamor of Beijing opera drums and cymbals. The older tykes dash up and down the aisles, or drag docile moms or dads on urgent trips to the john.

The men do a lot of the shopping. A large plastic bag—useful for carrying books and papers—often serves as a receptacle for fresh vegetables spotted at the roadside on the way home from the office.

Male chauvinism is diminishing as women's social and economic positions improve. In the cities, both husband and wife usually have jobs. In the rural areas, where roughly 80 percent of the population lives, a lot of the farm work is done by women. Drunkenness has never been the problem in China it is in the West, and wife beating is rare. The actual running of the household has always been the wife's job, including control of the family budget, although on any substantial expenditure the husband has the final say. Within the home the men behave pretty well, and help with many of the household chores.

Outside the home it's a different picture. Millions of rural families will not pay for even the most elementary formal schooling for their daughters since, when they grow up and marry, they join the husband's household and no longer have any financial obligation to their parents. Education for them would be considered a dead loss. Some of the girls leave home and find menial jobs in the cities. A few go to work in the newly formed rural factories and enterprises. But due to their limited training and skills their prospects are limited.

The chances for city girls are better. Most are able to attend primary school. Some get to middle school—here the limitation is due more to a lack of schools than to discrimination against female students. It is more difficult for them to find jobs when they graduate. While nominally entitled to equal pay for equal work, they generally end up getting less than the men. High rank in government positions or commercial enterprises is also rare—similar to the situation of their sisters in the West.

Most striking, and to me most distressing, is the overall social attitude to women. The reaction to rape, forced prostitution, kidnapping, and the sale of women is remarkably lenient. Many of these crimes go unreported, and even when the culprits are actually caught the courts tend to impose very mild sentences: four or five years, as compared, for example, to summary execution for some embezzlements. Neither the press nor the general public seems particularly incensed. Moralists angrily complain that a socialist market economy is not supposed to give higher rank to money than to female virtue and integrity.

After only a year in our garden quarters, *Chinese Literature* was again shifted. The new office building for the Foreign Languages Press was ready for occupancy in 1956, and we moved in. The various magazines and book departments, which had been scattered throughout the city, were finally gathered under one roof. I wasn't altogether pleased to be back in an office building. We were on the fourth floor, all concrete and dull colors, with four to six in a room. As a "foreign friend" I shared my room with only one person, our chief editor.

From a law office on the 14th floor of the Paramount Building in New York I had moved to the 11th floor of the Development Building in Shanghai, and now to the fourth floor of the Foreign Languages Press Building in Beijing. But there were other differences than a mere change of locale and moving down a few floors.

In New York I had express elevators and steel cabinets and a view of the water cooler of the air conditioning equipment on the roof of the Paramount Theatre next door. The Shanghai elevators were more sedate, the office had wall-to-wall carpeting and large Chinese-made desks of mahogany. Tea and perfumed hot hand towels were constantly available for attorneys and clients.

My Beijing office was five stories high, the ground floor, which had offices as well as a small lobby, counting as the first floor in the British manner. In the middle of the long rectangular building were broad staircases and an elevator reserved for invalids, and foreign visitors and staff. Hallways with offices on either side stretched in both directions, with more stairs at each end. The bright sunny rooms on the south side were allocated first to foreign personnel, the elderly, and those in poor health. Rooms on the chilly north side went to the younger and hardier members of our staff. Steam heat in winter was feeble at best, an economy measure designed to save coal. You had to wear almost as many clothes indoors as you did out, and the poorly insulated north side required full cold weather garb.

We worked an eight-hour day, six days a week, lunch hours not included. At 10:00 and at 3:30 (4:00 in summer) there was a 15-minute exercise break. Those who needed it most—the fatties and the bookworms—usually strolled around, chatting and smoking cigarettes. The young and eager types went through a series of calisthenics, an interesting combination of standard and traditional movements, to broadcast directions in cadence accompanied by music. A few fooled around on the basketball court in the rear compound. Here were three buildings, four stories high, of apartments, with steam heat and hot water, for both foreign and Chinese personnel, and a large garden.

Aficionados of *tai ji quan*, like myself, worked out on the flat roofs, along with practitioners of other ancient Chinese martial arts, attracting small audiences. There were always some who wanted to learn, and we formed classes. But in a few weeks the novices usually drifted away. It's a tough discipline and requires perseverance.

We had a canteen which served three meals a day. Food was cheap but mostly what my colleagues called "big pot" style, meaning that it ran heavily to dishes which could be cooked, boiled, or stewed in large cauldrons for a great number of people. Still, it was reasonably tasty and more convenient than going out to a restaurant. My favorites were the big grilled wheatcakes, which are similar to bread, and dough friters fried in deep fat. The pickled bits and small side dishes were also delicious.

There were no water coolers, or coke or coffee machines, but everyone had his or her own ceramic tea mug and cover. Each room was equipped with one or two thermoses, filled from special boilers on every floor. You kept your favorite tea in your desk drawer, and put leaves in your mug and steeped them when you arrived in the morning, replacing them with fresh leaves when the flavor was gone. People drank tea all day long, taking the mugs with them when they went elsewhere in the building for meetings or discussions.

Tea serves the same function in China as liquor in the West. When you call on anyone, in a home or in an office, a cup of tea is placed immediately before you, and is kept replenished throughout your stay. If workmen are repairing your house, you naturally keep them supplied with tea. There are dozens of varieties and grades of tea, and many Chinese are connoisseurs who can expound on how quality is affected by times of picking and methods of curing.

Our office had no air conditioning, no janitors. We did our own cleaning. On a rotation roster, we swept, mopped and dusted our rooms and the hall outside, and filled the thermos bottles. That meant each of us had a turn roughly once a week. It required only about 15 minutes. Another roster provided for cleaning the toilets. Since every able-bodied person on the floor took part, that job came up approximately once a month. Windows were also cleaned monthly, inside and out, mostly by the young and agile.

For a number of years in the 1950s the first hour was devoted to individual private reading of fundamental political theory. You could choose your author—Marx, Engels, Lenin, Stalin, or Mao, as you preferred. Two full afternoons a week, and sometimes an evening as well, were used for discussion of domestic and international political affairs, usually with people from your own office, in groups of five to ten. Occasionally talks were given on some important current topic during office hours by a senior official of the Foreign Languages Press or higher organization. These invariably were followed by discussion in the small groups.

In our frequent *Chinese Literature* work conferences we talked about planning, editing, translations, illustrations. Criticism was offered of methods and attitudes of the leadership and, on rare occasions, of each other. Among the rank and file self-criticism was more common than criticism. The shortcomings of a unit, including those of its members, were deemed to be ultimately the fault of the leadership—for not being more efficient or not giving better guidance.

To me these meetings and discussions were extremely fruitful. I was kept informed of the country's highest concepts and approaches to political, economic and cultural affairs. The agreement or disagreement or suggestions which any of us, including me, voiced on matters of major concern were, theoretically, relayed up to the top. We believed we were important participants in a democratic process determining and implementing government policy. Popular consensus was essential. If, for example, a person in my unit was applying for membership in the Communist Party, we all, Communists and non-Communists, discussed his or her qualifications. Applicants would not be considered unless they first won the approval of their peers.

While what was known as the "mass line" was often honored by its breach in national affairs, you certainly had a very direct say in how your own particular outfit was being run. You felt that your opinion counted, that you helped shape methods of leadership and management. As a foreigner I was not entitled to any of this, but I was nearly always asked to attend, and my views were courteously solicited.

Frequent confabs improved mutual understanding with my colleagues. They ranged in age from the 20s to the 60s and they came from different backgrounds. They illustrated what they had to say with examples from their own lives and experience. This gave me an insight into Chinese ways and mentality, and taught me a great deal about conditions in various parts of the country.

We seemed to spend an awful lot of time in meetings. Often we did more discussion than work. Democracy was a new phenomenon in China, and I wondered whether they weren't overdoing the free exchange of views aspect. It tended to create what my colleagues called a "relaxed start and a rush finish" syndrome. We

96

alternated between intervals of not much to do and intense scramble. Yet once everyone got the idea and swung into action the teamwork was impressive.

Our chief editor, Ye Junjian, was a tall, handsome Chinese novelist, with a fine command of English and several other languages. He had attended Kings College in Cambridge, and was active in China's literary world. Though not a member of the Communist Party, he supported its principles.

His assistant administratively, an attractive competent woman, was the head of the magazine's Communist Party branch. She had left her well-to-do Henan family as a teenager to join the thousands of young people flocking to the outlawed Communists in the hills of Yanan. There she studied literature and art, which brought her ultimately to her present post of literary editor.

The head of our translators section was a young woman from a wealthy family who had attended Shanghai schools run by American missionaries, and who had served for a few years as a translator in the UN. She spoke flawless colloquial American and was one of those geniuses known as a "simultaneous" interpreter. That meant she could convert your Chinese or English as fast as you spoke it, somehow rattling out your last sentence at the same time she listened to your next.

The other translators were mainly recent college graduates who had majored in English. (Our editorial personnel were usually Chinese lit majors.) In the early 1950s they came from middle-class or rich families, since only these could have afforded to give their children enough education in the old society to qualify them for university entrance. This changed gradually after liberation as more worker and peasant kids were enabled to attend school.

My relations with my Chinese colleagues were warm and friendly. They were curious about America and a bit puzzled by my American ways. I played ball with them during breaks; I wasn't "dignified." We talked freely about my family and theirs. There was a strong family atmosphere in the office. Some of our staff lived nearby and their children also ate at the office canteen. Kids wandered in and out at various hours of the day—to bring something mom or dad had forgotten, or to ask for a missing key, or to have a button sewn on. Preschool-age tots, when whoever was looking after them was ill or away, might stay with us for the day, kept busy at an empty desk with pencils and drawing paper. The Chinese love children, who are usually well-behaved, and someone would always be stopping by to play with or caress them.

My colleagues visited me and I them. Though I lived in a Chinese style household and Phoenix and the baby were both Chinese, I was still a foreigner, and seeing me in this environment was itself a matter of some fascination.

Their own homes varied. Both of the senior editors lived in traditional compounds like my own, with coal stoves for heat and coalballs for cooking, but with beautiful rosewood furniture, gardens, privacy and quiet. The younger staff pre-ferred the new apartments which had steam heat and hot water, and even gas ranges in some, but which tended to be adorned with a kind of Chinese Grand Rapids fur-niture, and gave me an impression of drabness. Beaming grandmothers and kids dashing about, and the unstinting hospitality of the inevitable tea, plus peanuts, or candy, or melon seeds, or whatever was the best the family had on hand, brightened the atmosphere considerably.

During the spring and autumn festival days we went on outings together—to the Western Hills, to the Great Wall, to the Summer Palace, to the Ming Tombs, carrying picnic lunches, always with full complements of kids. I often went along when the whole office volunteered to help bring in a harvest on a suburban farm, or dig an irrigation canal, or build a reservoir. The fact that I didn't mind sweating and straining and getting dirty, impressed some of my older colleagues, who came from a more genteel background.

Though on the whole we got along fine, we did have points of friction. I was inclined to be blunt and had a "let the chips fall where they may" attitude. It took me a long while to learn the custom of starting with a little polite palaver, then sidling up to the problem and circumlocuting all around it, before actually identi-fying it and diffidently suggesting a solution. I still don't do it very well. I consid-ered it pussy-footing, overemphasizing the saving of face, a fear of coming to grips with conflict.

But gradually I realized it's not a bad approach at all. You get the question solved just the same, with a minimum of ruffling of feathers. A strong objection by a translator to one of the editors might go something like this (I'm exaggerating of course): "You've done a marvelous job of editing this short story. I really admire you, I have so little talent in these things myself. The tenant farmer is particularly well done. There's just one small question. It's hardly worth mentioning. But could it be a tiny bit out of character to have him longing for a deluxe, fully automated car the day after he's acquired the bicycle he's never been able to afford before? It's simply a thought. I mention it in passing—for your reference."

Although this routine is a bit frustrating to Westerners raised on adages like "Time is money!" and "Do it now," it is what the Chinese are accustomed to, and evokes the best response. They are differently and more delicately attuned. A light touch on an electric organ can give you full volume. You don't have to pound it with two hands like a piano.

The attitude which aroused my greatest antipathy was the veneration for authority, rooted in centuries of unquestioning Confucian obedience to superiors and official pronouncements. I remember expressing doubt about some formula-tion in one of our *Chinese Literature* articles, and being told, "But that's how it appeared in the *People's Daily!*"

With this goes a scrupulous addressing by titles: "Bureau Director X," "Department Leader Y," "Section Chief Z," etc. Interestingly, those who have the best relations with the rank and file, and enjoy the solidest respect discourage ceremoniousness and are known simply as "Old Li" or "Old Wang," or whatever their name might be.

Mindless acquiescence to "higher wisdom" inhibits progress. Mao fought it for years. "Ask why more often," he urged. But paternalistic authority remained deeply embedded in the social and governmental fabric, continuums of two millennia of feudal society.

While I objectively understood the reasons for this, I wished China could learn a bit about methodology from countries like America, without sacrificing any of her principles and goals. And I wished America would quit mindlessly bashing China.

Since the day I arrived in Shanghai in 1947, although dealings between the two countries on a government level were virtually nil, I remained in touch by mail with my mother in New York. There were never any interruptions, even during the Korean War. I followed regularly what was going on in America and the rest of the world. You could subscribe to foreign news magazines, or read them in the office library.

And you could listen to the Voice of America, Armed Forces Radio, BBC, Radio Australia, and various other English-language broadcasts. They were never jammed. Once in a while there were visitors from the States.

They had to come quietly because America was at the height of the "Hate China" period. China was anathema. No fabrication was too fantastic. It used to make the Americans here laugh wryly. China was news, nevertheless, and American periodicals would buy stuff from foreign journalists and then slant and twist it as best they could.

Life in one issue in 1959 carried 18 pages of pictures taken by French photographer Henri Cartier-Brisson. Certain inescapable facts it reported: China was training 400,000 engineers annually, many of them women. Kids in nursery schools were well cared for. Elderly people kept check on neighborhood cleanliness. . . .

But this was all too positive. *Life*, in the same issue, quickly followed with a bit of pulp fiction on the horrors of Chinese communes. Although Cartier-Brisson had spent four months and traveled 7,000 miles in China, *Life* was unable to find one even slightly horrible photo among the hundreds he had taken, and had to rely on the imagination of a hired artist to supply the appropriate illustrations.

It wasn't that material wasn't available. Newsmen and press association representatives from dozens of noncommunist countries had been covering the China story for years, and their reports were accessible to any American editor who wanted them. There must have been many who knew the truth. But it wasn't wise to be considered "soft on communism."

America had built a crescent of military bases around China—complete with planes carrying nuclear-tipped rockets. American troops were stationed on Taiwan, the Seventh Fleet patrolled the Taiwan Straits. The US armed forces pushed toward Chinese borders in wars against China's Korean and Vietnamese neighbors, and made hundreds of intrusions into Chinese territorial air and waters. Any trade with China was strictly forbidden.

Yet, amazingly, the Chinese kept their cool. When the attacks came too close—as in Korea—they hit back. A few planes that flew in too deep were shot down. They gave the Vietnamese heavy logistical support. They made no wild moves, but they made it plain they were not to be trifled with. The American top brass learned that in the Korean War. While the US forces in Korea hadn't exactly lost, they hadn't won either, something that had never happened before in American history. In this, the new Chinese soldier had played no small part.

A grudging respect crept into American comments on Chinese fighting abilities. Important generals publicly concluded that a land war against China would be "suicidal." A major clash of arms between the United States and China, while certainly not impossible, was no longer inevitable. Or so it seemed to the armchair generals among my foreign intimates. Many of the Chinese I spoke to had the same feeling.

Where did that leave me, personally? If I were to go back to America, this would be the time. The hostilities had ended. My mother was a widow, earning a slim living at various odd office jobs. The modest sum my father had left her was running out. What I was able to send her occasionally just about covered her rent. Though she never labored the point, she sometimes asked when was I coming home.

I missed her, and my sister and my old friends. I remembered lakes in summer and green wooded hills, tree-lined residential streets, concerts in Carnegie Hall, comedians with the zany humor on which I had been raised, dancing to soft lights and sweet music, Fifth Avenue on a windy day. The unpleasant edges had been rounded off by time and distance. I was even nostalgic about subway rush hours and the frenetic bustle of Times Square.

I wondered idly about going back, but with no sense of conviction. There was too much against it. I talked it over with Phoenix, and we both agreed. I think she would have gone with me if I really wanted to leave. But she never had to make that decision because I never had any overpowering desire to.

America was still in the throes of McCarthyism. Witch-hunters were finding Reds under every bed. The China Lobby, furious over their loss of property and power, were constantly beating the big drum against Beijing. Even if I should not be subjected to persecution I would probably have to become a lawyer again in the commercial environment I had traveled 12,000 miles to escape.

And where would Phoenix fit in, torn from her familiar roots and plunged into a way of life she disliked? What could she, a professional woman used to decision-making and activity, do in a society like America's? Wouldn't she, and later Yamei, be discriminated against because of the color of their skin and the shape of their eyes? The disadvantages of returning to America far outweighed the advantages.

But the main reason we never seriously considered leaving was because we were stimulated and pleased by our life in China. We liked our jobs—I translating stories, Phoenix discovering new plays for the burgeoning drama companies. We had plenty of friends, more Chinese than foreign, who dropped in frequently, unannounced, in the Chinese fashion, although we had a phone. Yamei was growing prettier daily and more endearing. As to entertainment, we could have gone out every night in the week had we been able to stand the pace.

Financially, we were secure. Our combined salaries, high by Chinese standards, enabled us to eat and dress well, and put some money in the bank. Medical care was virtually free, as was education; rent was low. We had no mortgage to amortize, no insurance premiums to meet; retirement pay was guaranteed. Since there were no private cars, we had no installments to keep up, didn't have to queue for gas, or pay for parking, or mess about with repairs (the hours, the days, I spent on details like that in New York). We got around on buses, or trams, or rode bikes.

Most important, I admired the Chinese people and the brave new world they were creating. Though naturally there were a few exceptions, most Chinese I met were possessed of a gentleness, a courtesy, a reasonableness that to me were a revelation. They suggested rather than demanded, they were interested in your opinions, your comfort, your welfare.

The Communists, too, were not what I had expected. While I didn't believe in the bushy-bearded, wild-eyed "Bolshevik" with a bomb in his hand I used to see as a boy in the Hearst newspaper cartoons, I thought they would surely be dry, austere, sternly puritanical. But, if anything, they were more relaxed, more humorous, than the average Chinese. They drove themselves hard, inspiring by example rather than by words. But their relations with the people they worked with and among, were as intimate and comfortable as an old shoe.

I had seen something of what China had been like in the old society. Now I was not only witnessing the miracle of a people pulling themselves up by their bootstraps out of medieval squalor, but was directly participating. For the first time in my life I had a sense of purpose, and accomplishment, and a goal. I wanted not merely personal advancement—though there was that, too—but to move forward as part of a whole vibrant society.

101

I don't think I said to myself at that stage: "China is my country and my home. I want to spend the rest of my days here." But, though amorphous and unexpressed, that conclusion was beginning to take shape in my mind.

With the political and economic changes in Chinese society, moral values were also being transformed.

To the younger generation "landlord" and "capitalist" were dirty words. They didn't want any part of it. They had their jobs. Their futures were assured. In a social status sense the rich were all dressed up with no place to go. What good did it do businessmen to accumulate a lot of money? Their kids wouldn't accept it. Conspicuous consumption was considered vulgar. The motivation for acquiring a fortune was gone.

State planning now embraced almost all of China's industry and commerce. The capitalists were still capitalists because they continued to draw unearned income in the form of installment payments for the assets the government had bought, but they could no longer control operations. As salaried members of their old enterprises, they developed a new attitude, and their relationship with their former employees improved, as did their social standing.

By November 1956, 96 percent of China's peasants were members of farming co-ops, 83 percent of them in co-ops of a fully socialist type. Ninety-nine percent of private industry and 75 percent of private commerce had become state-private partnerships. Ninety percent of the handicraftsmen and service stores had formed special co-ops of their own.

I had no difficulty in accepting the idea of socialization of agriculture, industry and commerce. It wasn't utopian, it wasn't even new. The Mormons had a large prosperous cooperative economy operating in the state of Utah for well over 100 years. Nor had the Chinese invented government participation in business. The difference was that in China it was a socialist-oriented government, and all collective endeavor was part of national and local government plans. I saw no reason why it shouldn't succeed. It certainly seemed be working well enough.

Just as events in China were proceeding, for the moment, on a fairly even keel, we were fanned by the shockwaves of Khrushchov's bombshell at the Twentieth Congress of the Soviet Communist Party in February, 1956.

The Soviet Union had exercised a profound influence on Chinese intellectuals. The writings of Lenin and Stalin were the texts of study courses. Hundreds of Russian books were translated into Chinese and widely read. Good inexpensive primers on the Russian language were available at the bookstores. Russian plays and operas were staged. There was a flood of Soviet movies, skillfully dubbed here into Chinese. You heard Russian music on the radio. People sang Russian songs in Chinese. The best of the Soviet artists performed on the stages of many of China's big cities.

Stalin had been the symbol of the Soviet Union, of its Communist Party, of its achievements, besides being respected and admired in his own right. Yet now, three years after his death, Khrushchov, the new Chairman of the Party, was depicting him in the darkest of colors.

My own feelings were mixed. I knew that Stalin had sent help to the Spanish Republicans when Hitler was rehearsing his bombers over Madrid and Barcelona and Guernica for more ambitious future operations. I heard that he had offered to fight for Czechoslovakia after the betrayal at Munich, but that his French and British allies had refused to lend their support. Most observers agreed that life in the Soviet Union had climbed from squalor to, if not plenty, at least a previously unsavored adequacy.

Chinese friends had their reservations about Stalin. They said he destroyed thousands of good people labeled as "counter-revolutionaries"; he wasn't vigilant enough against Hitler's blitzkrieg; he wanted the PLA's chase of the fleeing KMT to halt at the Yangtze River; that he exaggerated the importance of his own role. . . .

Of Khrushchov they were even more critical. They said he had supported an appeasement of hostile foreign powers in international affairs and, domestically, a "revision" of socialist political and economic policies.

At the end of 1956, the Chinese Communist Party issued a formal statement. It affirmed the "tremendous success" of the Soviet Union in the 39 years since its inception. It said that Stalin's achievements far outshone his failings, although these were serious. But, to paraphrase, the statement went on: There is a difference between proletarian and bourgeois rule, between socialist and capitalist systems. No bourgeois country can become socialist without a proletarian-led revolution creating a state headed by the proletariat. You can't reach socialism by "evolution."

While "revisionists" engage in wishful thinking, said the statement, the imperialists are mobilizing their military, economic, diplomatic and undercover forces against the socialist countries. Deposed old regime boys, hiding at home or in exile abroad, are working every minute to stage a comeback. We must rally round common principles and close our ranks. The proletariat, through its Party, must lead the country, with no rights for its enemies and full democracy for the people. . . .

This was the first public pronouncement of China's stand against revisionism in the international arena. It marked the beginning of the end of the Big Brother concept. While the Chinese still voiced appreciation for the achievements of the Soviet Union, they were much more cautious of any concept or proposal emanating from Moscow. They were particularly opposed to the theory that the socialist lamb could now lay down with the bourgeois lion.

As if in confirmation of the Chinese contention, in 1957 a sharp class struggle erupted within China's own borders. It began as a "rectification campaign"—one of the periodic house-cleanings in which the Communist Party invites the general public to point out and correct its shortcomings. The targets set for this one were bureaucracy, sectarianism, and subjectiveness within the Party.

People with complaints voiced them freely and, on the whole, in a friendly and helpful spirit. But some became so carried away by their own rhetoric that they switched from oblique slashes at socialist theory and forms of government to direct assaults on the Party as such. They said that the people were suffering under Communist rule, that bureaucracy in the Party was a "more dangerous enemy than capitalism." They demanded that Communist Party organizations quit functioning in schools and government offices.

Public reaction was angry and swift. People gathered in factories, on the farms, in offices, on the campuses. Usually there was just a makeshift platform and a microphone. I attended some of these meetings. Audiences were anywhere from a few hundred to several thousand. They listened quietly while some critic went into his spiel. There was rarely any heckling, but you could feel the tension building. When he finished there would be a dead silence.

Then some man, or woman, would get up on the platform and begin, awkwardly and hesitantly at first but gradually warming into eloquence, and tell the story of their family under Chiang Kai-shek's Kuomintang, their poverty, their misery. They would compare it with their life today, the jobs they had, what their income was, the kind of foods they ate, the homes they lived in, the schools their kids attended. Could this have happened without Chairman Mao and the Communist Party? Some members of the Party might have faults, but why should anyone want to remove the Party from leadership?

But the attacks continued. Day after day articles, cartoons, appeared in the press, with never a dissenting comment. Indignant people deluged the editors with letters nailing the distortions, but the letters never saw print. Workers from a Beijing radio factory stomped into the office of the *People's Daily* and demanded to know which "people" they thought they represented. How could they publish such bilge without a word of refutation?

Only later did the reason come out. The Communist Party had instructed all its organizations and periodicals to say little for a whole month, and let the critics blow their tops. Irritated by the lies and exaggerations, the people defeated them easily in a big national debate.

This was a generally healthy exercise of free speech, but it soon developed into something else. Although thousands of protesters had voiced merely mild criticisms, a few insisted that the socialist experiment had failed, and proposed various forms of "Western democracy" which, in effect, would lead to a vitiation of Communist control. Chinese leaders, worried by anti-Communist uprisings in Poland and Hungary, reacted oversensitively and called their critics "Rightists."

A national witch-hunt against intellectuals followed, and many were tagged with this label. Some lost their jobs, or had cuts in pay, or were sent to work for long periods in the rural areas, their careers ruined. The social opprobrium stuck even when, years later, the majority were formally rehabilitated and their condemnation declared unjustified. Since Chinese intellectuals were then relatively few in number, the "anti-Rightist" campaign deprived China of some of the very people she needed most in her drive for modernization, and placed a pall on an open expression of views.

On a personal level I felt that those demanding Western-style "freedom" and "democracy" for China were naive, since I had seen in America that however attractive they seemed in theory, they were actually implemented very differently. At the same time I was disturbed by the mechanical "slaughter of the innocents" I saw among several of my colleagues and personal friends in the name of political purity. I didn't realize it, but this was a harbinger of the religious fanaticism, cloaked as "Marxism and Mao Thought," which followed 20 years later in the "cultural revolution."

Northwest Interlude
1957

Overall, my mood was up-beat. The country was clearly improving, and for a foreigner living and working in China life was never dull. If you had an interest in the past, well-preserved historical records went back 2,000 years. Strata of early dynasties lay only a few yards below the surface of the earth. Art, painting and sculpture, showing vigor and beauty and a great variety of styles, were everywhere in abundance. Huge figures hewn out of cliffs, a delicate frieze or drawing tucked away in some grotto, a splendid mural on the wall of a temple. Old operas reproduced the dress, the mannerisms, the speech patterns of people in ancient times.

And the present, with its promise of the future, was there under your nose, bustling, free-swinging, groping, but ever cheerfully driving ahead, with all the clamorous good humor of a wide-open frontier town. It was hard to see it all, to get the whole picture. China was so enormous, so complex. It was particularly difficult for a foreigner. Not only were there language barriers to overcome, but the culture, the customs, the habits, the code of conduct were very different from those of the West.

The most important of these differences was the magnificent experiment the Chinese were conducting. They were attempting to remold a whole society, to snatch it from a narrow-minded semi-feudal, semi-colonial past and thrust it into a new civilization, a highly civilized civilization, reasonable and scientific.

You got a good deal of the feeling of this in your daily job, your daily life. But to sense the scope of the thing, you had to get out and travel around. There were some conducted tours for foreigners working in government organizations, but there was too much formal hospitality, too many courteous limitations. You couldn't get very close to ordinary life. We stayed at the best hotels, which were always comfortable, with piping hot water and boxspring mattresses, but often not to my taste where decor was concerned. A few had been built by foreigners in the Victorian period, and were dark and massive and gloomy. Others were designed to satisfy tourist ideas of Chinese architecture, and were more Graumann's Chinese than China's Chinese—Hollywood temples with purple dragons entwined around vermilion pillars. The courteous attendants, mostly bright young boys and girls, seemed as out of place there as I.

In the summer of 1957 I decided to do my trip differently. I would travel as economically as possible. No VIP treatment, no set schedules. Only a general destination of Yanan, the "cradle of the revolution," visiting ancient Xian on the way up and historic Luoyang on the way back. There would be no formal lectures. I would just meet people and chat.

Working with me in the Foreign Languages Press was Singh, a young fellow from northern India. Short and stocky with a receding hairline, he came from a poor family in a mountain village. With dogged perseverance, he had worked his way through school, not easy for a poor boy in India. But Singh was very bright. His English was as fluent as his Hindi, and he translated from one into the other for a Hindi language magazine we were putting out. He also was picking up Chinese with astonishing rapidity.

When he heard about the trip I was planning he offered to come along. He too felt the formal tours didn't go deep enough, and he liked the idea of doing the trip economically, since he was saving to get married. I was delighted to have him. Lin, a young Fukienese from the Hindi section, agreed to accompany us as Singh's interpreter and guide.

At our request, the Press notified the authorities in the places we intended to visit that we wanted only ordinary treatment. Phoenix was too busy to get away. With some misgivings and a long list of do's and don't's, she saw me off.

We took the train to Xian one evening late in August, all three of us in lower berths in a "hard seat" sleeping car. The berths were in tiers of three athwart the car, separated by narrow aisles, with a passage running along by the windows. The berths were hard only in comparison to the spring upholstery you get in First Class. These were firm, leather-covered, and quite comfortable. The bedding, which you rented, cost only 80 cents from Beijing to Xian. It included a thick quilt, which I folded lengthwise and used as a mattress, spotlessly clean sheets, pillow and pillowcase, and a fresh blanket.

Above me was a 70-year-old peasant woman, returning home to Shaanxi after visiting relatives in Beijing. Lin changed berths with her because it was such an effort for her climbing in and out of an upper. The berth above Singh was occupied by a young woman with a baby girl, not quite two, cranky with a bad cold, who in her more cheerful moments sang loudly in a strong penetrating voice, regardless of the hour. The mother, around 25, was a native of Sichuan who had served in Korea as one of the Chinese People's Volunteers. After her discharge she received technical training in a school in the northeast, and was on her way to Xian with her husband, also ex-army, to work in a factory in Xian where there was a big growth in light industry.

Singh and I were charmed by a girl attendant in our car, one of two who shared shifts. About 18, very healthy, very pretty, she worked every minute she was on duty—sweeping, mopping, dusting, bringing bedding, answering questions. She was from Tangshan, a little place 100 miles out of Beijing, and was an elementary school graduate. The run to Xian and back took four days. The crew then got five days off. She used this time to attend a special school conducted for railway staff with irregular hours, and was taking political and academic courses.

I was restless the first night, but slept like a log on the second, except when awakened from time to time, roughly between two and four in the morning, by arias from the little girl. The mother chose this opportunity to "pee" her from the upper berth, aiming her at the chamber pot on the floor below. Singh confessed later he feared disastrous results might ensue from bad marksmanship and the lurching of the train. Fortunately we came through dry and unscathed.

In Xian we were escorted to something called "People's Mansions," a huge new white elephant of a hotel leaning heavily to the Confucian temple ambience. The roofs were covered with tons of glazed tile requiring extra-strong and expensive beams and foundations. And the dining room was graced with—wouldn't you know—purple dragons and vermilion pillars!

With some difficulty we managed to convince our hosts that we would be content with simple quarters and food, and that we didn't need any chauffeured vehicles or special escorts.

We set out after lunch and a short nap to view a few of Xian's fabulous antiquities. Because of its ideal location on a fertile plain beside a broad river, the city is one of the oldest sites of human habitation in China. Both paleolithic and neolithic remains have been found, including a 6,000-year-old neolithic village. It was the locale of Western Zhou (1100 B.C.), the earliest Chinese kingdom to have kept written records.

For centuries Xian, then called Changan, was China's greatest metropolis. It reached its pinnacle of splendor during the Tang Dynasty, from the seventh to the tenth century, when it was the nation's capital. Xian was then three times the present size and had a population of two million, including 40,000 foreigners. It was the largest city in the world, a great center of science, culture and trade, the terminus of the Old Silk Road, carrying goods between China, Europe, the Middle East, and other parts of Asia.

By the time it was liberated in 1949, the population had dwindled to less than half a million. It was dusty, dreary and decayed. As one jingle described it: "Dim lights, faulty phones, bumpy roads." It rhymed in Chinese: *Dian deng bu ming, dian hua bu ling, ma lu bu ping.*

But Xian was starting to recover. When we arrived in 1957 its population had jumped to a million and a half. The locals boasted they'd soon be back to Tang Dynasty size. We were inclined to believe them when we went to have a look at a government textile mill east of the city—Number Three of six built so far in the Xian area. Every piece of machinery was made in China. Of the mill's 6,000 workers, 2,000 were youngsters from Shanghai. Sixty percent were girls, primary or middle school graduates. China was very parochial in the old days. Now kids are often assigned to jobs hundreds of miles from home. They like the adventure of going to distant places, and it does the local people good to get infusions of new blood and new ideas. By government regulation, the kids get a paid trip home every year to see their parents.

After wandering through the fresh-as-paint workshops, we dropped in on the bachelor girls' dormitory. The effervescent southern kids made a great fuss over us. They ushered us into one of the rooms and served us hot drinking water. The room contained six beds and was very neat and clean. Colored posters of fat babies and scenes from romantic operas covered the walls. It was obvious what the girls thought about in at least some of their spare time.

They weren't a bit shy. Two of them sang arias from a Shaoxing opera—greatly favored in the Shanghai-Nanjing-Hangzhou area. Singh then sang an Indian poem and I did "Tavern in the Town." Both numbers were acclaimed by fervent applause. Singh took a group picture of the dozens of girls who had somehow managed to squeeze into the small room.

Next we had a look at the nursery. Apparently textiles were not all they were turning out at a great rate in Number Three. They had 1,000 children under the age of seven, with 600 women in varying stages of pregnancy. The six textile mills in the complex had a combined population of nearly 50,000, including the workers' families. They said they were starting a birth control education campaign.

A printing and dyeing plant was due to be completed that year. The textile mill area was becoming a city in itself. Nicely laid out and landscaped with trees and flowers, it had its own shopping centers, movies, clubs, restaurants, bath houses and post offices.

In the afternoon we took a bus to the famous Big Goose Pagoda. It had been within the sprawling confines of Xian in Tang times, but now the land around it had become farms again, interspersed with many new schools and institutes. A Chinese Buddhist monk named Xuan Zang had the pagoda built in A.D. 650 on his return from a pilgrimage to India. It was a round stone tower seven stories tall and covered with carvings of religious scenes. The wooden stairs inside were somewhat rickety, but they seemed strong enough. You got a magnificent view of the city from the top.

The pagoda stood in a compound with a few old temple buildings and was tended by seven monks who lived on the premises. These brethren belonged to a farming co-op composed of about 40 monks from neighboring Buddhist temples. They were tilling temple land, which they had pooled, and were doing so well that several had bought wristwatches and bicycles.

We were told that Xian's Taoist priests also had their own agricultural producers' cooperatives, and that the Buddhist nuns had organized a sewing co-op.

Singh said the clergy in India were very numerous and led a parasitical existence. They were a big problem. He thought the Chinese method was sensible.

In the evening we went to see a Qinqiang opera, a specialty of the region. China has at least a dozen major types of local operas. Some of these, like Sichuan opera, are still further subdivided into another four or five types. They are not nearly so stylized as Beijing operas and have a lot more comedy and local color. There is more dialogue and less singing, and the music is mainly derived from folk songs. Every word of the arias is understood by the audience. This is not true of Beijing opera, whose unnatural style of singing requires that the lyric be flashed on screens on the sides of the stage, which is tough on people who read slowly or not at all. Nevertheless, Beijing opera draws the largest audiences of all the opera forms, thanks to its superb artistry, and is nationwide in its appeal.

The Qinqiang we saw in Xian was called "Tale of Pu Mu." Pu Mu was a girl who caught the eye of the County Boss of Hangzhou several centuries back—a lecherous dog who tried to steal her from her sweetheart, who was also his friend. It was too long, but we stayed almost to the end. Not that we had any doubts about virtue triumphing, but because the leading lady was so beautiful.

For some reason the hero was played by a woman, though the other characters were cast according to their rightful sex. In old China all parts, male and female, were played by men, like in Elizabethan England, and probably for the same reason. No decent woman would be seen in the company of actors and mountebanks. Mei Lanfang, the most famous of China's Beijing opera actors until his death some years ago, was a female impersonator.

There were exceptions, however. In Yue opera, all roles are played by women. Taken over by idle wives and concubines of wealthy Shanghai merchants at the turn of the century, it is mostly historical soap opera, very weepy, about unrequited passion and dying for love. The music is melodious, though a bit monotonous. Its male impersonator approach may have seeped over into Qinqiang.

We spent all of the next day at Lintong, a resort amid wooded hills east of Xian. In the warm mineral springs here, the famous Tang imperial concubine Yang Yuhuan took her baths. Her private pool has been rebuilt many times, but it is in the same location and taps the same spring. You could still bathe in it for one yuan (20 cents) four times the cost of the ordinary pool. We examined it, a sunken pool of dark rose tile, then bathed in some of the cheaper ones.

Chiang Kai-shek stayed in Lintong in December of 1936, while conferring with Zhang Xueliang, the "Young Marshal," warlord of the northeast provinces, then called "Manchuria" by the Japanese. The Young Marshal wanted to cooperate with the Workers and Peasants Red Army, led by the Chinese Communist Party, and fight the Japanese who had occupied the northeast. Chiang was more interested in battling the Communists than the foreign aggressors. The young warlord sent men to arrest him in his house at the Lintong springs to force a showdown. Firing broke out. Someone put a couple of bullets through Chiang's front window. We saw the holes. They were still there.

Panic-stricken, Chiang hopped out of the back window in his nightshirt and scampered up the mountain. He hid himself in the small dead end of a steep fissure in the rocky slope, above a pavilion done in the classic Greek style. We climbed up with considerable difficulty and peered into the crack. Chiang must have been terrified to have made such a stiff climb so quickly. There he was caught, minus his false teeth.

Madame Chiang Kai-shek rushed up his Australian advisor W.H. Donald in a vain attempt to mediate. (I, the perfect Australian with a Brooklyn accent, played the role of Donald in a film made in the 1980s.) Only the intervention of Zhou Enlai, sent by the Communist Party, saved Chiang from being shot. The Communists wanted unity in the face of a common foe. The Kuomintang agreed to stop internecine strife and cooperate in driving out the Japanese.

That was the famous "Xian Incident." Chiang Kai-shek soon went back on his word. His armies seldom ventured against the enemy. They spent most of their time harassing the communist forces and gouging the people.

Local folk, to commemorate Chiang's little escapade, have installed a large stone plaque in the Grecian Pavilion at Lintong which reads: "Where Chiang Was Caught." But the popular name for the cul-de-sac in which he cowered is, contemptuously, "Dog's Hole."

The next day, September 1, we started for Yanan. We took a train at seven in the morning for Tongchuan, to the north, which was as far as the railway extended. The rest of the way we would have to go by bus. Our fellow passengers were young people from all over China who got off at various stops along the road. Loud, cheerful youngsters from Jiangsu, south of the Yangtze, were working in a local railway administration office. A moon-faced young man with round glasses, from Hainan Island, had become a forestry instructor at a university in Zhengzhou, in Henan, and was conducting his students on a field trip.

You saw these shifts of young population wherever you went, breaking down the old provincial narrowness, enriching the national culture, broadening people's outlooks. The bobbed hair and smart attire of the pert girl textile workers from Shanghai were being emulated by their sisters in Xian; the languorous southern Yue music shared popularity with the more decisive northern opera arias on the Shaanxi radio. There were jokes and laughter over the misunderstandings caused by regional differences in pronunciation, but the laughter was good-natured and friendly. The youngsters were enjoying the exciting adventure they were sharing in building a new China.

Our train was a local, with hard wooden seats. The weather was hot and we were climbing continuously. By the time we got to Tongchuan we were pretty weary.

111

But we perked up when we saw what lay before us. Tongchuan, meaning "Copper Valley," is a pass in the mountains guarding the northern flank of the Weihe River plain and the city of Xian. It was well-garrisoned in ancient times, for it was through here that Tartar and Turkic nomadic tribesmen poured through in raids on their more affluent Han neighbors to the south. The name indicated there had been copper mines at one time, but these must have been worked out, for coal mining was now the major industry. Tongchuan had the biggest coal mine in the northwest.

It's beautiful country, this land of the yellow soil, known as "loess" in the West. Sticky and adhesive when wet, it's fine for making bricks or building dams. When dry it is porous and light. Local people carve their homes out of yellow soil bluffs, merely boring a hole in the top for a chimney and adding a front wall of wood, with paper panes for the windows.

There are few real mountains, but you see great heights and depths, because centuries of erosion have incised the yellow soil plateaus with huge canyons, some hundreds of yards deep and stretching for miles across. With a little water, the soil is fairly fertile. The problem is it's dry most of the year, and then in late summer, usually August, heavy rains form torrents which race through the gullies and canyons, smashing everything in their path. The locals had started a drive to build check-dams and reservoirs, and to plant trees and bushes and grass. But it was difficult, for the population was small and the area vast.

After a late lunch heavily flavored with garlic in an earthen-floored restaurant carved out of a bluff, we walked into Tongchuan's old walled city. It had only one real street, lined with a few stores and government offices. We were followed by a large gang of kids, very friendly, in high spirits, average age about nine. They were neatly dressed, many in new cotton prints. We were struck by the beauty of the children, especially some of the girls. Tall, well-proportioned, they had large eyes, fresh complexions. A few were quite Western in their facial configuration. Raiding Central Asian tribesmen in ancient days were often exiled on capture to Yanan Prefecture, then a garrisoned border region, where they intermarried with the local girls.

The city had a Tang Dynasty pagoda—a nine-story tower. It was shabby and run-down. People are not impressed with antiquity *per se*. A mere thousand years is nothing in a land where recorded history runs back 3,000 years and detailed legends commenced four millennia ago.

Our bus would leave the next day. We were put up in a government office compound, in rooms of cadres out on field trips. Tongchuan had no hotel, only inns "not suitable for foreign guests." We were given bedding, hot water for washing, good tea. There was no charge. We went to bed at 7:30, worn out. They told us the Yanan bus, due to leave at five in the morning, might not. There had been rain up north, and water made the yellow soil slick and dangerous on mountain roads.

Most freight was hauled on two-wheeled carts, pulled by horses and mules in mixed teams of four, with one animal in shafts and three in forward traces. The squeal of their brakes—a wooden block pressing on a round metal drum on the axle—never stopped. It was the last thing we heard as we fell asleep and the first thing we heard on awakening in the morning.

At seven there was still no bus. They said at the station they wouldn't know about the condition of the roads until ten. We had breakfast in our cave restaurant, crisp oil fritters and soybean milk. As we sat dawdling over our food we felt strangely at peace. We had already become accustomed to the screech of brakes as the carts, laden with coal, checked their speed on the downgrades, and listened with half an ear to the Beijing opera and Shaanxi folk songs audible from loudspeakers across the valley through the clear mountain air.

We finally left on the bus at 11, due to reach Yanan by eight that night. Our vehicle, an ancient light Dodge pickup, had been converted by means of building a large wooden box on the chassis. It was intended to hold 20, but was actually crammed with about 30, plus their hand luggage and two live chickens in cages. You were distracted from the pain in your butt, thumping on the hard wooden bench, by the agony in your knees, jammed rigid and motionless against the back rest of the seat in front. What saved us was the frequent breakdowns of the bus, which gave us a chance to get out and stretch our legs while it was being repaired. The winding mountain road was still wet and slippery from last night's rain wherever it was in shadow, and we had to go slowly.

At three in the afternoon we had only reached Huangling, the halfway point. The bus couldn't get to Yanan that night. The driver was planning to go as far as the next county town and stay over, continuing on to Yanan in the morning. Singh, Lin and I decided to remain in Huangling, which we had heard a lot about, and catch another bus in the afternoon of the following day.

We were cordially received by Comrade Liang, deputy chief of the county. A soft-spoken, enthusiastic man of about 50, he was as easy and friendly as the old cloth shoes he wore with his faded cloth uniform. He had been a primary school teacher in a neighboring village and "joined the revolution" in 1937, operating as an underground agent until liberation. He became a county leader in 1950.

Liang put us up in the rooms of county cadres who were out on inspection tours of village administrations and farming co-ops. The county government office was housed in an old temple compound worn smooth with age, its tile roofs mellow in the shade of large trees. Temples and landlords' mansions were often used for government offices. They were generally the best constructed buildings, and taking them symbolized the ascendancy of the people over their former corporal and spiritual rulers.

113

The furnishings were simple. Our borrowed beds consisted of boards laid across a couple of saw horses. There was no electricity. Water came from a well. But the place was spotlessly clean.

Our warm-hearted host insisted on immediately going out and showing us around. He knew the county like the palm of his hand, and his relations with the villagers were more neighborly than official. As we strolled along, farmers, mule train drivers, boys and girls, hailed him affectionately as "Old Liang." People stopped him and asked him questions, told him their problems. Smiling and patient, Liang had a few words for everyone.

He wanted us to see the Tomb of the Yellow Emperor, which is what Huangling means, while it was still daylight. We climbed a long tree-shaded hill. It was crowned by a large mound 20 feet high. This was the last resting place of China's first ruler, Huang Di, the legendary Yellow Emperor, who reigned 4,000 years ago. With him began sericulture and weaving; people wore clothing instead of animal skins, built houses; wheeled vehicles and boats were invented; a written language appeared.

We asked Liang whether anything remained in the tomb. He said most ancient tombs had been plundered again and again over the centuries. Archaeologists had made no recent check. Liang grinned and told us local lore had it that it was not the emperor but only his boots that were buried here. The First Emperor was such a beneficent ruler that people were loath to let him go, even after his death. As he began his ascent to Heaven, they seized his feet. But the pull of the heavenly hosts was too strong, and the people were left holding his boots, which they entombed with due ceremony.

Liang told us that Comrade Wang, head of the Yanan Prefecture, which embraced 14 counties, was driving down that evening. Around seven p.m. a long black sedan rolled up to county headquarters. I'm not sure what I expected, but I was certainly surprised when the door opened and out stepped an old peasant. At least that's what he looked like in his loose-fitting tunic and trousers and patched cloth shoes. A man of about 60, he grinned engagingly when we were introduced, apologized for the "poor" accommodations, asked whether our beds were comfortable, whether we could take the food. We assured him the food was delicious, which it was.

We went into one of the large rooms, where a couple of lamps had been lit, and sat down on the big wooden chairs. Wang promptly slipped his shoes off and tucked his legs up under him. He passed cigarettes around as tea was served.

In response to our questions, Wang told us about himself. Sure enough, he had been a peasant, and had fought in the guerrilla forces, first against the Japanese, then against the Kuomintang. He gave a fascinating account of how the guerrillas and the PLA, closely coordinating, had smashed the army of Hu Zongnan, the Kuomintang general who, for a time, had taken Yanan. A self-educated man of keen

114

intelligence, Wang spoke humorously and with gusto, leaping from his chair and gesticulating as he warmed to his story.

His complete naturalness, his absolute contempt for the enemy, his supreme confidence in the way China was going, were typical of the old Party cadres we met. The northwest was one of the more backward regions of China, yet the atmosphere was almost festive. Sitting in the dim-lit room of an ancient temple high on a yellow loess plateau, we felt warm and excited, listening to Wang's witty, incisive tale. We knew why the revolutionaries had won, and would go on winning—if they could maintain that spirit.

We had a good weather forecast for the next day and should have gone to bed at a reasonable hour to prepare for the rest of our trip. But Wang wanted to know all about America and India and Beijing, and we had dozens of questions to ask him. It was quite late by the time we finally turned in. We slept beautifully.

The sun came out in the morning. It was a fine clear day. Since the bus wasn't due until noon, we went to call on the head of the county women's federation. A bright young woman of about 30, she came from Hebei, the province Beijing is in. It was a relief to hear the familiar accent again. The local pronunciation was understandable, but I had to strain to get everything.

She told us Huangling had been very feudal in the old days. Women had been restricted to "circling around the cooking stove." Only after liberation did they begin working in the fields, the real break coming with the formation of the cooperatives the year before, 1956, when large-scale farming had created the need for more labor. Since the women added substantially to the family income, the men's opposition petered out. Wives generally managed to do 140 days in the fields per year to the men's 200.

Nevertheless, the position of the women was still inferior. They had neither the experience nor the technique of the men and, consequently, were paid less. This was being remedied through more on-the-job training. Also they were too tied down by kids and housework to put in as much time as the men. The grandmas looked after the children during the harvests, when 90 percent of the women took part, but they couldn't do this all year round. Regular nurseries and kindergartens were being set up, birth control education had begun. The women were all for it. Some had four or five kids before they were 30. The men were not opposed to the idea either, particularly those with large families.

I also chatted with the county nurse, a young woman from Xian. One of her main jobs was to train midwives. A few were the old-fashioned kind, whom she instructed in modern methods, but most were ordinary farm wives. There was no charge for maternity services, only for the medicines, which ranged in price from 50 cents to one yuan. In the event of economic hardship, even this was paid by the county. The nurse said it had been difficult to convince the farmers at first that the services were free. Women would be in labor for two or three days before calling for help. Now everyone understood.

Medical and surgical treatment for China's hundreds of millions of rural people was, and still is, a big problem. How could it be financed? Where would the doctors, the nurses, the medicines, the equipment come from? In the 1970s, a start was made with the introduction of "barefoot doctors"—paramedics who do preventive medicine, deliver the babies, and treat all of the simpler common ailments—guided and aided by professional government medical units. Acupuncture and local home remedies are provided by traditional doctors, and everyone helps gather the needed herbs and roots. Today, various health insurance schemes are being tried.

But in 1957, when we were in the northwest, the country nurses ran the whole show. They led the fight against contagious disease—by inoculation and vaccination, by teaching hygiene. They did a good job. The kids were clean in Huangling. The town was virtually fly-free.

We got on the bus at 1:00 p.m., after warmly thanking Old Liang. Comrade Wang had left that morning. We wouldn't forget Huangling, toughly persisting through the ages and now, with youthful spriteliness, moving forward on the socialist wave.

Our bus ride was breathtaking. The road climbed and twisted to dizzy heights, and clung by its teeth to the edge of precipices. We traveled for miles along high plateaus so wide and flat we thought we were on the plains again, until suddenly yawning canyons, ten miles across, would open up to remind us where we were. Crops grew at 5,000 feet, a little sparse because of the water shortage. At least they had plenty of sun. Then we started down, staring at the terraced fields mounting like stairs to the very tops of the lofty hills. It must have taken people hours just getting to and from those fields, to say nothing of working them. What courage and persistence, wresting a yield from nature under such conditions.

Near the bottom, the road met a winding stream, yellow with eroded soil. We followed it to Fuxian, another county town. It was 5:30 in the afternoon by then, and we had to stay over. The buses didn't travel at night. The mountain roads were too dangerous.

We took a walk before dinner down the main, and only, street. Our eye was caught by a riot of flowers in a garden seen through a courtyard gate. The owner, a retired peasant whose kids were grown up and working away from home, invited us in. The interior decorations were interesting. Carved wooden partitions screened the kang bed, which was covered with small rugs and had a chest, painted with flowers by a local artist, at its head. There were excellent likenesses of the old man and his wife, in oils, on the wall. These had been done by their son in Hubei. Scrolls of Chinese calligraphy were also hung, paper-cuts decorated the windows. A delightful place.

116

The Chinese are very artistic. Everything is a creation, from a store window display of nuts and bolts that have somehow become a locomotive and cars chugging across a railway trestle, to the homely radish which has been carved into a blushing rose to garnish your plate in a neighborhood restaurant.

We strolled back and had dinner at the local restaurant, with an audience of about 50 curious kids staring at us through the plate glass window. The proprietor kept shooing them away, but they kept coming back. There were plenty of Young Pioneers among them. The little girls were darling. While we and the kids smilingly examined each other, big dogs nonchalantly wandered among the tables, looking for scraps. Not one of our most relaxed meals.

At five the next morning we were on the road again. By 8:30 our bus was rolling into Yanan. Before the Long March culminated here, it had been a small ancient walled city on the banks of the Yanhe River with a population of 3,400. The wide river valley was surrounded by hills of yellow soil, cut by gullies and gorges. People grazed sheep and goats, gathered meager crops from the arid earth, and paid exorbitant rents to tyrannical landlords.

Everything had been taxed when the Kuomintang government was in power. One yuan for getting married, one yuan for each son born, 50 cents for a daughter. There was a tax for having an ox, another for not having an ox. There was even a tax on chimneys from the cooking stoves. Magistrates collected two years' taxes in advance, and they did it every year. Some were decades ahead of the game. When in desperation a poor man sold his land, official "fees" ate up 40 percent of the price.

Oppression breeds resistance. By 1926 the province had a Communist Party, by 1935 a people's army controlled the entire region except for cities like Yanan, Suide and Mizhi. They instituted their own land reform, and drubbed the landlord home guards sent to crush them. Regular Nationalist (KMT) troops had to be called in. The people's army made monkeys out of them, though they had virtually no weapons. Peasants would rush into Nationalist strongholds with terrifying invented reports that huge well-armed forces were approaching, and the garrisons would flee.

The people knew every move the enemy made. Whenever a Nationalist Army expedition set forth, a peasant spotter on a mountain top would fling up a handful of yellow earth which would blossom out into fine dust and rise like smoke. The signal would be passed in the same fashion from mountain to mountain. The Nationalists never could be sure who was people's army, for they wore no uniforms. They were peasants working in their fields, until the call came. In 1937, when the Red Army, which had come to Yanan at the conclusion of the Long March, went off to fight the Japanese, the people's militia forces became primarily responsible for the defense of the Yanan Prefecture.

117

As the headquarters for the Chinese Communist Party, Yanan grew rapidly. Intellectuals flocked to it from all over the country. The population of the prefecture soared to 100,000 by 1939. The Nationalists, more afraid of the people than of the foreign invader, avoided clashes with the Japanese and imposed a blockade against the prefecture. Yanan met the challenge by setting up home industries which turned out most of their daily necessities.

On the food front every student, cadre and Party leader guaranteed to produce 90 catties (about 100 pounds) of millet per year. In the Nanniwan sector outside Yanan an Eighth Route Army brigade, composed mostly of southerners, hacked paddy fields out of the wilderness and planted rice, a crop the area had never known. They performed prodigious feats of production. Some of the men were jokingly known as *qi si niu*—"ox infuriators" because they could pull a plow through more acreage in a day than the average draft animal—which naturally aroused the jealousy and fury of the ox. The need for and feasibility of self-reliance became permanently impressed on communist thinking.

Yanan was the center of political and military leadership, the school in which cadres for these fields were trained. Tens of thousands passed through Yanan for short-term courses. In Yanan Mao wrote many of the profound articles which were to shape the destiny of China and influence the course of world history. Arts of and for the people got their start in Yanan. It became the beacon, the inspiration, for millions of Chinese.

Despite the Kuomintang blockade, its fame continued to spread across China and around the world. Canadian surgeon Norman Bethune, who had served in Spain, came to serve and die in the Chinese revolution. Young American journalist Edgar Snow came to observe and talk with Mao, and ended by writing the classic *Red Star Over China*. Young American doctor George Hatem (Ma Haide) arrived in Yanan and remained in China for half a century until his death, creating miracles of public health and nearly wiping out venereal disease and leprosy. Yanan also drew American military observers, for it symbolized Chinese resistance against the common enemy.

After the Japanese surrender in 1945, the Kuomintang, with heavy American backing, launched its final attempt to crush the Communist-led revolution. Kuomintang warlord general Hu Zongnan attacked the Yanan Prefecture with 230,000 troops. The defenders numbered less than 30,000. They had, on the average, only 500 bullets per machine gun, 30 bullets per rifle. The enemy boasted they would take Yanan in three days and capture the CPC Central Committee in three months.

Mao's strategy was to let the foe take cities but to destroy their troops. In March 1947 the Communists left Yanan. Chiang Kai-shek was delirious with joy. He held victory celebrations in the large Chinese cities, decorated Hu Zongnan, and sent reporters to cover the "triumph." Hu enclosed 1,500 of his own troops in ten different camps and had them pose as POW's. He exhibited heaps of old weapons as "battle trophies."

But it wasn't quite over. The whole countryside rose in support of the Communists. In the year that followed the two million population of the northwest area contributed 50 million workdays to the support of the People's Liberation Army, as it was now called, the PLA, delivering grain and serving as stretcher bearers. The women hand-stitched 580,000 pairs of cloth shoes. Guerrillas made life hell for the enemy. Hu Zongnan never dared spend a single night in Yanan for fear of being assassinated. Mines and booby traps were planted everywhere. Enemy soldiers were still being blown up months after the occupation.

The PLA wasn't idle either. With Mao personally planning and directing the battles, it destroyed 15,000 Kuomintang effectives in the first 40 days of the campaign, and eliminated another 61,000 by the end of the year. Then it switched over to the offensive. Early in 1948 it knocked out another 20,000 of the enemy. In April 1948, exactly one year and one month after their departure, the Communists recaptured Yanan. The enemy left in such a hurry that actors, performing for them in the city, fled with their costumes and makeup on.

Hu Zongnan had worked cruel havoc in the border region. He commandeered most of the farmers' grain; an estimated 400,000 people died of starvation. During their rout the enemy vengefully committed widespread destruction. Restoration took a long time.

When we arrived the city was still in the early stages of its growth, but the old Yanan spirit was going full blast. They had great plans: In the next five years the population would expand from 30,000 to 100,000. They would need that many for all their new projects. Irrigated land would grow from 10,000 to 50,000 acres. They would raise a lot more grain. While implementing water and soil conservation measures, they would move farming down from the hillsides to the valley floors and devote the slopes to grazing and orchards.

We got this story after we settled in at our temporary quarters. There was a bit of a hassle first. The hostel was halfway up a high bluff on what used to be the Yanan University grounds. On the lower level they had a fancy new building for foreign dignitaries, with steam heat, hot and cold running water, and no view at all, except for the tall chimney of the heating plant. Fortunately it was not yet completed, and the old hostel was still being used. We were shown nice rooms at 80 cents a head. No, thank you, we said. What we were looking for were cave dwellings. Friends like Dr. George Hatem who had lived here in the old days had recommended them highly.

Our hosts laughed and showed us a row of caves near the top of the bluff. Hollowed out of the yellow earth in vaulted arches fronted with a wooden frame which

119

held a door and paper-paned windows, they were clean and surprisingly bright. The whitewashing probably helped. Furnishings were simple. An electric light bulb, a few wooden beds, a couple of tables and some wooden chairs.

When we said these would be fine, our hosts looked startled. Only our earnest protests stopped them from carrying up spring mattresses and a few sofas. We liked the caves very much, and the location was ideal. There was a broad terrace in front of the caves shaded by several large trees. You could see for miles—the Yanhe River, the Tang pagoda on the hill on the other side, the large valley and the mountains beyond.

After supper that night, Comrade Huang gave us more background information. He had been one of the local guerrillas and still walked with a limp from arthritis contracted hiding in damp gullies. Like all the old cadres we met in this area he spoke with infectious enthusiasm. He said in the days when Yanan was the heart of the revolution, life was hard but everyone was cheerful. Wherever you went you heard singing. That buoyancy remained. The mountains were vast, the air was clear. The people were big, rugged, outspoken, and confident in their future.

The next day we visited the cave dwellings where Chairman Mao lived and worked during his stay in Yanan. They were simple and austere. We spoke with old peasants who knew him. They said Mao was always friendly and relaxed, just one of the people. He refused to accept any special treatment. While directing the course of the revolution and writing his famous articles, Mao tended his own vegetable patch and wore old clothes. Hearing that we were from Beijing, the peasants asked us to send him their regards. We could only smile and nod.

Yanan natives were a colorful lot. The men turbanned their heads in small towels, knotted in front. (Towel turbans were worn in many parts of northern China, but in most places they were knotted in the back.) The towels were a protection against the dust and handy for wiping sweat. Tunics, padded or lined with sheepskin, were held in place by a sash, often with a brass-bowled, long-stemmed pipe tucked beneath it like a dagger. Baggy trousers were lined or unlined according to season. Feet were shod with the ubiquitous cloth shoes, by far the most comfortable of footwear. Black cloth made the uppers. The shoes were light, they could "breathe." "Athlete's foot" among Chinese was virtually unknown.

Everybody sang, men and women, young and old. The northern part of Shaanxi Province was famous for it. There were plaintive shepherd songs, sometimes to the accompaniment of a flute. And there were the duets—between boy and girl, husband and wife—tender, funny, broad, as the case might be. China's first revolutionary opera, later a ballet, the *White-Haired Girl*, composed in Yanan, was based on north Shaanxi folk songs. Singing seems to come naturally to hill dwellers.

This being Saturday, the hostel threw a dance for us. American doctor George Hatem, who had been there in the early 1940s, told me the Saturday night dance was a regular feature of life in Yanan, a scratchy phonograph or a small pickup band providing the music. Our dance was a bit more elegant. We had the orchestra from the local operetta company. The singers and dancers also came, as well as doctors and nurses from the hospital, and cadres from half a dozen government units.

There was lots of dancing, with the girls inviting Singh and me in relays. Only when we pleaded the need to catch our breath were we allowed to sit a number out. We slept well that night.

In the morning we were taken to where the *Liberation Daily* had been printed when Yanan was the revolutionary center. Our friend George Hatem, when he wasn't doctoring, had helped produce the English edition. As a precaution against Japanese and, subsequently, Kuomintang bombings, the newspaper had been housed in the Cave of the Ten Thousand Buddhas—a cavern about 60 feet square which had been hewn out of solid rock over 1,000 years ago. Two huge pillars supported the ceiling. Every inch of the walls and pillars was lined with rows of carved Buddhas and female figures in the lush natural style of the Tang Dynasty.

They originally had been colored, but Hu Zongnan had set fire to the printing equipment when he retreated, blackening the paint. The figures were still beautiful. Each one was different in posture and expression, and had been created in sets by different sculptors over several centuries. Beside each set was a plaque inscribed with the names of the artists and the devout Buddhists who had sponsored the carvings.

We visited a large experimental farm outside Yanan. They had found a good wheat variety for cold climates and were trying to improve it. Their wheat expert turned out to be a man who had been studying agriculture at Cornell while I was there taking an army course in Chinese. Small world department. His English was very good. He had returned to China in 1945.

The farm was also pushing apples. For one thing they had discovered that the slopes held water better when strips of field were alternated with strips of orchard. For another, apples grew well here. They had several varieties. My favorite, and the one which seemed to thrive the best, was a type called the "banana apple." Crisp and juicy, it did actually have the flavor of bananas. The farm had given 100,000 grafts the previous year to the co-ops, free of charge, to improve the local stock. They would be bearing fruit within three years.

As any farmer will tell you, fruit is a risky crop. If you don't dispose of it all in season, it starts to go bad. You have to preserve it or refrigerate it, and that requires capital and equipment poor hillside regions don't have. Here again, the experimental farm people distinguished themselves. They found that the yellow soil caves were natural refrigerators, cool and dry. Apples stored in October kept most of their natural juice and flavor until the following May or June. Big cities like Xian could be supplied all during the usually apple-less first half of the year. Another source of income for the farming co-ops.

According to the lunar calendar it was Moon Festival Day, the time of the year when the moon is at its roundest and people celebrate the harvests. In the afternoon we bought moon cakes and lots of fruit and invited the kids from the operetta company over. The boys had a basketball match, but half a dozen of the girls came. A pretty Mohammedan girl from Kaifeng sang Henan opera tunes. (She was the only member of the troupe who had dietary scruples, but they had a special kitchen for her. It's government policy to respect the customs of ethnic minority people.)

Others did some north Shaanxi songs. We were amused by a cute number called "Husband and Wife Have a Tiff." Gao Min, a charming mezzo-soprano from Jiangsu Province, wrote out the words and rehearsed us a couple of times. She was surprised that I didn't have any of the pear-shaped tones some foreigners use for rendering Chinese folk songs. Obviously she had never heard of unpretentious Brooklyn speech.

The next day was our last in Yanan. We visited the famed Precious Pagoda. Built in Tang times, it stood atop a high hill from which there was a wonderful view in all directions. A big old bell of cast bronze stood in a wooden frame not far from the pagoda. Also made in Tang, it had hung in a local temple, long since gone. It was inscribed with the names of worshipers who claimed they had been cured of their ailments, and of women who believed their prayers for sons had been answered. They had all chipped in to pay for the bell and present it to the temple. An expensive gift. It had been used as an alarm in the Liberated Area days.

To my amazement, along with various holy figures on the bell, there was Pigsy. Old Pigsy was a folklore figure who allegedly accompanied Xuan Zang, a devout Buddhist monk, to India 1,000 years ago to bring back holy scriptures. Their other companion was Monkey, whose X-ray eyes could penetrate the disguises of the many demons who beset them on their way. The adventures of these three was an important part of Chinese children's fairy tales and puppet shows. They appeared, too, in Beijing opera.

Monkey was a typical children's hero. He could work powerful magic, was fearless, humorless, and treated women with disdain. Pigsy appealed more to the grown-ups, though the kids liked him too, as a raffish comedian. Brave enough when he had to fight, he was a good-natured slob the rest of the time, a glutton and a lecher whenever the opportunity presented. Due to certain minor deficiencies in my own character, I have always found Pigsy entirely lovable. But I never expected to see him commemorated on an ancient bronze temple bell. That must have been quite a congregation. No wonder Tang was a Golden Age.

We took off the following morning at 5:30 by bus, arrived in Tongchuan by 3:30 in the afternoon, got on a train at 4:30, reached Xian at 11:00 in the evening,

Cryptanalyst, US Army Signal Corps, 1944.

With Mom, Pop, and sister Ruth, Monticello, New York, 1925.

Yale University campus, 1946.

Just married, Shanghai, 1948.

Korea, 1951. Phoenix meets the Chinese
Volunteers.

Phoenix escorts Premier Zhou Enlai
to Beijing Writers Conference, 1950.

Our garden,
53 Nanguanfang,
Beijing, 1959.

Off to work, outside our
front door, Beijing, 1962.

Mom's visit, with Yamei
and Phoenix, 1963.

As the Commander-
in-Chief of the
US Army
Airforce in Korea
in the film *Eagles
of the Sky*, 1975.

Dancing with "Madame
Chiang Kai-shek" as
"W.H. Donald,"
Australian advisor to
the "Generalissimo,"
in the film *The Xian
Incident*, released 1980.

With an Uygur
rural official,
Xinjiang, 1984.

Dr. George Hatem at my
70th birthday party,
Beijing, 1985.

At the Asian-Jewish
Colloquium, Hong Kong,
March 1987.

On a CPPCC junket,
the Angang Steel Mill,
Liaoning, July 1987.

Israel, March 1989, a Roman amphitheater.

Tai ji quan, Rear Lake, Beijing, autumn 1990.

At home, November 1991, with son-in-law Guo Taiping, Phoenix, daughter Yamei, and granddaughter Stella.

February 1993, a toast with President Jiang Zemin in the Great Hall of the People, Beijing.

Shenzhen Botanical
Gardens, March 1994.

My 80th birthday party, Beijing, 1995. Blowing
with me are Wu Jieping and Huang Hua.

At home, Beijing, March 1996. On the far right, a picture of Phoenix.

returned to the hotel by pedicab, had a wash and fell into bed, bone weary, around midnight.

After a day or two of rest and a bit of sightseeing, Singh, Lin and I decided to climb Huashan, one of China's five famous mountains, before going on to Luoyang. Why I got involved in this madness, I'm not quite sure. Singh came from the mountains in northern India and had done a lot of climbing. Lin, as his interpreter, had to go with him. The highest I had ever reached on my own two feet had been the top of the hill in Brooklyn's Prospect Park. Perhaps I didn't want my Indian comrade to think the men of Flatbush craven. I was only 42, and in reasonably good shape.

But more likely it was because I wanted to examine Huashan closely, first-hand. It wasn't simply a high and beautiful mountain. Priests had begun building Taoist retreats on Huashan 2,000 years ago, during the Western Zhou Dynasty (ca. 11th century-771 B.C.). The mountain reached its zenith as a Taoist center in Tang Dynasty, when hundreds of hermit priests inhabited caves cut into the living rock. Devoted followers clambered up the steep cliffs daily to keep them supplied with food and other necessities. Temples were built. The caves, some of them only niches, and the temples were still there.

At eight in the morning we got on a train and arrived in Huayin at 10:30. We left our luggage in the county office and set out. We walked for an hour along a peaceful country road. Mountains reared abruptly out of the plain. We started up through a deep ravine, the path crossing back and forth over an icy stream filled with rocks and boulders. We had to step and leap from one to another, constantly climbing. Though it was a cloudy day, we sweated copiously.

Then the ravine widened out into gentler slopes, with groves and mountain flowers. About every mile and a half was a small Taoist temple where you could buy tea or boiled drinking water. Every two miles was a large temple which served food and had sleeping accommodations. The temples were old and dark and cool, set among shady old trees. Perfect resting places on a hot climb.

The caves were in the most inaccessible places all the way up the mountain, many perched on ledges above sheer rock. Taoism was a religion of withdrawal, of private contemplation. Among the priests in bygone days were alchemists and men with knowledge of herbal medicine. But particularly in later centuries "Tao"—the "Way"—led to an escape from society and personal problems.

From the hundreds of Taoists who had inhabited Huashan Mountain in the Tang Dynasty the number dwindled to only about 70 at the time of our visit, including eight women. They had all been organized into a service co-op which sold food, drink and lodging to travelers. This covered their expenses.

We talked with them wherever we stopped. They dressed in gowns similar to those of the Buddhists, but neither the priests nor the nuns shaved their heads as the

Buddhists did. They wore their hair long, gathered into a bouffant which protruded through an opening in the top of their hats. They were quiet-spoken, relaxed. In that cool stillness, amid the vast distances between towering peaks, we all instinctively lowered our voices.

"What brought you here? Why did you become a Taoist?" we asked.

One man said he had fled from being conscripted into the Kuomintang army. Another had dreams of becoming a second Sun Pin—a doctor who had earned fame centuries ago with cures he had learned as a Taoist. But most had run away from personal danger or tragedy they hadn't had the strength to face.

I asked one priest how he reconciled the Taoist retreat from the world with the socialist concept of serving the people. He couldn't, of course, and he admitted it. The government was paying for the repair and upkeep of the temples, but the priests had to work. Now they were providing food for the people instead of people bringing food to them. He said there were still believers among the old folk, but they weren't getting any new converts. Although people came long distances to Huashan during religious festivals, most came as tourists, not as pilgrims. He thought Taoism as a religion would be gone from China in another generation.

Wearily we began the last leg of our climb. We were determined to reach the northern peak before nightfall. We had to mount banks of steps cut into the rock at an angle of about 80 degrees, aided by swaying chains hung on both or only one side of the steps. In one or two stretches they were absolutely vertical.

I was pouring sweat. My heart pounded, I gasped for breath. At first I could do 20 steps at a time. Then ten. Finally, I had to rest after every five. In a few places, one misstep would have sent us hurtling down into the abyss. I remembered the priests' warning—you can look up, but don't look down. Surely, I thought, one little peek can't hurt. I tried it. Immediately, the gorge below and the mountains behind and the sky above began to rotate. I clung desperately to the chains and faced inwards till my dizziness passed.

At last, more dead than alive, we reached the temple on the north peak. The interior was gloomy and full of ancient trappings—worn stone pieces, faded tapestries and weathered bronzes. But the half dozen priests had the healthy ruddy complexions of mountain men. They provided us with a hot meal of rice and vegetables. I was so tired I could hardly eat.

I couldn't help feeling a little proud of myself. It was seven p.m. The climb had taken eight hours. It had been pretty strenuous in spots, but we made it.

"I don't suppose you get many visitors up here," I said to one of the priests.

"Not this time of the year," he said. "But in April during the Incense Burning Festival we sometimes have as many as 100 a day. They're all kinds—even little old women with bound feet."

124

That properly deflated me. I felt even smaller when, asked about how they got their supplies, they explained that a couple of men brought them up from the valley every day on shoulder poles, returning the same day. Since shoulder poles, weighted with loads at either end, have to be supported with one hand, that meant the men had only one hand free to scale the vertical cliffs. And they traveled so quickly they could breeze up to the summit and back to the valley in the time it had taken us to crawl to the top.

We fell into bed at eight that night, all three of us sleeping on a wide platform in a room perched on the edge of the cliff. I was overtired, and in that ethereal mountain stillness the squirrels scurrying around on the inside of the paper ceiling seemed to be making an awful racket. I thought I felt one of them run across my face, and woke with a start. Maybe I only imagined it. Anyhow, I slept badly.

The next morning I didn't have much energy. I let Lin and Singh go off to climb the other peaks. I stayed and chatted with the Taoist priests. They told me that when the Kuomintang armies fled, a gang of officers and men had climbed up to the temple and hid themselves, intending to hold out until Chiang Kai-shek made his "comeback." It was an ideal location. The only path leading to it was steep and narrow. A single man with a machine gun could hold off attackers indefinitely. All the other sides of the peak were sheer rock.

But a daring team of seven PLA men and a peasant guide scaled one of those "inaccessible" cliffs in the dead of night and took the enemy by surprise, killing some and capturing the rest. Looking at the precipitous rock face, I was amazed. They must have had incredible courage.

After Singh and Lin returned we had lunch and started back. Going down was relatively easy, but we were stiff and awkward, and Singh sprained his knee. The sun was out. It was hotter than the day before. We stopped at every temple for tea to replenish our streaming perspiration. The Taoist priests were friendly and talked with us freely. The vitality of the new society seemed to have broken the centuries-old silence imposed upon them by religious mysticism.

One of them presented us with some home-grown walnuts. They knew a bit about India and America, and a lot about what was happening in China. Newspapers were delivered almost every day. From time to time they went down to the county town for meetings. There was no longer any necessity to "get away from it all." But they were doing a useful job, running way stations for tourists, and would remain in the quiet mountains they loved.

We were fairly fresh when we reached the foothills, but fatigue caught up with us during the last hour's walk on the flat. We arrived at the county office at seven in the evening. After supper we washed our sweaty clothes and ourselves, read the newspapers, and were in bed by ten.

We rose early the next morning and shaved, for the first time in three days. In the rural areas the campaign against the Rightists was just starting. The office walls were plastered with cartoons and posters. After breakfast we chatted with the county cadres and thanked them for the excellent treatment they had given us. It was the same in every local government office we stayed at during the course of our trip—good food, clean bedding, and a friendly concern that was almost embarrassing in its solicitude. The men and women we met were modest, hardworking, competent, and full of optimistic plans for the development of their particular region or district. They gave you the feeling that China's rural foundations were solid, secure.

At 10:30 we boarded a train to Luoyang, arriving at 6 p.m. Although the hotel had been notified, no one was at the station to meet us. We telephoned them. A quarter of an hour later, a young man showed up. He said the section chief, who it later turned out had received our message, had "gone to the theater" without saying a word about us to any one.

When we got to the hotel we had a long argument over quarters, they trying to give us something lavish and expensive, we insisting on something simple and cheap. After the question was finally settled—to our satisfaction—we went to bed. Only to be awakened an hour later by the shriek of a train whistle which sounded as if it were right outside our window. The hotel was built much too close to the station. It had good expensive equipment, but it was dirty and poorly run. Our first and only encounter with bureaucracy throughout our journey, it was all the more upsetting because it was so unusual.

I think Lin, our Chinese comrade, worried the section chief, a languid fellow, with his critical comments when we met the next day. From then on, he left us strictly alone, except for a few cautious suggestions about points of interest we might visit.

We took pedicabs to the city's outskirts, then a bus for Longmen—the "Dragon's Gate"—site of huge idols carved out of the cliffs. Luoyang had been China's capital during most of the first six centuries A.D. When we saw it in 1957, what remained of the original city was very run-down. The outskirts were a different story. Schools and machine tool factories had risen. China's first tractor plant was in the process of construction.

The famous Longmen Grottoes lined both sides of the Yihe River, a wide shallow body of water. Remnants of two bridges blown up by the Kuomintang armies fleeing from the Japanese stood forlornly in midstream. There was heavy traffic of trucks and ox carts fording the shallows. Creaking carts, hauling coal from a mine across the river, over the years had spread a layer of coal dust inches thick on the cobbles of the ancient road. The tomb of Bai Juyi, great poet of the Tang Dynasty, as well as one of Chiang Kai-shek's villas, were visible on the opposite shore. Glory and disgrace, cheek by jowl.

126

Carving of the Longmen figures began in the fourth century with the growth of Buddhism. In that period China had as many as 30,000 temples and two million monks and nuns. The Longmen sculptures ranged in size from rows of figures only a few inches high, decorating the grottoes, to towering Buddhas of 30 and 40 feet, cut out of the cliffsides. In the more waterproof caves many of the images, their niches and ceilings, retained their original colors—soft and of beautiful artistry. The paints are believed to have had a mineral base, but the secret of making them is lost.

Considerable damage had been done by rascals who worked for foreign collectors. Hands and heads, artistically expressive and easy to ship, had been ruthlessly chopped off. Even larger operations had been undertaken for customers in a position to pay. The New York Metropolitan Museum had acquired two wonderful Northern Wei (535-556) frescoes of a devout king and queen. The Kansas City Museum got another. Lions and flying fairies ended up in the Boston Museum. Ugly scars of chipped stone were infuriating reminders to the Chinese of what imperialist countries meant by "cultural exchange."

A fresh layer of dust was churned up and spread on the classic sculptures with every passing ox cart. We were told the Ministry of Culture had allocated funds for paving the cobblestone road and repairing the grottoes. The whole area would be turned into a large public park.

The following day was our last in Luoyang. We spent it in the White Horse Monastery, a 20-minute train ride away. It was established in A.D. 68 for two Indian monks brought from India by an expedition of 19 Chinese sent to investigate Buddhism. Han Ming, the emperor, had heard of the influence of Buddhism in neighboring countries and was curious.

China had not merely tolerated outside religious beliefs over the centuries, she actively encouraged the establishment of their orders within her empire. Nearly every civilized religion has at one time or another been freely preached and practiced. This seems to have been inspired less by a desire for spiritual salvation than a search for new ideas. In ancient days it was generally only the clergy of the world who had any education. China gained quite a bit of her scientific information from resident foreign priests and monks and Chinese religious pilgrimages abroad.

After a lunch of fried noodles in the village we strolled over to the railway station. There wasn't any train due until nine p.m. We walked back along the rail line and reached the hotel at six.

Singh and Lin decided to spend a few more days taking in Kaifeng, Zhengzhou and possibly Anyang. I had already seen more than I could fully digest. I left Luoyang at eight a.m. on the 18th of September, traveling "hard seat sleeper," and dining on snacks of noodles and meat pies at station stops along the way. I was home before seven the next morning, in time for breakfast with Phoenix and Yamei.

The Big Leap Forward and
the Communes
1957-1958

The Chinese are as "racially pure" as the people of any other large society, mixtures in ancient times of many different local tribes, each with their own physical characteristics, then infused by Mongol invaders, Central Asian raiders, Arab traders and—with the advent of European imperialist expansion—Western paraders.

On first arriving I had some difficulty in remembering faces. (Chinese friends have confessed that, to them, "all foreigners look alike.") But it didn't take more than two or three weeks before I was easily recognizing varied, and quite distinctive, features. By the end of the month the Chinese no longer appeared "foreign." Another month after that and I was marveling to myself how many of them resembled people I knew back home. One day I prevented myself just in time from calling out to a man who, at a quick glance, was the image of my brother-in-law.

I developed a real interest in the movement and blending of peoples throughout history. At one point I harbored strong suspicion that Phoenix had gypsy blood, though I could find no basis in my anthropological studies for the presence of Romany caravans in China. I never met a girl with such a passion for moving. She had only to see an attractive vacancy and she was ready to go.

This is a family joke. Actually, we've had only five different homes in the past 50 years, which isn't much when you consider the hectic clip at which the new society is developing. I certainly enthusiastically concurred in each of our moves, being a bit of a traveling man myself. In fact in a couple of cases I was responsible for them.

A young woman we knew, who had learned American brashness by spending her teenage years in New York, called to see me. The first time I met her, in 1949, she got us both into hot water, herself literally and me figuratively. I was home alone one afternoon when a stunning Chinese girl came breezing in, introduced herself as a friend of a friend, and said she had heard we had a bathtub—then a relative rarity in Beijing. This was true enough, since we were still living in a foreign-style house in the old College of Chinese Studies compound. If I didn't mind, she added pleasantly, she would take a bath, and strolled off before I could close my gaping mouth.

Ten minutes later, Phoenix came home and headed straight for the bathroom. Twenty seconds later, she marched up and confronted me.

"Who is that woman?"

"I never saw her before in my life—"

"Hah!"

I was pure as the driven snow, but it wasn't until the lady herself emerged, pink and fragrant from her bath, and explained who she was, that the suspicious look faded somewhat from Phoenix's eyes.

Now, in 1957, this high-voltage beauty was amazing us again. She was planning to move, she said. Good housing was still pretty scarce, but somehow she had got on to not one house, but two. She asked whether we would be willing to take one of them off her hands. Since the place she offered was more conveniently located to both Phoenix's office and mine, besides being larger, brighter, and with more rooms than where we were living, we quickly agreed. Rent was not much. All premises where 15 rooms or more were let for profit had been taken over by the city. You paid your rent directly to the municipal authorities, who gave a fixed share to the former owner over a period of years until the value of his equity was paid off.

Moving was no problem. We had beds, a sofa, two wicker chairs, woven mat rugs, pots and pans, iron heating stoves—very modest. At the same time we had a good foreign-made radio bought from a departing Westerner, bureaus and clothes hampers (traditional Chinese homes have no closets), and several antique tables and mahogany bookcases. These last I had bought for a pittance in secondhand shops when the wealthy of the old regime were retrenching and flooding the market with beautiful hardwood furniture.

Our main item of kitchen equipment was the stove—a cylinder of sheet iron about three feet high, lined with thin firebrick, for cooking with coalballs. We were not encumbered by a refrigerator, since Chinese families buy only whatever perishables they eat that day. In the 1950s home furnishings of foreigners were a mixture of local and imported products.

It didn't take us long to move. My office sent a small truck and a couple of strong young men, and we finished the job in two trips.

Our new quarters were in another hollow square compound. It must have been very old. On either side of the front gate was a square stone about two feet high. These were mounting blocks, for getting on your horse, or into a sedan chair. The compound was a yard lower than the lane outside, always a sign of age in Beijing, for the dust of centuries, swept out of the courtyards daily, piled up and raised the level of the earthen streets.

Full of large trees and flowering shrubs, it was very pleasant. We were in the outermost courtyard, in a one-story structure built in a straight row which used to be the servants' quarters. The only trouble was that our rooms were paved with large stone flaggings laid directly on the earth. In the damp of spring and early summer our floors and walls sopped up moisture like a sponge, and we all developed aches in our joints. But houses were hard to come by, and we stuck it out for several years until we found our present place, which has wooden floors a yard above the ground.

Our neighbors—three families living in the handsome inner courtyard—were all connected with civil aviation. The main and best building, facing south, housed our landlord. He had been a manager in the KMT's China National Aviation Company (CNAC). When the old regime collapsed, along with other officials he had been pressured onto a ship heading for Taiwan. As they were leaving the harbor, he jumped overboard and swam ashore. The People's Republic gave him a position in the new airline at a high salary. He owned quite a bit of real estate in Beijing, of which the compound we lived in was part. With him was his wife, a sharp efficient woman disliked by the poorer people in our lane for her arrogant manner.

The family in the east wing, consisted of a young aeronautical engineer, kept on when the CNAC was taken over, his wife and two kids. Except for a tiny fraction of fervid counterrevolutionaries and crooks, everyone working in the numerous Kuomintang government offices and agencies had been retained when the Communists came to power. The wife was a typical middle-class housewife, rather beefy, and always expensively dressed.

In the west wing lived a bachelor, at least for the moment. A lean, good-looking fellow who had been married and divorced, he lived alone, when not being solaced by a young woman who wore high heels and form-fitting gowns. He had a good radio-phonograph combination, a stack of American dance records, and a well-equipped bar. I dropped in for a drink occasionally, and he told me his story.

He had been a commercial airline pilot under the Kuomintang, and had just finished a flight to Hong Kong when Chiang Kai-shek fled the mainland. The Communists broadcast a statement that they would welcome all returning airline personnel and would pay bonuses for planes brought back, the price ranging with the size of the plane. He had no illusions about the Kuomintang—"a pack of turds," he called them—and had no desire to spend his days in Taiwan. Besides, the bonus offered was substantial. He drove down to the airport, said he had to test his plane, took off and flew to Shanghai. Not only was he paid for the plane—in gold—but he also was given a job as a flight instructor with a very good salary in Beijing.

He should have been happy, but he wasn't. He had nothing against the new administration—he could see how much better off people were. But it wasn't the kind of life he was used to. He had no interest in the political study going on. His smartly cut clothes were conspicuous among his casually dressed colleagues. It was hard to rustle up a card game or throw a big party. People were busy. They didn't care much about such things any more. He had his girlfriend, of course. No one seemed to mind that they were living together. People only smiled and asked when was he planning to get married. Even his money didn't give him any special status. He could buy expensive canned goods with it, but who wanted food in cans when fresh meat and vegetables were plentiful and cheap?

He was pretty frustrated, but there wasn't anything I could do to help him. It was just part of a process all bourgeois-minded people, including myself, were going through. You had to decide. No one was opposed to fun and games, as such. The Chinese enjoyed their amusements as much as anybody. But it was a question of values, of emphasis. To what did you devote your main energies? What was your primary interest in life? Your personal comfort? Your immediate family? Or did you raise your sights and work for your local community, your national community, the world community? True, you could keep your nose clean, go through the motions on your job, say what you felt was expected of you and, on your own time, indulge in all the material pleasures and comforts you wished. You could live that way, no one would stop you, as long as it didn't infringe on the rights of others. Yet, unless you had the hide of a rhinoceros, you couldn't help feeling that most people—your colleagues, your friends, your children—watched you sadly.

That was what was disturbing our pilot. What was the good of a little ostentation if no one envied you, or—even worse—thought you vulgar? The braggart, the show-off was like a fish out of water in the new society. Our pilot was a dying breed. Yet even he might change. I'd seen it happen in worse cases. They suddenly realized that "Serve the people" was the only creed that brought any lasting satisfaction.

Or so I viewed the situation in China in 1957. I wish I could say I feel the same way about social morality today.

Yamei started primary school that year. It was two long blocks from the house, about a 20-minute walk, the way the kids dawdled along. We let her go and come back by herself. She was taller and leggier, and self-sufficient for a girl of seven. She was proud of her textbooks and covered them with fancy paper, keeping them scrupulously clean for two whole weeks. Then artistic doodles and decorations began appearing in the margins and inside the covers. Yamei was not the most conscientious pupil in her class.

It worried us a little because she was an only child and our standard of living was higher than that of her average classmate. To prevent her from becoming spoiled we taught her to keep her room clean, to help around the house and, when she was older, to wash her own clothes. She got, if anything, less candy and trinkets than her little pals. We often fed her coarse grains, like sorghum and millet, instead of only highly polished flour and rice. We probably overdid it, but while her grades didn't noticeably improve, she was a normal enough child, and very healthy.

Phoenix was then editing a monthly magazine for the Dramatists Association called *Playscripts*. She did a lot of theater-going in Beijing, and I almost always went along. I had been interested in the theater since my days as a lawyer on Broadway, and I liked the friendly, informal atmosphere. We usually went to dress rehearsals or opening nights. Sometimes a meeting and general discussion would be held backstage after the performance. I would be invited to listen in and once in a while was asked for my opinion. They talked mainly of staging, direction and performance. How to bring out the positive qualities of the hero without making him stuffy; how to show him as human without reducing him to a jelly of indecision and self-doubt. How to point up the villainy of the villain without making him a caricature; to portray him in depth without turning him into an odd type who was good to his mother. They were aware of the one-dimensional quality of some of their characters but, in trying to flesh them out, it was all too easy to go to extremes.

I had by then translated half a dozen novels for Foreign Languages Press and scores of short stories. These on the whole, perhaps because we were able to cull through and pick the best, were of good literary quality. Most dealt with war situations—against the Japanese, against the Kuomintang—and were dramatic and fairly straightforward. The difficulty arose in material concerned with the ideological struggles of the post-liberation period. To present these well required a thorough rapport with the thoughts and emotions of the workers and peasants who constituted 80 to 90 percent of the population. Many of the authors were petty-bourgeois in their background or upbringing and tended to superimpose their own attitudes upon their characters. Or for the sake of suspense they would create a mental conflict where none existed, at least typically or to any appreciable extent.

China was poor and backward, with dozens of engineering problems in urgent need of solution. Instead of waiting for money, special machinery or trained personnel, all sorts of people were turning out across the country and getting things done. Between October 1957 and January 1958, for example, 100 million co-op farmers pitched in and dug irrigation ditches and built check dams, converting nearly 26 million acres into irrigated fields. In four months they brought water to more land than their ancestors had been able to irrigate in the previous 2,000 years.

Ecological and medical problems were also tackled on a mass public participation basis. An intensive two-year (1957-1958) campaign was waged against the "Four Pests"—flies, mosquitoes, rats and sparrows. I was one of the warriors in the Beijing battle against the birds, which demonstrated the ingenuity and organizational skills of the Chinese.

Sparrows were listed for extermination because every year at harvest they descended on the fields in droves and consumed large quantities of grain. A spring day in 1958 was set as the time for the final crushing assault. On every building, in every street, in front yards, in back yards, people stood or sat and waved white cloths and shouted, whistled, and banged on pans, whenever sparrows appeared. I was perched on a high garden wall with a pillowcase, and I flapped and whooshed for hours.

Confused and hungry, the birds plunged into net snares, alighted on limed branches, ate poisoned food laid out in areas purposely left open. Thousands upon thousands were eliminated that day.

Later it was found that our enthusiasm had been misdirected, and that sparrows destroy certain insects which do much more harm to crops than the birds themselves. The authorities, with characteristic candor, admitted they were in error, and the birds were given a reprieve, though measures are still taken to keep them out of fields when the grain is garnered. Bedbugs were substituted for sparrows as the fourth pest. The experience reminded the Chinese of the need to maintain an ecological balance.

They do that pretty well. Although wide use is being made of chemicals, the main fertilizer is organic waste—human and animal manures, sewage and garbage. Human waste is carefully hoarded and collected. In the cities and towns big trucks siphon it out of public toilets. If you have a cesspool, you can expect a visit every spring from the organization that cleans them out, free of charge. In Beijing, the stuff is carted to special areas in the outskirts where it, together with the city's garbage, is processed into fertilizer. Some cities, like Shanghai, have huge mains piping the waste directly to communes miles away.

With the rats (and mice), flies and mosquitoes we had an even harder job, but we did very well. The favorite stamping grounds for city rodents were the sewers. First we drove them out of homes and buildings by plugging their holes, setting traps, spreading poisoned baits. Then, on a given night, powder that emitted poisonous smoke when ignited was lit and lowered into the sewers, and every surface opening tightly sealed. The same routine was repeated a few nights later, and then again several nights after that. Everything depended on full intelligent public participation. You did not utterly destroy the rodent population. No one had discovered how to do that yet. But you sure as hell discouraged them, and if you repeated the process periodically you could keep them down to a minimum.

A slightly different approach was used with flies and mosquitoes. Flies were attacked first in the grub and larvae stages. Kids knew where to dig them out—in soft spots along the bottoms of outer walls, and a lot of other places I would never have thought of. Swatting was taken seriously against those flies which managed to get born. People were embarrassed if you saw a fly in their home, and the whole family, and the guests, promptly zeroed in on the offending creature.

With mosquitoes, everyone checked around his own house and lane or street to make sure there were no puddles or water-filled cans or jugs in which they could breed. Stagnant pools anywhere were flushed out or filled in. Several nights during the summer at fixed hours you fumigated your house with smoke bombs, keeping the doors and windows closed while you stayed out in the garden. Then you aired the house and let the surviving mosquitoes, if any, stagger out, and you went inside and shut all the doors and windows. At this point, planes came skimming over, spraying insecticide. About half a hour later there was an all-clear signal and you emerged into a virtually bugless evening.

The glue that stuck all this together was the neighborhood committees—mostly retired oldsters and housewife volunteers. They were part of a city-wide organization, and notify you of the time schedules, issued the smoke bombs (at a few cents a pack), supervised the operations, and checked the results. Quite efficient. The kids helped a lot, as messengers doing most of the legwork. They got a big charge out of it, and so did the adults. It was very satisfying being part of a positive community action, particularly when you felt you are helping got rid of dirt and disease, quickly and cheaply. Of course the campaign against the "Four Pests" was never-ending, but it got easier and more effective with each succeeding year.

This "do-it-yourself-with-what-you've-got" approach was spreading like wildfire all over China, always carefully watched and encouraged by the Communist Party. Someone would have what looked like a good idea. He would need time or money or conditions to try it out. These, the local Party organizations would provide. If it worked, it would be tried on a somewhat larger scale. If that also succeeded, a complete report would be sent to the Party Central Committee in Beijing. After investigation, it might be introduced nationally.

One of the most important developments in modern Chinese history—the advent of the communes—occurred in just this manner. It began in Henan Province early in 1958. Henan for centuries had been tormented by floods and droughts. Determined to put an end to these disasters once and for all, the high-level cooperative farms to which most of the rural population belonged began to merge. This offered obvious advantages in dealing with the vagaries of a river. The co-ops on the lower reaches couldn't do much without the help of those on the upper.

And they discovered other benefits as well. With manpower and capital pooled in large concentrations, they were able to allocate their personnel more rationally and invest in costlier projects. They could make more appropriate use of their fields, according to terrain and soil conditions. The coal in the hills of one cooperative farm, for example, could be combined with the iron ore of another to make iron and manufacture farm implements.

Mergers proceeded apace. Encouraged by the Henan provincial committee of the Communist Party several thousand more communes—as people began to call them—were formed on an experimental basis. In addition to agriculture, the communes did small-scale manufacturing—mainly of things they needed themselves—set up their own supply and distribution companies, ran their own schools and their own militias. They organized mess halls, tailoring and mending shops, laundries, homes for the aged, medical dispensaries, maternity clinics,

134

nurseries, kindergartens. Women were freed from much of their household drudgery and could play a fuller role in the work and administration.

I was eager to see the communes in action in Henan, the province where they were born, but had to delay my visit for several weeks because of the arrival in China of A.L. Wirin, defense counsel in the Powell case. I was in the legal section of a committee of Chinese and Westerners in Beijing supporting Bill Powell, his wife Sylvia, and Julian Schuman, charged in a San Francisco federal court with "conspiracy to incite sedition."

As spelled out in the indictment this consisted of publishing in *China Monthly Review*, the English language-magazine founded in Shanghai by Bill's father, statements regarding the use of bacteriological weapons by the US forces in Korea and China during the Korean War, of revealing the extent of US casualties, of exposing American stalling at the armistice negotiations, and of suggesting that Chiang Kai-shek was corrupt! The charges were brought in 1956 when the China Lobby—big business and missionaries who had been shown the door by the new regime—were hysterically fulminating against the Beijing government. By then the Powells and Julian had closed down the *Review* and returned to the States.

The defense of the accused was truth. They said they could and would prove everything they had published in the *Review*. But they needed a fair chance to prepare their case. For a year and a half defense counsel had been struggling, against strong opposition on the part of the US government, for an opportunity to interview potential Chinese witnesses. The State Department had persistently refused to give Wirin a passport for China. It broke down only when the judge threatened to throw the case out if the government continued obstructing the defendants' constitutional right to secure evidence in their own behalf.

In China Wirin was able to meet over 40 people in Beijing, Nanjing and Shanghai willing to testify for the accused. Character witnesses included a former president of the World Council of Churches, the Chairman of the National Committee of Three–Self Patriotic Movement of Protestant Churches in China, the Secretary General of the Chinese YMCA, and an Episcopal bishop. There were military men ready to identify the dog tags taken from the bodies of GIs killed in Korea. (Long after the names, ranks and serial numbers of these men were published in *China Monthly Review*, the US Defense Department continued to torment their parents and wives with false hopes by listing them as "missing in action.") Scientists and civilians by the score were prepared to come forward with eye-witness accounts, present special bomb canisters which had carried the insect hosts, produce reports of elaborate tests . . . to prove the commission by the United States of germ warfare.

Wirin was anxious to get these people and their evidence before the court, but the US government refused to conclude a judicial assistance pact with China. These pacts are standard international practice. Without them some countries—

Switzerland, for example—won't permit a foreign lawyer to even interview a potential witness. No country will allow its citizens to give depositions or go into a foreign court in the absence of such an agreement. Since the judge of the federal court trying the case had written to the Chinese Ministry of Justice requesting that judicial assistance be granted, the Chinese delegate then attending ambassadorial talks in Geneva demanded the execution of a proper pact. The US representative refused to consider it. Premier Zhou Enlai commented on the inconsistency.

"The proposal that judicial assistance be given came, in the first instance, from American judicial authorities," he said. "The Chinese government is quite willing to see this brought about. But until the US government changes its inflexible and hostile attitude, all efforts by the Chinese government are in vain."

Wirin returned to San Francisco empty-handed. Stalemated, the case hung fire. Eminent scientists from half a dozen European countries who had made on the spot investigations of germ warfare in China and Korea offered to testify. American scientist Dr. Theodore Rosebury published his book about the extensive bacteriological warfare experiments conducted in Fort Detrick, Maryland, in which he personally had taken part. Protestations of innocence from Washington grew weaker. After dragging on for five years, the case was finally dropped.

A few weeks after Wirin's futile visit to China in 1958 I was able to arrange my trip to Henan, where the communes started. That summer I traveled with a young photographer from *China Pictorial* who was looking for material on this interesting new subject.

We went first to Xuchang, an ancient city in the center of the province, and spent the night in the compound of the prefectural Party committee. It was situated on a square half-acre of land that rose abruptly some 20 or 30 yards out of the surrounding plain, with four almost vertical sides. Legend had it that this had been the headquarters of Cao Cao (A.D. 155-220), a general and statesman, one of those dynamic figures who keep cropping up in Chinese history, and who had been the subject of centuries of debate. Was he a hero or a villain? Either way, he was a familiar figure to all Chinese theater-goers, and Xuchang was proud to be the site of his old stamping grounds.

The Party committee was generous and helpful. They provided us with a jeep and a driver, and one of their cadres to show us around. We set out the next morning for Two Temples, a township in the county of Xiangcheng. Two Temples had formerly contained several high-level farming co-ops. Recently these had merged to become one of 13 subcommunes in a commune embracing the entire county. Though not all communes were as large, their general structure was similar. A dozen to several dozen families formed a team. A dozen or so teams constituted a brigade. A dozen or so brigades made up the commune. The brigade leadership also functioned as village government. The commune leadership, depending on the area the commune embraced, governed either the township or the county.

Even before we reached Two Temples we could see the enthusiasm the formation of the communes had generated. As we rolled along in our jeep, I was struck by a series of little signs that lined one side of the road, each carrying a few words of a slogan, like the Burma Shave ads you used to see along US highways. Later we learned that these were the wooden covers of the family pots, no longer needed because the pots had all been donated to be melted down in the drive to make iron. A staggering mistake, one of the many silly excesses committed in the initial stages of what became known as the Big Leap Forward.

There were as many women as men in the fields we drove through, all bright with red banners. On arches of boughs built over the road were announcements by brigades challenging each other. The harvest was in, and they were turning the soil to make it more fertile for the next planting. The brigades were vying to finish their respective fields first.

At my request we stopped our jeep and walked into one of the fields. It was like stepping onto a stage. The brigade members—mostly young—were working steadily and fast in a long moving row, turning over the soil with spades.

Behind them, actors and actresses, in full makeup and historical costumes, were singing rhythmic arias, to the accompaniment of pounding drums and cymbals, while dancing around on stilts—a peculiarity of the local opera. This gave the shovel-wielders added vigor, though they didn't seem to need any encouragement. They were chatting and laughing as they worked, some of them singing along with the performers.

We were introduced to the brigade's Communist Party secretary. He looked harassed and tired. He said they had estimated the earth-turning job would take two weeks, but the kids had made up their minds to finish in one. It looked like they were going to do it. They had been working in shifts, 24 hours a day for three days, and were already more than halfway through. The brigade's Party committee had been begging them to slow down, but in vain. Everyone was determined to make the communes a quick success.

Formerly, in that part of Henan the ploughing had been too shallow. Government agronomists had advised a depth of three inches. "If three inches is good," the young people cried, "we'll turn over three feet and make it ten times better!" With great gusto they dug up the underlying sand and buried the good topsoil three feet under.

This was typical of the joyous frenzy of the Big Leap Forward which was sweeping all China. Much of it was clearly unscientific and impractical, but it was difficult to control. Wishful thinking swamped the objections of common sense.

In Guangdong Province, dizzied by a sudden large increase in rice harvests, some communes allowed their members to eat as much they liked in the public dining rooms the brigades had established, free of charge. They soon consumed not only the expanded yields, but much of the reserves, including the seed grain. In many places, while harvests were honestly calculated according to the condition of the crops in the fields, they were less than anticipated when actually gathered. Too many commune members were busy digging irrigation ditches, building dams, making iron, and engaged in the many new collective enterprises the communes had made possible. "Overpopulated" China was suffering from a labor shortage. Crops went to seed, toppled in the fields, got soaked on the threshing grounds. The difference between estimated and final harvest figures was not always corrected in reports to higher authorities.

Many farmers were not keen about joining the communes. Traditionally cautious, they did not want to give up their right to decide what, and when, and where to plant. Willy-nilly, public pressure forced them to comply, but the next few years proved that their reservations were correct. Rules created to determine shares in the harvest, for example, based on quantity and quality of work in the fields, were implemented instead in accordance with old-fashioned neighborly considerations or outright favoritism. Output quickly dropped. In some parts of the country people went hungry. The communes and the Big Leap Forward, on balance, were a failure. It is not possible to leap from backward foundations into utopia.

Yet despite their failings they had a lot to their credit. Large parts of China were able comprehensively to control their floods, drain their fields, and provide irrigation when needed. Thousands of miles of dams, dikes, canals and roads were built. New agricultural techniques were evolved and spread. Small home-grown mills and workshops sprouted like mushrooms. There were many inventions, some mechanization, even a little automation. In science and the arts there was a lively ferment of new methods, new ideas.

At the Two Temples Sub-Commune tobacco and wheat output had risen considerably. Everyone was delighted, the women most of all. They were into everything—agriculture, industry, the schools, the militia. At least half the trainees I saw in the Two Temples iron foundry and farm implements factory were girls.

For the first time some families had a little money left over after buying their necessities. A few people were beginning to accumulate savings.

"In four or five years, you'll have quite a pile," I said jokingly to one of the women. "What will you do with it all?"

"Buy more machinery for the commune."

"Don't you want anything for yourself?"

She hesitated. "Maybe I'll buy a car. Walking to and from the fields wastes so much time."

"I'll come and see you and take a ride."

"Don't bother," she laughed. "I'll drive to Beijing and pick you up."

New horizons had brought new outlooks. Women in the old society, the oppressed of the oppressed, were blossoming out. They wore colorful cotton prints to the fields, they took more pains with their appearance. One of them recited a jingle she had composed. I wrote it down:

Nurseries, kindergartens, tailor shops,
You don't do the cooking, or feed pigs the slops.
Machines make the clothing and grind fine the flour,
When you give birth you're cared for every hour.
Freed from household drudgery let's produce more every day,
And drive ahead to communism, it isn't far away.

Wildly optimistic, of course. Even socialism, to say nothing of communism, was a long way off. Many of the measures taken were unrealistic, some were downright harmful. But there was no doubt that the Big Leap Forward and the communes lent wings to the imagination of China's millions.

We climbed into our jeep again and took off for Yuxian County, where 9,000 homemade furnaces were going full blast, turning out thousands of tons of iron per day. People had known for a long time that the Yuxian hills contained coal and iron, but they had no skilled workers, no decent roads, no large investment capital.

The communes had brought a unique strength—huge concentrations of well-organized manpower, people who had learned to think boldly and big. In September, after the harvests were in, 150,000 commune members—half the county's working population—moved into the hills. First they built a road, 250 miles in eight days. They dug coal and iron with pick and shovel. Transport consisted of anything that could carry. Trucks, rubber-tired mule carts, wooden-wheeled ox carts, wheelbarrows, people with shoulder poles and baskets . . . traveled in endless procession up and down the slopes, bringing iron ore and coke to the flame-belching furnaces, food and supplies to the busy workers. I watched them doing it.

The furnaces were miracles of ingenuity. Guided by only a few dozen persons with any technical training, the farm folk in two or three weeks learned to improvise furnaces and blowers that were cheap, quickly built—and that made iron. At the time of our visit a variety of furnaces were in operation, producing from half to three or four tons each, daily. Most of them had thick earthen walls and used little or no firebrick. Some cost only 20 yuan apiece to build. The majority of the blowers were hand-operated. Teams of two, in relays, rotated vertical wheels connected to the motors of the blowers by leather belts—the cow hair still on them more often than not.

In all of these operations women played a large part. I saw them digging ore, toting it in big baskets slung from poles supported on their shoulders—one woman

139

in front, the other behind. Others sat on the ground pulverizing chunks of ore with small hammers. Many tended the furnaces, from the mixing to the tapping, and pouring the liquid iron into molds.

The policy was to give the men the heavier jobs and the women the lighter. But in one mill of 500 people the women outnumbered the men three to two, and they insisted on running the whole show. Ranging in age from 13 to 35, the women were strong, healthy, and mostly single. They had tried to restrict their volunteers to young women with no family ties, but this had proved difficult.

One lady in her sixties had demanded that they teach her to make iron. She said she had learned to do everything there was to do on a farm, she didn't see why she couldn't learn to tend a blast furnace. After much persuasion, they finally induced her to go home. Another woman came—she was only 48—and refused to leave. She just wouldn't take no for an answer. They had to keep her on as a cook.

I asked Wei, an unmarried girl of 21 who was the leader of the mill, what brought her to the rugged hills. She said she had learned to read and write. When the co-ops merged into communes and the drive to expand industry started, she was among the first to volunteer to learn to make iron and steel. As a Communist, she felt she should set an example. Before long, she mastered all the processes, from prospecting for ore to casting the pig iron ingots. Recently, the women had elected her leader. She loved her job and hoped she could stay with it permanently.

Another woman, 34, mother of two small boys, knew precisely why she had come. China needed steel, she explained. Steel would make guns and tanks to protect the nation and machines that would raise farm yields. She said she hated to leave her kids, but it was only temporary, and she was working for their sake and the sake of all the children.

About half of China's iron and steel production was coming from crude furnaces in the countryside, close to sources of iron and coal, and tended by people fresh from the farms with no previous experience. Later it was found that too many had left agriculture. The communes were short-handed, and the quality of much of the iron produced was not worth the effort. Most people returned to their farms, and many of the "mills" were abandoned.

But part of the iron had been good enough to be turned into farm tools. Mass prospecting had unearthed a large number of previously undiscovered mines. More important, homemade iron and steel production had given millions a basic familiarity with tools and machinery, sadly lacking in a country just emerging from feudal backwardness. When small and medium-sized iron and steel plants were subsequently set up all over the country these people were a reservoir of technical trainees. Some became the indispensable "handymen" who serviced the machines increasingly demanded by the communes.

As we traveled back to Beijing we stared from our train window in awe at the little furnaces spewing flames into the night sky for miles along both sides of the railway. All China was making iron and steel. In the city our taxi had to drive slowly. Some streets were so thick with smoke it was difficult to see. We could have been in Gary, or Pittsburgh. Every school, every government office, had its backyard furnaces. Teachers, pupils, civil servants, took turns tending them.

Inefficient, yes, but exciting, stimulating. I doubt whether the iron turned out behind the Foreign Languages Press served any practical purpose. The cost of transporting coal and iron to the center of the nation's capital far exceeded the value of the steel we produced. But the value to intellectuals, rising from their swivel chairs and sweating beside a blast furnace they had built themselves, carbon smudges on their noses, was incalculable. They were identifying, for the first time, physically and directly, with industrial production. They weren't just talking and writing about things—they were doing them. It was very satisfying.

The atmosphere was positively festive. There was a great feeling of togetherness. "Me" and "mine" tended to give way to "us" and "ours." Doctors of traditional medicine made public prescriptions which had been jealously guarded in the family for generations, and even then passed on only to first-born sons. City people also tried to form communes. Although as economic structures they were not yet feasible in the cities, many of the social amenities they brought were very useful.

Older women neighbors whose children were grown, would call at the homes of young working mothers, if desired, with thermoses of water already boiled for drinking and washing, let them leave for their jobs, dress the kids, feed them, and get them off to school. They would also do the housework and deliver the dirty clothes to another, specially organized, laundry group. In the late afternoon they would feed a snack to the kids returning from school, clean them up a bit, and put the kettle on, so that all mama had to do when she got home was cook supper.

There were also tailoring and mending services, and grocery and butcher shops that delivered right to the door. Unfortunately the small home industries organized by the city communes could not earn enough to pay for all these amenities, especially when the rest of the city was being run on a different financial basis. They gradually dwindled away and vanished. Like so many of the ideas and approaches attempted by the Big Leap Forward and the communes, they looked fine on the surface but lacked the foundations and preconditions needed to implement them.

Some cooler heads recognized this from the start. Tried and true veteran Communist Peng Dehuai in a private letter to Mao voiced concern that China was moving too fast. For his pains he was removed from office as a high military leader, and blasted openly by Mao at a national Party convention. Mao was not a man to brook disagreement gracefully.

I and most of my friends, and much of China, had been carried along by the ecstatic environment. Today, with the wisdom of hindsight, we see that the Big Leap Forward and the communes were flawed by an impetuosity which ran ahead of reasoned judgments. Adjustments had to be made, China's countryside was not ready for communes operating as economic entities. The unit of accounting was returned to the village production teams, rather than the brigade or the commune as a whole.

Past mistakes and excesses were examined and merits recognized. What should be the priorities in China's economy? How do you build up a backward country starting virtually from scratch? Some wanted to mechanically copy the Soviet Union and put the stress on heavy industrial complexes. First steel, machine tools, modern transport, chemicals, power. Then, and only then, an expansion of light industry and agriculture.

The Chinese Communist Party felt this was not suited to China's conditions. China lacked heavy industry, but she had enormous rural manpower. Agriculture should therefore be recognized as the base of the economy, with industry providing the drive. This was the blueprint embodied in a new General Line. A rising agricultural output would supply the grain and industrial crops and the finances (through taxation) for industry, and provide it with workers. As industry grew it would turn out the farm tools, the chemical fertilizer, the consumer goods needed by the people on the farms. Agriculture and industry would complement each other. "Walking on two legs," the Chinese called it.

The same dialectical approach was taken to all aspects of the economy. Developing in tandem would be light and heavy industry, modern factories and the home-grown kind, small and medium-sized plants as well as large ones. Most factories were then concentrated in the coastal areas. These would continue to be used. But new enterprises would also be developed in the interior. In administration, too, the "two legs" pattern was maintained. The central government held overall control and ran certain enterprises directly. But the initiative of lower levels of government and their management of local plants was encouraged.

Working out a comprehensive viable economic policy in less that ten years after coming to power was no small accomplishment. It all had to be done by trial and error. China's progress was unique among socialist countries.

This was positive. At the same time there were signs of a growing intolerance of criticism within the Party leadership, and harsh measures against those who dared to voice contrary opinions. This had already been manifested in the anti-Rightist campaign. It was to grow and plague China until its ultimate eruption in the form of fascist takeovers by the Gang of Four during the disastrous "cultural revolution."

142

Integration Accomplished:
An American-Chinese
1959-1963

The late 1950s had been exciting, inspiring. But they were also preludes to the trouble the 1960s would bring.

While China was leaping forward, various poodles were yapping at her heels. New threats were muttered in America of "unleashing" Chiang Kai-shek. In December 1958, Khrushchov, in a talk with Hubert Humphrey, labeled the Chinese communes "essentially reactionary." At the 21st Congress of the Soviet Communist Party early in 1959, he said that China was "skipping over a stage," that the communes were a form of "egalitarian communism." Khrushchov was so thoroughly hated in China for his hectoring and bullying, and he was so clearly wrong in international matters, that no one wondered whether his remarks about the communes might be true. Some years later, the Chinese themselves reached the same conclusions.

More harassment came from the southwest. In March 1959, the ruling nobles and the Buddhist lama hierarchy in Tibet staged a rebellion. In August and October, Indian troops attacked. The Chinese drove them out.

Tibet had been part of China for centuries. Though it had mineral and metal resources of some potential, it was so high in the Himalayas and so lacking in transport that they were never developed. The Indians, across the border, had a few trading posts in Tibet, where they did a bit of business. The British had sent a military expedition at the turn of the century, occupied Lhasa, and built a sphere of influence which they continued to maintain, via India, until October 1951, when the Chinese PLA marched in.

Everything was owned by the nobles and the high Buddhist lamas. The people were slaves and serfs living in conditions that would make medieval Europe look like the Age of Enlightenment. For any infraction of the "rules," eyes were gouged out, hands or legs cut off. Floggings were an everyday affair. Human skins were used for drums, skulls mounted in silver were popular as bowls among the high lamas. Thigh bones of virgin girls were said to make the best flutes for religious services.

Beijing tried to encourage gradual reform, but did not interfere in local government and left the big land holdings intact. The clergy and the nobles were not content. In collusion with British, American, Indian and Kuomintang agents,

143

they staged an uprising in 1959, nominally headed by the Dalai Lama, which was quickly put down. It was only then that Land Reform was commenced, starting later, and moving through mutual-aid team and co-op stages more slowly than in the rest of the country. Today Tibet has its own autonomous people's government.

At the time of the 1959 rebellion crocodile tears gushed copiously in the West over the loss of "freedom and democracy" by the poor Tibetans.

Imagine the jolly celebrations if restoration of the old order had succeeded, quaffing toasts out of skull bowls, while virgin thigh-bone flutes tootled sweet songs to the soft beat of drums of human skin. . . . I saw some of these mementos in an exhibition in Beijing, including a neatly flayed skin, complete to the very finger tips, an offering to the gods in a lama temple. It was sickening. Holy lamas, soul brothers to Ilse Koch!

Nineteen fifty-nine was the first of what was to become known as the Three Bad Years. When it wasn't floods, it was drought, or insect plagues. Farm output dropped sharply. The supply of food was short, and China was paying for a good part of Soviet "aid" in foodstuffs. Could these payments be delayed a few years? the Chinese asked. Nothing doing, replied the Soviet leaders. The contracts had to be observed to the letter.

The first signs of the malaise had surfaced in 1956 after Khrushchov made his dramatic "secret" exposure of Stalin at the 20th Congress of the Soviet Party, which somehow immediately found its way to the pages of the *New York Times*. He alleged that Stalin had a "persecution mania," that he indulged in "mass repressions and terror," that he was a "criminal . . . bandit . . . idiot . . . fool. . . ."

The Chinese, in two newspaper editorials, politely but firmly disagreed. They said Stalin had committed serious errors and it was correct to criticize him. But his accomplishments far outweighed his failings. After all, it was under his leadership that the Soviet Union had built a solid economy and defeated Hitler's Nazi hordes. Stalin also made important contributions to Marxist theory and stood for working class rule. He preserved harmony among the ethnic and national entities within the Soviet Union. Racial and religious persecution was effectively stamped out. Why try to negate him completely? In Beijing Stalin's portrait continued to be prominently displayed. Translations of his writings remained on sale throughout China.

The next clash occurred in 1957 at a world conference of Communist parties in Moscow. China obviously thought the meeting important. Mao Zedong personally led the Chinese delegation—his second, and final, trip abroad. (The first was in 1949 when he went to Moscow to negotiate with Stalin, who had been supporting Chiang Kai-shek's Kuomintang. Stalin reluctantly concluded a Treaty of Friendship, Alliance and Mutual Assistance, with the new, liberated China.) The Soviet delegation with characteristic modesty touted the "majestic results" of the "splendid"

20th Congress, reiterated their attack on Stalin and tried to steamroller through a declaration confirming their brand of "peaceful transition," plugged by Mr. K.

According to him the world had changed, and it was now possible to go from capitalism to socialism by following the "parliamentary road." In other words, vote capitalism out of existence and the rulers, the boys scraping the cream off the top, would meekly give up if only you mustered enough votes at election time.

Absurd, said the Chinese. Even if, in a particular country, you might get a majority vote for socialism, the power gang would definitely come shooting and blast you out of the chairs of office. That didn't mean the Left shouldn't take part in elections and public debate. These were a means of educating the public. But you were mad if you thought they would create any fundamental changes in the system.

As for the 20th Congress, one of its "majestic results" was to delight the enemies of communism. The greatest fear in the West was that the social and economic forms in the "communist" (read "socialist") lands would prove superior to those in the capitalist world. Might that not make people in the West question the alleged superiority of the political systems in their own countries, and—worst of all—decide to change them and get rid of their monopoly rulers? It was the terror at this prospect which accounted for the intensity of the hatred of the socialist experiment.

But now, happily, the antics of Mr. K were putting the unity of socialist nations in disarray. The director of the US Information Agency said Khrushchov's speech had "never so suited our purposes." A *New York Times* editorial acclaimed it as a "weapon with which to destroy the prestige and influence of the communist movement." And John Foster Dulles had mused thoughtfully it might even help to bring about a "peaceful transformation" of the Soviet Union.

Due mainly to Chinese efforts, and despite the wheeling and dealing of the Soviet Party, several important principles were included in the Declaration which was finally adopted. It said that US imperialism was the center of world reaction and the sworn enemy of the people. That it was not the people who would be destroyed in a new world war but imperialism itself. That a socialist country had to fight bourgeois influences within and imperialist pressure without, or it would lose its principles and the people would lose their power.

Mr. Khrushchov's love for the Chinese Communists was not enhanced. They were spoiling his pitch. He was trying to tell everyone how sweet and reasonable the American power structure had become, while chilling doubters with the prospects of an atomic war if they didn't knuckle under to imperialist threats. The Chinese were saying that while the tiger doesn't change its stripes, and possessed a full set of atomic teeth, in the face of solid resistance by people the world over it was only a paper tiger, hollow inside.

Though irked, Mr. K doggedly pushed ahead. In September 1959, he had his Talks at Camp David. "A turning point in history," he called them. Gromyko said they marked "a new era in international relations." The Soviet leaders praised the "sensibleness" and "goodwill" of American presidents. They foresaw "a world without weapons, without armed forces and without wars," and burbled that universal disarmament would "open up literally a new epoch in the economic development of Asia, Africa and Latin America."

To their Chinese allies and friends they were not so kind. In 1958 they put forward demands "designed to bring China under Soviet military control," as the Chinese cryptically described them. Beijing coolly declined.

Nikita's rage was mounting. The Chinese would not allow themselves to be browbeaten. They would not join Comecon—an economic grouping of socialist states serving mainly as suppliers to the Soviet Union of raw materials and semifinished products at lower than world market prices, in exchange for Soviet manufactures at higher than world market prices. The Chinese stressed self-reliance. They were following their own interpretation of Marxism in the light of their own national conditions. They treated the Soviet Party as an equal but not as a superior.

The Soviet Union squeezed harder. In June 1959, they unilaterally abrogated a treaty on technical military assistance concluded less that two years before, and refused to provide China with a sample atom bomb, previously promised, or any data concerning its construction. On the eve of Khrushchov's departure for America in September 1959, a *Tass* statement blamed China for an Indian incursion across the Chinese border.

Khrushchov was splitting the communist camp wide open with his pronouncements on imperialism, war and peace, revolution, and how a socialist country should be governed. The Chinese Party had to speak out. In April 1960 it published an article entitled "Long Live Leninism," restating its views. Yet even at this point the Chinese refrained from openly criticizing the Soviet Party or its leaders.

A week later, as if to underscore the Chinese contention that imperialist enmity had not abated a whit, an American U-2 spy plane flew over the Soviet Union, aborting a scheduled four power summit conference. Moscow, instead of closing its ranks with Beijing, only intensified its invective. At a Romanian Workers Party Congress in Bucharest in June 1960, which other Communist parties attended, Khrushchov took the opportunity to sound off in typical style. He said the Chinese Communists were "madmen" who "wanted to unleash war," that they were "picking up the banner of the imperialist monopoly capitalists," that they had behaved in a "purely nationalist" manner in the Sino-Indian border clash, that their attitude toward the Soviet Party was "Trotskyite." Delegates from satellite parties chimed in with charges that the Chinese Party was "dogmatic," "sectarian," "pseudo-revolutionary," "worse than Yugoslavia."

The Chinese would not be cowed. They issued a calm, reasoned statement, sticking to their guns. A number of parties, notably the Albanian, supported them.

Khrushchov simply blew his stack. In July 1960 he abruptly broke all 343 contracts under the "Sino-Soviet Treaty of Friendship, Alliance and Mutual Assistance," canceled 257 projects of scientific and technical cooperation, and called home 1,390 Soviet experts, instructing them to bring the blueprints with them. (Many were hard workers eager to help China. Some, outraged by Khrushchov's behavior, rushed day and night to copy the blueprints for the Chinese before leaving.) Suddenly there were incidents on the Soviet border and unrest fomented in the autonomous region of Xinjiang.

It was summer, and Phoenix and I were enjoying a vacation at the beach in Beidaihe, along with some of the Westerners living and working in China. We had heard stories about the friction between Beijing and Moscow, but we were astonished that Khrushchov should resort to such a vicious stab in the back.

From the Chinese point of view the Soviet Party was going from bad to worse. Khrushchov showered sticky kisses on the rump of the US imperialists, scrupling at nothing to fawn and win favor. The Soviet Union supplied transport for UN troops to suppress revolutionaries in the Congo. It agreed, without consulting the Cuban government, to "inspection" in Cuba during the missile crisis. It called the bloody slaughter of the Algerian people an "internal affair" of France. It announced that it would "stand aloof" when the United States invented an "incident" in the Gulf of Bac Bo as an excuse for escalation in Vietnam.

Though Communists the world over had long proclaimed their goal to be the emancipation of all mankind, the objective of the Soviet Communists, according to Mr. Khrushchov, was "a good plate of goulash." "Goulash communism" was the new ideal. This rewriting of Marxist political theory became known as "revisionism."

With bourgeois values revived, chauvinism in international affairs inevitably followed. And, of course, ruthless attacks on anyone who tried to stop them.

To the West, Khrushchov was a hero. He was definitely on their side. "Nikita Khrushchov has destroyed, irrevocably, the unified bloc of Stalin's day. That is perhaps Khrushchov's greatest service—not to communism, but to the Western world," said *Newsweek*. "We ought to be grateful for his mishandling of his relationship with the Chinese," said *US News and World Report*. "We should be grateful for his introducing disarray into international communism by a lot of quite bumptious and sudden initiatives." Again *Newsweek*: "The administration is now convinced that the United States should offer Khrushchov maximum support in his dispute with Red China."

By July 1960, the handwriting was on the wall. The Soviet Union was moving back toward capitalism, it was itself becoming an imperialist power. China would not bow; China made pointed comments; China, therefore, had to be crushed. What better time than now, when her harvests were failing and she was beset by economic difficulties?

147

But the Chinese proved to be surprisingly uncrushable. In the first place, they understood the situation. Every office, school, farm and factory, every branch of the armed forces, held formal political study sessions several times a week. In these, Mr. K's antics were closely analyzed. The nature of revisionism and how it manifested itself in socialist countries was discussed. Though Khrushchov and the Soviet Party were never criticized in public, all China was aware of their growing hostility.

Yet the savagery of the open attack, when it came in the summer of 1960, was something of a shock. Reaction among Chinese friends and colleagues went from incredulity to anger to determination. There wasn't enough to eat. Rationing tightened. Protein was in short supply. (This was thought by doctors to be a factor in the hepatitis epidemic which followed a few years later.) Several young people in my office swelled up with edema. Foreigners, as usual, received special treatment. But there wasn't much food to buy, and who had the heart, anyhow, to stuff himself when everyone else was plainly in want?

Incredibly, there was little grumbling. Unruffled, even cheerful, some of them, people went about their regular tasks. Several large vats were set up in the backyard of the Foreign Languages Press. They were raising algae—served in daily soup to fill in the protein deficiency. Calisthenics and sports were out, and we were advised to rest when possible and go to bed early. But we kept the same office hours and did the same amount of work. Matronly ladies laughed and said they were wearing clothes they hadn't been able to get into for years.

Privation and hardship were real enough, however. While Chinese freight cars continued rolling toward the Soviet Union with foodstuffs, as per contract, there were cases of starvation in hard-hit parts of the country, and relief supplies had to be rushed. What saved China was the faith of the vast majority in the country's leaders, in spite of the failures of the communes and the Big Leap forward, and their response to calls and exhortations by the Communist Party. Huge, well-organized forces of men and women built dams and dug canals to bring water to parched fields. They drained off floods and replanted quickly and extensively. They turned out by the thousands and flailed locusts to death. They hewed roads and railways through mountains and rough terrain. . . .

The Soviet betrayal left China with newly started or half-finished projects which, in a way, were worse than none at all. For they were being built according to Soviet plans and specifications, were designed to be equipped with Soviet machinery, and the plans had been taken home and delivery of the machinery canceled. I continued my annual tours, and everywhere I saw empty silent plants and factories. Only two and half of the six planned rolling mills in the Wuhan steel complex had been completed. Projects had to be abandoned or completely redesigned and equipped.

No help could be expected from the West. America and countries under US domination were boycotting China. Those willing to trade demanded exorbitant prices. The Chinese had no choice but to make their own plans, design their own projects, supply their own equipment. They had to practice self-reliance rooted in the earliest traditions of the revolution.

It was slow hard work, but China made a virtue of necessity. The Soviet betrayal and the American boycott turned out to be blessings in disguise. Chinese machines, Chinese industrial processes were born. There were new and original approaches in science and scientific method. But China was still very backward economically, and there was strong disagreement on the methods to be used and the pace at which to advance the new socialist stage.

In spite of the failings of the communes, there was no suggestion of doing away with them. Overall, there had been a rise in the people's standard of living. The question was how to improve them. Should markets be permitted, for example, at which commune members could sell produce raised in their own gardens? Were some of the communes too large for efficient operation? Should they be cut down? How should the small ones be strengthened? What about industry? Was some retrenchment necessary? How should it be effectuated? Was the social system too advanced for the existing technology?

Mao's position was that it was not. He said it was true there were some imbalances between the social system and technology, but the advanced quality of the social system was precisely what was enabling labor organization and technology to develop quickly. What was holding things back was bourgeois ideology, bourgeois methods. This was because class struggle and the battle of ideas still existed in China. It was too early to be complacent and say that socialism had won. Contradictions existed everywhere, they were a law of nature and of human society. In socialist society, too, this law had to be recognized and applied, giving due consideration to the differences between antagonistic contradictions with the enemy and non-antagonistic contradictions among the people. China's socialist system had to be strengthened and problems met as they arose.

This was the essence of "Maoism," and the majority of the Chinese thought he was right. Phoenix and I, and most of our friends, also agreed. Most everyone was swept along by his broad visionary optimism. All that was needed was a firm grasp of "class struggle," conviction, dedication, and hard work, and all problems could be solved. It was an enticing concept, and we were happy to embrace it. Certainly there were thousands of instances of great individual heroism, of miracles of construction wrested by thousands of virtually bare hands.

Unfortunately, as a matter of economic policy, it didn't work. You couldn't pressure a farmer to "invest" the land his family had tilled for generations into a large impersonal commune which decided when and where and what to plant, regardless of original boundaries. His share of the income from sales of the annual yields was supposed to be based on the quantity and quality of his work, but this rule was loosely, and sometimes dishonestly, enforced. If he tried to earn a bit from some sideline occupation, he was criticized for having money-hungry bourgeois weaknesses. The "bourgeois" epithet was carelessly thrown about. Often it was used to label anyone who didn't stringently toe the current line.

The farmer's family life was disrupted. His children scolded him for being too cautious and hesitant. There was no more gathering together at meal time—they all ate in the canteen. Their own kitchen was gone, the pots and metal utensils delivered to the maws of the home-made iron and steel furnaces. A large part of the furniture was smashed to make wood to feed them. Everyone marched to and from the fields, singing, with banners unfurled, divided into units called platoons, companies, brigades. . . . Not surprisingly, among the middle-aged and older farmers there was little enthusiasm.

The weather was good in 1959, 1960 and 1961, and the crops were large. But they withered and rotted in the fields because the majority of the young farmers were away digging iron and making steel, and there weren't enough people to bring in the harvests. There were severe food shortages during what were called the Three Bad Years, but they were not due to any inclemency of the weather, as some Chinese media claimed.

Looking back today the errors and excesses of the Big Leap Forward and the communes are clear and obvious. Why do we recall that period with nostalgia? I think it is because of the feelings we had of togetherness, of striving for a common goal, of discarding selfish motivations, of the joy of believing that what you as an individual were doing would really help bring about the greatest good to the greatest number. People were kinder to each other, more solicitous about their neighbors' welfare, families were harmonious, crime nearly vanished.

For this we have to thank Mao. It was his social philosophy, the attitudes he exhorted, the human relations he urged, the work style, the democratic approach, the free expression of ideas, of dissent, on all of which he commented and preached. . . . These created an idealistic, utopian atmosphere in which we, for a time, basked.

He gave us an ethical code of conduct which worked beautifully, combining the best of the feudal tradition and the advanced enlightened ideas of the modern world. The pity was that he had failed to live up to his own code, and that in the economic field he was ignorant, stubborn and inept.

Today, we are again confronted with the age-old problem: Must we choose between morality and affluence, between greed and love? Or is it possible to create a society which is both decent and prosperous? In China that remains an open question.

150

In 1961 I began translating my twelfth novel for Foreign Languages Press, a lively affair called *Tracks in the Snowy Forest*. The author Qu Bo came from a poor peasant family and rose through the ranks of the People's Liberation Army to the post of regimental political commander. The story is based on his experiences in the 1946 campaign to wipe out Chiang Kai-shek forces in the wooded mountains of what was then "Manchuria," and the local bandits—long a scourge of the impoverished population—with whom the Chiang soldiers had combined. The style is strongly influenced by the blood and thunder tradition of classic folk tales about heroes. The characters, though stereotyped, are stereotyped in the manner of Beijing operas, particularly the main protagonists—exaggerated, and strikingly colorful.

Take Butterfly Enticer, who appears in our story as the daughter of the nasty Chief of Police of Peony River City. Qu Bo offers an earthy sketch of how the lady got her name:

> Her looks were enough to turn your stomach. An incredibly long head perched on her neck like an ear of corn. In an attempt to disguise her fantastic ugliness, she covered her enormous forehead with bangs right down to her eyebrows. But nothing could help. The combination of dry yellow skin and the black freckles made her face even more revolting. She coated it with powder, so thickly at times that the powder flaked off when she blinked her eyes. Because her teeth had turned black from opium, she had them all crowned with gold. When she smiled the glare was painful.
>
> Since Fatty Chiang had no son, but only this precious daughter, he announced that he was seeking a son-in-law to enter the Chiang family and inherit his property. Sons of officials and landlords came flocking to his door.
>
> Of course, these young gentlemen weren't interested in his daughter, they wanted his money. The competition put a high price on the prospective bride. Fatty Chiang forgot his unhappiness over not having a son. He carefully picked through the list of suitors.
>
> The lady had her own method of selecting a mate. Bedding down three days with this one and five days with that, she soon became very notorious. In spite of her ugliness, not one of her gallants failed to tell her that she was "as beautiful as the Heavenly Maidens."
>
> Old Fatty and his daughter became prouder than ever. Standing with his big belly poking out before him, holding his cane, Fatty Chiang announced one day with heartful satisfaction, pompously enunciating each word:
>
> "A fragrant flower attracts a swarm of butterflies. My daughter is truly a butterfly enticer!"
>
> Thus the name originated. The story spread from one person to ten, from ten to 100, and soon the name was known far and wide.

Whoever heard it, snorted. Someone composed a line to match Fatty Chiang's:

"A pile of shit brings the dung beetles in droves. Miss Chiang is truly food for the dung beetles!"

Several good writers came out of the army. The soldiers had fought the Japanese, the regular armies of Chiang Kai-shek, the battalions of local tyrants, and all sorts of scum and riffraff. In addition they were deeply involved with the people of the areas in which they operated—protecting them, enforcing reductions of land rent and interest on loans, organizing the women, the youngsters, bringing medication, sanitation, education. The relationship between the army and the people was, as the popular saying put it, that of "fish and water."

Of course there were problems. The army lads were handsome and brave. The village girls were pretty and impressionable. It was inevitable that some should fall in love and want to marry. But army policy did not permit this during wartime, and emotional conflicts were created. Shi Yan, an army writer, deals with this theme charmingly in *It Happened in Willow Castle*, which I translated fairly early. We hear the political officer talking:

> I explained to Li Jin carefully: The peasants were still full of feudal concepts, especially in the newly liberated regions. They weren't educated yet to the idea of freedom of choice in marriage. The girl's father would raise a row if a man he didn't select himself married his daughter. Furthermore, if Li Jin were given permission to take a bride, every other soldier should have the same right. What kind of army would we have then?

[The boy and his squad were billeted in the girl's home. He answers:]

> "You know I've always listened to you. As I talk here with you, I think— break it off and be done with it. What's the use of dragging it out? But when I get back to the house and see her, my ideas change fast. I can't make up my mind. You don't know what it's like—the way she's been looking at me the past two days. Her eyes shine like she wants to cry. Living with her in the same house—it . . . it upsets me!"

The political officer finds another billet for Squad Four.

Zhao Shuli, one of China's most gifted writers, dealt mainly with life in the Liberated Areas, when the Kuomintang enemy had been driven out and local governments established. He humorously describes the battle between the new enlightened ideas and the old backward feudal practices. In *The Marriage of Young*

Blacky he relates how, with the support of the local government, two young people fight off the attempts of their parents to choose their mates for them. The young lovers are in the district office when Liu the Sage, the boy's father, storms in:

Pointing at his son, he exclaimed: "Trouble-maker. They've let you off. Why don't you go home? Are you trying to worry me to death? Shameless wretch."

"What's all this?" the district chief interjected. "Is the district office a place to swear at people?"

Liu the Sage fell silent.

"Are you Liu Xiede?" the chief asked him.

"Yes," replied the Sage.

"Are you raising a girl at home to be Young Blacky's wife?"

"Yes."

"How old is she?"

"Twelve."

"She's too young to be engaged. Send her back to her mother. Young Blacky is already engaged to Qin."

"She has only a father, and he's a refugee who's gone heaven knows where. There's no place to send her back to. I know the law says she's too young to be engaged, but at her age lots of girls in our village are. Be merciful and let this engagement stand."

"Any party to an illegal agreement who's not willing can break it."

"Both families agree."

The district chief asked Young Blacky: "Do you agree?"

"No, I don't," replied the boy.

Liu the Sage glared at him. "That's not for you to decide."

"You didn't ask his consent when you made the engagement," said the district chief. "He doesn't need yours to break it. Today people choose their own partners in marriage, old neighbor. You have no say in the matter. If that little girl you're raising has no other home, you can consider her your daughter."

"I can do that, all right. But I must beg you to be merciful and not let him be engaged to Qin."

"You can't interfere in that."

"Be merciful, I beg you. Their horoscopes don't match. They'd be miserable all their lives," cried Liu. He turned to Young Blacky. "Don't be such a muddle-head. This will affect your whole life."

"Old neighbor," said the district chief, "don't you be such a muddle-head. Your son would really be miserable all his life if you forced him to marry

153

a 12-year-old girl. I'm telling you this for your own good. If Young Blacky and Qin want to get married, they can whether you agree or not. Go home now. The little girl can be your daughter if she has no place else to go."

Before Liu the Sage could renew his plea for the district chief to "be merciful," a messenger escorted him to the door.

Because our historical and cultural backgrounds were so different, I frequently had difficulty in comprehending the thought processes and motivations of my Chinese colleagues and friends. I came from a bourgeois background, imbued with the ethical values of Western democracy. My Chinese counterparts were profoundly influenced by 2,000 years of feudal traditions. These were manifested in almost everything almost all of them said and did. I had only a vague inkling of why this should be so, and what precisely these traditions were. Today, after decades of living and working in China, I understand much better.

My career as a literary translator helped a lot. I had to read and analyze many works of Chinese fiction—novels, plays, short stories. These describe the deeds and thoughts and emotions of various persons in various walks of life, in depth. And, of course, they clearly reflect the many feudal influences. Two of the books I translated, *The Family* by Ba Jin and *Spring Silkworms* by Mao Dun, are good examples of what feudalism meant in China even as late as the start of the twentieth century.

It is important to bear in mind that hangovers of the feudal mentality still persist in China at every level.

The Family is about the hopeless love of a young son of a wealthy household for a sweet bondmaid in Chengdu, Sichuan, in the 1920s, against a background of warlord strife, student unrest, and the ferment of new ideas. The boy writes in his diary:

She seems to be avoiding me lately, I don't know why. Today, for instance, when she saw me coming she turned and walked the other way. I ran after her and asked, "Why are you avoiding me?"

She stopped and looked at me timidly, but the light in her eyes was warm. She dropped her head and said in a low voice, "I'm afraid . . . I'm afraid Madam and the others will find out."

Very moved, I raised her face and, smiling, shook my head. "Don't be afraid. It's nothing to be ashamed of. Love is very pure." I let her go. Now, at last I understand.

After lunch I went back to my room and started reading the English translation of *Resurrection* that Juemin had just bought. Suddenly I grew frightened, and couldn't go on. I was afraid that book might become a portrait

154

of me, even though its hero's circumstances were very different from mine. . . .
Lately I've been daydreaming a lot, wondering how families like ours are going
to end. . . .

I'm so lonely! Our home is like a desert, a narrow cage. I want activity, I
want life. In our family I can't even find anyone I can talk to.

That book Grandfather gave me—*On Filial Piety and the Shunning of Lewdness*—was still on the table. I picked it up and skimmed through a few pages.
The whole thing is nothing but lessons on how to behave like a slave. It's full
of phrases like "The minister who is unwilling to die at his sovereign's command is not loyal; the son who is unwilling to die at his father's command is not
filial," and "Of all crimes, lewdness is the worst; of all virtues, filial piety is the
best." The more I read the angrier I became, until I got so mad I ripped the
book to pieces. With one less copy of that book in the world, a few less people
will be harmed by it!

I felt depressed and weighted down by all manner of unpleasant things.
Everything in the room is so dull and tasteless; outside my window, too,
it's always so gloomy. I wished I could sprout wings and fly away, but the
silent house engulfed me like a tomb. I threw myself on the bed and began
to groan.

Many Chinese intellectuals, and not a few older leaders of the Communist
Party, came from a similar background.

Spring Silkworms is a collection of short stories—a dozen on the Japanese war
period, and one regarding an ancient slave revolt. Mao Dun writes graphically
about the little man—and woman—disrupted by cataclysmic forces beyond their
control. The peasant, the shopkeeper, the office employee, the worker, the student,
even the concubine of a local gangster, are wrenched out of the normal tenor of
their lives. In *Epitome* the author gives us a glimpse of the hell in which the mistress
of an opium runner lived:

About 11 that night the Master finally returned, his face pale and splotchy.
His bloodshot eyes looked smaller than usual. His head was steaming with
sweat and he reeked of drink. He took out his pistol and thumped it down
on the table. With palsied fingers Miss Ling helped him remove his clothing.
Suddenly, laughing boisterously, he grabbed her, lifted her up and tossed her
on the bed. This had happened often before, but this time it was unexpected.
Miss Ling couldn't tell what kind of a mood he was in; she lay motionless, not
daring to stir. The Master strode up to her and angrily yanked open her
garments, the black gleaming pistol clutched in his right hand. Miss Ling
went weak with terror. She stared at him, her eyes large and distended. He

155

stripped her and placed the icy muzzle of the pistol against her breast. Miss Ling was shivering so violently the whole bed creaked.

"I'll practice on you first," she heard the Master say . . . "let's see how good my gun is."

There was a roaring in Miss Ling's ears. Tears coursed down her cheeks.

"Afraid to die, slut? Hah! Don't worry, I still want to play around with you for a while yet!"

Laughing cruelly, the Master flopped into bed, and instantly began to snore, deep in slumber.

Miss Ling huddled to one side of the bed. She was afraid to sleep, she was unable to sleep. If only he had pulled the trigger, she thought, my misery would have ended, quick and clean. Stealthily, she took the pistol, looked at it, and closed her eyes, her heart beating fast. But finally she put it down again. Life was bitter, but death was too frightening.

Most of the people fought back. Take Mr. Li, the typesetter in Shanghai's prestigious *Commercial Press*. In Mao Dun's *Wartime*, he was at home with his wife and three children in the late 1930s, hoping the war would go away, when the Japanese started their saturation bombing:

The three children had already eaten their fill. Holding on to a chair for support, the youngest was chattering animatedly in a language all his own. The two older children were out playing in the courtyard, chasing things that flew like small black butterflies. As Mr. Li watched his three lively little youngsters, he was oppressed by the thought that this happy home which he had spent ten difficult years building might be blotted out in an instant by a shell or a bomb. Tears came to his eyes.

Suddenly, Mrs. Li came running out of the kitchen, a dish-cloth still in her hand.

"Do you know what happened? Do you know?" she cried, distraught. "The Commercial Press was bombed! The whole plant is in flames!"

"What! Then that big fire is at the Press? Who says so?"

"Xiang's wife, next door!"

The seven-year-old boy bounded into the parlor with the little black things he had caught in the courtyard, his little sister right behind him. Mr. Li's eyes opened wide. Those little black butterflies were bits of burnt paper! It was all clear to him now. His heart beat fast. The Japanese had smashed his livelihood, they had broken his rice bowl! Destroying China's biggest publishing house, they had broken the rice bowls of thousands of workers and employees! A savage laugh burst from Mr. Li's lips. His pale face became tinged with an angry purple.

"Those Japanese have gone too far!" he cried.

He forgot all about the danger of bombs. His "rice bowl" was broken. What more was there to fear! He rushed out of the door, why or where he had no idea, nor did he care.

Mrs. Li ran after him. "Don't go out!" she wailed. "Where are you going?" But the howls of all three kids bawling in unison pulled her back to the house.

Mr. Li ran to the entrance of the lane in one breath. Xiang and another printing press worker were just coming in. Mr. Li greeted Xiang like a long-lost friend.

"What's the fire like at the Press?"

"Dozens of big blazes!" Xiang retorted angrily. He was in the uniform of the plant's fire-fighters. His clothing was half drenched, his face brick red. On his head was a brass helmet. Wiping his mouth with the back of his hand, he said hotly:

"Japanese bombs fell like rain. Wherever they burst, fires started. There were fires all over the place. Our fire-fighting squad couldn't handle them all. And the Japanese wouldn't let the fire-engines through from the concessions. The dirty bastards! I'm going to show those dogs a thing or two!"

"Plant Five is the only one left now," put in Xiang's workmate, "but sooner or later the Japanese'll bomb that too!"

Mr. Li didn't know the man's name but recognized him as another type-setter. Mr. Li's heart was pounding hard. It seemed to grow bigger with each beat. Standing with these two valiants, Mr. Li felt like a new man.

There was no respite however for the Chinese people when the Japanese were finally defeated after eight years of savage fighting. Chiang Kai-shek, with four million troops equipped with billions of dollars worth of US arms and munitions, boasted in 1946 he would crush the relatively small People's Liberation Army in three to six months. That never happened. Instead, in 1949 a new China was born, facing new problems, and still bearing many traces of the old society.

It was a difficult past and a complicated present for anyone, to say nothing of a foreigner, to understand. Still, I had one advantage—my job. Translating Chinese literature was my profession and my pleasure. It gave me the opportunity to "meet" more Chinese people, and "travel" to more places than I could possible have done in several lifetimes. The literature contained the flesh and bone and sinew that many of our articles lacked.

It seemed to me no ordinary person in another land could help but like and admire the Chinese once they got to know them as I did. Short of actually meeting face-to-face—very difficult in the existing "hate-China" atmosphere—

the literary medium was probably the next best thing. I wondered whether the day would ever come when Chinese and Americans could mix in large numbers, not just on a literary level, but personally as well. The prospects didn't look very promising.

The Three Bad Years, the increasingly vituperative attacks of the Khrushchov gang—China weathered them all. The realities proved that the people supported the government's policies. In the spring of 1962 Premier Zhou Enlai announced that the country's economy had taken a turn for the better.

We could see it in our daily lives. Food and clothing became more plentiful and varied. Beef had been hard to buy, and pretty tough even when you could get it. Now we were eating fillets again. There was plenty of fruit and vegetables, and very cheap. Six communes in the outskirts specialized in supplying these to Beijing. More factories went into production.

The "zeppelins" disappeared. When Khrushchov broke the commercial contracts with China in 1960, he stopped supplying gasoline. Bus service had to be sharply curtailed. But not for long. The next thing we knew, buses were rolling again, on schedule. They looked queer, for on their roofs lay huge floppy bags. These were filled with marsh gas which some clever people remembered was rising in abundance from outlying swamps. Piped into the big bags and fed into converted engines, the gas did the trick. The fact that the bags were now dispensed with meant that China was developing a respectable petroleum industry.

The crisis had passed but fresh problems were right around the corner. Chiang Kai-shek chose the first half of 1962 to launch a flurry of assaults and incursions against the mainland, aided and abetted by US armed forces. They were squashed, of course, but still it was annoying. The Indians, who had been raiding China since 1959, made a large-scale invasion in October. In November, the Chinese army drove them out, chasing them all the way down to Assam, to the alarm of the British tea plantation owners there, then turned around and came home.

In spite of the shortcomings, I was stimulated by life in New China. The people were going on, cheerfully enthusiastic, striving to turn a country which had been backward and oppressed into a land of plenty. I was learning about their fabulous cultural heritage, their epochal revolution, their bold vision. I felt Mao and his Communist Party were the true humanitarians, men and women to whom the grass roots were the source of all strength and creativity, who worked with the ordinary folk, learned from them, and taught them.

My Chinese friends and neighbors, and most of my colleagues at the office had shortcomings, too, as individuals. But they generally were warm, considerate, intelligent. They wanted a better China and a better world, and they worked toward that aim. I had a Chinese wife in the thick of the intellectual ferment and a Chinese daughter who regaled me with insights on Beijing teenagers.

I could and did read Chinese books, magazines, newspapers. My grasp of the language was not bad. I could listen to the radio, see movies, go to the theater, chat with people, joke, laugh, discuss, argue. None of my intimates treated me as a foreigner, except to ask me occasionally for my views and interpretations of American events. I was flattered and embarrassed, for often they knew more of what was going on in the States than I did. Anyhow, I was accepted.

I was still very much the boy from Brooklyn, and everyone accepted that, too. I read the airmail editions of *Time* and *Newsweek*, listened to the Voice of America, kept up on the more important new books, talked with visitors from the old country, played a tape library ranging from Sophie Tucker to The Supremes. I missed a lot of things and places and a few people.

Yet swept along by the Chinese revolution, I was coming closer to socialism, at least in mental outlook. By the early 1960s I knew that in China I had the kind of life I wanted most. I agreed with Chinese aims and policies, I liked the political atmosphere, the cultural and social life. I had a home, a family, Chinese and foreign friends. I felt I could do more useful and satisfying work in Beijing than in New York. In short, I decided I wanted to remain permanently.

And so, in 1963, I applied for Chinese citizenship. The proceedings were simple. I wrote out an application, stating why I wanted to become a citizen of China. There were no forms, no interviews. A few months later I was asked to fill out a small form, giving my name, date and place of birth, country of origin and present occupation, and to submit three photographs. A week or two later I was issued a certificate of citizenship with the state seal on it and signed by Premier Zhou Enlai. That was all. No ceremony, no oaths of allegiance.

From that day on, I could vote in the elections, travel anywhere in China without restriction, take part in political study and movements, hear confidential reports. My Chinese colleagues had always been friendly, but now there was a new intimacy, a closer rapport. I felt a heightened sense of responsibility toward my work and what was going on in China. I had stopped being an interested helper and became a full participant. It was good to know at last exactly where I was going.

I was somewhat troubled by the special privileges which the Chinese insisted I retain. I drew the same relatively high pay as before, went on the annual free travel tours, still got a month's paid vacation, received complimentary tickets to the theater and sporting events, was invited to state banquets, had a place in the reviewing stands on national holidays. My status was, and remains to this day, that of "foreign expert."

It didn't seem right to me having it both ways. During the next few years I tried sporadically to reject some of it. Chinese friends said I was wrong. They said it was Communist Party policy to respect the customs and habits of different nationalities. Didn't they have special kitchens for Chinese Muslims? Weren't the various ethnic entities encouraged to wear their national dress, speak their national languages? A person from a foreign country had more expenses than the Chinese. Foreign-style meals cost more; he might want to buy books and magazines from abroad. He sometimes was supporting dependents in his own country.

I let myself be persuaded. Most of the activities arranged for foreigners were useful for anyone who wanted to learn more about China. And having a place on the reviewing stands and attending state banquets, I told myself, couldn't do any harm as long as I remembered I was there only because of the courtesy extended to foreigners, not because I had done anything particularly commendable. But I drew the line on the question of salary. I managed to cut it down a third. I was no flaming revolutionary, I simply didn't want to live too far above the general average.

I wouldn't take more than 300 of the 440-yuan monthly salary to which I was entitled, but it was still too much. Phoenix was getting around 200, giving us a total of 500 yuan. Our rent was only 17 yuan 50 cents a month. Food came to less than 100. Our cook-cum-housekeeper, who slept in, received a monthly wage of 30 yuan. Even after sending 100 or so to some of Phoenix's relatives, entertaining frequently and spending without stint on extras like fruit, liquor, candy and tobacco, we lived very comfortably indeed, in Chinese style in a Chinese household, and had a surplus of 200 or 300 each month.

The stuff kept piling up and we didn't know how to get rid of it. To make matters worse the government, while indulging me in my request that I not be given more than 300 yuan a month, banked the rest in a special account, and frequently reminded me that I could have it whenever I wanted. Only when I went to the States in 1971 was I able to dent the bankroll a bit.

It took some adjusting, learning to be a "foreign" Chinese, but on the whole it was a fairly happy transition. The difficulties were mainly in my own mind and, eventually, I was able to work them out. I had my Western music, my Western books, my Western friends, as well as their Chinese counterparts. That was not only acceptable, it was useful to one translating Chinese literature for Western circulation. I had already been eating Chinese food and wearing Chinese cloth shoes in summer and tunics padded with silk floss in winter. That was because I preferred them, but whenever I felt like eating or dressing differently, no one minded.

The superficial trappings didn't mean anything to most Chinese. Foreign "super-revolutionaries" who wore old clothes and struck Spartan poses did not impress them. What mattered was your attitude toward your job and the people you worked with, your social behavior in your community. For an egocentric American from a high-pressure, impatient, materialistic society, it was an enlightening experience to start learning to be self-critical and think in long-range community and world terms.

To add to the excitement, a few months after I obtained Chinese citizenship my mother came to visit us. We had been talking about getting together for years. I might have gone to New York when I was still a US citizen, but my American passport had long since expired, and what with the atmosphere of implacable hostility to China prevailing in Washington, I wasn't sure I could get another one and be able to return to China. Besides, my mother wanted to see my wife and daughter, see how we lived, see this place which had so enchanted her darling boy that he was willing to forgo the joys of Brooklyn.

She was over 70 when she boarded a Northwest Airlines plane at Kennedy airport, a brave venture for a lady who used to get seasick on the Staten Island ferry and had never been on a plane in her life. During our summer family tours when I was a child she was accustomed to giving invaluable admonitions from the back seat to my father as he drove the Buick through New England mountains. On the plane, after a first uneasy half-hour, she had no choice but to relax and let the pilot drive the plane himself. To her surprise, they reached Anchorage in one piece. By the time they arrived in Tokyo she was such a veteran traveler that she didn't trouble to stay over and rest a few hours but took the next available shuttle to Hong Kong. There, a China Travel Service man met her and took charge. The next day he delivered her to the border at Shenzhen, where Phoenix and I were waiting.

I recognized her immediately as she walked across the short iron bridge linking China and the Territory of Hong Kong. Older, but not much grayer, and the same ramrod-straight back. She stared at me, then threw herself into my arms. Later, she told me she thought for a moment I was her brother Jerry. I looked more like him than the much younger impression she had retained of me in her memory.

She and Phoenix were promptly enamored of each other. The exchange of letters over the years had made them somewhat acquainted, but both were very pleased with what they found in person. The normal courtesy and solicitude of the Chinese toward older people was, in Phoenix's case, underscored by a strong warmth and affection that went straight to Mom's heart.

We rode back to Guangzhou (Canton) on the comfortable air-conditioned train which plies between that city and the border, and drank fragrant tea. Mom, like all in-coming travelers, was struck by the contrast with what she had seen in Hong Kong. "It's so clean here," she said. "And they're so bright and fresh and darling," she added, indicating the pretty girl attendants pouring tea and handing out scented washcloths.

She liked our hotel, too—a huge sprawling affair surrounded by lawns and palm trees and lush tropical flowers. Everything was new, everything was interesting—and very different from what she had been led to believe. But her main interest was me and mine. So we strolled around a bit and the next day took the train for Beijing.

The train was crowded, and we shared our first-class compartment of four berths with a big stocky Hunanese about the same age as my mother. He was obviously an armyman. We knew this not only from the dark green trousers he wore with his plain white shirt, but because of the young orderly who came in from time to time and spoke to him.

We introduced ourselves and he told us his name. He said he was on his way to a meeting in Beijing. I asked what sort of work he did.

"I'm a soldier," he replied, raising an imaginary rifle to his shoulder and pulling the trigger. We learned afterwards that he was the commanding general of the whole provincial border region, and that the "meeting" he was attending was the National People's Congress, of which he was a member.

He knew half a dozen complicated card tricks that he patiently taught us, and a version of solitaire I hadn't seen before. We showed him a few American kinds. He wanted to hear all about us, and was as pleased as we were that we could be reunited after so many years.

His own story, which he told at my urging, was laconic. In the 1920s he had worked in a weaving mill in Changsha. Conditions in Hunan Province were terrible, so the peasants staged a big uprising and the workers went on strike. Mao had led the peasant revolt. For a time they were in control of a large part of the province. He himself had been a member of a workers' patrol. Then the reactionaries came back with modern weapons and artillery and slaughtered thousands. The people had only spears and knives.

"So what did you do?" I asked. "Head for the hills and fight on from there?"

"Oh, no. The enemy was too strong. I went back to work," he said. "But they treated us worse than ever at the mill. We couldn't live. So finally we had to go out and join the guerrillas."

People weren't really fired by romantic idealism like it says in some novels, he explained. They revolted only when there was no alternative, when their backs were to the wall. Even then, their aims were limited and simple. A decent wage for the worker, a piece of land of his own for the peasant.

"I was very ignorant when I first joined the revolution," said the general. "I couldn't even read or write. Many of us were like that. We fought through many provinces. Gradually we came to see that it wasn't just this boss or that landlord who was at fault, but the capitalist and landlord classes. They were the same everywhere we went. They had better weapons than we, but we were many and they were few. We took their guns away from them, and the poor people in their armies came over and joined us, and so we won and changed the social system."

We discovered that he had a very bad heart, and that he kept a small oxygen inhalator in his berth. The orderly was a medic, who was always within calling distance. But the old soldier was blithely unconcerned. He mentioned these things casually, in passing. He had installed himself in an upper berth and we had a devil of a time getting him down. Only after repeatedly vowing that Phoenix and I both

162

abhorred lowers, did he agree to change places. Our journey to Beijing was very pleasant, and the general promised to come and see us.

Yamei and her grandmother were mutually delighted the moment they met. They could hardly speak a word at first, but they soon picked up enough in each other's language to enable them, adding gestures and drawings, to engage in long conversations. Both of Phoenix's parents were dead, and Yamei keenly felt the lack of a grandmother. In her schoolmates' families the grandma often outdid even the grandpa in pampering the children. Coming from a similar tradition herself, Mom certainly didn't let Yamei down.

We gave Mom our room and borrowed a daybed for ourselves. She found our meals quite palatable, asking only for bread instead of rice. She spent hours in the kitchen with our housekeeper, who had not had the benefits of even a few weeks of "the English of southern England" which Yamei was then absorbing in her first year of junior high. Nevertheless, the ladies managed a fruitful exchange of recipes, beef in oyster sauce heading for Flatbush, and potato pancakes with onion grated in passing into Chinese culinary lore.

Mom brought me up to date on the births and marriages and deaths among relatives and friends in the States, briefed me on the rise in prices and crime and the drop in moral standards. We did our best to explain what we could about China. But mainly we let Mom see for herself—in the stores, on the streets, in the residential lanes. We didn't make a Red out of her, but she agreed that it was a fine society "for the Chinese."

Our friends and colleagues—Chinese and foreign—were marvelous. Both Phoenix's office and mine gave dinners in Mom's honor. Chinese friends were constantly calling, presenting her with little gifts, showing her around. We were overwhelmed by their kindness. Mom had a whale of a good time.

A few things took a little getting used to, on both sides. Fresh from the land of the youth cult, she bridled a bit at their frequent reference to her "great age." We had to explain that this was said admiringly, that the term "venerable" was a mark of respect. Mom finally accepted this, though only, I'm afraid, reluctantly.

To our Chinese friends, she was something of a phenomenon. Red—one of her favorite colors—was worn in China mostly by young brides. They were puzzled, too, by smartly cut dresses, lipstick and permed hair on a woman of 70. But they liked her honest modesty, her courage, her independent spirit. When they learned that she was a widow and had been working for a living until only recently, they paid the highest accolade in urging me, her son, to "learn to be like her."

We had been separated for 16 years. Mom confessed that she had frequently worried about me, wondering, in spite of my letters, whether I was "really" alright. Now she had come and seen that I was very much alright indeed, that my life and family were everything I had said they were.

But you couldn't deprive a mother and grandmother of her "worries." Having disposed of the Chinese branch of the family, she was able to concentrate her full attention on the American side. Could she be positive that they were getting along without her? There was no way to reassure her. After nine weeks in Beijing she was burning to get back to New York.

Farewell dinners, some last minute shopping, then the return trek to Hong Kong, Phoenix and I accompanying her to the border. We stopped over in Nanjing, Shanghai, and Hangzhou, taking in ancient and revolutionary sites, communes and factories. Mom enjoyed it. She was impressed by things we had learned to take for granted.

"Isn't that wonderful," she said when we visited the creche of a Hangzhou silk embroidery factory, where mothers had time off to nurse their infants. "They use to fire us when we got pregnant. In a lot of places you had to deny you were even married if you wanted a job."

The border again, everyone being very tight-lipped until, half-way across the iron bridge, Mom turned and waved. Then I couldn't see her for my tears. Was this the last time we would meet? Very possibly.

A few hours later she phoned us in Guangzhou from her hotel in Hong Kong, and her brisk cheerful voice restored my optimism. In the long run our people were winning and the reactionaries were losing all over the world. Things were bound to improve, including Sino-American relations. Who knew? I might even get to the United States. A wild thought in 1963.

Mom arrived in New York before Phoenix and I reached Beijing. The gallant State Department canceled her passport, on the theory that she had violated some ruling of theirs against using a US passport to visit China. Actually, China did not acknowledge American passports and refused to stamp them, issuing their visas separately. But the Hate-China crowd was still strong in Washington, and any decent intelligent attitude toward Beijing had to be smothered.

In China meanwhile among certain philosophers it became fashionable to deny the dialectic principle that contradictions can only be solved when one side conquers the other. These gentlemen claimed that opposing factors could harmoniously and permanently blend into a single entity. Like Jonah and the whale, perhaps, or Mount Vesuvius and the people of Pompeii. Equal opprobrium was heaped on the aggressor and the victim—"all wars are bad." Forget about exploiters and exploited, they urged, "classes and class struggle no longer exist."

Again Mao warned: If class struggle was forgotten, if working class rule was abandoned, capitalism would make a comeback, the Chinese Communist Party might go revisionist, fascist; the country would "change color."

How could this be prevented? You had to have people who would carry on, said Mao, who would keep the Party and government leadership in the hands of the

164

revolutionaries, who would stick to Marxism. You had to teach them to serve the people of China and the world. They had to learn how to unite with the majority, including those who disagreed with them—but not with the phonies and opportunists. Communists had to be democratic, and listen to the masses as well as lead them. They had to be modest, self-critical, to admit and correct their mistakes. A man's ability to meet these requirements was judged by his behavior in the "great storms of revolution."

In the international arena the battle for men's hearts and minds also raged, with the Chinese and Soviet Parties both mapping very different courses to socialism and, ultimately, communism. They disagreed on every fundamental—the nature of revolution in capitalist countries, in colonies, the continuation of class struggle and revolution within socialist countries, relationships between socialist and capitalist countries, between socialist countries, among communist parties, the nature of imperialism, attitudes toward war, the atom bomb. . . .

The conflict which had been flaring up sporadically ever since Khrushchov's keynote speech at the 20th Congress of the Soviet Party in 1956, reached a climax in 1963 and 1964, when he and his gang launched a series of vituperative attacks on the Chinese Communist Party. Every one of these was carried in full in China's *People's Daily*.

The Chinese did better than that. They published, in translation, the complete works of Nikita Khrushchov, put them on public sale and begged people to read them. These masterpieces were analyzed and solemnly discussed, along with the various denunciations in *Trud* and *Pravda*, in China's millions of study groups. In my group we found Nicky rough going. He was always windy and frequently incoherent. Still the nuggets of pure revisionism were worth the dredging. It was so easy to take them apart.

At the same time, the Chinese Party replied with a series of articles of its own, which came to be known as the Nine Polemics. In November 1964, China's *Red Flag* added a neat little coda: *Why Khrushchov Fell*. In these lucid incisive documents we thought we detected more than a little of the Mao touch.

None were published in Moscow. The Soviet people knew nothing about them. They did get around, however, to many other parts of the world. Their revelations of the degeneration within the Soviet Union were more of a shock then than they would be today, when the situation is worse and more widely known. But their main value was that they laid out the gut issues for those who claimed to be, or hoped to become, revolutionaries. They showed the way the Soviet and other revisionists were going, and the results. They stated what the Chinese position was, and why, bolstered by common sense and plenty of facts. Subsequent Soviet behavior and world developments further strengthened the Chinese case.

From then on, the die was cast. China no longer considered the Soviet Union a socialist country. It was "social-imperialist"—an imperialist superpower with socialist trimmings, but imperialist nevertheless, with all of imperialism's typical exploitative, chauvinistic, military-bases-abroad characteristics. The Soviet Party was not communist, but revisionist—building "socialism" on a bourgeois goulash basis, bringing back capitalism in disguise, selling out ordinary folk and sucking up to their oppressors.

To the Chinese such policies were utterly reprehensible. The breach between the two Communist Parties which inevitably followed was irreconcilable, for it went to the heart of what a communist party, a socialist country was, by Chinese standards, and ought to be.

In the summer of 1962 I was asked by the Beijing Motion Picture Studio to play in a film they were making about what was known as the "Executive Headquarters" period of 1946. After the Japanese surrender in 1945, fighting broke out between the Communist and Kuomintang forces. American military representatives in Beijing acted as "mediators," while American ships and planes were busily ferrying Kuomintang troops to points of strategic importance.

At the same time America was trying to build a "third force" among China's intellectuals, hoping that these could form a government partial to the United States.

The only thing wrong with the idea was that the country was split roughly into 89 percent suffering oppressed humanity and ten percent feudal fascist tyrants plus-capitalist compradors. The other one percent—if it was that much—was comprised of worshipers of the bourgeois West who represented no one but themselves.

I was offered the role of an American professor in a major Chinese university who attempts to pull his Chinese colleagues into the ranks of the "third force." The ham that lurks in every man rose quickly to the surface. I couldn't resist the temptation to immortalize my profile on celluloid, and graciously accepted. I was sure it would be a thrilling experience and very glamorous.

It turned out to be anything but.

My first problem was with the makeup man. I relaxed and let him have his way with what he thought an American academic in a Chinese university should look like. I watched the mirror, intrigued, as he fitted me with a bald head, mustache and goatee. It dawned on me that he was turning me into the foreign intellectual whose image he knew best—Lenin!

A hurried consultation with the director resulted in the removal of the shrubbery. When exposure on the set to high-voltage lamps in the middle of August caused me to sweat so profusely under my rubber headpiece that all my makeup washed away, the baldy was also discarded. We settled for parting my hair in the middle and heavy horn-rimmed spectacles.

I found that movie-making is hard work, alternating with long boring periods when you do nothing. In the intervals I had time to translate a book of rhymes by

166

poet Yuan Shuipai. He was wickedly sarcastic about Washington's refusal to allow transshipment of a Chinese cargo destined for Canada.

In "Soy Sauce and Prawns" he jibed:

Neither canned prawns nor soy sauce
May America's borders cross:
Canadians, amazed, confused,
Are irritated and amused.

Soy sauce endangers security,
The reason's there for all to see,
So deeply red it's purple nearly
—Criminal nature proved clearly.

And as to Chinese big prawns canned,
They obviously must be banned;
In armor cased from tail to head,
When boiled they turn a fiery red.

An Iron Curtain America binds,
Hysteria grips the White House minds;
"Strategic goods"—what if they're edible?
Such idiocy is scarcely credible!

He was also amused by an earlier news item that the House Un-American Activities Committee had investigated "communist influence" in California schools among children between the ages of five and seven. It inspired him to write a jingle called "Babes to the Barricades." It ran:

Infant subversives, they're news, they're hot,
Will they revolt, or will they not?
(Naturally, their teachers too
Must answer legal process due.)

Outer bluster, inner dread,
Everyone a potential Red.
Seek them under every bed
(Big and small, suspect them all.)

No matter if they're five or six,
Those communists are full of tricks;
Preserve our precious Liberty,
Put kids and teachers under lock and key.

While becoming a movie star, most of the time I just hung around, waiting. Before each shot there were a few practice run-throughs and endless fiddling with lights. For economy reasons they did only two actual takes. We merely mouthed our lines. The actors dubbed in their own voices later. The foreign stars were dubbed by Chinese professionals. Mine gave me a rather reedy tenor.

Even observing the lovelies wasn't much fun. Their beauty was obscured by the heavy make-up they had to wear.

When the film began its nationwide run, theatrical friends who saw me on the screen said I looked very authentic—just like an American. They politely refrained from commenting on my acting. Phoenix, with wifely candor, pronounced it "vapid." I was reluctantly compelled to agree. I vowed I would never set foot before a camera again. A dozen years passed before I broke my word.

The picture turned out quite well in spite of me. It's called *After the Armistice*, and is frequently revived.

The "Cultural Revolution"
1966-1976

For some years in certain areas of Chinese society negative attitudes and methods had been growing. In the arts, for instance, a few quite decadent things appeared. Educators tended to be conservative and stodgy, waspishly feuding among themselves as to which of their alma maters—be it Oxford or Cambridge or Harvard—was the most prestigious.

Phoenix and I attended the graduation ceremonies of an English class in the Foreign Languages Institute. For a triumphal conclusion they put on an act from *The Importance of Being Earnest* by Oscar Wilde. The poor kids looked ridiculous in putty noses, crinoline skirts and top hats. What use 19th century English of the British upper class was supposed to be for fledgling socialists never seemed to have entered their teachers' minds.

How typical or widespread such phenomena were I had no idea. The Central Committee of the Chinese Communist Party—with Mao's backing—evidently considered the situation very serious. On August 8, 1966, it promulgated its *Decision Concerning the Great Proletarian Cultural Revolution*—the famous "Sixteen Points" which set the guidelines:

> Although the bourgeoisie has been overthrown, it is still trying to use the old ideas, culture and habits of the exploiting classes to corrupt the masses, capture their minds and stage a comeback. The proletariat must do the exact opposite: it must meet head-on every challenge of the bourgeoisie in the ideological field and use the new ideas, culture, customs and habits of the proletariat to change the mental outlook of the whole society. At present, our objective is to struggle against and overthrow those persons in power taking the capitalist road, to criticize and repudiate the bourgeois reactionary academic "authorities" and the ideology of the bourgeoisie and all other exploiting classes and to transform education, literature and art and all other parts of the superstructure not in correspondence with the socialist economic base, so as to facilitate the consolidation and development of the socialist system.

This document reflected the confusion in Mao's thinking. He felt that with the defeat of the landlord ruling class the main danger lay more with bourgeois than

169

with feudal concepts. It is true that some intellectuals, having been shaken by the indiscriminate attack on dissenting opinions during the "anti-Rightist" campaign in the late 1950s and the economic errors during the drive for communes and the Big Leap Forward, wondered whether Western social and political systems might not be superior.

They were very small in number, and had little influence except among themselves. While they had no particular enthusiasm for socialism they did not actively oppose it. At the same time, they respected the Chinese Communist Party for its accomplishments. This was also true of the relatively tiny number of capitalists, who had been on the verge of bankruptcy when the Communists came to power and saved them with partnerships that brought them money and respectability. Some were given high rank in government and other responsible positions.

There were also others who, no doubt, would have liked nothing better than to destroy socialism and the Communist Party and replace them with bourgeois alternatives. Mao was quite right in warning against them. Where he and his supporters went wrong was to concentrate their big guns on them almost to the exclusion of the feudal elements.

The most serious threat to socialist China at that time was, in fact, "persons in power" still imbued with a feudal mentality, and the persistence of feudalism in "ideas, culture, customs and habits" in China generally. These were manifest in everything, from the way the government and the Communist Party conducted affairs to the approach to education, arts, sciences and the professions. When Mao called for a thorough shake-up and reform in these areas, and encouraged bringing new fresh forces into play—particularly the young—most of us approved.

One result was the spontaneous creation of "Red Guards" all over China. They were teenage students who took Mao's dictums "to rebel is justified" and "impediments must be smashed before the stream can flow" literally. Cultural treasures were destroyed, teachers were beaten, courses were drastically cut, some schools were closed completely. Any thing and any person labeled "reactionary" was attacked.

Primary targets were "persons in power" who bestowed on themselves valuable perks and special privileges, who were dictatorial and autocratic, who populated China's stages with historic princes and courtesans to the exclusion of modern day individuals, who made the better hospitals a haven for medical treatment of high officials, who rewarded their supporters and punished their detractors . . . all in a typically feudal manner. Bourgeois ideology had nothing to do with it.

Most of them were leaders in government organizations. Their attackers, while genuinely and justifiably indignant, were also often hostile factions seeking to replace them in office. Each side wrapped itself in the red flag, so to speak, and claimed to be the only genuine orthodox proponents of Marxism and Mao Zedong

Thought, while labeling the opposition as political philistines and heretics. Invariably, government heads who came under fire as "capitalist roaders" were simultaneously leaders of their units' Communist Party organization.

Why Mao permitted the campaign to degenerate to such foolish, and at times very harmful, levels, is a subject of continuing debate. One theory is that he felt the quality of Party leadership had deteriorated. He wanted to shake out those who had gone bad, the stuffy overstaffed bureaucracy, to restore the verve and imagination and daring of his lieutenants, to "weed through the old and let the new emerge," to create a vibrant, positive, typically Chinese socialism. For this, he was willing to stand aside for a while and let events take their course, even if it meant allowing some mistakes and injustices. He was confident that the intelligence of the people and the integrity of the majority of the Communists would ensure an ultimate correct resolution. Toward the end of the battle, when he himself was old and feeble, he regretted the excesses but was unable to stop them.

Another theory is that he was impatient, rash, as his handling of the communes and the Big Leap Forward had proven. That he resented opposition from leaders who counseled caution, that he feared they wanted to usurp his power, and had no objection to their being victimized by self-proclaimed revolutionaries.

That may have been a factor, but I believe his main motivation was a passionate desire to regenerate the Communist Party and free people's minds. He was convinced that this was essential to China's future. The need for a "cultural revolution" was sound enough. The way in which it was implemented was something else again. Mao had released from a Pandora's box forces whose instability he had not foreseen.

I participated, directly or indirectly, in several aspects of the "cultural revolution" at the same time, joining a "battle team" in *Chinese Literature*, and later, a "revolutionary" group formed by foreigners. I had missed the very beginning at the Foreign Languages Press because I was holed up in the Friendship Hotel, rushing out a translation of a new novel. By the time I moved back home again, Beijing was a different city. Walls were plastered with posters, with fresh ones going up at all hours of the day and night, denouncing and defending Party leaders at various levels and excoriating manifestations of the backward and reactionary left over from the old society.

Red Guards were raiding the homes of former bigwigs and digging up the most amazing things. Before liberation many of the rich absentee landlords and bureaucrats and top Kuomintang officials had their retirement homes in Beijing, living in genteel leisure, far from the sources of their harshly accumulated wealth. These ladies and gentlemen, even before the details of their pasts became known, were invariably the most hated people on the block. For although a new society had been established, they rarely changed their insolent manners and avaricious habits.

171

During the "cultural revolution" the Red Guards made for them with unerring instinct.

In the compound across the lane from us was a retired businessman who got his original capital from extensive land rents, a common evolvement in the old society. Though only about 60 and in vigorous health, he had himself pushed around in a wheelchair of shining tubular aluminum because he liked his comfort. He and his wife, a fat, pasty-faced woman, never spoke to any of their neighbors—mostly working people with a sprinkling of office staff, who heartily returned their antipathy. When the Red Guards went in, they found trunks filled with ceremonial Kuomintang uniforms—reminders of the old boy's days of glory, and some outlandish ancient costumes—burial clothes which would enable them to join their ancestors in swank feudal style.

I went to view some of the treasures unearthed by Beijing's Red Guards in the first stage of the "cultural revolution." They filled two galleries in the city's Exhibition Hall. There was money, pots of it, gold and silver coins and solid gold bars, illegally hoarded. There was memorabilia of the days when the former privileged were riding high. Tricolored hats, fringed epaulet uniforms, medals, decorations, autographed pictures of Chiang Kai-shek. Weapons galore, from sword canes to submachine guns. Several radio transmitters. Kuomintang flags. Carefully cherished were land title deeds, originals. One cautious chap had his photostated as well. Pre-liberation account books neatly listed every debtor and exactly what he owed, capital plus compound interest. The old regime crowd were apparently all set. Just waiting for Chiang to make his comeback.

As we see it now, these people were merely a bit of fuzz on a miniscule lunatic fringe. But at the time you had the feeling that fiendish counter-revolutionaries were lurking everywhere, and this added several degrees of temperature to the already over-heated atmosphere.

Red Guard raids didn't help. While the kids' antipathy to musty remnants of China's feudal past was understandable, they did considerable damage, smashing and defacing cultural relics, confiscating "reactionary" private library collections. Friends of ours still haven't been able to track down their books.

Worst of all, it seems to me, the Red Guards, spurred on by inflammatory slogans from above, set a pattern of lawlessness. According to the ground rules laid down by the "Sixteen Points," the "cultural revolution" was to be conducted by means of wall posters and large open debates. Searches and seizures violated the Sixteen Points, to say nothing of China's Constitution. In the ten years that followed they became a widespread and accepted practice, not just among adolescent hot-heads but in mature groupings as well—all in the name of "revolution."

Yamei and most of her schoolmates were members of the Red Guards. I was interested to observe their reactions. Political issues were coming up all the time. Some kids took a stand, some wouldn't stick their necks out, some tried to play both ends against the middle—just like their parents. The majority—depending on their own position—formed opinions and drew conclusions. They were learning to separate the wheat from the chaff, not on the basis of the usual childish petty squabbles and jealousies, but in their relation to the political strife of the adult world.

This sudden broadening of vision made them hungry for more. All of China was in ferment, and the kids wanted to see for themselves. They began traveling—in groups of tens, hundreds, thousands—to schools, factories, to other cities, other provinces. They simply swarmed on to trains and went. When a government regulation proclaimed they could travel without charge it was only confirming a fait accompli.

Millions came to Beijing. Mao received them—*en masse*—on eight different occasions at Tiananmen Square. The Beijing kids traveled to other parts of the country. It was very casual. Yamei went up to Dalian because the train to Chongqing—where she had planned to go with a dozen of the girls from her school—was too crowded that day. Of course it raised hob with the nation's transport facilities, and local authorities went mad trying to amass enough food and water and accommodations for unpredictable numbers of kids daily descending upon them without notice. Yamei slept on a high school gymnasium floor in Dalian and paid a few cents a day for her meals. She said everyone was "very nice," accepting it all as quite a matter of course. The local teachers looked after them.

The brakes were not applied to this great children's crusade for many months. The Red Guards helped spread the "cultural revolution" and learned a lot from the experiences of others. In old China most people spent their lives within a few miles radius of their little village. It was good for youngsters to break out and see something of the world. But their travels disrupted rail traffic. A few kids got uppity and tried to tell people how to run their local struggles. Gradually, they were channeled off the trains and on to "Long Marches" in the tradition of the old Red Army. Wherever they stopped, whether in communes or in factories, they worked and earned their keep, in addition to discussing the "cultural revolution." Finally it was felt there had been enough cross-fertilization and everyone—workers, students, commune members—was urged to concentrate on solving the problems of his or her own organization.

The influence of the anarchistic manner in which the children behaved was deep and persistent. They had got out of the habit of going to school, of studying. They had become accustomed to being a law unto themselves. Discipline, application to their books, examinations, respect for elders were not "revolutionary." Even after the "cultural revolution" ended, it was several years before the smashing of schoolroom windows and insolence to teachers could be halted, and some semblance of normality restored to the process of learning.

In the Foreign Languages Press the battles were intense, the walls of our office corridors were papered with written posters immediately after the universities and colleges put up theirs. Then "work teams" were sent in to "guide" the campaign, and the youngsters who had dared to speak up—most of them were young cadres—were cross-examined, accused of being "anti-Party" or even "counter-revolutionary." The written posters dwindled to the vanishing point.

Mao followed with his blast against these suppressive tactics and said, in effect: "Fire away at anybody, however high, who puts a spoke in the wheels of socialism." Unfortunately, each person interpreted this edict in his own way, and many good leaders were extravagantly attacked in a flood of posters. Now the walls in the Press weren't enough. Two strings were run the length of either side of the hallways, with posters hanging from each. The dining room was co-opted as well. You couldn't walk—you literally had to plow your way through the posters from one room to another. Arguments and debates raged in every office, heated and straight from the shoulder.

Young men and women—the girls were very active in the "cultural revolution"—would get up and speak before audiences of hundreds, sometimes thousands, and calmly and effectively make their points. I wondered what had happened to the traditional Chinese reticence. It was a healthy change from the feudal habit among intellectuals of indirection and circumlocution.

Power in the Press was seized by first one side, then the other. There was some violence and a small Army group—unarmed—came in to sort out the differences and get the arguments back on a reason and debate level. Eventually a leadership group was formed, consisting of a few Army men and representatives from both sides. The work of the Press—turning out books and periodicals in foreign languages—never stopped all during the "cultural revolution." But due to the bitter factional strife our publications were often late, and quality dropped. While the factional differences didn't end automatically with the creation of a leadership group, production was able to proceed more smoothly.

Meanwhile, all over China extremists who called themselves "revolutionaries" began to appear. Lin Biao had set in motion a "suspect everyone, down with everything" campaign. He was vigorously supported by Jiang Qing and other influential figures who were later to become known as part of her Gang of Four organization. The slogan misled millions of ardent young people, and perverted the "cultural revolution," for a time, into a kind of witch hunt.

Chairman Mao had said that the "Party persons in power taking the capitalist road"—the targets of the "cultural revolution"—were a "mere handful" of whom "only a few are absolutely unrepentant," that is, actual class enemies. Extremists at the top responded by attacking almost every leader, whether a Communist or not. A friend of ours was accused of being a "non-Party person in power taking the capitalist road"!

174

Equally important as targets of the "cultural revolution" were decadent ideas, culture, customs and habits—hangovers from centuries of a repressive feudal social system which provided the environment for a revival of exploitation and tyranny, But "suspect everyone, down with everything" encouraged a strengthening of the very attitudes and concepts Mao was battling to change.

A fanatic "orthodoxy" developed that had distinct Confucian elitist overtones. Young men of worker or peasant background, who described themselves as having been "born Red," claimed to be the only true revolutionaries—everyone else was suspect. Chairman Mao had indicated that the main stress in the arts should be on contemporary themes. The extremists wanted to ban Chinese classics and foreign arts completely. Chairman Mao thought the education system needed reform. Fanatics wanted to eliminate teachers and let the students teach themselves. Egged on, utilized and manipulated by Lin Biao and the Gang of Four, China's confused youth carried everything to its ultimate absurdity.

Throughout the country they formed new "revolutionary" teams and regiments. Bigoted and highly factional, their members behaved like brothers in a feudal robbers band, and bickered riotously with rival groups.

In many places radicals temporarily seized power. For 48 hours they held the Foreign Office, sending out cables giving orders to embassies. Their adherents burned the British Mission in Beijing. They raided the Chinese Foreign Office and broke into the Secret Archives. The influence of their ideas filled the periodicals sent abroad with preposterous nonsense—categorical condemnations of Shakespeare, Beethoven, "jazz," a plethora of stories about heroes, all of whom died, some needlessly. Red flags and pictures of Mao appeared on covers and throughout the magazines.

Meanwhile, in the name of "defending" Mao, they sniped at the tried and true Communists around him—from high Party leaders down to solid hard-working county Party secretaries—inventing "material" about them, slandering, spreading rumors, trying to undermine and topple the best in the Communist Party structure so as to facilitate obtaining complete control. The very methods of oppression applied by the extremists were feudal, medieval—and this was painfully apparent in spite of all attempts to envelop them in a "revolutionary" aura.

Almost every person in authority in the Foreign Languages Press was accused of "taking the capitalist road," and almost all were suspended from their duties. They were compelled to write detailed summaries of their pasts and analyze their "mistakes." Some were not allowed to go home and lived under guard in a special section know as the "monsters' enclosure," in the top two stories of a five-story building in the rear yard. These naturally did not include the few who supported the extremist crowd or were their secret backers and instigators.

The prisoners, in the early stages, were loaded on to open trucks, placards stating their "crimes" hung around their necks, and "paraded" through the streets—

an old feudal custom for those accused of capital offenses—somewhat to the puzzlement of the local populace. Each morning they were assembled in the meeting hall before a large portrait of Mao, where they bowed and recited passages from the Chairman's works regarding lenient treatment for counter-revolutionaries who made a clean breast of things.

They were also required to perform various menial tasks, like scrubbing the toilets. Each had turns of being questioned and lectured by various "struggle groups." Most of the time they sat at improvised desks in dim office hallways, interminably writing "confessions" and "exposures."

I found this confusing, and a bit nauseating, and most of my Chinese colleagues felt the same. True, there were wall posters up about the detainees, alleging all sorts of misdeeds in their past and while in office. But these were only claims. I was raised on the tenet that a man is innocent until proven guilty. Why should people be denied their freedom before any legal evidence was produced? Many of these were men I knew well, and for whose integrity I had the fullest respect.

There were rumors of torture of prisoners in the "monsters' enclosure." On six different mornings one of the detainees was found dead just outside the building where they were confined. Their captors alleged they were "suicides" who had jumped to their deaths. One of them was found with his wristwatch and eye glasses still neatly in place. Police investigations dragged on for years without ever reaching any conclusions.

I didn't like the bowing before the portraits of Mao and Lin Biao, and the incantations which were required ceremonies for all of us every morning. It was straight out of old Chinese mysticism, exactly the sort of thing Mao angrily opposed. Nor did I care for the enforced dirty jobs routine. Chairman Mao affirmed the dignity of labor. He said it was good for intellectuals to work with their hands since it enabled them to appreciate the contributions made by workers and peasants. But it was necessary for everyone to participate. To impose physical effort as a punishment on a minority of prejudged pariahs bespoke a contempt for labor, not respect.

Why didn't those of us who disapproved of the practices protest against them? I think it was partly lack of courage, and partly because those doing the detaining were the group which had seized power and which had been given the seal of approval by the Army team then overseeing "cultural revolution" activities in the Press. You couldn't help wondering, under the circumstances, whether there might not be something in at least some of the charges. In that case, might it not be better to let matters take their course for a while?

I felt sure, moreover, that the highest Party leadership was firmly in control of the situation and that, sooner or later, they would straighten out any temporary injustices. Actually, control in a few sectors, like the media and the arts, was already

176

in the hands of the extremists, and they were working feverishly to grab the whole thing. There were several very rotten apples quite near the top of the barrel.

The going was increasingly rough. What had the most immediate impact on me was the incarceration of Phoenix. In the Dramatists Association, where she held the post of chief editor on one of the magazines, she was accused of being a participant in the "evil" arts of the 1930s. This sweeping condemnation of an entire era is something Jiang Qing dreamed up in 1966 when, in collaboration with Lin Biao, she called a conference of army people in the arts. Since the accomplishments of writers and artists in this period had earlier been hailed by Mao Zedong, it seems astonishing that no one spoke up in their defense. Perhaps the explanation is that several of the leading figures in those days were currently under attack for various other "crimes," and people hesitated to come forward, even indirectly, as their champions.

Then, early in 1969, Phoenix was told she could not come home, but would have to live in the office, and continue her "study" there. No explanation was given. We were mystified. I visited her almost every evening. The first few times a guard—usually some young woman colleague we knew well—dutifully remained within earshot. But gradually she grew bored and wandered off, and we could talk freely.

Phoenix said she was informed her history was being investigated. We tried in vain to guess what this might mean. Since student days in Shanghai she had worked under the leadership of the Communist underground. In Chongqing, during the Kuomintang-Communist cooperation period of the anti-Japanese war, she had been one of the many people in the arts receiving direct guidance from Zhou Enlai, who was there as the Communist representative.

I queried members of the workers and army teams which had been sent in to supervise the "movement," as well as the "revolutionary" colleagues who were conducting the proceedings in the Dramatists Association. None of them could shed any light. They knew simply that instructions had come from "higher up."

Only after the downfall of the Gang of Four did we learn that the order was issued by Jiang Qing as part of her campaign to smear anyone who might have some knowledge of her loose living and unsavory past. Phoenix had never met her, but both were playing on the stages of Shanghai in the 1930s, and Jiang Qing was no doubt nervous about what Phoenix had heard. Out of respect for Chairman Mao veteran theater people never gossiped about Jiang Qing. But during the "cultural revolution" she was gambling for top stakes, and this was her way of discrediting possible detractors in advance.

In early 1969 we didn't realize this. Phoenix, an emotional, active person, fretted under the restraint. I was worried about her health. We spoke of other things, and reassured each other that all would turn out well in the end, and to "trust the Party and the masses." Had we realized to what extent the high Party leadership

177

was infiltrated by traitors and renegades, and what ruthless fascists Jiang Qing and her Gang of Four organization were, we would have been a lot more frightened than we were.

On the lower working levels, the Party as an organization ceased to function. The encouragement, or at least the tacit approval from above, of a review of the records of all Party functionaries—during which they were suspended from office—had created a power vacuum. This engendered rival factions, all attempting to take over the running of the day-to-day affairs in their respective units, that were generally floundering.

Most of the members of the "battle teams" and "revolutionary regiments" they formed were sincere. But they also included a number of rogues and criminals who saw the chaotic situation as an opportunity to gain power for themselves. They, and the "revolutionary" units that they soon controlled, provided ready-made "troops" for the big wheels operating behind the scenes. The Lin Biao-Gang of Four crowd could and did utilize such organizations to ruthlessly crush their opponents, or even those they merely disliked.

Hundreds of persons in the arts who had for the most part followed Mao's line, and matured politically and artistically under Zhou Enlai's guidance, were confined on various trumped up charges issuing from Jiang Qing's headquarters. There were many mysterious deaths among them—scores in Shanghai alone. Famous writer Lao She was alleged to have "killed himself" in Beijing. Peasant novelist Zhao Shuli was proclaimed a "suicide" in Shanxi. Later we learned that Lao She had drowned himself, unable to bear the humiliations inflicted upon him. Zhao Shuli, desperately ill, had died because no hospital would accept him for treatment.

We got only occasional odd bits of news. Rumors were so rife we simply scoffed at the more lurid tales. Moreover, the "revolutionary comrades" imposing the detention in Phoenix's office mainly were people who had worked with her for years, and liked and respected her. They were quite pleasant, and obviously honest. Their treatment of her was considerate, often kindly. Once, when a group of rampaging teenage "revolutionaries" broke into the Dramatists Association looking for "reactionaries" to parade through the streets, Phoenix's people hid her and other "suspects" in the cellar until they were gone.

At the end of 1969, she and her entire organization moved to a "May Seventh Cadre School" in the country. People in offices are usually out of touch with the vast majority who produce the food and daily necessities. Chairman Mao had proposed, on May 7, 1969, that they should put in periodic stints in field and factory. Outfits like the Dramatists Association created their own small rural settlements, and these came to be known as "May Seventh Cadre Schools." Instead of individual members going by turns for a few months as Mao envisaged, whole organizations remained at the "schools" until 1973, and the Dramatists, like the other associations in the arts, became completely dormant.

The exodus was hastened by a prevailing rumor, namely that the now unfriendly Soviet Union was likely to atom bomb China. It was necessary to move the intellectuals far from the cities in order to "save" them. The fear of attack was widespread, and there was much digging of bomb shelters. Mao approved, wary of Soviet intentions. He insisted that China's war preparations were purely defensive. "You can't attack anybody from inside a bomb shelter," he observed drily.

The Dramatists Association moved twice in the course of their rural stay, ending in a lowland between Beijing and Tianjin where they raised meager rice crops on sandy alkaline soil. As it turned out, they had little to do with the neighboring communes, and consequently not much opportunity to "learn from the laboring masses." They did learn to sustain themselves, however—making bricks, building their own houses, tilling, planting, harvesting.

Phoenix enjoyed the exercise. They didn't let her do much, but she liked the *gung ho* spirit, and working in the fresh air. She insisted on going along on the morning jogs, from which she was exempt, and wrote me proudly that she could run half a mile and had slimmed down nicely. The problem was that when the others came home on periodic holidays, she was not allowed to leave the "school." She was miserably homesick, and increasingly depressed by the long time it was taking to finish "investigating" her. She developed heart flutters and had fainting spells. Although psychosomatic, they were none the less dangerous. Several times she had to be given oxygen.

I was concerned. We didn't think it wise for me to visit her in the extremist anti-foreign atmosphere, but Yamei went once, remaining a week or so. She said her mother was well-treated and tried to appear cheerful, but she clearly was very unhappy. Phoenix was permitted to come to Beijing to see me off when I left for the States in 1971 on my first "home leave," and when I returned a few months later, early in 1972.

In 1994, when Phoenix's memoir was published, I learned how this had been made possible. I had written a letter to Premier Zhou Enlai requesting it, and his office's foreign affairs section had telephoned instructions to the "May Seventh School" where Phoenix was under house arrest!

All during the "cultural revolution" Zhou navigated an extremely difficult course, trying to steer the Ship of State between the Scylla of Jiang Qing's fanaticism and the Charybdis of the erratic pronouncements by the aging Mao. While Zhou could not simply order the release of the thousands being wrongfully detained, he did his best to make their lot more bearable.

Jiang Qing hated Zhou Enlai with an undying venom. He had been one of the Communist Party leaders who had opposed Mao's marriage to her in the Yanan

179

days. They softened their stand only on condition that she be kept out of all political affairs.

In the turmoil of the "cultural revolution" she had finally been able to slip her leash. She directed vicious attacks against Zhou, always oblique, never open—he was too well loved for that. But he now represented not just those she regarded as personal enemies. He was also the spokesman for reasonableness and moderation, which were the main obstacles to her anarchistic "revolutionary" program.

At home I was coping, but lonely and bored. Yamei, on finishing middle school in 1969, had been assigned to a paper mill about 50 miles from Beijing in Tongxian County, the former terminus of the old Grand Canal. She came home only on weekends. I rode my bike to the office every morning, and returned every evening to an empty house. Except for our *bao mu* housekeeper, I was alone. Since my own needs were simple, and no one was doing any entertaining, I let her go.

Foreigners working in government organizations and schools, stirred by the "cultural revolution," were eager to take part, but there were differences of opinion as to how. Some wanted to be treated exactly the same as the Chinese. One passionate fellow who objected to the comforts of the Friendship Hotel where most of the foreign experts lived, wrote a poster which he hung in the dining room saying the place ought to be "burned down." To the bottom of this proclamation some joker sarcastically tacked a packet of matches. Several wanted to criticize the Foreign Experts Bureau. Others were mainly interested in the units in which they worked. Everyone wanted to be kept informed of the overall developments.

A meeting of foreigners working in Beijing was called in January 1967, and was addressed by Chen Yi, then Minister of Foreign Affairs. He said they could participate in all "cultural revolution" meetings, read and write posters if they wished, criticize and exchange views with their Chinese colleagues. If some wanted to live more simply, that was up to them. The foreigners came from 60 different countries. They had their own ideologies, their own opinions, their own life-styles. Under no circumstances would China try to impose the Chinese viewpoint on them. Those who wanted to take part in "cultural revolution" could form their own rebel organizations or join existing Chinese ones. About 100 of us joined a foreigners' group called "Bethune-Yanan."

It was beset from the start with special difficulties. The Chinese rebel groups functioned mainly within their own schools and places of work, and dealt with people and problems with which they were familiar. The foreigners worked in various organizations. Most of them were unable to speak or read Chinese and could act only on second-hand information, which was frequently unreliable. "Bethune-Yanan" had to grope half-blind in a very fast Chinese ball game.

It was a very complicated situation of a kind none of them had ever experienced. Unfortunately for them, they were tutored by a "revolutionary" American named Sidney Rittenberg.

In 1946 Rittenberg, who spoke fluent Chinese, had gone as an interpreter for American journalist Anna Louis Strong to Yanan, where she interviewed the greats of the Communist Party. He remained on after she departed in 1947. In 1949 she was accused of espionage and deported from the Soviet Union. Because of his close association with her, Rittenberg was put under house arrest by the Chinese, pending investigation. The "investigation" lasted eight years, until the Soviet Union admitted the accusation against Anna Louise had been groundless. Rittenberg was then released by the very embarrassed Chinese with profound apologies.

From then on, they bent over backwards to make amends, and he quickly rose in rank. When the "cultural revolution" started in 1966 he was the director of all the foreign language broadcasts on Radio Beijing. Leaping into the forefront of the Chinese factional squabbles, he became very active and very visible. As part of a trio consisting of a girl, a young man and himself, he seized control of Radio Beijing—the government's official broadcasting station, beamed to every corner of the globe.

He boasted of his close association with Jiang Qing, leader of the fanatic Gang of Four. As new head of the broadcast administration, in order to meet a "quota" the Gang had imposed, he pressured innocent victims to "confess" to being "revisionists." They were exiled to the rural boondocks. He made fiery speeches at mass meetings of various organizations, and induced enthusiastic foreign experts to join him on podiums and march in demonstrations, which sometimes resulted in bloody clashes between hostile factions. He later admitted to having kept tabs on the foreign experts in Beijing and reporting on them to the "Party," i.e., the Gang of Four.

Two or three of the foreigners became so enmeshed in the factional warfare that, encouraged by Rittenberg, they openly and actively took part. When the opposing factions seized power, these foreigners were easy targets. They were cast into prison to be "investigated" for a variety of suspicions and accusations. If it was any consolation, Rittenberg soon joined them. He had become in such bad odor among the Chinese "revolutionaries" that Jiang Qing turned on him, and threw him to the wolves, denouncing him as a "CIA spy." The foreigners were released in 1973, with regret expressed for the discomforts they had endured. Rittenberg remained incarcerated several years longer. He was allowed to leave the country.

While young Chinese dizzy with "revolutionary" fervor might conceivably have been impressed by a foreigner who could intone the slogans in their own language, and strike heroic Red Guard poses, I was surprised that Westerners could regard Rittenberg with anything but amusement. He was an obvious hustler, a typical high-pressure salesman. Broad-smiling, back-slapping, he would have been spotted immediately in any Western metropolis. Yet quite a few normally well-balanced foreigners lost their sense of judgment, so infectious was the euphoric "revolutionary" atmosphere then pervading Beijing.

Still, the experience was a useful one. We certainly learned a lot about class struggle in China, and among ourselves, and the Chinese gained a better understanding of the foreigners in their midst.

It was Mao's opinion that revolutionary changes were taking place not only in China but all over the world. A poem he wrote in 1963 expresses beautifully his lofty scorn for pip-squeaks like Khrushchov who thought they could stop China, and his own conviction that the surge of global revolution is irresistible. I translated it thus:

Reply to Comrade Guo Moruo

On our small globe a few flies
Bump against the wall,
Droning, groaning,
Shrilling, moaning.
To ants a locust tree appears
A land of vast enormity.
Do midges really dare imagine
They can shake a mighty tree?
The west wind showers leaves on Changan
And whistling arrows fly.
Many things are urgent,
The earth turns, days fleet by.
Ten thousand years are much too long,
The time is nigh.
Mid boiling seas, 'neath angry skies
The five continents stir tempestuously,
All vermin shall be swept away,
All, inevitably.

Changan—today Xian—was the ancient Tang dynasty capital. Autumn Changan, deluged with enemy arrows, was on the verge of collapse. A simile for the Soviet revisionists? For the old order throughout the world? Mao lets readers provide their own explanations of his poems.

In the autumn of 1971 we became aware that strange things were going on. The annual National Day parade in Beijing on October 1 was suddenly called off. For several weeks the name of Lin Biao did not appear in the press. All kinds of rumors were circulating. The Western media said that a plane from China had crashed in Mongolia, but that the bodies had been charred beyond recognition.

When Lin Biao was named as Mao's successor in the new Communist Party Constitution in 1969 many of us were puzzled. It didn't sound like something the Chairman would agree to. Mao was still healthy and mentally alert. How could you be sure a "successor" would not change in political nature? Why couldn't the Party select a new chairman when the need arose? Later, we learned that Lin Biao had committed serious errors in the past, and that Mao had criticized him. With so many fine members of the Communist Party why, even if you had to choose a successor in advance, pick Lin Biao and not someone else?. These questions troubled me then, and still do today.

Lin Biao had a shrewd Machiavellian angle. Mao, he said, was divine. Like all divinities he had to be unquestioningly obeyed. "Carry out the Chairman's directives whether you understand them or not," said Lin. "Mao Zedong Thought is the pinnacle of Marxism."

Subtle. Mao was undoubtedly one of the great men of history. But as a Marxist he had always maintained there is no "pinnacle"—man's understanding of the world, the universe, continues ever to grow as his experience and knowledge increase. To petrify Mao Zedong Thought was to attack its very essence.

Further, Lin's call for blind obedience contained the implication that Mao's ideas were mystic, obtuse, in need of interpretation. And who would be better suited for this task than Lin Biao the man who, according to the new Party Constitution, "consistently held high the great red banner of Mao Zedong Thought," who was the "sincerest and most dedicated of all in carrying out and defending the proletarian revolutionary line of Comrade Mao Zedong," who was Chairman Mao's "close companion in arms" and designated successor?

Mao was hailed as the incarnation of courage and wisdom. Whoever recommended careful appraisal of the reckless and extreme proposals set forth in his name was excoriated as sabotaging "revolutionary" advance and opposing Mao personally. There was a strong emotional public reaction which took the form of people by the millions wearing Mao badges, buying busts and pictures of Mao, putting up statues in his honor. Lin Biao saw this as an opportunity to deify and mysticize Mao for his own purposes, and spurred it on to extremes. Lin affixed the titles "Great Teacher, Great Leader, Great Supreme Commander, Great Helmsman." All four appellations had to be appended every time Mao was mentioned. No meeting could open or close without everyone standing and facing a portrait of Chairman Mao and wishing him "long life." It also became the custom to wish "good health to Vice-Chairman Lin Biao." Lin's words were frequently quoted in speeches and in the press. To question Lin Biao was tantamount to questioning Mao himself.

All of Lin's private inclinations—military "cooperation" with Moscow, soft living for a small elite—drew him toward the Soviet revisionists though publicly he adopted the pose of a dedicated Spartan. In 1966, after America stepped up the war in Vietnam, a few leaders proposed that China send a delegation to the 23rd Congress of the Soviet Party to restore the alliance between the two parties. Mao refused. A self-reliant, united China, fighting a people's war, he said, could cope with both US imperialism and Soviet social-imperialism. The majority of the Party leadership supported Mao. So Lin kept his opinions to himself.

In August 1970, at a meeting of the Central Committee, he proposed that the post of Chairman of the People's Republic, equivalent to that of President, be restored. Mao, he said, should occupy this position in addition to the chairmanship of the Communist Party. Lin knew full well the burdens would be considered too heavy for one man, and hoped he himself would be given the chief executive command. This proposal was rejected by the Central Committee, after being criticized by Chairman Mao.

Lin didn't have much string left to his bow when the Nixon visit was announced in 1971. He couldn't drum up any real support in the army, which was overwhelmingly loyal to Mao. His attempt to build a rank-and-file fascist corps—May Sixteenth—had failed. Lin was desperate. He decided to assassinate Mao, frame "evidence" against Mao's strongest supporters, rush in, weeping copiously, as the named "successor," and proceed to "restore order."

The scheme was discovered and he fled, frantically, with his wife and son and a few of his closest associates. In the mad scramble they didn't take on enough fuel, and their plane crashed in Mongolia, in September 1971, killing all on board.

Although the Soviet Union was not mentioned by name, the Chinese press accused that country of complicity with Lin Biao. "Plots against the Party are not isolated or fortuitous. They have their international connections. . . . Domestic and international class struggles must be regarded together." No facts were given, but the direction in which Lin was heading when his plane went down was obvious.

The revelation of the story to the general public was a shock, in view of Lin's position as the successor to Mao. How could a man so trusted, who voiced "revolutionary" sentiments so often and so loudly, turn out to be a traitor plotting to establish a revisionist regime? How could this happen in socialist China? The net effect was to make the Chinese more wary of demagogues. They proved to be less susceptible to flag-wavers and tub-thumpers when the Gang of Four came out into the open only a few years later.

China's growing strength at home and abroad, political and economic problems within the big countries, the contradictions among them, cracked the wall of antagonism Washington had erected to isolate Beijing. More visitors came from America. Among them in 1971 was a Chinese professor who had obtained American citizenship and who had returned to see his aged mother in Shanghai. A Chinese colleague spotted the news item first.

"If a Chinese who's an American citizen can visit his mother in China, why can't an American who's a Chinese citizen visit his mother in America?" he asked.

I hadn't given the matter much thought in years. Without diplomatic relations, it hadn't seemed possible. There were still no formal ties, but clearly things were changing. I talked it over with my Chinese family. Phoenix was busy with the "cultural revolution," and Yamei was finishing her three years in the paper mill and intending to apply for medical school, but they urged me to go, if I could. My office fully agreed. Then it was announced that Nixon would visit China. If ever the atmosphere was conducive, this was the time. I applied for and obtained a Chinese passport with no difficulty.

So far as Washington was concerned, I was now a "foreigner." I would need a visa to get into the States. I would have to make an application at a US embassy or consulate, and there was no assurance they would grant it. I decided to apply in Canada. If I couldn't get into America, at least my family could drive up and see me. The Canadian Embassy in Beijing granted me a visa, and I was ready to go.

China was stable when I left for America in November 1971. My wife and daughter and a few friends saw me off at the Beijing Airport in properly reserved Chinese style—no tears, no embraces. I was to be the first New Yorker to visit New York as a Chinese citizen from Beijing.

The cultural shocks began when I boarded the Air France plane the next day in Shanghai. Softly piped Parisian jazz, the perfumed cabin, chic short-skirted hostesses—I had forgotten this world, it had slipped into some recess of my mind. The transition wasn't too abrupt, for the majority of the passengers were Chinese, heading all over the world on diplomatic and trade and technical missions. I was still talking more Chinese than English by the time we reached Paris. Here I parted company with the most distinguished of the passengers—China's delegation to the United Nations.

They were going to New York and I was heading for Montreal first, and then Ottawa, to apply for an American visa. I was switched to a Canadian Airlines plane at Orly, having missed the Air France connection. Our Shanghai-Paris flight had been late. Dignitaries appearing at every stop along the way to greet the Chinese UN delegation had tended to be long-winded.

The huge 747 was more than half empty. I don't remember too much about the flight. I slept most of the time, worn out from 21 hours on the Shanghai-Paris leg, with touchdowns in Rangoon, Karachi, Cairo and Athens. Between dozes I watched a John Wayne movie about the Civil War. I felt pretty nauseous. It could have been the bumpy air off Labrador.

Immigration at the Montreal Airport was brief and friendly. Customs just waved me through. "Wanna look at this stuff?" I asked the inspector, indicating my smart Chinese zip bags. He was chomping a cigar and had a pistol belt around his

185

bulging middle. It must have been my Brooklyn accent, which seemed to have come back automatically. He barely glanced at me.

"Nah, go ahead."

I was "home."

I spent the next ten days with a Canadian friend, whom I had met at the Trade Fair in Guangzhou, where he was buying corduroy, eight years before. He had invited me to stay with him if I ever came to Canada. I never thought I would take him up on it. He and his wife lived comfortably in the pleasant West Montreal section. Their pretty teenaged daughter was finishing high school. Their 20-year-old son, a good-looking boy with rather a lot of hair, was in college. He was sarcastic about the social order and thought the future looked bleak.

Several of my host's business acquaintances, whom I met in the next few days, were also pessimistic. All of Canada's major industries were controlled or owned outright by the Americans. Inflation was rising, the cost of living was high. Drug use was spreading among the youth, though crime was not as rampant as it was in the States. There was trouble with the French-speaking population, a depressed minority with the usual syndrome of low-paying jobs, therefore less opportunity for a good education, qualifying them therefore only for low-paying jobs. Unemployment among the French was much higher than in the English-speaking communities.

The Canadians I met were warm-hearted, intelligent. I liked their clean, well-lighted subways, their beautiful shopping centers. They are a talented people. It seems a pity their social gains haven't kept up with their technological progress.

Actually, I didn't see much of Canada. Besides Montreal, the only other place I visited was Ottawa, where I was given a glorious Sichuan luncheon at the Chinese Embassy. At the American Embassy I applied for a visa. They were a bit startled, but polite and helpful. It came through in a little over a week, and I picked it up in the US Consulate in Montreal.

I had telephoned my mother as soon as I arrived in Canada, and she and my sister Ruth and her husband Jack had come tearing up the next day in their car with a carton of lox and bagels, positive, and rightly so, that nothing could compare with the genuine Flatbush variety. They stayed one day, then rushed off again to prepare for my homecoming while I awaited my visa.

We used to spend all day driving up from New York to Montreal when I was a kid. Today, what with the superhighways and supercars, it was only six hours. Everything had speeded up. I, the sophisticated New Yorker who used to weave through Times Square traffic with the ease and grace of an All-American fullback, found myself leaping wildly to avoid being smeared by the rapid-acceleration monsters from Detroit.

You go through US Immigration and Customs in the Montreal Airport. All you have to do, on landing in New York three quarters of an hour later, is pick up your bags and go. It was dark when I arrived, and I remember only walking dazedly to a huge parking lot with my mother, sister and brother-in-law, then whisking along a broad highway for 20 minutes or so and pulling up before a one-family house on a quiet tree-lined street. Here Ruth and Jack lived, directly in back of James Madison, my old high school, and a few blocks from where I had grown up as a child.

We went in. A large Boxer dog flung himself on me in a frenzy of welcome and licked my nose with a slobbery tongue. My mother sat down on a sofa and tried not to look exhausted. She was 80, but insisted on living alone in an apartment nearby. Jack showed me to my room. All the kids were away and there were three empty bedrooms. Ruth made some coffee and sliced a deep-dish blueberry pie. We ate at the kitchen table, with the dog wheedling for scraps, just like the old days. Twenty-five years. Incredible.

A lot had changed, as I discovered in the succeeding weeks. Some of it I liked— good music on stereo FM radio, small inexpensive TV sets, fast travel on super-highways and on planes, cheap useful gadgets for the home, clothing of synthetic knits and fabrics, lively imaginative styles, convenient supermarkets, handsome new office buildings.

Most of all I liked the young people. Americans were always outspoken, but now they seemed particularly articulate. There was nothing "beat" about the kids I met. They were very critical of the social order and those running it. They wanted new concepts, new values, though few had any clear idea of what this new America should be like, or how to bring it about.

Some of the youngsters were on hard drugs—I saw a few ashen, dull teenagers in Union Square Park one morning—and almost everyone smoked pot. But most of the dulled minds I encountered were among the hard-core Old Left who clung to the faded charms of the Soviet Communist Party, and the starry-eyed liberals still hoping for a knight in shining gray flannel to come riding up and bring them the best of both worlds. The Chinese in feudal times had a wish-fulfillment figure they called the "clean official." He was the high-minded gent, within the Establishment of course, who would dispense even-handed justice to rich and poor, and bring peace and prosperity. After vainly waiting 2,000 years for this messiah to appear, they decided to try something else.

I watched TV, went to the theater, saw as many movies as I could, and thought how sad that such artistry should not be devoted to a better cause. The pornography was overwhelming. Breasts and buttocks were thrust at you from film screens and news stands in indiscriminate abundance. People were becoming bored with public sex, and Hollywood was turning to cruel and bloody violence in an attempt to prop up the sagging box office.

187

I spent two weeks in California with Jerry Mann, with whom I had crossed half of America on freight cars many years before. Jerry had "made it" as a manufacturer of ladies' sportswear, and lived in Hollywood Hills. He had a beautiful home, and telephone connections with long lines that could be dragged out to the side of the kidney-shaped swimming pool, a Philippine houseboy who cooked, and no pictures on the walls. Jerry shared the place with Jay Weston, a film producer who was actually making a picture. Only three major studios remained of the original dozen. Both men were divorced, had no children. They were intelligent, troubled by the way America was going, but too "practical," or spiritually weary, to attempt to change things.

Intellectuals generally, particularly those with social consciousness, or artistic ability, were fed up with their jobs and way of life. A few of the older generation were fighting back, but not many. Some had reconciled themselves to finding what pleasures they could. One or two of the braver ones were talking about leaving. A well-paid TV writer in New York told me he was seriously thinking of moving to Paris with his whole family—they had a big apartment on Central Park West—and opening a delicatessen.

These were mostly well-to-do middle class liberals, a relative minority. The vast majority of the people were as I remembered them—riding crowded subways in the morning to tend a machine all day or do some mindless office job, then coming home tired in the rush hour to an "economy" meal and sitting before the synthetic excitement of TV until bed time. The unemployed and semi-employed lived in vermin-infested leaky flats, nursing their hatred of slum-lords who stalled or refused repairs until misery and frustration impelled the inevitable blow-off. I saw the burned-out hulks in Brownsville and Bedford-Stuyvesant.

There was new life in the city, thanks to the large infusions of new blood—mainly Black and Puerto Rican. Dark-skinned kids seemed to comprise about a third of the student body of my old high school, James Madison. The subways were crowded with them, traveling to and from various schools, bright, lively, talkative. A hush fell whenever one of the teams of policemen, who patrolled the subways day and night, always in pairs, entered the car. Half of the kids usually got off quickly at the next stop. Experience had taught them to hate and fear the cops. Blacks and Puerto Ricans were moving into the city as whites moved out toward the suburbs. They would make or break New York, depending on how they were treated. Racial tensions were high, not a good omen for the city's future.

I had the feeling that the whole society, not just the poor, was hemmed in, restricted. Kids couldn't learn much in school that "related" to them and their problems. The country's leaders were pursuing the same dreary futile policies. Jobs were dull and hard to find. The average man was revolted by American-made carnage—in Vietnam, and on the streets at home.

People had to live behind double- and triple-locked doors, and it was wise to keep a dog. You couldn't stroll in the park at night. Old ladies were fearful in apartment house corridors and elevators. Girls had to be careful anywhere, any time. Even if you had a car—once the magic carpet to open spaces—you couldn't use it much. There were just too many of them. Highways were crowded, there were frequent traffic jams, parking was expensive and distant from places of work. Most people left their cars at home during the week in front of the house. The fancy tin on front and tail made them too long to cram into the old garages.

There was little in the way of intellectual fare. Movies were so awful that people stopped going. Friends told me they hadn't seen a movie in, literally, years. Neighborhood theaters which used to run continuous performances 12 hours a day were now open only a few hours in the evening, and on weekends. Theatrical fare was generally inane. I saw one off-Broadway show which breathlessly announced the discovery that the Vietnamese were human, like the rest of us. That left only TV, which did ball games beautifully, was great on "funny" shows, and had brought the afternoon tear-jerkers intact from radio without breaking a soap bubble. Who needed religion as "the opiate of the people" when you had TV?

The greatest inhibitor was inflation, high prices. No decent apartment for anything under $150 a month for two rooms. Five dollars for a haircut that used to cost 50 cents, 35 cents for the nickel subway ride, half a dollar for a ten cent hamburger—and they didn't even toast the roll. (This seemed outrageous to me in 1971. I was still thinking in terms of 1947 prices when I left America.) It was less a question of keeping up with the Joneses than of keeping your nose above water. The ordinary American dared not lose his job. He had to toe the line. Within his "free" society he was compelled to lead a cautious narrow existence.

I found useful gadgets and technological marvels in America after 25 years, but not much joy.

Many of the people I met realized they had been had on the China story. In anticipation of Mr. Nixon's visit to Beijing a new kind of China coverage was appearing in the press. The mindless "blue ants" now turned out to be civilized, efficient, likable people who had pulled their country up by its bootstraps and were making good progress. With the removal of restrictions from above, the inherent long-standing friendliness of Americans toward China overflowed. There was a China craze. Chinese blue denim work clothes and fishing baskets sold in department stores for ridiculous prices. High school and college students snapped up copies of the Little Red Book. Anyone who had been to China, however briefly, wrote articles, or a book, and appeared on TV. China was the "in" thing.

I basked in the reflected glory. Coming straight from Beijing at such a time, I was bombarded with questions on every conceivable topic. They ranged from China's internal politics to her international relations, from Mao's philosophic

189

concepts to everyday life in Beijing. I did the best I could, within the limitations of my knowledge and ability. The majority of my listeners accepted without demur the purely factual information I had to offer—that living standards were improving, that China had no aggressive intentions but would fight if attacked. A few of the Old Left wanted to know about China's differences with the Soviet Union, a few Zionists wanted an explanation of China's "hostility" to Israel. A few young people were worried about China's "friendliness" to Nixon.

Though I couldn't always satisfy the questioners, I think in the process I satisfied most everyone else.

My greatest difficulty, and where I was least successful, was in persuading Americans that the average Chinese worked mainly to serve his fellow men, and had no particular interest in making a lot of money or becoming famous. They said this was inconceivable. As China's prosperity grew, people would surely become more acquisitive. It was human nature to be selfish. You could never change that, they assured me.

The Chinese don't agree, I said. They are trying to end selfishness. I admitted it would take some years to see whether it really could be done. Usually, we left it at that, with many wishing China well for the sake of the future of mankind. The older idealists reserved judgment. They had been burned too badly by the recrudescence of "human nature" in the Soviet Party.

At last it was time to go. It was the end of January, 1972. I wanted to make a short stop-over in London and be back in Beijing in time to witness Nixon's arrival on February 21. My parting with my family at Kennedy was not solemn. We felt the ice had been broken. There would be more coming and going between China and America, and our chances of meeting again were good.

I flew to London where I spent a pleasant two weeks, visiting friends, seeing the sights, taking in a few shows and concerts. I also paid a courtesy call at the Chinese Chargé d'Affaires Office. A few days later they telephoned and said Edgar Snow was dying in Geneva. The only other American with him from China was Dr. George Hatem, his old friend. Did I want to go? I said yes, of course. They helped me get a Swiss visa and booked my passage.

I dashed off as soon as the arrangements were made, but Ed was already gone by the time I arrived. He had terminal cancer. Although the Chinese had flown George and their best doctors and nurses in from Beijing and Algiers, where they were setting up a hospital for the Algerians, they couldn't save him.

Ed was a fabulous guy. As American as apple pie, yet with a deep feeling for the Chinese people and a perceptive understanding of the aims and methods of their driving force—Mao Zedong and the Communist Party. As a result of his trip to the northwest in 1936 and lengthy interviews with Mao in Yanan, Ed wrote his classic *Red Star Over China*, stating with remarkable clarity, though he himself was never a Communist, what the Chinese "Reds" were doing and where they were heading. I met him on his first return to China in 1960, and again on subsequent visits in 1964 and 1970. It was a pleasure talking with Ed. He probed and dug away at every little thing, but he was so modest and relaxed no one minded.

Head and shoulders above 90 percent of the journalists writing on China, Edgar Snow was maligned and boycotted by the "respectable" press in America for 20 years. Even after his long talks with Mao in December 1970, when the Chairman's comment that he would be happy to discuss Sino-American problems with Nixon led to momentous international breakthroughs in the Far East, Ed's offer to do a series of articles was turned down by a leading New York paper. They were ultimately published in the Italian journal *Epoca*.

Edgar Snow never flagged in his admiration of the new Chinese and the new China. He recognized and pointed out shortcomings, but the warmth and friendliness of his approach was keenly appreciated by the Chinese. Zhou Enlai cabled a message as Ed lay dying. Huang Hua, another old friend, then China's ambassador to the UN and later Foreign Minister, flew in from New York. Mao sent Lois Wheeler Snow, Ed's wife, a letter of condolence. "His memory will live forever in the hearts of the Chinese people," wrote Mao.

Ed's passing was more than a personal loss to those who knew and loved him. It was a departure from the scene of one of the most articulate proponents of friendship between the Chinese and American people. Ed had done his work well. It must have been a source of great satisfaction to him in those final days to hear of Nixon's impending visit to Beijing and to feel the balance of the American press swinging toward that cordial and appreciative appraisal of New China for which Edgar Snow had labored so mightily and well.

After the memorial service ended and friends who had flown in from all over the world had gone, I stayed on with Dr. George Hatem to keep Lois company for a couple of weeks. George and Ed had gone to the Red Areas together in 1937, when they were both young men in their twenties, and they had remained close friends over the years. George had rushed to Geneva with a Chinese medical team when Ed fell ill and had been working feverishly ever since—as liaison between the Chinese and Swiss doctors, coping with the press, meeting visitors, doing a million and one things. Lois and Ed's children—the boy Chris and the girl Xian—were there, as well as Lois' able sister Kashin. We thought it might be good to help take Lois' mind off things a bit now that the tension had relaxed. And so we gladly agreed to her proposal that we all go up to a friend's chalet in the Swiss Alps.

I spent about ten days with them, high amid magnificent mountains covered with snow. It was rugged country but the accommodations weren't exactly austere. Our two-level house, beneath its cuckoo clock trim, was steam-heated by an oil-burner furnace, and had piping hot water all day long. In the nearby ski resort center shops sold all the blessings of civilization at prices to suit the altitude. The kids skied every day, while we older folks went staggering through the snow drifts or rode to the top of impossible peaks in cable cars. Everyone was glad to collapse before the fireplace in the evening and muse on world affairs.

In Geneva we had watched on TV Mr. Nixon's almost silent entry into Beijing. The visit and its significance was the main topic of conversation. There was a division of opinion as to where this move was leading. Lois and Kashin were afraid that receiving Nixon in the Chinese capital would improve his chances of re-election and hurt the antiwar forces in the West.

Those of us familiar with the ways of the Chinese Party advised them to keep their shirts on. There was more than one way to skin a cat, we said. In Asia the underlying long-term contradiction was between the drive toward socialism—as represented by the socialist countries and the people's movement there—and the attempts of the imperialists to maintain and extend their grasp. There was also an acute global contradiction between the two major imperialist powers—America and the Soviet Union, the latter having earned the label both by its internal policies and its foreign military and economic incursions. A dialogue was possible between China and America because people's war had made the American positions in Asia untenable, and it was the Americans who had to make the concessions.

These were mainly an acceptance of the inevitable. The US military had to get out of Vietnam, Laos and Cambodia as rapidly and with as much grace as they could muster. This had first priority. Taiwan and the Chiang Kai-shek crew had gradually to be abandoned. No further impediments should be placed in the way of trade and diplomatic relations between China and Japan. Sato and his *Bushido* warriors had to go. Washington should stop interfering with the urgent desire of the Koreans, north and south, to reunify their homeland.

In the months which followed we saw China continuing adamant in her support of the three small Indo-Chinese countries. American planes no longer attacked from the convenient proximity of Taiwan. Korean troops began withdrawing from Vietnam. The fall of Sato and his war gang sparked large public demonstrations in Japan against the manufacture of arms for the US invaders and interference with their shipment. The new Japanese government placed restrictions on American use of bases and fort facilities.

Japan established diplomatic relations with China. Australia and New Zealand elected Labour governments which did the same. Since calm fruitful discussions were obviously possible with Beijing, America's main theoretical prop for the invasion of Southeast Asia—"the need to contain China"—was knocked out from under.

All this followed the Beijing visit, and was of considerable encouragement to anti-Vietnam war forces the world over. It could hardly have helped Nixon in his election campaign since his trip to China was recognized as an admission of the failure of US Far Eastern policy. Moreover, the American people were judging him on how quickly he ended the war in Vietnam, and that he showed no signs of doing, merely switching from ground attacks to massive bombings.

Most of these events had not yet transpired when we armchair analysts were batting around the possible effects of the Beijing meeting in our Swiss chalet. Arguments waxed hot and heavy, both sides lacking facts to back their contentions. Now we know.

Lois was in fairly good spirits. She was talking about going to New York later in the year to put the finishing touches on Ed's book and getting out one of her own—on the Chinese theater. George and Kashin and the kids were staying on for a while, but I had to get back. I was already several weeks over my planned leave.

They drove me down the misty, snowy mountain into the sunny valley below and put me on the train. From then on everything happened fast. In a few hours I was in Geneva. The next day I went by car to Berne. The following noon I was at the Zurich airport with Dr. Huang Kuojun, the cancer expert who had tended Ed. The flight to Paris took one hour. From there to Shanghai was another 17. We changed planes and landed in Beijing at nine o'clock that evening. The drive home from the airport, where I was met by cheering wife, daughter and a few friends from the office, was 30 minutes.

I dispensed the delicious Swiss chocolates and cheeses with which I had crammed my luggage to the limit of my weight allowance, assured everyone I wasn't a bit tired, washed, got into bed and slept, on and off, for the next two days. When I came out of my stupor I was briefed on family affairs. Phoenix's Dramatists Association was still awaiting reorganization, but Yamei was about to start medical school—a three-and-a-half-year course in Western and traditional Chinese medicine. We were all very excited about that.

It was no effort for me getting back into the swing of things. I was a Chinese. Beijing was my home. But my office told me to "rest." So for the next couple of weeks—it was already the middle of March—I rattled around, chatting with friends, popping into the office, wandering through shopping centers and along the streets. I was in great demand as a speaker on "America Today."

When I could stand it no longer I went back to work. The morning of April 1, 1972, twenty-five years to the day of my arrival in Shanghai, found me on my trusty Coventry Eagle, pedaling leisurely down the lane on my regular half-hour ride from house to office. Sunlight, filtering through the morning mist, gilded the tiled roofs rising behind the compound walls. Three old men were sweeping the lane with big bamboo brooms. The air was fresh, trees were beginning to bud.

Phoenix had been granted leave from her "May Seventh School" to greet my return. She had to go back in two weeks, and 1972 was a troublesome year for both of us. In writing to family in America I said nothing about her true situation, but it was difficult to explain to foreign friends in Beijing, or to visitors from abroad, why my wife was never around.

That summer, although I was transferred from *Chinese Literature* to *China Pictorial*, another division of the Foreign Languages Publication Administration Bureau, I continued to devote most of my time to translating novels.

The grip of the Lunatic Left loosened perceptibly in 1973. In January Phoenix was allowed home for the Spring Festival. At the end of April she came again for two weeks. After sampling my cooking, she promptly hired a new *bao mu*. In August she returned on a sick leave that extended until April 1974. Only two months later, in June, she came again, and never went back. Her trunks in the School were packed by colleagues still there in January 1975 and shipped home. She was assigned to a special study group for the "old, infirm and ill" who lived in Beijing.

She was bitter about the long agonies she and others like her had endured in the May Seventh Schools and the devastation the "cultural revolution" had inflicted on Chinese society. As she says in her memoir:

> I can't forget what I experienced in the "cultural revolution," the inhuman scenes I witnessed.
>
> Although I was not put in prison, I lived in a state of constant fear. I was insulted, humiliated, and had to write innumerable reports about my background. It was as if people were born bad. You had to recall as a confirmed sinner everything you had done. Otherwise you would be "exposed," criticized in public meetings. No one trusted anyone.
>
> Nothing was private. You had to tell everything. You had to backstab even your own loved one, if he or she were under investigation.
>
> It was Dante's *Inferno*. I didn't die, and I didn't want to die. But hearing the shouts to "Confess!" by the whip-carrying interrogators while their victims groaned and protested their innocence, seeing their arms twisted up behind their backs so that they were forced to lean forward almost to the ground, hearing the savage yells of the "revolutionaries" . . . rivaled any hell Dante could have imagined.
>
> Criminals had fixed terms of imprisonment. But they were better off than people being "investigated" during the "cultural revolution." We had no way of knowing when we might regain our freedom.
>
> I stopped looking at the calendar. I didn't know what day, month or year it was. Like a simple rustic I was aware only of sunrise and sunset. We had moved from our office in the city to a crude farm "school" in the country. I had indeed "become a new person," as demanded.
>
> In autumn 1975, I was finally allowed to return permanently to Beijing. Home had become a strange place. I was with my husband and daughter again,

but we had nothing to say. We were separated by an invisible curtain. I had lost any sense of happiness or sorrow. My emotions were dead. There was no "me" any more.

Sha Boli was also quiet. Our daughter Yamei had married and given birth to a little girl into whom she poured all her love and dreams and aspirations. There was no future for Yamei's generation. We could only hope that children born in the 1970s could have a normal life, receive an education, and enjoy the proper rights of a citizen. May they never endure another "cultural revolution" and the madness of so-called "class struggle determines all"!

That same month, on Chairman Mao's proposal, Deng Xiaoping was appointed Vice-Chairman of the Party Central Committee, Vice-Premier of the State Council, Vice-Chairman of the Military Commission of the Central Committee, and Chief of the General Staff of China's Armed Forces. Deng was one of the veteran revolutionaries who had stood with Mao in the early days. The Gang of Four had victimized him and sent him into exile in the backwaters of Jiangxi. His appointment was a clear sign that Mao had decided to weaken the power of the radicals and create a more rational balance of leadership in the Party and government.

In June 1975 the result of the investigation into Phoenix's past was formally announced. She was completely exonerated of all charges.

At long last our life was returning to normal. Yamei finished med school in 1975 and was assigned to the Beijing Traditional Medicine Hospital, only a 15-minute bike ride from the house. She was put into the Growths and Tumors Division, which treats both benign and malignant tumors with the combined application of Western and traditional techniques. She married a classmate, Guo Taiping, from Shanghai. After a year in a mountain hospital in Henan he was assigned to the Drum Tower Clinic in Beijing, actually a small hospital, to work as an opthalmologist. They moved in with us, and set up house in a bungalow in our rear garden.

We were conscious of a slackening of ethical standards. Nothing like America, but serious in a country which had been so clean. By the end of 1975 it was very apparent. Yamei and her girl friends stopped skating on our nearby lake because boys were deliberately bumping into people and knocking them down. A friend's son was badly cut on the forehead because, when waylaid by a gang who demanded his fur hat, he didn't hand it over quickly enough. Purse snatching and burglary were more frequent. There were cases of murder and rape. Children sassed teachers, broke windows, went to school only when they felt like it. Sales people were surly. Even the bright young waiters and waitresses in the Beijing Hotel where foreign tourists stayed were inattentive and rude.

Living standards also declined. There were all sorts of shortages. Coal, which 90 percent of the Beijing population used to heat their houses, was difficult to get.

195

Power shut-offs were frequents. Friends who visited family in their old homes in the provinces returned with stories of real privation.

Nor was the situation in the arts any better. For nearly 30 years, I had specialized in translating contemporary Chinese fiction into English. Now there were virtually no new creations. The few that were written were contrived and dull. On the stage we had only the "model operas"—traditional Beijing opera with modern themes. Their stories were intrinsically good, but little else was performed. People got tired of seeing the same thing over and over again. Painting appeared limited to posed, photographic-type oils. Musical composition was repetitious, trite.

What was going on? We couldn't understand it. China seemed beset by countless problems. There was a pervading sense of uneasiness. Articles and editorials in the press didn't help. They railed against veteran cadres, claiming they were "empiricist" and "bourgeois" and relied too much on practical experience. Their worst sin, thundered the editorials, was that they pushed production—or scientific research, or study, or artistic creativity—when every true Marxist knew that all you had to do was stress "political revolution" and the other things would take care of themselves. It was the duty of the arts to attack those "capitalist-roaders." Above all, the press exhorted, be "revolutionary"—"Better a socialist train which runs late than a capitalist train which runs on time. . . . An illiterate proletarian is superior to an educated bourgeoisie."

The result was great confusion. In the name of "revolution," college students, regardless of their major, spent six to eight months of the year on farms, "learning from the former poor peasants," most of whom were still quite poor. Library sections containing foreign books were locked. You risked being called "a slave to foreign culture" if you persisted in a demand for access. Ancient Chinese writings were all categorically branded as "feudal" or "Confucian," and were also taboo. In several parts of the country trains stopped running when vociferous factions brawled and vilified their "capitalist-roader" ministry leaders. Similar strife paralyzed local government organizations, right down to the county level, badly disrupting agriculture. Steel and other industrial output dropped sharply.

It gradually became evident that the radicals who called themselves "revolutionaries" had regrouped their forces and were again on the offensive. We weren't sure who was heading the ultras' clique, though Jiang Qing, the Chairman's wife, was a prime suspect, mainly because we had been exposed to her strange mentality in our work.

She had a thing about pianos. Quite early in the "cultural revolution" she announced that the piano had always been the instrument of the bourgeoisie and that she, Jiang Qing, was going to see to it that it be made available to the broad masses. It would be brought to them "down in the country and up in the mountains."

I could just picture 14 men heaving and straining and hauling a piano up some summit and delivering it to an astonished woodcutter.

Another of her brilliant innovations was the principle of the "Three Stresses." This demanded that in any artistic creation the positive be stressed, and within that the heroic, and within that the most heroic. The net effect was that you had a hero or heroine of sheer cardboard who, already being most heroic, had no room for development. All the other positive characters could serve only as foils and echoes, and under no circumstances surpass the main protagonist.

As for villains, they got the opposite treatment. On stage they often wore makeup of a bilious green. For the cinema, the camera usually panned down on them from a height to make them look smaller. To stress their murky natures they were filmed in such dim light it was difficult to discern their features. They skulked around in the sinister manner of the baddies in old-fashioned melodramas, their wickedness immediately apparent to everyone in the audience. It usually took the "most heroic character" a full three or four acts to see through them, which made you wonder whether the author was trying to equate nobility of spirit with thickness of wit.

Then there was Jiang Qing's attack on Beethoven, out of a clear blue sky. It came not long after she welcomed Eugene Ormandy and the Philadelphia Orchestra and complimented them on their performance. Their programs had featured the music of—guess who—Beethoven!

Jiang Qing was not just a screwball, she was an unprincipled egomaniac. The "new" model opera and ballets for which she claimed credit were vehicles which had been on the boards from 10 to 20 years. She simply hijacked them, made a few trifling changes, often for the worse, and prohibited any mention of the original creators. Feature film and TV adaptations also credited Jiang Qing.

Phoenix and I in July 1975 were at the Changchun Motion Picture Studio in the northeast where I was continuing my illustrious career as a movie star. Again I was an American villain—this time upgraded to the role of commanding general of the US Air Force in Korea. For the sake of our family reputation as thespians, Phoenix insisted on coaching me personally. While we were shooting, the studio received a written comment by Chairman Mao on *Pioneers*, a film they had made about the Daqing Oilfield. Jiang Qing had assailed it, listing ten "flaws" and demanding that it be suppressed. Mao said there was nothing seriously wrong with the film and approved its release. He indicated that nit-picking criticism hampered creativity.

The studio's reaction was ecstatic. A mass meeting was called which Phoenix and I were invited to attend. Everyone turned out, beating drums and gongs and carrying big banners. When Chairman Mao's rebuke to Jiang Qing was read, the audience cheered. It was not only because this particular film was vindicated. What mattered was that the erratic virago who had been raising such hell in the arts was at last being publicly rebuked. Surely this signaled a turn in the tide?

When we returned to Beijing we were amazed to find that no one knew anything about Mao's blast. Jiang Qing had managed to prevent it from being circulated. Yu Huiyong, then the Minister of Culture, was subsequently revealed to be her man.

We heard through the grapevine that Mao had also said: "People are afraid to write articles or plays. There is nothing in the way of novels or poetry. People come under fire for the slightest fault. No one is allowed to offer any opinion. That's no good."

In spite of this, Jiang Qing continued to ride high. We didn't know then about the other three in her Gang of Four (Zhang Chunqiao, Yao Wenyuan and Wang Hongwen), but we were very much aware of the lady herself and the damage she was doing in the arts. Though very few writers were responding, she was pressing for plays and scenarios attacking "capitalist-roaders"—meaning the tried and true Communist Party leaders.

How could she flagrantly oppose Chairman Mao's policies and remain in a position of power? Was her backing so strong? Did it mean that Mao and the veteran revolutionaries were losing control? We were growing concerned.

The tension tightened. Chairman Mao's health was plainly deteriorating. He looked weak and haggard when we saw him on TV. To make matters worse, Premier Zhou Enlai was in the hospital, gravely ill. In January, 1976, he died.

It was a staggering blow. Zhou Enlai, whose remarkable talents had been devoted totally to implementing Mao's policies for 50 years, whose selfless drive and warmth and gaiety had endeared him to millions as the ideal revolutionary, was gone, at the very moment Mao, and China, needed him most. What was going to happen?

We soon found out. Letters from friends in Shanghai said posters had been put up attacking Deng Xiaoping, who had been chosen Vice-Premier in 1975, and demanding that Zhang Chunqiao be appointed Premier. Mao responded swiftly, with all of his old fire. On his recommendation the Party Central Committee named Hua Guofeng as Acting Premier. Stories were already circulating that Zhang Chunqiao was part of a "Shanghai Mafia" in which Jiang Qing was also involved. Zhang's defeat was welcome news. Hua Guofeng was not yet a familiar figure nationally, but Mao's endorsement reassured us.

The next clash came in April. In 1976, Clear and Bright, the traditional day for remembering the dead, fell on April 4. People were angry at what they considered inadequate funeral services for their beloved Premier Zhou. Their hatred for Jiang Qing had intensified when they saw her on TV, standing by his bier with her hat on. In the surge of emotion that swept all of China they began preparing wreaths and poems of eulogy days in advance. The Monument to the People's Heroes in the center of Tiananmen Square would be the natural focal point in the capital.

Late in the day of April 3 an order was issued by the Beijing municipal authorities: "Stay away from Tiananmen Square tomorrow."

I never saw such a combination of grief and cold fury as gripped the people of Beijing. The following morning they poured into the Square by the millions, on foot, in trucks, in many instances led by their local Communist Party secretary. They bore large wreaths of paper flowers, beautifully and lovingly made by themselves, and marched solemnly to lay them at the foot of the Monument to the People's Heroes.

The wreaths soon overflowed into the Square. Groups stood in silence, tears coursing down their cheeks, some raising a clenched right fist in communist salute as their spokesman, or spokeswoman, read a statement, or recited a poem.

My whole office turned out. I went by car that afternoon, and we stopped for a few minutes. I noticed plain clothesmen jotting down license numbers. We ignored them and gazed at the stupendous scene. The evergreens and hedges forming the background to the Monument looked as if they were covered with snow. White paper carnations with wire stems are also symbols of mourning in China, and thousands of people had attached theirs to branches as small personal tributes.

These were expressions of homage to a great statesman and dear friend, pledges to carry on the cause of Chairman Mao for which Zhou had so valiantly fought, and thinly veiled defiance of Jiang Qing and her Gang. Many poems reviling them by innuendo were also put up.

Processions were still arriving, endlessly, as we drove slowly away, our own eyes wet.

The trouble came the next day, April 5. Someone had ordered that the wreaths be removed. As they were being carted away, new ones kept arriving. One mill brought a wreath of solid steel weighing several tons on a flatbed truck and lowered it carefully into the Square. "Let's see those bastards move that!" said one of the steelmen grimly.

Tempers flared, a clash occurred, and suddenly "militiamen," swinging truncheons, tore into the crowd. The fighting spread, many were hurt. There were, it was rumored, some deaths. Scores were arrested.

"A counter-revolutionary incident," cried the Gang of Four the next day in their controlled press. "Deng Xiaoping is behind it!" Praise was heaped on the militia, which Wang Hongwen directed.

The Tiananmen disturbance was a fatal blunder for the Gang. While previously many Chinese had been confused by their "revolutionary" rhetoric, the venomous treatment of people who wanted only to pay respects to the memory of Zhou Enlai was something everyone understood. If the Gang of Four were against Chairman

Mao's most loyal and dedicated supporter, they surely were bad. Public opinion crystallized against them.

Again Chairman Mao acted. He recommended that Hua Guofeng be appointed Premier and "First Vice-Chairman" of the Chinese Communist Party. This ensured that Hua, and not anyone from the Gang of Four, would lead the country and the Party in the event of Mao's illness or death. At the same time, Deng Xiaoping was removed from office. Had the Chairman been misinformed about him? Was it a tactical maneuver in the battle against Jiang Qing and her faction. We still don't know.

Though the Gang had won a victory in having Deng, one of their most out-spoken critics, expelled, they had suffered a stunning defeat when Mao destroyed any chance they may have had for a legal take-over. They retaliated by intensifying their efforts to pin "capitalist-roader" labels on all leaders, high and low, who adhered to Mao's principles.

Everyone in the Ministry of Culture, to which Phoenix was attached though not yet assigned to a specific job, was subjected to interrogation: "Did you go to Tiananmen Square on Clear and Bright? What did you see? Did you copy any of the poems? Did you see anyone there you knew? What were they doing? Have you heard any rumors circulating against Comrade Jiang Qing?"

Because at last word of Mao's stringent criticism of the lady had leaked out and was being happily spread. No one was foolish enough to answer directly. The usual response was an innocent expression and the counterquery: "What rumors?"

I too was involved in a brush with the Gang of Four. Foreign Languages Press had been translating Chairman Mao's poems into English for circulation abroad. Late in 1974 I had participated in a discussion of a draft translation with very per-functory footnotes. A number of us had pointed out that all of Mao's poems, replete with literary or folk allusions, referred to specific persons, places and events. For-eign readers would not be able to understand and appreciate them fully without detailed explanations.

Now, at a second meeting in 1976, we were shown a final version, in page proof, with no comments or footnotes at all. I and one or two others really ripped into the editors. Why invite us to discussions if you don't heed our advice? we said. Don't you want readers to understand Mao's meaning?

Behind all this was Jiang Qing. One of the poems praised Yang Kaihui, to whom Mao had been married and who was killed by the Kuomintang in 1930. Jiang Qing didn't want the world to think of anyone but herself as Mao's wife. To delete only the footnote to Yang Kaihui would be too obvious an exposure of her own jeal-ousy. She found a simpler device. She forced the editors to omit footnotes and amplifications to all the poems.

Our strenuous objections angered the lady. There were dark hints of reprisals. A few persons at the meeting, who had not been introduced, had assiduously taken notes. Later, I heard they demanded the editors give them the names of those who had criticized, and asked why the Foreign Languages Press was "using foreigners to attack Chinese"?

This was disquieting at a time when some Chinese friends, appraising the general situation, were gloomily forecasting that "heads will roll." I remembered Mao had warned that under certain circumstances it was not impossible for China to go fascist.

Certainly the attacks by the Gang of Four (though most of us still didn't know them by that name, or as an organized faction) were becoming more open, yet we could see no countermeasures to restrain them. Among our friends the consensus was that there must be a split in the highest echelons. No one was sure which way the struggle would go. Would all the blood and sweat of the previous decades prove to have been in vain? Was China to be plunged into another civil war? We were very worried.

Mao passed away on September 9, 1976. For at least a year we knew he was dying. Yet, when it finally happened, we were shocked. Who could imagine a new China without Chairman Mao? He had conceived it, raised it to maturity, guided it through shoals and storms. Not for nothing was he revered as the teacher and helmsman. What would we do without him, particularly now, when China was in such dire straits?

Even while the Chairman's body was lying in state, Jiang Qing was demanding his papers. The Party custodian refused her. The Gang of Four stepped up the pressure. They notified local Party and government units to take orders from the "Wang Hongwen Office" of the Central Committee, rather than the regular Office of the Central Committee. Wang had his "official photograph" taken. Zhang Chunqiao wrote a memo proposing "executions" and the "suppression of counter-revolutionaries." More arms and munitions were handed out to the Shanghai militia, which was put on battle alert.

On October 4 the Gang published an article in the *Guangming Daily* threatening Hua Guofeng and other top leaders of the Central Committee. Implying that the Gang of Four were in possession of a "testament" left by Chairman Mao recommending that government and Party control be given to them, the article said: "Any revisionist chieftain who dares to tamper with the principles laid down by Chairman Mao will come to no good end!"

That was it—an open declaration of war against the Party. On October 6, the Gang of Four were arrested. Their chief lieutenants were rounded up the same evening. Strongholds such as Shanghai, and Qinghua and Beijing Universities, were taken over in the days that followed.

Relief was universal. Huge celebrations were held all over China. Foreign newspaper correspondents noted their obvious spontaneity and genuineness. We could breathe again.

From various parts of the country reports began coming in of the depredations of the Gang of Four. It added up to a pretty horrendous picture. They had used their power and position to build a coterie of the worst elements in China and tried to wreck the existing structure of society by persecuting the people and their veteran leaders. As part of their attempt to discredit these leaders they sabotaged the economy. Between 1974 and 1976 industrial output dropped in value by 100 billion yuan (worth then about US$62 billion), steel fell by 28 million tons, 40 billion yuan worth of state reserves were lost. China's economy was on the brink of collapse. Where the Gang was able to put their cronies in, production ground to a halt.

They disrupted administration in the rural areas so badly that many communes quit farming. Sichuan, once known as "China's Rice Bowl" because of its bounteous harvests and annual surpluses, couldn't feed its own population.

Higher education and scientific research stopped. There was virtually no creativity in the arts. Ancient Chinese classics and foreign cultural fare were banned.

The groundwork for these machinations was laid in 1966 when Jiang Qing, in collaboration with Lin Biao, published a critique which claimed that a bourgeois revisionist line predominated in the arts from the very inception of the People's Republic. The Gang later extended this smear into every field of endeavor—agriculture, industry, the armed forces, education, health, the media, science, security, the judiciary, foreign trade, even foreign diplomacy. On this basis, they could, and did, set aside many leaders who had been implementing Mao's policies, and exaggerated their errors and inadequacies into major proportions.

Their scenario was simple. If they could persuade the country that Mao's policies had never been properly carried out, that the havoc which they themselves were creating was due to the failures of the existing Party leadership, they could then pose as the only true defenders of Mao's line, and modestly offer themselves for the highest Party and government posts in the land. Naturally their organization would participate in the take-over at every level.

The designation of Lin Biao as Mao's successor and the appointment of Jiang Qing to the Politbureau and to the "cultural revolution" leading group had been interpreted by some as an endorsement of their extremist policies. Because of this, many people—myself included—for a time were fooled by their ultra-"Left" sloganeering. Eventually most of us realized they were talking rot. The general public was disgusted by the Gang and their methods. When the Gang of Four were arrested there was wild rejoicing.

In 1977, after 11 years, the "cultural revolution" came to an end. Due to the disruptions of Lin Biao and the Gang of Four it had lasted too long, and at times radical elements had got out of hand. It will be some years before historians can offer a comprehensive appraisal. Among our Chinese friends the feeling seems to be that not all of the facts have been revealed, that more information may yet be forthcoming.

Certainly some good came of the "cultural revolution." The turmoil bubbled a lot of scum to the surface—class enemies, sycophants, opportunists, cowards. At the same time the honest, the courageous, the dedicated showed their colors in overwhelming numbers. For millions of young people who never experienced exploitation in the old society it proved graphically what class struggle was all about.

China indeed had class enemies, only they were Lin Biao, the Gang of Four, Chen Boda and perhaps others yet unnamed—not, in the vast majority of cases, those originally accused of being "Party persons in power taking the capitalist road."

The people and the leadership have learned that while no one can guarantee that no demagogues will ever again appear in China, they can make it impossible for them to remain undetected for long. For this the formula is, as Deng Xiaoping indicated, democracy, mass line, and an atmosphere in which everyone, inside the Party and out, can raise questions, voice opinions, criticize defects, and supervise the work of the leadership.

As if these events weren't momentous enough, nature joined in with an earthquake in July of 1976 which killed hundreds of thousands. Its epicenter was the industrial city of Tangshan, only about 100 miles from Beijing.

I was awakened before four in the morning by the violent shaking of our bed and Phoenix yelling: "Earthquake! Earthquake!" Still half asleep, I clumsily dressed and staggered into the front garden. Everyone was present and accounted for—our *bao mu*, our next-door neighbors and their kids. Yamei was honeymooning in Shanghai with husband Taiping. The house seemed intact. Later we found a big crack, right through the foot-thick wall, running from ceiling to floor.

Others didn't get off so lightly. Many of Beijing's picturesque buildings have plastered-over walls of rubble and mud. Quite a number collapsed under the initial tremor—nearly eight on the Richter scale at Tangshan, six or seven around Beijing. Casualties were higher in Tianjin and towns in the earthquake zone, where people rushed out into the narrow crowded streets and were killed by flying bricks and tiles. In traditional single story homes, where pillars and beams support the roof, it was relatively safe indoors. The walls were only to ward off the weather, and tend to fall outward during quakes. Prefabricated tall modern dwellings were the most dangerous. The huge cement slabs which formed the floors and ceilings came down flat, directly, crushing all beneath.

We learned these things, and other quake lore, in the next few days. The unthinkable had happened. Centuries before, Beijing had been chosen as the capital partly because it had been free of the serious quakes which periodically rocked other parts of north China. We should have been warned, according to the stories going round. The seismographic instruments had recorded suspicious signs. More-over, snakes and burrowing animals had come out of their holes, horses had refused to enter their stalls, domestic fowl had roosted high in trees. Certain officials had been lulled by a false sense of security—or had been criminally negligent.

Recriminations were no use. The situation had to be met. Immediately, the Chinese genius for organization and self-discipline swung into action. Food and medical care were rushed to Tangshan and other badly stricken areas. Teams began clearing away the rubble and erecting shelters.

In Beijing, the parks and playgrounds were filled with makeshift shacks of every description. They lined the sides of broad avenues, and mushroomed in gardens and on campuses. It was feared there might be another quake. Indeed, the ground never stopped trembling, and there were minor shocks every few days. Many homes were destroyed. Of those still standing, several needed only one more good shake to bring them down as well. For about a week everyone was urged to stay out of all buildings, regardless of condition, except when absolutely necessary.

Fortunately, the water supply in Beijing was not disrupted. Electricity, which had been cut, was restored for certain hours of the day. Trams and buses ran. Most work resumed. But vigilance was constant. Yamei, who had hurried back with Taiping from Shanghai, was among the doctors on duty in the hundreds of first-aid stations set up all over the city.

With our next-door neighbors, we erected a temporary shelter in our common front garden. We built it of poles—supplied by our respective offices—plus tarpaper, matting, and plastic sheets. Our beds were planks laid on benches and chairs. We all slept there at night. There had been a little looting—which was severely punished. The main danger was a new tremor. Someone had to remain awake at night to hear any shouted warnings, and listen for a possible ringing of the phone, which was in the house.

I rather enjoyed my shifts. Beijing was very beautiful in the summer moonlight. The stillness was almost absolute, broken only by the occasional wail of a far off train. You could feel beneath your feet the solidity of a city which for 1,000 years had been a major center of civilization. It would take more than an earthquake to destroy Beijing.

Gradually, as the weeks went by, those who could began moving back into their homes. Outdoor living was inconvenient, and the nights were turning cold. Remembering my army training, I dug a drainage ditch around the shelter, but when it rained the inside of our flimsy structure was damp from leaks and drips.

For a time, after returning to the house, we continued to be cautious. Chinese beds are simply a mattress on a board platform. We, being more effete, had man-aged to buy a box-spring affair, but still retained the board platform of our old bed. We suspended it above us by tying it to the bedposts in the pious hope that this

204

would protect us should the ceiling fall in the night. Similar contraptions were erected for the rest of the household. We kept banging our heads every time we sat up, and finally decided repeated concussions might prove more injurious than what, by then, seemed a highly unlikely collapse. We dismantled the thing and resumed more or less normal living.

That was the state we were in when Joan and Doug arrived in early October of 1976. Joan is my sister Ruth's daughter, and Doug was her husband. (They are now divorced.) Both were young lawyers, practicing separately in Chicago. Joan was a pretty girl who some kind Chinese friends said looked like me. Doug's face was so covered with the then fashionable American youth whiskers it was difficult to tell who he looked like—unless it was Santa Claus in his twenties. They got to Beijing shortly after the Gang of Four had been nabbed, and all China was in a mood of wild exultation. We had a hard time trying to answer their whys and wherefores about things we understood only imperfectly ourselves.

My *China Pictorial* office was more than generous in extending hospitality. Although the kids paid their own fares and hotel bills, we provided the "interpreter"—actually the man in charge of our English section. The head of our Foreign Affairs section, a very competent woman, also accompanied us on our subsequent tour of south China. Phoenix and I helped show them around Beijing—street committees, factories, the Great Wall, the Ming Tombs. . . .

We had them over to the house almost daily. They sampled Chinese home cooking and met some of our Chinese friends. Yamei was in the nauseous stage of early pregnancy, which didn't add much to my suggestion to Joan and Doug that they ought to consider starting a family. (Something must have persuaded them, because they had a little girl in 1978.) Yamei and Taiping were roughly the same age as our visitors, and the two couples were mutually intrigued. They exchanged information on how they lived, what they thought, what they hoped for.

Phoenix couldn't get away, but I went with Joan and Doug and my two colleagues on their swing through the south. We visited Nanjing, Shanghai, Yangzhou, and Guangzhou. The streets of the first two were jammed with demonstrators, joyously celebrating the downfall of the Gang of Four. These cities had been strongholds of the Gang, and their persecution of opponents was brutal.

In Shanghai we stayed at the Peace Hotel, formerly Sassoon House, a great Victorian pile on the Bund. We each had a big room with twin beds, a curtained alcove containing a couch, a large closet with a timed light switch, and a bathroom with pure brass plumbing fixtures bearing the trade mark "Crapper & Sons, Ltd." (etymologists please note). Not exactly a simple proletarian life-style, but that's where they put us.

Right on the corner, where Nanjing Road meets the river-front drive known as the Bund, was a wide strip of park backed by a huge billboard. Plastering the

205

board were cartoons in lurid colors exposing the machinations of the Gang in strongly uncomplimentary terms. We could see them from our hotel windows. Joan and Doug wanted to take pictures and know what they said, so we went down for a closer look.

As I translated the captions aloud into English, we were soon surrounded by a crowd of thousands. They were smiling and friendly. Some understood English, or maybe they just liked the idea of us laughing at lampoons of their hated oppressors. They were pressing so tightly, the kids were having difficulty in taking notes. We decided to move on.

Everywhere it was the same. Marchers pounding enormous kettle-drums on open trucks, girls with streaming broad ribbons tied around their waists dancing the vigorous *yangge*—all heading for the Shanghai Municipal Government headquarters on the Bund to present pledges of support from their factory, their farm commune, their office, their school . . . and denunciations of the local henchmen of the Gang of Four. Knots of people gathered in front of cartoons and posters on walls in many parts of the city.

There wasn't nearly so much visible evidence of the reactions in Guangzhou. The persecution hadn't been as bad—though there was plenty. Besides, the annual autumn international trade fair was in session, and the city was bursting at the seams with businessmen from all over the world. We were in another posh hotel, with semi-tropical gardens, opposite the fair grounds.

At Doug and Joan's request a meeting was arranged with a few officials from the local judiciary. It was not very satisfactory. Some of their answers to the kids' questions were evasive and vague. One man in particular struck me as a likely sympathizer, at least, with the Gang of Four network.

Nevertheless, on the whole our young visitors were pleased and impressed by our tour. They had seen a lot that was positive. They also had hours of opportunity to quiz my poor colleagues who, out of their years of experience, were able to provide them with honest comprehensive information on a great number of topics.

They were going back via Hong Kong. When we saw them off at the Guangzhou Railway Station they were effusive in their thanks. Doug dashed out of the train at the last minute to present us, on the platform, with Frisbees they had brought with them from America to give to Chinese children but had forgotten.

Both had taken hundreds of pictures. They wrote later to say they were kept busy giving slide shows and talking about their trip. Doug became active in the Chicago chapter of the US-China People's Friendship Association.

My colleagues and I spent another two somewhat less hectic days in Guangzhou, then returned by plane to Beijing.

Turning Point
1977-1980

Phoenix was working again, this time as an editor of a film magazine. Friends we hadn't seen in years, many of whom had been under attack by the Gang of Four "purists," called to see us. They too had resumed their careers in Beijing, in Shanghai, as writers, actors, directors, administrators.

I had visited the States in 1974 and now went again in 1977. Happily, I found my mother still thriving at 85, my sister and family doing well, most of my old buddies still around. Yamei had given birth to a little girl named Xin, or Fragrance, in May 1977. Well-wishers overwhelmed me with gifts of the latest in New York and Hollywood infant wear. Fragrance looked as cute as the dickens in them.

It seemed to me that America was continuing to slide downward. Unemployment was higher, particularly among young Blacks and other ethnics. No one appeared able to stem the inflation. The 35-cent New York subway fare which had so aroused my indignation in 1971 was now half a dollar. The value of US currency was falling on the world market. Crime was worse, moral disintegration was accelerating. I was in New York during the blackout that summer evening in 1977. I watched TV films, after power was restored, of thousands of poor people looting stores, cheerfully and matter-of-factly. Why not, since corruption was so widespread, and extended to the highest offices in the land.

In China reconstruction was under way in all fields of endeavor. Some had been merely fractured by the Gang of Four syndicate, others were virtually shattered. The question you heard most frequently was: How could such a pack of scoundrels, obviously inept and unsavory, gain such high positions and hold them for so long? No one I knew had a satisfactory answer. It didn't come, to me at any rate, until January 1979, when an article in the *People's Daily* by a "Special Commentator"—meaning a top-ranking leader in the Chinese Communist Party—gave the frankest and most convincing explanation I had seen to date.

He indicated that some of the causes were the Big Leap Forward and the people's communes of 1958, and the "anti-Rightist" purges of 1962. Other factors occurred between 1959 and 1961, when China was beset by floods and droughts and food shortages, and this was compounded by the Soviet Union choosing, in 1960, to pull out its experts, with blueprints, and cancel contracts for over 100 major engineering projects.

Commentator stressed that, in addition to these objective conditions, the leaders' personal deficiencies were a major cause of the disaster. "There were subjective factors as well," he said. "Certain leaders cast aside the practice of investigation and research, the factual approach, and gave orders blindly. They wouldn't listen to contrary opinions, they rejected criticism, and crushed [dissenters] with horrific labels. As a result, it was impossible to correct errors and failures in our work which originally were not difficult of solution. In fact it made them worse."

He went on to say how, after a brief interval of relative democracy, Lin Biao and the Gang of Four plunged the country into near anarchy.

People want to know, he said, "how the great Chinese Communist Party could permit [them] to run amok for more than ten years? Our tens of millions of Communists, especially our many old cadres—veterans of hundreds of battles—could handle the Kuomintang reactionaries, could cope with the imperialists. Why were they helpless in the face of a few petty clowns like Lin Biao and the Gang of Four? There is only one answer: For years political life within the Party was extremely abnormal and undemocratic. In consequence, our society was undemocratic as well."

During the Communist Party Central Committee meeting at the end of 1978, the drive for modernization by the end of the century was announced. Stress was placed upon the restoration of democracy and legality and the correction of errors committed by the leadership during the "cultural revolution" and before. Many people were interviewed by *People's Daily* and asked for their reactions. Workers in a Lanzhou plant were particularly blunt.

"Whenever the economy made a little progress, whenever our livelihood improved a bit," said one man, "we'd be hit by another 'movement' and they'd go smash."

Another worker expressed the wish that the impracticalities and wild boasts of the Big Leap Forward would not be repeated. "No matter what, we mustn't run our four modernizations program like 1958. This time we must be strictly objective," he said.

Through strongly in favor of modernizing China, he cautioned: "You can't do it without democracy. In the past we didn't encourage democracy very much and we were always getting into trouble. It's not surprising that people couldn't liberate their thinking. Before each 'movement' we were told we could speak frankly. But when we did, we were blasted and labeled and harried. We hope this time we'll have real democracy, not some watered-down version, and that people, no matter what their ideas, will be able to say whatever they please. History proves that when the Party Central Committee listens to the voice of the working people it makes fewer mistakes."

One accidental good which came to me out of the "cultural revolution" was that since few writers dared touch pen to paper and no outstanding novels had appeared, I was asked whether I would be willing to translate the famous classic *Outlaws of the Marsh*. I delightedly agreed.

Written in the 14th century, it is a fictional dramatization of 12th century Song Dynasty events. Over 100 men—and women—are forced by a harsh feudal officialdom to take to the hills. They band together and ingeniously defeat every attempt of the government troops to quell them. Within this framework we find intrigue, murder, sex, mystery, warfare, adventure . . . in a connected series of fascinating individual tales, recounted in the suspenseful manner of the traditional storyteller. It's a smashing yarn, a kind of Chinese Robin Hood—but definitely not for the kiddies.

The project brought me again into conflict with the Gang of Four. Jiang Qing got wind of my intention to call the novel *Heroes of the Marsh*. I thought this more appealing than *Marsh Chronicles*, which is what the Chinese title *Shui Hu Zhuan* literally means. The lady angrily protested that Song Jiang, leader of the rebels, was a "traitor" because, at the request of the emperor, he and his forces crushed the Golden Tartars who were attacking China from the northeast. This episode is in the final chapters of the novel. True heroes would not have impeded the Tartars, she implied, since they opposed the reactionary imperial court.

The fact was that the Song Jiang rebels were never anything but completely loyal to the emperor. They claimed that he was deceived by wicked ministers, and they had to fight the troops sent against them. Their sole aim was an imperial amnesty, which the emperor finally granted. Only then did they move against the Golden Tartars threatening the Song Dynasty.

I was in no position to offer a lesson in Chinese history to the queen of the "super-revolutionary" radicals.

"If you don't like 'heroes,' how about 'outlaws'?" I countered to her emissaries. "People outside the law?"

"People outside the law? Like bandits?"

"It's true, bandits are outside the law."

"Alright, then."

And so the matter was settled. Fortunately the English of the Gang of Four was as weak as their comprehension of Song Dynasty history. They didn't know that "outlaw" is a "good" word in common English usage, that its main connotation is a folk hero who stands up against unjust persecution of the ordinary people by the establishment.

When our translation appeared it was entitled *Outlaws of the Marsh*. China's Foreign Languages Press published it in three handsome volumes, with striking Ming Dynasty woodcuts which originally had illustrated the 15th century Chinese edition. Reviews in the West were laudatory. Indiana University Press requested and received permission to duplicate an edition for America.

I felt I could never find another Chinese work of fiction of higher quality, and decided this would be my swan song as a literary translator. From then on, I did no more translations of Chinese fiction as such. But I have made extensive use of my abilities as a translator to compile source materials for books of my own. More of that later.

In the spring of 1978 Phoenix and I went on a three-week tour of southwest China, visiting Nanning in Guangxi and Kunming in Yunnan. The highlight of our junket was a fabulous little town called Jinghong on the Lancang River, which becomes the famous Mekong after crossing the Chinese border not very far to the south into Burma, Laos and Thailand.

Jinghong is the capital of the Xishuangbanna Dai Autonomous Prefecture. Thirty percent of the prefecture's 620,000 population are Dai, who are ethnically the same as the people of Thailand. Settlements of other racial minorities are scattered mainly in the heights where, we were told, occasional tigers and wild elephants can be found. Fortunately we didn't meet any of these face to face.

We arrived just in time for the Water Splashing Festival, celebrating the destruction of the Fire Dragon, who had a nasty habit of collecting beautiful Dai maidens to be his wives. Though Dai in origin, the holiday is observed by all the minority people, as well as by the numerous Han (the majority population of China's millions) who have settled in the Dai communities. The festival lasts for three days and marks the start of the Dai New Year.

The first day, we trouped down to a high bank along the Lancang. On the slope, and for about a mile along the broad sandy flat between the bank and the river, were some 30,000 national minority people, all decked out in their beautiful folk garb. They had come to watch the Dragon Boat Races and the Rocket Contest, to see the dancing and just wander around enjoying the color and merriment.

A cannon's boom signaled the start of the races. Each Dragon Boat, so named because of the dragon's head carved upon its prow, was paddled by 60 to 80 men, or young women, half on each side of the craft. One person wielded the rudder in the stern, two or three more stood pumping with their legs on the prow to give the boat added impetus.

They shoved off in heats of four from the opposite side of the Lancang, angled against the swift current. Crowds moved toward the river's edge as contestants from their brigades, or militia units, competed. The winners marched, dancing and singing, to a special stand where each was rewarded with a traditional tot of the potent local rice wine. It wasn't enough to get any of the paddlers drunk, but the poor county head, who had to imbibe with each set of victors, was pretty glassy-eyed before the morning was over. I didn't know who won the finals. Nobody seemed to care. The fun was all that mattered.

In the meantime the rocket competition was proceeding full blast (no pun intended) further down the bank. The idea was to see whose homemade rocket could fly the highest and the farthest. The Chinese invented rockets centuries ago, and most of them soared off swiftly. A few had booster devices which shot them even higher.

The crowds were fluid, drifting after the sword-play demonstrators, dragon manipulators, peacock dancers, and performers of Dai and Hani dances. The ethnic minority costumes were a dream. Together with their ornaments they were fairly expensive, but obviously the pretty girls could afford them.

The second day of the holiday was the water-splashing carnival itself. We went well into the countryside to Manting, a village production team of a Dai commune. All gathered in a large open square, equipped with small basins of water, constantly refilled.

Then the dancing began. Half a dozen youths, heads bound with strips of mauve silk tied in the back, wove through the crowd in a large circle, dancing and rhythmically beating their elephant foot drums.

Everybody joined in, the Han and foreign visitors trying awkwardly to imitate the graceful gestures of the dancers' hands. Villagers splashed cadres and local army personnel, who laughingly returned the compliment. Water flew madly in all directions, regardless of race or rank. I and our entire visiting group were soaked from head to foot. I can't remember ever having had a more hilarious time.

General merry-making was the item on the agenda for the third and final day of the festival. For this we went to Manqinghong, a commune headquarters village. Here too the people were predominantly Dai, but many ethnic Hanis lived among them, plus a goodly number of Hans from other parts of China who had been assigned here on finishing school. There was considerable intermarriage among the races.

Bananas, mango, papaya, oil palms, fine timber trees and the like abound throughout the prefecture. Folk handicrafts are superb. At the moment the absence of a railway prevents these from getting to market in any real number. A lot of their income today comes from increasing numbers of tourists, who can fly to Jinghong directly from Kunming.

On the return leg Phoenix and I spent a few days in Kunming, visiting ancient landmarks and temples which didn't interest me much. But in their museum they had 2,000-year-old bronzes recently unearthed, cast by a people called the Dian who had a kingdom which then ruled that region. Detailed etchings on their bronze vessels show them to have been remarkably like the South American Incas in dress, in weapons, even facially. They raised humpbacked steers which no longer exist in China, and buried bronze models of them with their dead. There were several in the museum. I bought a replica of one, of bronze from Yunnan's famous copper, and brought it home with me on the plane.

211

In the months that followed there were momentous developments in foreign affairs. The first big breakthrough occurred in October 1978, when Deng Xiaoping, representing China, went to Tokyo to sign a Treaty of Peace and Friendship with Japan. It contained the much debated anti-hegemony clause, to the fury of the Soviet Union. It also paved the way for vastly expanded trade between Japan and China.

Next came an even bigger thunderclap. On December 15, then Chairman Hua Guofeng and President Jimmy Carter simultaneously announced the establishment of formal diplomatic relations between the People's Republic of China and the United States of America as of January 1, 1979, and the opening of embassies on the first of March. America's defense pact with Taiwan would not terminate until the end of 1979, and China did not renounce the use of force to liberate the island. But subsequently the United States declared a cessation of arms sales during the final year of the pact, and China ended its shelling of the off-shore islands, pulled its navy out of the Taiwan Straits and offered to negotiate with "Mr. Jiang Jingguo." The Hua-Carter announcement also inveighed against the attempt by any country to impose hegemony "in the Asia-Pacific region or in any other region of the world."

The rapport was expected sooner or later, but none of us thought it would happen so quickly. Clearly, the atmosphere was improving. The Guangzhou Motion Picture Studio sounded me out about playing the role of a "good" American—the friend of Wen Yiduo, the liberal professor in Southwest Associated University who was murdered by Kuomintang gunmen for supporting student protesters. I courteously declined.

The Beijing Hotel was thronged with American tourists and businessmen. I met quite a few. Everyone wanted interpretations of what was going on. I had no special wisdom, but at least I could figure out what was bugging them and talk in words they understood. Many of them found it difficult to communicate with their hosts, due not so much to language as to their very different backgrounds.

For me personally formal Sino-American relations was a heartening development. China was my home, America was my roots. My wife, my daughter, my granddaughter, many dear friends, and I myself, were Chinese—in principles to which we were dedicated, in our attitudes and way of life. At the same time, in the States I had family I loved and friends I was fond of. I recalled with nostalgia all manner of American places and things. For 30 years these two aspects of my existence had been kept pretty much apart. The blending of the best of both had now begun.

One evening shortly after diplomatic ties were established Phoenix and I were invited to a banquet in celebration given in the Great Hall of the People by China's Association for Friendship with Foreign Countries. Attending were

Leonard Woodcock and members of the American Liaison Office—soon to become an embassy, four visiting US senators, and a number of Americans living in Beijing. An orchestra played Chinese tunes and *America the Beautiful* and *Home on the Range*.

A new era had begun, not just for me and mine, but for all the people of both countries. We had much to offer each other. From my own experience I felt confident that Chinese and American would be a very happy combination.

After acquiring Chinese citizenship in 1963 I had joined, to a greater or lesser extent, in the various mass campaigns urging ideological purity according to Marx, Lenin and Mao Zedong. While I could not always understand the reasoning, I assumed that my low level of political theory, plus a limited knowledge of the facts, were the main causes of my obtuseness.

What I felt I did understand, and completely agreed with, was that China's main contradiction, the basic condition which had persisted throughout Chinese history, was the struggle between the oppressors and the oppressed. The vast majority of the honest, hard-working Chinese had been sweated, squeezed, exploited for centuries by the men who held the whips, the guns, who ran the governments ruling in their names, who invented philosophies and moral precepts justifying their depredations.

Every few hundred years when the cruelty and the pain became unbearable the common folk rose up and smashed the current regime—only to replace it with a new dynasty, a new broom that swept clean for a number of years, before lapsing back into the same autocratic feudalism it had replaced.

There had to be a better way. In the late 19th and early 20th centuries Chinese intellectuals heard about "democracy" and "bourgeois economy" in the West, and "Marxism" and "socialism" in the Soviet Union. Limited superficial experiments with them failed in China. Obviously, no reforms of any nature could be even attempted until the monstrous old structure was demolished. This time the battle had to be thoroughly won, and tyrannical rule supplanted by a government of, by, and for the people. The Chinese revolutionaries called this class struggle.

It was not a new concept to me, though not by that name. From my earliest years in New York I had seen countless examples, and heard about countless more, of how the haves, as a class, squeezed and crushed the have-nots. It was a fact of life known to millions who had never heard of the *Communist Manifesto*. The British in their pubs sang with bitter humor over their pints of ale:

It's the same the whole world over,
It's the poor wot gets the blaime,
It's the rich wot gets the pleasure,
Ain't it all a bloody shaime!

In China I had seen much worse horrors with my own eyes. I needed no convincing that only demolition of the old society could put an end to them.

During the next 30 years the country experienced one momentous event after another. The People's Republic smashed the feudal hierarchy by giving land to hundreds of millions of tillers—an accomplishment no other country in the world has been able to match, and instituted major social reforms.

At the same time China was constantly harried by remnant armed forces of the big landlords, air-dropped CIA spies, boat-landed wreckers from Taiwan, a blockade by the Seventh Fleet, a US-imposed economic boycott, foreign armies just across the border in wars threatening to spill over into China, an unremitting stream of propaganda from abroad urging the overthrow of the new republic.

In addition, although Mao didn't talk about it publicly, we heard that the Soviet Union, under Stalin, and later Khrushchov, maintained incessant pressure to extort economic, political, and military concessions.

People in parts of China were living in the depths of poverty, some were starving. But ignorant, complacent officials were unconcerned, and clung stubbornly to an education system based on dead memorization and abhorred original thinking. Merit and skill were less important than having the right connections.

And so, when in 1966 a national drive began, later known as the "cultural revolution," to bring in fresh ideas, new approaches, and shake up the existing feather bolster, most of us welcomed it. We approved of the attack on bureaucracy, on the outmoded educational system, on clumsy governmental structures long overdue for reform.

But the campaign soon acquired feudal, almost religious, overtones. Mao was invested with a god-like infallibility. His words, or things he was alleged to have said, were quoted with breathless reverence. Various unsavory types proclaimed themselves his most faithful disciples, and alleged that much of his divine aura had rubbed off on them. Their highest leaders, commanded by Mao's wife Jiang Qing, were known as the Gang of Four. (I privately dubbed them "Holier than Mao"). Although their behavior became increasingly outrageous, they picked up hundreds of thousands of adherents. Most were young idealists angered by what they considered the abandonment of revolutionary principles by the ruling authorities. They quickly embraced the dictum of the Gang of Four, embellished with appropriate quotations from Mao Zedong, calling for a complete destruction of the old and starting everything *de novo*.

Mao saw everything, without exception, in terms of "class struggle," and carried the concept to extremes. "Every person in a class society lives in the environment of a particular class," he said. "Every type of thinking bears a class brand." During the "cultural revolution" Chinese intellectuals (and I include myself among them), accepted this without reserve. It was an easy, pat explanation for

214

everything people thought and said and did. We felt guilty about our instincts and preferences, considered our mentality inferior to that of China's workers and peasants. Intellectuals willingly spent long hours of soul-searching, verbally and on paper, analysing their failings. They were glad if given a chance to work in factories or on farms, believing that proximity to farmers and proletarian laborers would provide inspiration to a nobler character. When examining the real or imaginary shortcomings of another intellectual the tendency was to tag them as being of this or that class origin.

Mao himself, unwittingly perhaps, had set the tone for rabid persecution. As early as 1957 he had stated that while "the stormy class struggles are ended," they may at times again "become very intense." He called for the criticism of "all poisonous weeds, all demons and monsters. Do not let their ideas spread freely." And he added: "Of course this should be done in a reasonable manner, analytically, persuasively. . . ."

These comments provided the rationale during the "cultural revolution" for the wholesale mistreatment of the best of Party and government leaders, and the near obliteration of China's intellectual community. Mao's recommendation of "reasonable" criticism was cynically ignored. Surely he must have realized that an *a priori* labeling of independent ideas as "poisonous weeds," and reviling those who expressed them as "demons and monsters," were hardly conducive to calm, analytical discussion. The frenetic witch-hunts which were the curse of the "cultural revolution" proved how damaging his comments had been.

It was late in the day by the time most of us woke up to what was happening. A nationwide organization under the Gang of Four had taken control of most government bodies, the schools, the media, the judiciary, and many Communist Party organizations. Opponents were slandered, made the objects of public inquisition, reviled, beaten, some were killed. Phoenix was among the thousands of intellectuals confined under "investigation" for long periods in special camps.

Mao's simplistic, bulldozer approach to curing China's ills, the naive response of millions of mostly young enthusiasts, the shrewd manipulations of ruthless opportunists, the assumptions of guilt by self-deprecating intellectuals . . . all contributed to stretching out the "cultural revolution" for ten long years. The social and economic damage was tremendous.

The nightmare ended in 1976 with the arrest of the Gang of Four. But thousands of their former supporters who still agreed with the Gang's rabid, fanatic views had proliferated in government and Communist Party structures.

And other formidable problems remained: China's economic base was weak. Her science and technology were 20 to 30 years behind those of the advanced countries. The amount of arable land was limited. The bulk of the population were

215

illiterate poor farmers. There was much confusion as to which of the old concepts were worth preserving. An enormous effort was required to clean the organizational and intellectual Augean stable.

By March of 1979 Deng Xiaoping felt able to say that while not all of the debris was gone, most of the hostile forces had been defused, and that leadership of the Communist Party, the government and the army was again in the hands of those "worthy of the people's trust."

Like Mao, Deng cautioned that class struggle would continue in China. But he differed sharply from Mao in predicting what form it would take and who the opponents were. No longer the "exploiters from cohesive and overt classes," but "anti-socialist elements" such as "counter-revolutionaries, enemy agents, criminals, [those] who undermine socialist public order, [and] new exploiters who engage in corruption, embezzlement, speculation and profiteering." While describing what he called a "special form" of class struggle, Deng pointedly did not say that it might become "very intense."

We all were greatly relieved at no longer having to look for "class enemies" under every bed. (Americans had similarly been exhorted to search for "Reds" in the same manner during the McCarthy period.)

I have only one criticism of Deng's formulation. He does not sufficiently distinguish between the political and the social offenders. Counter-revolutionaries and enemy agents who commit treason and sabotage, and persons who engage in corruption, embezzlement, speculation and profiteering, all violate the law. But only the former are guilty of deliberate attacks on the government and the socialist system. The latter are ordinary, run-of-the-mill offenders, whose crimes should be treated more leniently. They want to make money, and have no interest in the system of government one way or the other. They are not engaged in class struggle against socialism in China any more than ordinary criminals in the West are engaged in class struggle against capitalism.

Still, I can understand why Deng continued thinking in terms of class struggle. He and many of China's most respected leaders were victims of a virulent form of class struggle during the "cultural revolution" only a few years before. They had survived ten years of chaos under what Deng called a "feudal fascist dictatorship." Is it any wonder he was wary of malefactors in China's still fragile, convalescing society?

The country's leaders agreed that stability was of primary importance to China's future, and that this stability could be guaranteed only by democracy among the people and within the Communist Party, bolstered by a good legal system, a clear understanding of social and political goals, clean government and dedicated leaders.

Deng was confident in 1979 that the fundamental groundwork had been laid. He said a "great turning point" had been reached in China's history, and proposed the immediate commencement of "socialist modernization," that is, the creation of a modern society based on socialist principles.

Then he struck a blow at the very foundations of China's failings—what he called "rigid dogma," in other words the Maoist approach to socialism. We must have open minds, he insisted. China has to start a new course.

What Deng was saying was what many thinking Chinese, including many dedicated Communists, had thought for years. While they appreciated China's accomplishments during Mao's leadership, they felt that he had committed serious errors—great purges of any who dared offer criticism, spurring a population explosion, autocratic, patriarchal leadership, tacit acceptance of a rebirth of feudal practices—in a dogmatic atmosphere of immutable rigidity. But few had dared to protest.

Among my Chinese friends and colleagues in private conversations I had heard frequent sarcastic and angry comments on the state of affairs. Intellectuals— that is people in the arts, sciences and professions—had been victimized in the "anti-Rightist campaign" of 1956. While attacking opponents of the socialist system, the campaign had wrongfully purged thousands of honest loyal critics. An unofficial censorship existed in the theater, in film, in literature and art, which hamstrung creativity. Tight control by the orthodox hierarchy made it difficult to express dissent.

Now Deng had driven the opening wedge. From then on the People's Republic would deal pragmatically with social problems, would experiment with new and daring (for a socialist country) forms of ownership and control, would open to the outside world. The goal was what became known, in the nineties, as "Chinese socialism."

As we prepared to enter upon previously uncharted waters, we were all asking ourselves: How can a repetition of the same errors, or the commission of new ones, be prevented?

Analysts abounded, in China and abroad. I had a tiff with American playwright Arthur Miller whose views on China were, I think, fairly typical of Western liberals. He had visited me in 1978 and wrote about it in an article carried in the *Atlantic Monthly* of March 1979. I was irritated by some of the things he said about me, but was more interested in refuting his views on the role of law in China. *Atlantic* published my reply in July of the same year. It ran as follows:

> In his "In China," . . . Arthur Miller fabricates material we never mentioned, distorts my remarks, engages in erroneous speculation about my past and in scurrilous innuendoes against my integrity. He even writes the dialogue to fit me into the role he has created.
>
> The facts are these. Miller called on me in my home in Beijing in 1978, at his request, to ask about law in China. I told him that . . . criminal cases are

brought to trial only after thorough investigation—and without presumption of guilt. The court will not entertain a criminal proceeding without at least enough pretrial evidence for a prima facie case, but the charges still have to be proved beyond any reasonable doubt. Provisions have long existed regarding the right of appeal.

During the "cultural revolution," as Miller says, thousands were unjustly imprisoned. This was not due to a lack of laws—China has plenty, though uncodified—but to an abandonment of legality. I agreed with Miller that China's laws should be amplified and improved, noting that this was already being done. Of course, I added, while not deprecating the value of laws and judicial process, these do not in themselves guarantee equity and justice.

Yet this infuriated Miller. I couldn't see why, at the time, but having read his article, I do now. Miller rejoices in "post-Renaissance parliamentary capitalism." He finds it superior to Marxism, which he describes as "infinitely close" to feudalism. He speaks lovingly of the "victorious revolutions against feudalism" of the 18th century "whose first business was the writing of laws demarcating the powers of the government and the governed." All China needs are laws like these and "justice . . . institutionalized and put beyond the reach of even the Party itself."

The Chinese—and several tens of millions in various parts of the world—have learned differently. They know that bodies of laws and concepts of justice are conceived by and for those who rule in any given country. That unless the people really govern, unless their leaders—in China's case their Party and their government—function in a democratic manner, legality and justice are, so far as the majority are concerned, empty abstractions. It is with this in mind that China is revitalizing her political approach. New laws are useful appendages, but only that.

Miller tries to write off Marxism, socialism, and the Communist Party of China. But in spite of the excrescences committed in their name during the "cultural revolution," the experience of the past 30 years has confirmed in Chinese minds their inherent soundness. At the same time they are being modified and improved in the light of present realities, and shall keep pace with developments of the future.

Miller's reply was published along with my letter. He said:

I do regret it if there seemed anything personal in my writing. . . . The question my article raised is whether the so-called excesses of the "cultural revolution," which have set China back for a decade or perhaps more in her development, could have been at least mitigated by a real system of appeal

218

within the judicial system and in the society at large. And whether the lack of it practically invites another period of chaos.

There the argument stands. Well-meaning liberals like Miller miss the point. "A real system of appeal within the judicial system" is useless without a democratically elected government genuinely representing the people in control and responsive to their appeals. It is substance, not form, that counts. Would an ostensible right of appeal to Hitler have saved the Jews from the gas ovens in Nazi Germany? Could Willy Loman, in Miller's fine play *Death of a Salesman*, when fired by the boss after 40 years of service, have saved his job if he had a right of appeal to the company's board of directors? Miller understands real life much better than he understands political theory.

Phoenix and I were living in half a tile-roofed, bungalow-style house, which we shared with another Chinese family. The husband was Sun Shengwu, a quiet scholar, an authority on Russian literature, who later became one of the leaders of the Chinese Translators Society. He and his wife had two children, a boy and a girl, both of whom were born deaf-mutes, throwbacks to unremembered ancestors who must have had the same affliction. There was nothing wrong with their vocal chords—they couldn't speak because their deafness prevented them from learning how.

They and our daughter Yamei had been warm friends since childhood, and she was completely "fluent" in their sign language. Yamei, a few years older than they, was then about 29. She and husband Taiping lived in a small bungalow, also tile roofed, we had built in the backyard, with our two-year-old granddaughter Xiang, whom we of course adored.

The house was the envy of Chinese and foreign friends alike—especially long-time Western "experts" living in special apartment-hotels. We lucked into it only because the former occupants wanted the place we were then living in because it was nearer their office. We arranged the formal exchange through the Municipal Housing Bureau which owned both properties.

A corridor, running from the front garden to the rear yard separated our flat from the Sun's. We had trees and flowers and, even more precious, quiet and fresh air. Our courtyard fronted on Nanguanfang—South Officials Lane, a modest dirt road, not paved till a few years after we moved in, in 1960. It got its grand-sounding title in the Qing Dynasty, when it was inhabited by minor eunuchs and junior Manchu officials. The whole area is very old. Here and there were princes' palaces, quite run-down but bearing traces of their former beauty. Secluded as we were, a five-minute stroll took us to Shishahai—the Lake of the Ten Monasteries. Five minutes more to Beihai—North Lake—a major bus junction on a main highway.

The house had wooden floors, about three feet above the ground, so that it did not sop up the moisture from the earth every spring, as the picturesque traditional home we previously lived in had done. In winter we heated with small coal stoves burning "beehive" cakes of pressed coaldust. They were warm enough, but ash dust covered everything whenever we cleaned the stoves.

We cooked with methane gas, from canisters which had to be fetched from a local supply depot. Not expensive, but it was a nuisance returning empties and picking up new ones. Eventually, we had a service which delivered them to our door. Rent was 14 yuan per month. (Today, it's around 80.) Our Municipal Housing Bureau "landlord" gave excellent maintenance and care, keeping the roof in good repair and the building structure generally sound. We were responsible for rent, water, gas, and electricity, and did our own inside painting. Together, rent and upkeep commanded only a small fraction of my salary, and my office reimbursed me for the entire cost, anyway.

We led a very comfortable existence. At no time were we without an *ah yi*— a general maid of all purpose. She was usually a girl or middle-aged woman from the farms seeking better wages. *Ah yi* was given food, lodging, and a small wage. She did the shopping, cooked, washed, mended, cleaned the house, and freed us from 90 percent of the household chores. We loved her as part of the family, and she cherished us and bossed us around, and was completely indispensable.

Most middle-income families had an *ah yi*, and so did many in the lower income category where both the husband and wife had to work, if they had a small child and there was no grandma to take over. Wealthy visitors from America would stare incredulously when I told them about our *ah yi*. Who can afford a full-time, live-in maid! Although it was very pleasant enjoying such a luxury, I had to confess to my visitors it was not one of the fruits of either socialism or modernization, but an out-and-out feudal hangover. My only merit was that I did not strike the pose of a dedicated revolutionary and pretend it was anything else.

I had my own "great turning point" in 1979. That year I completed my last project as a literary translator. For 30 years I had been transforming Chinese fiction into English for publication in China and sale abroad. I had produced a large number of translations, ranging from ancient to modern, from short stories to novels, plus some essays and poetry. During the "cultural revolution" I had the chance to translate China's great classical novel *Outlaws of the Marsh*.

China's first major novels were created in the Ming and Qing dynasties. Their milieu was the feudal era, which lasted roughly from the second century BC to well into the twentieth century. Feudalism was based on the control by a small landlord minority over the vast majority who tilled the soil in an agricultural society. In medieval China these were mainly tenants or serfs. The tenants, who had to pay the lion's share of the yield as rent, were compelled to borrow seed or food grain at exorbitant interest from the landlords to tide them over after bad harvests. Usually,

220

it was only a question of time before a crushing burden of debt reduced the tenant to serfdom or beggary, or forced him to sell his wife or his children.

This was the economic foundation of a political pyramid which extended upward through layers of bureaucratic officialdom, backed by armies and courts and police, all the way to the emperor. He was China's biggest landlord, since theoretically he owned all the land, sublet by him to lesser landlords.

He was also the infallible fountainhead of justice and wisdom, modestly known as the "Son of Heaven." Every few hundred years, when China slid into chaos, popular uprisings might remove a particular emperor, but only because he was deemed to have "lost Heaven's Mandate." Another emperor was quickly put in his place. Feudalism as an imperial political and social system was never questioned.

Prevailing religious beliefs and philosophic concepts praised submissiveness and respect for authority as the supreme virtues in a male chauvinist world. Women, at the bottom of the ladder, had to obey their husbands who took their orders from the local magistrates—euphemistically called "the parents of the people." The magistrates were under the command of the provincial governors who were ruled by the emperor. He had a direct pipeline to God—popularly hailed as *Lao Tian Ye*—the "Old Lord of the Sky."

It was an autocratic, paternalistic society in which the average Chinese respected the traditional ethical values and was generally law-abiding. At the same time he recognized the venality of the bureaucracy and the corruption of the clergy, and harbored no illusions about many who called themselves his superiors. If they harried him beyond endurance, he might rationalize resistance or even crime, always in the name of upholding righteousness and opposing immorality.

China's creative writers were of course thoroughly saturated with the concepts and attitudes of feudal China. This is very evident in *Outlaws of the Marsh*, the most popular of the Ming novels. A rip-roaring tale, even the violence and carnage of its protagonists are always presented as manifestations of the purest virtue.

During the final years of Song Emperor Hui Zong, who reigned from 1101 to 1125, 100-odd men and women fled persecution to band together on a marsh-girt mountain in what today is Shandong Province. They became the leaders of an outlaw army of thousands and fought bold and resourceful battles against the powerful military forces of the corrupt ministers who, the outlaws alleged, were deceiving the emperor. While the outlaws used no-holds-barred tactics against evil officials, they were not opposed to the imperial establishment, in fact they staunchly supported traditional feudal rule. They were rebels, not revolutionaries. They did not, and could not, conceive of changing the existing social and political system. They ran their internal affairs in a strictly "correct" manner, and took a high moral benevolent tone in their relations with the local populace.

221

The trials and triumphs of these brigands became the fabric of one of the best-loved episodic thrillers of the professional story tellers, and their tale was polished and elevated into the 14th century Ming Dynasty novel *Outlaws of the Marsh*. Most of the events actually occurred, and most of the *personae* actually existed, although much liberty was taken in the novel with the facts. During the Ming and Qing dynasties it appeared in numerous editions ranging from 70 to 124 chapters, the denouement changing with the political temper of the ruling monarch. Arguments over the authorship and the authenticity and dates of the various editions continue to this day. The prevailing opinion is that Shi Nai'an and Luo Guanzhong, Jiangsu Province *literati*, should be credited with the original creation.

The authors committed many inaccuracies. Fourteenth century dress, weapons, government offices are superimposed on the twelfth. Some time sequences and place locations are wrong. The authors often put their native Jiangsu Province colloquialisms in the mouths of Shandong provincial characters. . . .

This is of little consequence to any but the most nit-picking scholars, for the novel is intriguing and beautifully constructed. In spite of its enormous cast, the characters come across as distinct personalities, convincingly and in depth. The reader finds it difficult to remain objective and neutral as he becomes enmeshed in the complexities of Song Dynasty society.

In many respects it was the most advanced society in the twelfth century world. China was already using inventions like gunpowder, the compass and movable type. Her great merchant ships plied trade routes between China and southeast Asia and northern Africa. The arts flourished. There was heavy commerce between the cities and the countryside.

But the court and the bureaucracy were corrupt. By the late 12th century the empire was beginning to crumble, hammered by continuous attacks by tribal nations from the north. Internal disturbances gave rise to the formation of gangs of "brigands," such as the one described in *Outlaws of the Marsh*.

The novel has fascinated Chinese readers, young and old, for 600 years. It has been adapted for stage and screen, for television, for puppet theater, for picture books. Children know the tales by heart. Commented upon by decades of literati, it has been frequently quoted by eminent personalities, including Mao Zedong. In Japan it has long been appreciated in translation, and has exercised a considerable cultural influence. A few translations are also available in English and in European languages. My rendition is the first to have been done in China under the direct guidance of Chinese scholars.

The novel is important not only as a literary tour de force but because it brings out vividly the feudal, Confucian concepts, the attitudes and standards, which are still very much a part of the Chinese psyche. It is an ideal guide to understanding China today. I felt I could not have chosen a better vehicle for my "swan song" as a translator of Chinese literature.

That did not mean I had given up translating Chinese literary materials. On the contrary I found that Chinese sources provided valuable information I was able to use in writing books of my own on themes which interested me. *An American in China*, my first venture in original writing, was published in Beijing in mid-1979. Another personal "turning point"!

I was inspired by the magnificent 16th century Italian sculptor and goldsmith Benvenuto Cellini. He opens his *Autobiography* with this modest statement: "All men of whatsoever quality they be, who have done anything of excellence, or which may properly resemble excellence, ought, if they are persons of truth and honesty, to describe their life with their own hand. But they ought not to attempt so fine an enterprise till they have passed the age of 40."

Although I knew I was a million light years behind Cellini in talent and accomplishments, I was well past 40. (Today, I am double that age.) At least I could match him in effrontery! That is what decided me to write my autobiography.

Joking aside, it required a certain amount of courage—or stupidity—to include political events and attitudes that had been sensitive, even dangerous, during a tumultuous ten-year period only recently passed and whose meaning I still didn't fully comprehend. But I felt I had already lived 30 years in the People's Republic of China, and had directly participated in many of the new developments. If I waited until I knew everything there was to know about China—and myself—I would never write the book. My story, it seemed to me, would be a useful means of giving readers some insights on this vitally important country about which so little was known in the West.

I tried out drafts on a dozen different Chinese colleagues whose English was good, and received invaluable information and suggestions. After New World Press, a division of the Foreign Languages Publication Administration Bureau in Beijing, published it in hardcover, beautifully bound in silk, photo illustrated, in 1979, NAL (New American Library) did it as a paperback in New York later the same year. It was the first book by a Chinese citizen, generally favorable to New China, to appear in the States.

A published author. Incredible. My pleasure was mixed with concern over what the reactions to the book would be. Apparently I didn't have to worry. In China it was published a few years later in Chinese. In the States it made me something of a media curiosity and brought invitations to speak. I had no illusions about myself as a literary stylist, but I saw that I could put things down on paper about China in a way that people enjoyed reading. Not long after, I found the courage to try my hand again.

For Phoenix 1979 was also an outstanding year. It was a time of righting of wrongs and recognizing merits and talents. In 1979 her long wish of joining the Chinese Communist Party was granted, and this was followed by appointments to high Party and administrative positions within the Dramatists Association.

A few friends were surprised that she still wanted to be a Communist after the suffering she endured during the "cultural revolution." To Phoenix the matter was perfectly clear.

"It wasn't the Party that persecuted people like me," she said, "it was Jiang Qing and the Gang of Four. They pretended to act in the Party's name, but actually they opposed everything the Party stands for. Now that the real Party is back in power, being a Communist is an honor and a privilege."

I myself never joined the Communist Party. I was still too much of a maverick, reluctant to accept any organizational strictures or discipline. But I had the greatest respect for the Chinese Party, and fully supported its principles and goals.

Phoenix flew with me to the States in September, 1979. Although a Chinese citizen, I had Foreign Expert status, entitling me to a home leave approximately every two years. My office paid our plane fares. It was Phoenix's first trip, my fourth.

It had been awkward trying to explain to my mother why I hadn't brought Phoenix with me on previous trips. During the first, in 1971, Mom had been very disappointed that Phoenix hadn't come. She and Phoenix had been charmed by each other during her visit to Beijing in 1963. Since there had been no assurance that I could get into America via Canada in 1971, my explanation that I hadn't wanted to expose Phoenix to a tiring and possibly futile journey had sounded plausible.

I had much more difficulty allaying Mom's suspicions when I visited again, alone, in 1974 and 1977. Mom knew nothing about the insane "cultural revolution," and I couldn't very well tell her that her Chinese daughter-in-law was being held in a preposterous adult camp on unstated charges. My excuses that Phoenix was "too busy" to get away sounded pretty lame.

And so, it was a red-letter day for all of us when Phoenix and I took off from Beijing on a Chinese plane on September 5, 1979. There were as yet no direct flights to America, and even the route via Europe had to be circuitous. A brief war was waging between China and Vietnam. We went first to Teheran, stayed overnight, took a Swiss plane through Belgrade to Zurich, and then flew across the Atlantic to New York.

Sister Ruth and brother-in-law Jack Steinman were waiting at Kennedy, and drove with us to their home on a tree-lined street in Flatbush. Most of the houses were modest one family dwellings, two stories high, with small gardens in the front and garages in the back. Phoenix was struck by the absence of walls around them, which most buildings have in Beijing. She asked me later whether they were safe, and whether people minded the lack of privacy.

Ruth and Jack were fascinated by her. We had sent them letters and pictures, and my mother, whom we all called "Kate" in the informal American style (shocking the ceremoniously respectful Phoenix), had told them about her visit with us in Beijing in 1963. They had never had an opportunity to talk freely with a lady from China, who was also their sister-in-law.

They chatted incessantly, doing their best to field each others' questions. Phoenix, who had a large vocabulary, but no grammar to speak of, astonished everyone, including me, with her fluency. Jack and Ruth were enchanted. An active admiralty lawyer, Jack on one occasion told Phoenix about some legal battle he was involved in, throwing off phrases like "interrogatories" and "subpoenas duces tecum." Not understanding a word, Phoenix nodded politely from time to time.

Jack turned to me indignantly. "What do you mean, her English is poor?" he demanded. "It's excellent!"

The first order of business was visiting my mother. "Kate" had her own apartment a few blocks away. Although in her late eighties, she was fiercely independent and insisted on living alone, despite Ruth's pleas that she move in with her and Jack. Phoenix was amazed. Such a thing could never happen in China. A child naturally had to take personal care of an aged parent.

She was very happy to see my mother again. The two had formed a deep affection during Kate's stay in Beijing. Phoenix was nagged by what she considered a failure of propriety on her part. After a marriage it was the duty of the daughter-in-law to visit the mother-in-law first, not the other way round. Now, at last, she was able to set things right, and she felt much better.

September tenth was Kate's 87th birthday. We decided to celebrate with a grand luncheon party, in Ruth's house. Kate's grandchildren were scattered in different parts of the country; her only son was living as far away as China. It was a rare opportunity to get all of us together. Phoenix, after some urging, agreed to make a few Chinese dishes. We drove down to Chinatown in lower Manhattan on the ninth and bought the needed ingredients, with Phoenix muttering outrage at the prices.

The luncheon went marvelously well. Kate was blooming. We didn't know it marked the start of the decline of her sturdy health. Two years later, on our next visit, we would find her in a wheelchair. But this day in 1979, everyone was in high spirits.

The Washington Post had got hold of the Beijing edition of *An American in China*, and their interest was sufficiently aroused to send one of their crack feature writers, Lee Lescaze, to interview me in New York. The piece he did was entitled "China: Once-in-a-Lifetime Choice," and it appeared on the *Style* page of the *Post* in November.

He quotes me with amusement as saying that a producer who had been considering making a movie of *An American in China* had told me I could not play the lead because, he said, "You're not the Sidney Shapiro type." Lee also noted Phoenix's first impression of New York: "The people are very clean and the city is very dirty."

225

The interview was long, friendly and perceptive.

I was particularly happy with this visit to the States because Phoenix was able to come with me. I wanted to show her as much as I could of the reason for my infatuation with my old home. "You can take the boy out of Brooklyn, but you can't take Brooklyn out of the boy," as the saying goes.

Although I bitched and grumbled like any native, I loved Brooklyn and Flatbush, with its tree-shaded streets. And I was still thrilled by the noise and color and excitement of Manhattan. I took the grime and the squalor of the great metropolis in my stride.

Old friends were eager to help. George Hartman and his wife one sunny Sunday morning drove us out to Jones Beach. It was too cool for swimming, and the beach was virtually deserted. We picnicked on the sand, gazing at the waves and the scudding clouds in a crisp blue sky, and reminisced about our days in James Madison High School, and classmates, some already gone.

Phoenix and I had swum leisurely in the tranquil Pacific Ocean at Beidaihe in north China and in the tropical paradise of Sanya on the southern tip of Hainan Island. The powerful Atlantic was very different. Phoenix could sense its underlying menace, and she watched it somewhat uneasily. But before long she like the rest of us was lulled into drowsy relaxation by the steady booming of the waves, the calm sunshine, and the pure clean air. We returned to Flatbush much refreshed.

Again George was our host when we went to the restaurant in one of the towers of the World Trade Center. From 110 stories high in the air, people below looked like ants—an enlightening sight for any who may harbor inflated ideas of their own worth.

Phoenix, who had been years in the theater as an actress, script doctor and drama critic, wanted to see plays, and we gave her a very large dose. We started with an Irish vehicle called *Da*, delivered in a thick brogue as incomprehensible to me as it was to her. We both liked the exciting production of *Sweeney Todd: The Demon Barber of Fleet Street*.

Our hosts, meaning to impress us, invited us afterwards to supper at Sardi's. It was crowded with glamorous celebrities, dripping mink. As we entered, all eyes turned to Phoenix. The head waiter immediately recognized quality.

"You are welcome, my lady," he murmured, as he bent over and kissed her hand. It was our hosts who were impressed.

Buried Child, an off-Broadway Pulitzer prize-winning show, was performed in a small theater in Greenwich Village just above a subway station. The audience shook and trembled every time a train came in, which perhaps heightened their sensitivity to the nuances of the play.

Phoenix particularly enjoyed *Equus*, an off-off-Broadway vehicle, and was enchanted by *Loose Ends*, which we saw in the Circle in the Square in the Broadway theater district. She brought the script back to Beijing, hoping to have it performed in China, but was unable to interest any of the theater companies.

We met a number of young hopefuls. A small part-time acting group of Taiwanese were putting on plays in Chinese for Chinese-American audiences. A girl from Ohio invited us to her mid-town apartment, then took us to lunch at Curtain Up, a cooperative restaurant where the cooks, waiters and waitresses were all unemployed actors and actresses. Our friend, though she trained and studied hard, was unable to get a role on the stage, and supported herself doing bits in television commercials. She was discouraged, but stubbornly determined. She explained that most Broadway plays were staged by companies specifically organized for their production, and everyone hired—actors, actresses, electricians, stage hands . . . were out of work again when the play ended its run. But there were always new vehicles, she insisted, always a chance. . . .

Phoenix told her most theatrical companies in the big cities in China were funded by the government. Actors and actresses were on regular salary, whether they were performing or not. In addition they had medical insurance and retirement pay. The company would even hire the adult son or daughter of the person retiring whenever possible.

This arrangement provided financial security, Phoenix said, but there were too few good vehicles, and entirely too many people waiting for roles to play. As a result, most of them sat around doing nothing for years, but were afraid to abandon the modest benefits they were receiving and strike out for themselves. To the artists professionally this was deadly, said Phoenix. As a former actress, she wondered whether the American method wasn't better despite its shortcomings.

She was curious about Wall Street, "with the river at one end and a graveyard at the other." I showed her the steps of the Sub-Treasury Building where I used to bask in the sunshine after a lunch of nutted cheeseburger and a glass of grapefruit drink when I was a clerk for a prosperous law firm on Pine Street. Custom-made limousines softly tooled by. Later, driving along Second Avenue, we had to close the windows to keep out the pleading hands of drunks and panhandlers.

In front of one manicured lawn in Flatbush we saw a perfectly good sofa waiting to be picked up by the sanitation truck because a spring was poking through the seat. We agreed that such profligacy could not happen in China, where things were rarely thrown away, and patching and repair work has been raised to a high art.

I explained about the difficulty and the costliness of finding persons to make repairs in the States, but said that was only part of it. The advertising industry had done a thorough brain-washing of the American public. People were ashamed of holding on to things too long. They felt that having the newest model car, the latest fashion clothes, was a confirmation of their status, their sophistication. Phoenix said poor and middle class people in China could not afford ostentation.

In October we went to Wilmette near Chicago and stayed with my niece Joan Steinman and her husband Doug Cassel, who had visited us in Beijing exactly three years before. They lived in a big old frame house in a neighborhood of trees and gardens, and drove us to a famous pancake house for Sunday breakfast. Phoenix and I relaxed and enjoyed the kind of American environment I love best. Friends of Doug, bright young people who knew a lot about China, brought us back to reality with sharp questions about the failure of the model farming commune Dazhai, the problems of creative writers, the clumsiness of Chinese PR promotion. They asked us to give our appraisal of Mao Zedong. I don't think our answers satisfied them.

Jerry Mann was our host in Los Angeles. Recently divorced, he had given up his house, and was baching it in a marina miles from the city. He was determined to find us more centrally located quarters, and set us up in a house which had been entrusted to him by a lady artist who was away in New York, in return for his promise to feed her large dog daily. Jerry, involved in a dozen different activities, wasn't a very good dog-feeder. He was relieved when I agreed to take over the mission. Phoenix and I then became the occupants of a charming residence in Beverly Hills, and remained there until the end of our stay.

Why didn't we live in a hotel, or at least a motel? Under my "foreign expert" status, I was drawing a respectable salary, by Chinese standards, equivalent to about 100 US dollars per month. I was allowed to send half of it regularly to my widowed mother. Since that left me only another 100 dollars I had no money to put aside. My trips abroad were always on a financial shoestring. I couldn't have managed without the hospitality of friends, and at times of warmhearted people I scarcely knew.

They were glad to have me because as a Brooklyn lawyer who had lived for years in "mysterious" China I was the man from Mars. My hosts would give parties where I would be displayed as the guest of honor. I didn't mind being lionized. It gave me a chance to answer questions by people who previously had little interest in China, or who had been subjected to a lot of preposterous bilge.

Jerry and I had crossed long stretches of America atop boxcars during the Depression 1930s, and later had been classmates in St. John's Law School in New York. When we were riding freights together Jerry entered copious notes in a diary he carried. He hoped to write up our adventures as a sort of modern Jack London. Neatness was never Jerry's strong point. He soon lost the diary and instead of becoming a famous author, had to settle with becoming a very rich manufacturer of women's slack suits.

And so when I showed up as a live author, with hardcover copies of a genuine published book, accompanied by a beautiful Chinese wife, Jerry was overcome with admiration. He exerted every effort to have *An American in China* made into a motion picture. We had a couple of near misses, but no feature film.

Jerry spent most of his time with us, chauffeuring us around, introducing us to his friends. Marian, the divorced wife of my nephew Hank, lived on the shore further down the coast. We phoned to say hello, and she drove up to see us. A former airline stewardess, Marian was a beautiful blonde, with a complexion like a Dresden doll. We took her to lunch, and of course Jerry joined us. Although they seemed to get along well, we didn't think anything would come of it. Jerry had been friendly with a whole series of girls, including an Austrian tennis champion. To our surprise, a few months after we got back to Beijing, we were informed they had married.

This turned out to be a very good thing, not only for them, but for our then two-year-old Chinese granddaughter. I will explain when we get to her story at the age of 11.

China's economy had come a long way since the days before the establishment of the People's Republic in 1949, when poverty, unemployment, exploitation and oppression were commonplace. Still, the rate of improvement had been slow, even before the "cultural revolution" nearly brought it to a halt.

Chinese economists ascribed this to excessive government control on both a national and local level, to treating producer units as mere appendages of the administrative organs, and to a general lack of material incentive and reward to those doing the primary work.

Now, the proclaimed goal was "Chinese socialism." By 1980 national newspapers were telling about something called "economic reform" in the province of Sichuan. But the reports were general and, to me, rather vague. I decided to go down to Sichuan and see for myself how, as a practical matter, this reform was being carried out.

My office appointed a young man named Guo to accompany me and help in every way he could, including interpreting Sichuan dialect, which in some areas was very heavy, into standard Chinese. A warmhearted intelligent fellow, Guo solved all manner of problems regarding travel, accommodations and appointments. Unfortunately his Shanxi accent (he pronounced his name "Guo" as "Gua") was thicker than the local Sichuan variety, and more often than not I had to serve as *his* interpreter. But Guo was great company and, between us, we managed to interview all the people I wanted to see, mainly in the Chongqing and Chengdu areas.

We talked about agriculture, industry and commerce in new permutations and combinations—within themselves, with one another, and with governmental organizations. It was fascinating. They had really "liberated" their thinking, and had come up with many practical measures which were working well. Although they stressed that these were experimental, other provinces were already following Sichuan's example, adding touches of their own.

229

Zhao Ziyang, then the provincial Communist Party secretary of Sichuan, was credited with having shaped the new approach. Partly on the strength of its success, he was later chosen Premier of China.

The spirit of reform had spread into other fields as well. Chengdu had the best family planning record in the country. They had brought the birthrate in 1978 down to nine per thousand, from the 1970 rate of 30 per thousand, the first place in China to drop below one percent.

They promoted male sterilization by having government cadres undergo the operations first. Although quick and requiring only a short period of recuperation, many of the wives were opposed. They were afraid it would lessen their husband's strength for physical labor. (Also, though no one said so openly, if the operation didn't take and the wife became pregnant, she might be suspected of having a lover.)

More effective were other deals offered: A monthly cash subsidy to any city family with only one child. In the country a private plot of land was given to the parents at the birth of their first baby. The village took it back if they had another. But people were better off, and grandparents proved formidable opponents to family planning. They wanted grandchildren and were willing to pay for their upkeep. Many parents, too, were in a better financial position to have a second child if they really wanted one.

Old concepts, as usual, tended to put a spoke in the wheel of progress. Local government administrations were helping unemployed youth to form co-ops, financed by their parents, in the service fields. But the older folk, with fresh memories of the "cultural revolution," were reluctant to get involved in any commercial enterprise which might be labeled "capitalist."

The arts, too, had to battle against traditional conservatism. At the Sichuan Academy of Art, the director told me a funny-sad story: The city of Chongqing had paid the Academy a large sum to create four figures, each eight meters high, to stand as bridgeheads at both ends of the new span across the Yangtze River. They were to be cast in expensive sheenless aluminum. Two female figures would represent spring and autumn, two male figures would be summer and winter. They would range in age from around 20 to 50. Spring would be youthfully nubile. Autumn would be as lush as the hoped for harvests. All would be nude from the waist up.

Pictures of the plaster of Paris mock-ups were published in the Chongqing press to elicit public reaction. Several readers were so outraged they threatened to smash the aluminum ladies unless they were clothed. As a compromise, the sculptors put T-shirts on them.

"But that looked so awful," said the director, "they were finally draped in a diaphanous material more in keeping with the rest of their ancient style attire."

In spite of the peripheral problems, I came away with the conviction that Sichuan was leading the way in economic reform, and that I had learned something

230

about what the words meant in practical terms. Since then, economic liberalization in China has become much broader, but I was glad to have seen it in Sichuan at its inception. New World Press published my report in 1981 under the title of *Experiment in Sichuan.*

After my less than splendid performance in 1975 as the commanding general of the US Air Force in Korea in *Eagles of the Sky* I had sworn off acting in the movies. This steely determination was not shaken until 1980 when I was approached with a new offer. A big-budget, wide-screen modern epic called *The Xian Incident* was about to go into production and they needed someone to play W.H. Donald, Australian adviser to Chiang Kai-shek. They said I looked like him and showed me pictures to prove it. Major parts on the Communist side would include Mao Zedong and Zhou Enlai. Also prominently featured would be the Generalissimo and Madame Chiang Kai-shek, T.V. Soong (then foreign minister), and the Young Marshal Zhang Xueliang. The picture would reflect a vital change in Chinese history. And I, at last, could be a "good guy." After some dithering I capitulated.

The first scene in which I was involved was shot in Nanjing, China's capital in the 1930s. Madame Chiang was giving a party attended by foreign guests, played by foreign students at the university who had happily volunteered to be our extras. Donald, the Australian adviser, was also present. People who knew him said he was a soft-spoken, relaxed Australian who dressed very informally. I found the costume department had fitted me out for the Nanjing party in banker's pinstripes.

Fortunately, a gentleman from Vienna whose daughter was one of our student extras had come to China to visit her and had dropped in at the set. He was wearing a loud plaid sports jacket. When I explained my predicament he laughed, peeled it off and exchanged it for mine. Not only that, but he joined the dancers. A Viennese, he was easily the best waltzer on the floor.

In that same sequence I am dancing with Madame Chiang when we are suddenly interrupted by Foreign Minister T.V. Soong who comes rushing in to tell her the Generalissimo has been arrested in Xian. She announces to her guests that she must leave and hurries out. A foreign young lady asks me (Donald) what is going on. "I have no idea," I reply.

At that time Chinese directors had the actors dub in their voices after the shooting was complete. Since that was my only line in Nanjing and I wanted to get back to Beijing, I asked the director to have someone else dub it for me. He agreed, and I left. Some months later, watching the first preview I was horrified to hear me replying to the young lady's query with: "I haven't the faintest ideah," in flawless British upper class tones.

In my main scenes, however—with the Young Marshal acting as my "interpreter" during meetings with Chiang Kai-shek—I speak my own English, and did my own dubbing. Dr. George Hatem, who attended the preview with me, said

231

I deserved an award for being the only Australian character in Chinese cinema history with a Brooklyn accent.

As to the veracity of my performance, there seems to be no solid consensus. While preparing to do another scene I was seated in an ancient Packard with the Young Marshal. We were parked on a country roadside waiting for the sun to come out from behind the clouds so the camera could roll on an interior car-shot. A crowd of farm folks surrounding our vehicle was attracted by our costumes and makeup.

"That man," one old lady said to her friend, pointing at me. "Do you think he looks like a foreigner?"

The other old dear peered at me quizzically, then shook her head. "Not a bit," she said firmly.

Despite my sterling performance, the film is very good, and was a great success. It is shown on Chinese television every December 6, the anniversary of the "Xian Incident."

I nevertheless decided this was my farewell appearance as a Chinese movie personality.

Beijing Bagels and
Chinese Jews
1981-1984

In the summer of 1981 Phoenix and I again visited America. We stayed first with Barbara and Norman Bernie in their beautiful home in Hillsborough outside San Francisco.

Barbara had been suffering from an ovarian cancer pronounced terminal. In desperation she went to Shanghai, where a combination of Western and traditional Chinese medical treatment cured her. Convinced of the value of such an approach, she created the American Foundation of Traditional Chinese Medicine, with offices in San Francisco. After intensive lobbying, she persuaded the State of California to recognize acupuncture specialists as doctors if they passed state medical exams. Through the Foundation there is a constant exchange of doctors between China and America for short-term research.

Traditional Chinese medicine is very big in California. Dozens of American doctors go to China every year for special courses ranging from six months to two years. On return, they include this as part of their practice. It is quite profitable for some.

Phoenix and I encountered an interest in China wherever we went. The Bernies took us to see *Mao to Mozart*, a documentary violinist Isaac Stern had filmed of his tour of China. We had attended one of his performances in Beijing, where the audience gave him a tremendous ovation.

Not all interest was favorable. The media had fully covered the "cultural revolution," and Americans had been shocked by its excesses. Those who had long proclaimed "you can't change human nature," said it proved that Chinese socialism was a failure. They were skeptical about alleged gains. A man we met from Taiwan was worried by stories of turmoil on the mainland. He had no desire for unification. "Your economy is so backward," he said. "You only want to pull us down to your level."

Most shaken of all were the "friends of China," people who had always blindly exaggerated China's merits. I called it "the higher the praise the harder the fall." We tried to help put the picture into a more rational perspective, generally without much success. It was going to take a while for China to rehabilitate herself in people's minds. First she would have to rehabilitate herself on her own ground.

233

In New York we stayed with sister Ruth and brother-in-law Jack in their large one family house in Flatbush, dispensing gifts left and right. To Mom, in addition to our own, we presented a jade pendant and a Chinese style painting of a chrysanthemum from George Hatem the American doctor who had been so warmly solicitous during her visit in Beijing.

Mom was 88, and showing her age. She was frightened by the violence she saw on TV, and worried about the loss of family security her generation had known. Among many of her friends, parents and children were living separately.

Harold Lerner, a pal from high school days, was now a wealthy manufacturer of women's wear, the head of Fire Islander. We reminisced about touch-football games on the streets of our old neighborhood. He took us to see the Broadway musical *Sophisticated Lady*, the story of Black jazz composer and conductor Duke Ellington—further stirring my nostalgia.

Moss Roberts, NYU professor and China scholar (he was later to do a fine translation of the Chinese classic *The Three Kingdoms*), drove Phoenix and me up to Riverdale to visit Carrington Goodrich, famed Sinologist and former head of Columbia University's Chinese department. Moss and I had both studied under him. It was an exhausting ride. Moss liked to take his eyes off the road and look at you when he talked. In addition, his hands shook violently. He claimed it didn't influence his driving, but I'm afraid my own hands were shaking by the time we got to Riverdale.

Dr. Goodrich had been born and raised in China, a son of long-time missionaries. He loved China and knew China thoroughly. His *Short History of the Chinese People* is a fascinating and indispensable guide. He and his wife were still living in an old frame two-story house squeezed between tall apartment houses rising on both sides. He refused to sell, though offered a whopping price. I don't blame him. It was a homey comfortable house, with a garden and trees and flowers. Carrington Goodrich insisted he would stay there until he died, and he did. A fine man.

In Washington we visited the White House and the Jefferson and Lincoln Memorials, and audited a session of the Senate. They were debating South Africa. We were impressed by the pervading dignity and quiet. We tried in the Library of Congress to find a Chinese film Phoenix had played in during the anti-Japanese war. There were no copies left in China. Although the librarian in the Chinese Section, a scholarly Chinese-American, hunted high and low, we had no luck.

The Washington Post invited me down for an informal chat. The atmosphere was friendly, but they really grilled me about recent developments, and were sharp on the absence of freedom of the press in China. I could only weakly agree.

I seemed to be of particular interest to the Post. It had carried a long piece as a Sunday feature in July about my "meteoric rise in the Chinese cinema firmament" (which I coyly wrote myself), and then an even longer book review the following

Sunday by leading Post critic Joseph McLellan about *Outlaws of the Marsh*. His review of the novel and its translation was very able.

"*Outlaws of the Marsh* is a work of social protest," he wrote, "just as the Robin Hood legend is under its quaint Olde Englysshe trappings. It is also a classic and, by the time the end is reached, many readers may be willing to argue that it is a masterpiece."

Other critics were equally laudatory. A few made unkind comparisons of Pearl Buck's translation with mine. Her version, done in the thirties was entitled *All Men Are Brothers*—a nice thought but not quite in keeping with the murderous state of human relations today. Said China scholar Cyril Birch in the Wilson Quarterly:

> Pearl Buck's *All Men Are Brothers* brought parts of *Outlaws* to the West. But Shapiro's effort represents a three-fold improvement: His knowledge of Chinese makes this version more accurate, his straight-forward English proves more graceful than Buck's Sinicized patois, and his reliance on earlier editions of the original produces a more comprehensive text. . . . A saga of medieval derring-do, it has the advantage of being the genuine article.

That autumn I took Phoenix to places I myself had never been. In El Cerito, California, we stayed with the Schachmans (Howard is a scientist) and were startled one morning to see wild deer grazing on their lawn. We were the guests in Portland, Oregon of Dr. Charley Grossman and, his wife, Frosty, frequent visitors to China. They lived on the side of a mountain amid huge sequoias. In Seattle, Washington, our young hosts were Lloyd Ellingson and his wife.

I had run into both Charley and Lloyd the year before in the posh hotel where they and I were living outside Xian when I was taking part in the filming of *The Xian Incident*. "Come and stay with us if you're ever in our part of the country," they each had said. Neither they nor I had expected I would take them up on it so quickly.

The Ellingsons drove us in their car above the tree line on Mount Rainier, where we took pictures and had a snowball fight. I spoke about Chinese literature, and Phoenix about the theater, at Washington University. We lunched with some profs in the faculty dining room. Very pleasant.

George Foster interviewed us for the Seattle Post-Intelligencer. His piece was featured with a picture of Phoenix and me, both looking very well-fed after two months in the States. He placed me considerably in advance of the economic reforms then unfolding in China, saying earlier that year I had "opened a bagel shop on a back street behind Beijing's famed Forbidden City."

The rest of his article was more accurate. He quoted my analysis of Mao and thereafter in some detail.

"Mao had a fabulous track record," Foster noted me as saying, "and he certainly was the leading spirit in converting China from a degraded, backward and poverty-stricken society to a viable society that has a comparatively low standard of living, but where people have enough to eat and work to do and a degree of confidence in their own future.

"However, what we are criticizing now is that at some point in development, Mao and many of his colleagues went off the track and began adopting a radical speeded-up approach that was not in keeping with the realities of China.

"There were some dreadful errors made and the most awful of these culminated in the 'cultural revolution (1966-1976).'"

Foster noted I gave "little credence" to reports that lingering support for Mao and a more orthodox brand of Chinese Marxism posed an internal threat to the more pragmatic regime of Premier Zhao Ziyang.

To end his article, Foster quoted me thus: "It is true that in China we have our two schools of thought, just like every other country," Shapiro concluded. "But I would say that as of this moment those who are hoping for a very rigid, very doctrinaire, dogmatic keeping to the old line regarding social and economic development are very much in the minority. Their position is so weak they could not influence the present course of events."

I was grateful to Foster for letting me state my opinions so fully before a wide reading public. That was indeed what I believed at that time and what I still believe today.

Our last stop in the States was Los Angeles. Old St. John's Law School fellow graduate Jerry Mann was living with new wife Marian (to whom Phoenix and I had introduced him) and new baby (the first for both) in a small apartment near the Beverly Hills Tennis Club, and had no room for us. Tennis for Jerry ranked a close second to his wife and child. When not on the courts, he sat by the pool-side eating large bagel sandwiches and swapping lies with other rich retired habitues.

Jerry found us quarters in a mansion on a hilltop in Bel Air, a large walled estate occupied by even richer residents. Our host was the owner of the King Cole supermarket chain, a pleasant fellow who evidently worked too hard. He proudly showed us his maid's room, with its own color TV set and handsome furniture. He looked impressed when I told him we also have a full-time maid and housekeeper— then a rarity even in Bel Air. I neglected to go into detail about the quality of our Beijing equipage.

Back in Beijing we learned that Indiana University Press, having requested and obtained permission from FLP to publish my translation of *Outlaws of the Marsh*, had just released an American edition.

It was a good way to end the year.

236

When I was a callow youth in Flatbush I used to imagine "Letters to the Editor" writers were grumpy old fuddy-duddy types. I know now that is not true, but in any event I joined their ranks with a hot letter of my own, published in *Beijing Review* in February, 1982. It ran as follows:

> The writer of an unsigned article in your issue No.52 for 1981 regarding the proper treatment of love in Chinese literature summarizes what he alleges to be press comment. He says, in a paragraph entitled "Vulgar Interests," that proponents of "healthy" values and "proper moral approaches" are "particularly critical" of themes like "love relations between Chinese people and foreigners" because these are "corrupt subjects created for the sake of novelty."
>
> Such a statement is a misunderstanding of the Chinese press and attributes to it a chauvinist attitude it does not possess. . . . The press has never said that themes of love between Chinese and foreigners are in themselves "corrupt."

The editors of *Beijing Review* hastily agreed. "The article referred to indeed fails to clearly and accurately represent the opinions of Chinese literary critics," they admitted.

I was irritated by the narrow prejudices of the writer, and equally by the failure of editors of a periodical being circulated world-wide to read carefully the material they were about to publish. More instances of irresponsibility in other areas of the bureaucracy were to arouse my ire in the future and provoke more "letters to the editor."

Barbara Isenberg was in Beijing that summer and visited us at home. Sensibly devoting most of her attention to Phoenix, Barbara sought information on the state of Chinese contemporary drama. What she learned was carried in August in the Calendar section of the *Sunday LA Times* in a piece entitled *Theater in China*. I quote from her report:

> Visitors like myself are more likely to wind up at acrobatics, dance or opera performances when traveling in China, but theatrical companies abound. A recent feature on rural culture, published in the weekly *Beijing Review*, noted that besides all of the "big city theatrical troupes" touring the countryside, there were another 3,000 county troupes which spend two-thirds of their time in the villages.
>
> According to Phoenix, there are about 100 legitimate theater groups in this primarily agricultural country. Most, she said, are new since the "cultural revolution," but others predated it and were restored at its end.

237

The "cultural revolution" also temporarily halted *Play Scripts*, the theatrical monthly that Phoenix has long served as editor. Today, in contrast, Phoenix points to a theatrical magazine of some sort in every Chinese province and says *Play Scripts* alone had more than 50,000 subscribers.

(Just like nearly everywhere else in the world, movies remain China's most popular art form, Phoenix says a comparable movie magazine has about 10 million subscribers.)

Phoenix said that more than 100 original scripts come in each month, and she can publish only two monthly at most. Sometimes, too, she uses a portion of that limited space for "outstanding" foreign plays.

That's what happened a few months ago, when she published Lillian Hellman's *Another Part of the Forest*. Phoenix and Sidney visit the United States every few years, and one of the things they do on their sojourns is attend theater. They saw *Another Part of the Forest* last fall at Seattle Repertory Theatre, returned home to Beijing and, Phoenix said, had the play translated by a Chinese translator who specialized in Hellman's work.

In his booklet "Experiment in Sichuan—A Report on Economic Reform," published last year, Sidney interviewed Lu Peifen of the Chongqing Culture Bureau in Sichuan Province about theater there. Lu told Sidney that young people weren't much interested in formerly stressed heavy political fare or in traditional opera. What was popular, he said, were such contemporary dramas as "Save Her," described as a play "about a girl who gets mixed up with a gang of young hoods" or another "concerning the machinations of a female witch doctor."

We had a fairly steady stream of visitors from the West every year. Not a few of them had heard stories of Jews in China, and they frequently questioned me.

"You're Jewish," they said, "and you've lived in China for many years. You must know all about them. Please tell us."

The fact was I knew very little. I was a very secular Jew, completely nonreligious, with my interests centering heavily on the cultural and gastronomical aspects of Judaism. But even as my kind of Jew I was embarrassed and ashamed to be so ignorant. Moreover, I was now a Chinese, and here were people coming to my door and asking questions about an element of Chinese history. I felt I had a duty to find out. Besides, I myself was curious. I began searching.

I found that since the "discovery" by the West of a small remnant community of Jews in the city of Kaifeng in the 17th century, there had been an impressive assortment of books and articles and treatises, well in excess of 200 in number, written in English, French, German, Latin, Italian, Portuguese, Russian, Japanese, and Yiddish. In their original languages and in translation these were disseminated throughout the world, primarily in academic circles, but some in the popular press as well.

Travelers, Christian missionaries, Jewish scholars and Western Sinologists, all contributed to the reports. But there was nothing in the West by Chinese scholars.

With the help of Chinese colleagues I was able to track down two detailed works by Chen Yuan and Pan Guandan, made available only after the termination of the anti-intellectual "cultural revolution." I also discovered three other articles which touched on the Chinese Jews.

These five pieces are fascinating and of major importance. For they not only comment on existing theories of Western Sinologists, but offer the findings and views of Chinese historians from the vantage point of a thorough understanding of China's language, history and culture, so often limited in Western scholars.

But they had been written decades ago, and left many questions unanswered. Had there been any new research by Chinese scholars, any new findings, in the years which followed?

If there were, they certainly eluded me. My inquiries among scholars in Beijing proved fruitless. It seemed to me the only thing to do was go to those places which scholars like Chen Yuan and Pan Guandan listed as once having hosted Jewish communities, and try to persuade the local historians to undertake the necessary research. And surely I could arouse the interest of at least some of the scholars in Beijing.

Traveling by plane, train, and bus in the autumn of 1982, I visited Fuzhou, Quanzhou, Xiamen (Amoy), Guangzhou (Canton), Hangzhou, Yangzhou, Shanghai, Ningbo, Zhengzhou, Kaifeng, and Yingchuan. I met historians, archaeologists, and sociologists. They were helpful and provided valuable insights. Several promised to write articles for me. All agreed that the new government policy of actively encouraging academic studies had created a favorable environment for research.

Those whose field was foreign religions said they were already probing into the development in China of such creeds as Nestorianism and Manichaeism, but had not previously considered Judaism. They were pleased I had brought it to their attention, and said it was a "blank spot" which they would attempt to fill. In Beijing I also received a number of enthusiastic responses and soon was able to obtain remarkable new findings regarding the Chinese Jews.

As a result I was able to translate, edit, and compile a volume of 12 essays by prominent Chinese scholars on the Jews of China. Together they trace the history of the Chinese Jews from their beginnings to the present. The book is called *Jews in Old China: Studies by Chinese Scholars.* (It was published in New York by Hippocrene in 1984.) Like scholars the world over, the Chinese disagree among themselves on some of the events and with their foreign counterparts. Although their accounts are intricate, I found them highly stimulating.

The scholars dug far back into history to trace the events leading to the migration of the Jews to China, and described what happened to them after their arrival. The following is a rough summary of what the Chinese scholars concluded:

930 BC: The Kingdom of Israel split into Israel, in the north, and Judah, in the south. Ten of the 12 tribes lived in Israel, two in Judah.

722 BC: Assyria conquered Israel and exiled the ten tribes, which gradually vanished. Various modern travelers claimed to have found remnants of them among the Tibetans, the Chinese Qiang people, and the American Indians. The Chinese saw no proof for any of these.

Eighth century BC: Isaiah prophesied the Jews would return from "Sinim." Some Western authorities asserted the word was derived from "Ch'in" (Qin), the first dynasty to rule over a unified China. But the "Ch'in" Dynasty did not come into existence until five centuries after Isaiah. Such a derivation was therefore not possible. Biblical scholars today believe Sinim meant Aswan in Egypt.

Fifth and fourth centuries BC: The Persians moved a large segment of the Jewish population to Persia and Media, south of the Caspian Sea.

Mid-fourth century BC: The Greeks, under Alexander of Macedon, conquered Palestine.

176 BC: Oppressive rule by Greek king, Antiochus IV.

175 BC: Some Jews fleeing the persecution arrived in Bombay.

164 BC: The Maccabees reconquered Jerusalem. The event was thereafter celebrated as the festival of Hanukah by most Jews, but not by those in Bombay or Kaifeng. This proves the Chinese Jews left their homeland before the Maccabean victory.

143 BC: Judah was re-established under the Hasmonean Dynasty.

63 BC: It was conquered by the Romans and named Judea.

AD 70: After a series of national revolts, it was again conquered by the Romans.

136: The Romans crushed the Bar Cochba revolt, and expelled the Jews from Jerusalem.

At this point the large-scale Diaspora, or dispersal, began. Over the next 500 years, many Jews migrated to Alexandria in Egypt, and thousands more to Persia and Arabia. Part of these continued north into Afghanistan, Balkh, Samarkand, and Bokhara in Central Asia, all on the Great Silk Road. Some, around the seventh century, moved overland into China's northwest, also called Chinese Turkestan, where they settled, though not in large number. A few advanced further into north China.

According to Chinese scholars, during the Tang Dynasty (618-907) large numbers of Arab and Persian merchants began sailing to China along what became known as the Silk Road by Sea. Jews, who by then had been living in Persia and Arabia for half a millennium, came with them. Because the Jews were similar to them in physical appearance, wore the same clothes, spoke the same language, and had adopted Arab and Persian names, the Chinese could not distinguish between them. They placed all in the same category: *se mu ren*—"people with colored eyes." Some of the Jews settled in seaport cities such as Guangzhou, Quanzhou, Yangzhou and Ningbo. Some moved north up the Grand Canal and the Bian River (which today no longer exists) to Bianliang (Kaifeng) and other northern cities.

There is some evidence that Jews traveled with the caravans that came overland via the Silk Road, perhaps in the first and second centuries, and certainly by the middle of the Tang Dynasty. In the arid deserts of Xinjiang in far northwest China two important finds were made in the early years of this century. One was a letter, never sent, by a Persian Jew. It was written in Persian, using Hebrew script, and on paper, which, at that time, only China manufactured. The other was a scrap of Hebrew prayer, also on paper. Both have been carbon-dated as eighth century.

Camel caravans were arduous, long and dangerous, not the kind of journey on which a man would bring his family. Chinese historians concluded that only when the constant wars among the small kingdoms in Xinjiang made the overland Silk Road too risky, and sea trade opened up in the eighth century, did a fairly large-scale immigration become possible. So far no tangible evidence has been unearthed testifying to a Jewish presence in earlier times, although Chinese silk, which then could only have come by land caravans, possibly including Jewish traders, was popular among Roman women.

For Northern Song (960-1127), during the reign of Emperor Zhen Zong, we have a date. A young Chinese scholar claims to have found an entry in a Kaifeng immigration registry noting the arrival of a number of Jews in 998.

After the Mongols conquered China and established the Yuan Dynasty (1206-1368), Jews were often mentioned in official documents. The Arabic *Jahud*, the Persian *Djuh*, both from the Hebrew *Yehudi*, were transliterated into Chinese phonetic equivalents such as *Zhuhu*, *Zhuwu*, or *Zhuhe* in laws and regulations concerning taxes and military service. Several Chinese historians believe that when the Mongol armies returned from their conquests in the Middle East and southern Europe many Jews came with them, either voluntarily or as captives. From a Yuan Dynasty regulation referring to Jews "wherever they may be," it is obvious there were Jewish communities in several parts of China.

The fullest documentation we have of the history of the Jews in China was written, in Chinese, by the Jews themselves. Three stone tablets dated 1489, 1512, and 1663 engraved to commemorate rebuildings of the Kaifeng synagogue, plus a tablet dated 1679 of the Zhao clan, together comprise a fairly complete story. They also created considerable controversy.

241

They called themselves "Israelites" and said they came from the "Western Regions," a vague term which embraced India and the Middle East. But they disagreed on the date of arrival. The 1489 inscription says Song (960-1279), the 1512 inscription says Han (206 BC-220 AD), and the 1663 inscription says Zhou (c. 11th century-256 BC). The later the inscription the earlier, and therefore more venerable, the claimed arrival date! But the inscriptions contain a wealth of material on religious practices, philosophical concepts, and relations with other Jewish communities.

The consensus of Chinese scholars is that 1163, the date given for the construction of the first Kaifeng synagogue, is probably correct and that the Jews must have arrived in Kaifeng a few decades earlier. They also agreed with the statement in the 1679 tablet setting the number reaching Kaifeng as 73 clans of some 500 families. Most of the argument centers around where the Jews lived between the time of the diaspora in the first century and their arrival in China, probably in the tenth.

Chinese historians note that except for a group that migrated to Alexandria in Egypt, the majority of the Jews who left Israel in the first century moved east into Arabia, Persia, Central Asia, and India. One school believes the Kaifeng Jews came from India because the inscriptions at the synagogue state they brought cotto goods, then manufactured in India but not yet in China. Annotations to the Kaifeng prayerbooks, however, are partly in Persian without a single word of any of the Indian dialects. Of course, they could have called at an Indian port en route, or even spent some years there, but apparently not long enough to have forgotten their Persian.

It is true there were and still are Jews in India near Bombay, as well as in Khaibar. Also in the seaport of Kolaba, about 40 miles south of Bombay. In the Junjira district of Kolaba there are people who call themselves "B'nei Israel" ("Sons of Israel"). They say they fled from persecution by Seleucid Greek King Antiochus IV in 176 BC, when the Greeks were ruling Israel, and settled in Kolaba a year later. The Khaibar Jews claim a much earlier arrival—the sixth century BC after the destruction of the First Temple in Jerusalem.

The Durani, an ethnic tribe in Afghanistan, also refer to themselves as "B'nei Israel" and claim descent from "Afghan," an alleged grandson of King Saul, who preceded David as king of the Israelites. Some of the people of Kashmir say they are descendants of the Ten Lost Tribes.

All the foregoing stories are noted by Chinese scholars without judging their authenticity. They agree there were Jewish populations in those areas as well as places like Balkh (formerly Bactria), Bokhara, and Samarkand in Central Asia, from which it was possible to enter China overland via the Silk Road, or to move south to the Indian seacoast and travel north by ship.

Several other Chinese cities undoubtedly hosted Jewish communities. The beautiful city of Hangzhou became the capital of what was known as Southern Song

(1127-1279) when the Song court fled Kaifeng under the onslaughts of the conquering Golden Tartars. Yang Yu, a Yuan Dynasty (1206-1368) historian noted that "all officials of the Hangzhou Sugar Bureau are rich Jews and Muslims."

Jews in Yangzhou, Ningxia, and Ningbo are credited in the Kaifeng stone tablets with contributing scriptures and money for restoration of the Kaifeng synagogue in the tenth century, after it was destroyed by a Yellow River flood. In 1982 I visited Ningbo, a large seaport south of Shanghai, and was shown the former "Persian Street" where the "Persian Hotel" once stood. In Tang and Song times "Persian" was the popular appellation for all Middle Easterners, including Jews. Fujian Province's major seaport from the seventh to the 14th century was Quanzhou. Chinese scholars quote Andrew of Perugia, the Catholic bishop of that city, who complained in a letter to his superiors in Rome: "We are able to preach freely and unmolested, but of the Jews and Saracens [Muslims] none is converted."

Marco Polo, Chinese historians say, spent several years in the Yuan capital, then called Khanbaliq and now Beijing. The 13th century Venetian wrote in his famous *Travels* that Mongol Emperor Kublai Khan reproached the Jews for deriding Nestorian Christian rebels who were defeated in battle in 1287 despite the cross emblazoned on their banners.

Chinese scholars believe the list of cities once containing Jewish communities will be expanded as historical and archaeological research progresses in China. It seems unlikely that most major commercial and cultural centers did not have at least some Jewish residents.

The Jewish community in Kaifeng was the largest and lasted the longest. From 1161 to 1663 its synagogue was built and restored ten times, proof of the strength of its congregations, the support they received from Jews in other cities, and the benevolent attitude the Chinese authorities maintained toward the Jews.

It was China's policy through the ages to welcome all foreign races and religions—not only because the Chinese are a highly civilized people, but because doing so was very much to China's advantage. The scientific and cultural knowledge they gained from foreign sources, both in China and abroad, was of incalculable value. The Jews flourished in this environment, particularly during the Ming Dynasty when China was the most advanced country in the world.

Difficulties grew in later years. A devastating Yellow River flood in 1663 destroyed the Kaifeng synagogue and nearly all of the scriptures. During the 18th and 19th centuries the Manchu rulers harshly repressed China's ethnic Muslims who were seeking autonomy. Because the Jews lived in close proximity, resembled them physically, and had similar religious practices, they were often mistaken for Muslims, and mistreated. Many Jews therefore concealed their identities and ceased their religious observances.

Several Chinese scholars pondered over this question: Why was it that Jews in other parts of the world managed to survive the cruelest oppression, while in China, under generally favorable conditions, they were gradually assimilated and finally vanished as ethnic and religious entities?

Their answer is that it was due to a combination of economic and cultural factors. In discrimination-free China, Jews, like everyone else, were entitled to compete in the civil service examinations for official posts. That meant memorizing, from childhood, the thousands of Chinese characters a person needed to be able to read and write, and then learning the voluminous Confucian classics which were the basis of the tests. No time was left for becoming well-versed in Hebrew and Judaism.

Starting in the 14th century an increasing number of Jewish merchants and scholars succeeded in the civil service exams and were appointed to office, a few to quite high positions, bringing them under the sway of traditional Chinese thought and Confucian teachings. In an environment of feudal officialdom and daily contact with Chinese bureaucrats, they changed their philosophic concepts. Ethnic consciousness dimmed, particularly among those Jews who had become powerful and prominent, and this in turn influenced all the members of the Jewish communities.

The breakdown of other boundaries followed. There was much intermarriage. After a few hundred years the Jews were virtually indistinguishable from the local Chinese in outward appearance, speech and way of life. Intermarriage, no longer an isolated phenomenon but a common practice, gradually eliminated religious traces from Jewish family life. It also weakened the cohesiveness of Jewish society and culture, and eradicated the Jews' unique character as a race.

By the middle of the 19th century, Chinese historians point out, even Jewish religious ceremonies were identical with those of the Han and Muslim populations with regard to mourning for parents, weddings and funerals. The Jews also adopted Chinese-style sacrifices to ancestors. On one of their stone tablets they noted with pride the similarity of the feudal Confucian "Three Duty Relationships" and "Five Cardinal Virtues" to their own spiritual ideals.

Soon no one could read Hebrew or conduct religious services. The synagogues, which had been the centers of social and cultural, as well as religious, life, physically collapsed during the severe financial depression which struck China in the late 19th century. Only a very small number remembered their Jewish origins. Most left their old communities and scattered to other parts of the country. With their language forgotten, their religious observances abandoned, their thinking and way of life and very names changed, in every aspect they had become Chinese.

In modern times there have been a few minor influxes of Jews into China— from Iraq in the early 20th century, Jews fleeing the 1905 and 1917 Russian revolutions, German and Austrian refugees from Nazi persecution in the 1930s and 1940s. These did not become Chinese, they remained Jews, unlike their ancient predecessors who for a time were both Jews and Chinese—and thus the only ones who could truly be categorized as "Chinese Jews."

Nearly all of the modern refugees have moved to other lands. At present there are probably several hundred Jews in China—students, scholars, diplomats, business people. But these are only transients, most of whom have never met. They are Jews in, but not of, China. There are no synagogues, no Jewish communities.

A few Chinese today know they are of Jewish descent. I went to Kaifeng immediately after the new government was established and was introduced to two men, both of whom worked in municipal government offices. If you looked at them closely and used your imagination you could see faint Middle Eastern traces. They said their grandfathers had told them that *their* grandfathers had said their family were Jews. They knew no more than that.

Time and *Life* and *Newsweek* sent reporters when word of these men got out. Their memories miraculously improved with each succeeding interview, and they were given considerable coverage in the Western press. The fact that some Kaifeng residents had the word "Jewish" entered on their identity cards was reported as proof of the presence of a Jewish community.

These people could very well have been of Jewish descent, but their sudden eagerness to state this was not due to a desire to affirm their Jewish cultural or religious identity. "Ethnics" were entitled to buy beef and mutton in special butcher shops from which the majority Han population was barred. Jewish descendants in Kaifeng were very few in number, and did not live together as a community, nor did they express any desire to revive their Jewishness. Some of them, however, grew curious about their roots and began delving into their family histories.

A growing number of Chinese and foreign academics are today studying the subject. My book, the first to present in English the findings of Chinese scholars, created a stir. I became something of a "mavin" in the field. Jewish visitors, and persons simply interested in an unexpected site of the Wandering Jews, sought me out. I attended conferences in China and abroad. I was invited to lecture about the Chinese Jews, I was interviewed in the media. While it didn't make me a practicing Jew, a sense of Jewishness was thrust upon me, I became more aware of myself as a Jew. The absence of discrimination among the average Chinese, the respect of Chinese scholars for Jewish achievements through the ages, stirred and strengthened my pride in being one little ripple in the Jewish cultural mainstream.

In 1982 my *China Pictorial* office asked me if I wanted to retire. I was well over the official retirement age (60 for men, 55 for women) but had stayed on because they were having difficulty in finding a foreign English-language editor. Now they had one, and I quickly acquiesced. Pic's work didn't keep me very busy, but I wanted to be able to devote all of my time to writing.

Because I had "joined the revolution" before the People's Republic was established I was put in a retirement category which provides full pay for life and a continuation of all my other perks—complete medical care, paid home leave vacations (round trip to America, wife included), and so on. Very generous.

Early in 1983, though one thing had nothing to do with the other, I was informed I had the honor of being appointed to the national body of the Chinese People's Political Consultative Council. Each province, and several of the major cities, has its own council. The national CPPCC was formed when the new government was proclaimed in 1949. It consisted mainly of members of various political parties and associations, and outstanding persons in every field of endeavor—the arts, sciences and professions, ethnic and religious leaders, businessmen, overseas Chinese. . . . It acted as an interim legislature. Its main task was to create a government structure and a congress.

Once this was done the council assumed its permanent function of watchdog and friendly gadfly. In addition to criticizing legislation and policy, it can propose amendments and alternatives. Its members, chosen by their colleagues, are usually tops in their particular sphere, and serve as a bridge between their own grassroots and the government. Although pretty much of a rubber stamp at first, the council has played an increasingly important role in shaping and implementing China's development.

American doctor George Hatem was the only foreign-born member until March 1983, when it was decided to invite about a dozen other foreigners who had become Chinese citizens. I was one of them. I was assigned to the News and Publications Committee. We had about 30 members, men and a few women, who had been leading journalists, editors and executives in the press, publishing, radio and TV. Because of the nature of their professions, they knew more of what was going on than most. Our committee meetings were lively, outspoken affairs at which some astonishing (to me) facts were revealed.

The national body had around 2,100 members divided into some 30-odd committees. It met in full plenum once a year, in spring, at the same time the National People's Congress met. We audited each other's sessions and exchanged documents. We took turns in meeting in the Great Hall of the People, a handsome building that can accommodate audiences of 10,000. Members who register to speak can address the full session.

The Standing Committee of the CPPCC meets constantly throughout the year. Members of the regular committees go off on frequent junkets in groups formed of persons from the various committees to investigate targeted areas which are having problems. I went on at least one such junket every year since 1983 and found them enormously rewarding. Not only was I able to get close-up pictures of

246

special situations, but I could also travel in the same group and talk for hours with some of China's most talented individuals.

Every place the groups visit has complaints or criticisms or requests for the Beijing administration. We submit full reports of our investigations and add our own recommendations. In addition, individual members can and do send in written criticisms and proposals regarding anything and everyone, including government leaders and organizations. These are forwarded to the persons or units concerned, which must formally reply in writing. Both the complaints and the replies are published in a special CPPCC journal. The communication continues until the critic, and the superior unit of the one concerned, are satisfied.

Of course not all problems are solved, but nearly all are aired. Many are also covered in the public press. It's a good form of democracy, eminently suitable for China at its present stage.

My mother died in May 1983, at the age of 90 years and eight months. Sister Ruth phoned from New Jersey to tell me. The grandchildren, who loved her dearly, called her "Kate" in the modern manner. But to me she was always "Mom"—warm, pretty, courageous. She had been going downhill in the past few years. On our last visit in 1981 Phoenix and I had pushed her in a wheelchair to a nearby park. Still, it was a sad day when we heard she had gone.

When I went to the States again the following year, 1984, this time without Phoenix, Ruth and I went through things Mom had hoarded as her most precious possessions. Included were my infant booties. They were of soft mauve flannel shaped like high button shoes and decorated by very small mother-of-pearl buttons. The booties were only about two inches long, but apparently they were too large for my infant feet. There was still some cotton wool stuffed in at the toes. A lump rose in my throat. The image of the chubby blond infant that was me was surely one of the last things Mom remembered when she died.

Nineteen eighty-four was a hectic year. In March I addressed the whole body of the CPPCC in the Great Hall of the People. I spoke on behalf of Israel Epstein, Ruth Weiss and Betty Chandler, three other foreigners who had become Chinese citizens. They were also on my News and Publications Committee. We drew up a joint statement criticizing the manner in which China was editing books and periodicals in foreign languages and promoting them abroad. Due to my Beijing-accented Chinese tones I was chosen to read it.

The Great Hall was full, with all of the CPPCC, auditors from the National People's Congress, ladies and gentlemen of the world media, and some of China's highest leaders. I stood on a podium bristling with microphones on the left side of stage, backed by a tier of members of the presidium. It was my first experience of speaking to an audience of 10,000. Fortunately, the klieg lights concentrating on me for the benefit of the photographers, blinded me to everything but the script in front of me. I had no time to be scared, and read slowly and clearly and, I was told, quite well.

I felt good about the experience, and not just because it was rare and exciting. It proved that we foreign-born members of the CPPCC could really participate and be useful. The Chinese call people in organizations who were more decorative than functional *hua ping* ("flower vases"). We had shown that we were no mere exotic appendages. From then on, I became busier in public life.

In April, with a letter to *China Daily* I began what is probably a quixotic battle with the education establishment to promote the use of romanization of the Chinese written language. I followed this with another letter in January 1986 to *China Daily*, and an article in *Beijing Review* at about the same time. To paraphrase, what I said in substance was this:

> The Chinese written language has a vocabulary of some 7,000 or 8,000 ideographs, commonly called characters. They are almost completely arbitrary with little logical connection between them. A minimum knowledge of at least 2,000 is needed to read a newspaper, 3,000 or 4,000 for slightly more complicated material.
>
> They are a great cultural heritage, and calligraphy is a beautiful art form. Those who have mastered them can read valuable literary, historical and scientific material of centuries past.
>
> The problem is that in modern China they are an impediment to literacy. This has been recognized by Chinese scholars from Lu Xun to Mao Zedong, both of whom called for the introduction of romanization, that is, spelling out the sounds of the words in the English alphabet.
>
> The traditionalists are vigorously opposed. Their argument is that the ancient written heritage would be lost, that the art form of calligraphy would vanish, that the one means of written communication between the main areas of different dialects would be gone. They grant that the complexities of the ideographs make them very difficult to memorize, read and write. They offer as a compromise some 2,000 simplified characters for daily use. They say computers make writing, type-setting and electronic communication much easier.
>
> With emphasis being placed more and more these days on earning money as early and as quickly as possible, there is less desire among young people to spend time in school. You can hear the news on radio or TV, or learn farming and mechanical techniques, or whatever else interests you, without being able to read. While estimates vary, the extent of functional illiteracy is horrendous, and growing worse.
>
> For those who wish to learn—except for the tiny minority who are able to get into and remain in school—the problem remains, as a practical matter,

248

insoluble. To attain an ability to read and write even 2,000 characters, which is the absolute minimum required, a person must spend endless hours practicing and using them, time few people are able to afford.

Simplification helps somewhat, but knowing only the simplified characters means you are unable to read the material written in the older complicated characters. You would have to know both the old and the new. And learning the simplified characters is only slightly less arduous than the traditional ones.

The contention of the old guard that because of regional pronunciation differences it is impossible to use a common alphabetical written language does not hold water. The example of England, Ireland, Scotland and Wales immediately comes to mind. In fact using the same written alphabetized English helps them iron out the differences in pronunciation, and this is further expedited by films, radio and TV programs in "standard" English seen and heard by millions in the United Kingdom every day.

Computers are fine, a scientific advance, but you still have to learn and be facile with some 2,000 Chinese characters before you can convert them into computer symbols—usually by spelling them out in alphabetical phonetics—and write them on a computer. You have to do the whole thing in reverse to read what someone else has written. It is so complicated that when I asked a Chinese scientist friend how he manages to communicate with foreign colleagues abroad, he said: "Why, we use English, of course."

What, then, is the solution? My proposal is this: Continue teaching the present simplified Chinese, with courses offered in the old characters for those who wish to specialize in earlier and ancient writings. At the same time adopt an alphabetized, romanized system of Chinese writing, and provide textbooks and other teaching materials in this form, to be used simultaneously and parallel with the materials offered in simplified characters. (There is talk of simplifying these even further.) Let the student learn both, but use whichever system enables him or her to move ahead fastest.

This should be done in both the regular schools and in adult literacy courses. There is no doubt that the ability to read and write will spread rapidly in China, creating a huge demand for books and newspapers in the easy romanized form, and facilitating every aspect of written communication.

Gradually the "simplified characters" can be abandoned, but the ancient ideographs should be taught as an integral part of calligraphy as an art form.

While it is not necessary that the entire population pronounce Chinese words the same as a precondition to the conversion of the written language, it is certainly useful and desirable that they should as early as possible. Attaining a standard national pronunciation is not nearly so difficult as it has been made out to be. (Foreigners erroneously call standard Chinese "Mandarin." Mandarins were the hated officials of the Qing Dynasty. The Chinese use the terms *guo yu*—"national language," or *putong hua*—"popular speech.")

Zhou Youguang, a friend of ours, tells an interesting story. He was the head of the Alphbetization Committee for the Reform of the Chinese Written Language. Not long ago, he and a team of experts went down to a small village in Fujian, a province where they speak a patois which other Chinese jokingly say sounds like "the twittering of birds." The team set up in a primary school, taught the kids *hanyu pinyin*, and how to pronounce it. This is the system of spelling Chinese in the romanized alphabet approved by the Chinese government. In two weeks they could handle it, by the end of a month they were almost at the level of children in any major city.

The point was if you can teach *putong hua* to natives of Fujian, you can bring standard speech to every nook and corner of the land. But none of this will happen unless the government gets seriously behind a drive promoting on national and local levels the widest possible use of *hanyu pinyin*.

If that is done, in one generation, China will have the biggest literate public in history, and the Chinese will be able to communicate easily with one another and all of the outside world.

This is the dream of many Chinese educators and intellectuals. But the hardcore traditionalists are still in control. We probably will have to wait until they pass on to their Great Reward before we can see some change. A pity. The potential benefits one and a half billion educated Chinese could bring to humanity are dizzying to the imagination.

Xinjiang, formerly called Sinkiang, and earlier still Chinese Turkestan, is in the far northwest. A huge autonomous region, it occupies one-sixth of China's area but holds only about one percent of the population. It has always been important historically, strategically and economically, abutting on India, Pakistan (part of which had once been Persia), and Afghanistan. Today, it also shares a 1,800-mile border with the former USSR. Although largely mountains and desert, it is found to possess extensive oil fields. A start has been made in exploiting them with the help of foreign investors.

I went there in September 1984 as a member of a CPPCC investigative team. We flew first to Urumqi, capital of the region. Paved roads, water, gas and electricity were only just becoming commonplace. The main body of the population were Uygur, a Turkic people, some of whom migrated to what became present-day Turkey. There were also Kazaks (forerunners of the European Cossacks), Kirgiz, Tatars (Tartars), and Uzbeks—all of Turkic stock. We met many Mongols and a few

Tajiks—a Persian people from the western border The Han—China's overwhelming majority, were a very small minority in Xinjiang.

They did, however, control most of the governing positions, and Han chauvinism was not entirely expunged. A performance of kindergarten children was put on for us in a park. The tots looked darling in their various ethnic costumes. There were about 200 of them.

"You must have a large kindergarten to accommodate so many kids," we said.

"Actually we have several kindergartens," our hosts explained, "separate ones for each national minority."

With the growth of industry, tourism and commerce, Urumqi is becoming more of a melting pot. In the library of the local university I met a lovely Tibetan girl reading a Chinese translation of a French novel *(Les Miserables)*. Her parents were both professors. Tibet is immediately south of Xinjiang. She was surprised that I was surprised.

A member of my CPPCC group from the Chinese Academy of Social Sciences was an expert on Middle and Far Eastern religions. Like me he was interested in the possible presence of Jews in ancient times. The main arteries of the old Silk Road from Central Asia, Europe and India had run through Xinjiang.

We called on scholars in the Xinjiang branch of the Chinese Academy of Social Sciences. They said they had no new evidence, but that a large cache of Tang and pre-Tang documents had been unearthed near Hotan, one of the great ancient cities. It was so voluminous, and they had so few specialists, it would take years to translate them all. They promised to get in touch with us if they found anything relating to Judaism and Jews. We never heard from them.

From Urumqi we backtracked east and a little south to Turfan, an oasis town famed for its mummies and grapes. The grapes grow everywhere in luxurious profusion, about a dozen varieties, each more delicious than the other. You sit under arbors of grapes around tables laden with fruit, nuts, a variety of mutton dishes, baked flat breads, and melons from Hami, which is still further east. There are several different types of Hami melon, all succulent and fragrant. One, resembling honeydew, is called the *wa lai se* melon because when vice-president Henry Wallace, an agricultural expert, visited the region in the early 1940s, he introduced the seed.

The mummies are less profuse than the grapes, but there are a lot of them. Particularly in the Tang Dynasty wealthy local officials chose Turfan as a propitious place for their tombs. We visited one of them, going down about ten steps to a long corridor tastefully decorated with murals on either side, pictures of processions of women and their maids, or troops of mounted warriors in full regalia. They were very striking. Their colors had faded only slightly, preserved by the dry desert air.

251

The mummies, too, were in almost perfect condition. These were not bandage-wrapped Egyptian royalty, but Chinese aristocrats wearing their own clothes and jewelry. There were so many of them that Xinjiang archaeologists were no longer impressed. In the museum they were simply lying on trestle tables, their features a bit dried out, but otherwise looking more or less the same they did the day they died over 1,000 years ago. Except for astonished visitors like us, no one paid much attention to them.

Depending on the condition of the bus, it is three or four days of bad road through mountains and desert from Turfan to Kashi (Kashgar), along the northern branch of the Old Silk Road. Since this was ill-advised for elderly members of our CPPCC junket, we were glad to accept the use of the governor-general's plane to cover a distance of 1,000 miles as the crow flies, though no crow in his right mind would attempt the journey.

If you were shipping a caravan of silk for the Middle East and Europe in the eighth century Tang Dynasty, you would leave China at Kashi, go through Samarkand and Merve, across Persia to Baghdad, and up the Euphrates to Antioch on the Mediterranean, dropping some merchandise off at stops along the way and picking up others. Kashi was a major station, coming and going.

It was, and still is, a metropolitan city. The population is predominantly Turkic Muslims. They are very religious, and pray several times a day at the numerous mosques, or wherever else they happen to be. Kashi is one great bazaar. You can buy horses, cows and camels—or shawls from Russia or Kashmir, or pressure cookers or color TV sets from I don't know where. There are no set prices. What you pay depends on your bargaining ability. The Kashis love to bargain. They look positively disappointed if you immediately give their asking price without a counter bid. I bought an exquisitely mounted dagger and a few Uygur skull caps, hand stitched, beaded or embroidered. They were joyfully received when I gave them as gifts in Beijing and New York. I kept one for myself, and wear it as a yarmulke at occasional seders.

On the return leg we spent another few days in Urumqi. We were taken to see Tianchi (the Heavenly Pool)—a large glacial lake surrounded by hills about 50 miles outside the city. In spite of its remoteness it was filled with Han and ethnic tourists, who took trips around the lake in large motor launches.

Though I didn't expect to see anyone I knew, I suddenly found myself face-to-face with someone I knew very well—my wife Phoenix. I had heard, of course, that she would be visiting Xinjiang with a group from the Dramatists Association, but I hadn't expected our itineraries to coincide so exactly. She was all smiles until she saw one of the members of my CPPCC group—Shen Zui.

He had been the head of the KMT gestapo in Chongqing. She was on the list of persons he had orders to arrest during the anti-Japanese war, but the war had ended before he had a chance to get around to it. He greeted her effusively at the Heavenly Lake, but she coldly ignored him. Our CPPCC was an open-door haven for all sorts of former enemies. It was Communist Party policy to forgive and forget. For those who had been on the receiving end it was difficult to be so generous.

When we returned to Beijing I learned that the Sanlian Book House had published a Chinese translation of *An American in China*. It was a truncated edition, since they cut material I had included to explain Chinese history, culture and customs to foreign readers. Still, they kept most of my photo illustrations and had a good drawing of me on the cover. I didn't mind a bit being something of a foreign celebrity.

"You Don't Look Very Chinese"
1985-1988

My sixth visit to the States was a long one. It lasted from November 1984 to January 1985, and centered mainly around the publication of *Jews in Old China: Studies by Chinese Scholars*. News of the event and favorable reviews appeared in major newspapers, and I was interviewed on talk shows for radio and TV. I spoke at the Asia Society, and was extremely touched that Carrington Goodrich, distinguished China scholar then in his nineties, came all the way down from Riverdale on the subway to hear me.

I was also surprised and pleased to be interviewed by *Maariv*, a leading Israeli newspaper. They carried an article in Hebrew a few weeks later, extending over four pages of a special supplement with photos in full color. In addition to the story of why and how I wrote the book, *Maariv* added a box entitled "Relations Between China and Israel in the Not Too Distant Future." An English translation runs as follows:

"I don't know whether there is a possibility of diplomatic relations between China and Israel. I don't know of any Israeli sales to China in the industrial or security fields. Personally, I hope there can be diplomatic relations between China and Israel in the not too distant future. The two countries can benefit each other in many ways, especially in trade and technology."

It is difficult to learn more from Sidney Shapiro about Sino-Israeli relations. He reveals nothing about this delicate matter. He speaks like a Chinese diplomat, choosing his words carefully, and referring only casually to his special status in China. Though he jokes that it was just "to save the cost of a hotel," he admits that during his present visit he was the guest of the Chinese ambassador in Washington for a few days. He knows the top men in China, and is very informed about what is going on in that country.

"In the 1950s there were conversations between the Chinese government and Israel," says Shapiro, carefully pointing out that he heard this from an American-Jewish rabbi. "Ben Gurion broke them off, under pressure from American Secretary of State Dulles, who was very hostile to China. I know of no further conversations, although of course that doesn't prove there haven't been any. From my personal experience I can tell you that the Chinese people have a very warm feeling toward Jews all over the world. The fact that I was able to write *Jews in Old China* is proof of that. Otherwise, how could I have received the help of local scholars, of expert historians, of members of the Chinese Academy of Social Sciences? Several of them even contributed articles to the book. Although the academy is not a government body, its members would not do anything against government policy. I am happy to be both a Chinese citizen and a Jew. I want to see good relations among all peoples."

Q: Do you know anything about a purchase by China of Israeli military equipment?

Shapiro: I would be the last to know. I have no involvement in such matters.

Q: What does a Chinese citizen know about Israel?

S: The average person doesn't know much. We read in our newspapers about the conflict between Israel and the Arab countries, about Israel's internal problems. News agency reports tell of Israel's economic crisis and the efforts of the government to solve it. We read about and see pictures of political demonstrations in Tel Aviv against the war in Lebanon.

Q: What is the Chinese attitude toward the Palestinians and Yasser Arafat?

S: The Chinese have no wish to be involved in the Middle East.

They are concentrating on their own problems, on developing their country and raising their standard of living. Intellectuals in the big cities discuss international affairs. This includes some of my friends. I cannot speak for the Chinese government, but China has stressed many times that she is part of the Third World, and has no interest in interfering in the affairs of other countries.

Jews in Old China brought me to the attention of the American media. The interviews were mainly about me and, through me, about China today. My questioners ranged from one end of the political spectrum to the other. The coverage on the whole was fair and impartial, although one or two fished very hard for items which would discredit China, or me. While still on the east coast I was telephone-interviewed from Washington by Jim Bohanan in December. Here is a sampling of some of his questions and how I fielded them:

Q: Why did you go to China and stay? What did China offer?

S: China offered excitement and a fabulous experiment in human endeavor, an attempt to pull up a country from the depths of degradation into a decent kind of society against tremendous odds. I was curious to see whether they could do it.

255

Q: Have they?

S: Yes, I would say on balance they certainly have, although Lord knows they've made plenty of blunders and have had some very rough times.

Q: The "cultural revolution" must have been one of them.

S: Yes, that was devastating. It almost finished them, but fortunately they came out of it. Certainly in the last three or four years they've made remarkable progress economically.

Q: Have you run into any discrimination as an Occidental?

S: No, I have not. The present administration has continued a tradition of 2,000 years of an open-arms policy toward all races and religions. That's always been the case in China.

Q: Are you at all sorry you made the move? You cut yourself off really from the bulk of your cultural heritage both as a Jew and as an American.

S: Well, not exactly. You know it was strange. All through the years, even when there were very bad relations between Washington and Beijing, we were able to listen to the Voice of America, for example, every day in the year. I had a subscription to a famous American news magazine, and people did come and go from time to time. Also, starting in 1971, I was able to make periodic visits to the States. This is one of them. It's the seventh in the past ten years.

Only Yue Sai Kan treated with *Jews in Old China* in depth. She taped two interviews of me for her TV series Looking East—one personal, one on the book—enlivened by color slides of the illustrations. Both programs were aired in February and March of 1985.

I was in Los Angeles early in 1985, preparing to return to Beijing, and was able to meet, at last, Albert Maltz. One of Hollywood's foremost film writers, Albert had run afoul of the McCarthy era witch-hunt. A blacklist of the best writers and directors in the motion picture industry—men who had the courage to speak out against incipient fascism in America—had been circulated among the big studio moguls by the Rabid Right. With their customary courage these gentlemen immediately surrendered and refused to employ any member of what became known as the Hollywood Ten. Several, including Albert Maltz, moved down to Mexico, where they continued to write scenarios under assumed names. One of them won an Oscar, and caused considerable confusion when he failed to appear at the award ceremony to claim the prize. The whole thing was ridiculous, but not a bit funny for the Hollywood Ten who were compelled to sell top-quality material to the studios at bargain prices.

Albert had been very interested in modern Chinese writing, but had not agreed with China's literary theory of "socialist realism." He carried on a heated correspondence with Mao Dun, Chinese novelist and subsequently Minister of Culture. After the Hollywood Ten again became "respectable" and Maltz returned to LA, he still felt it wiser to keep his exchanges sub rosa. I had volunteered to play mailman, and the letters were relayed through me.

Mao Dun had invited Albert to visit China several times. Meeting him now in LA I renewed the invitation, but he continued to hesitate. Maltz died a few years later without ever having come to continue his argument in person.

In June of 1985 I went to Qinghai with a CPPCC investigative group. The Qinghai-Tibet Plateau, the world's largest and highest plateau, is commonly known as "the roof of the world." It has an average elevation of over 4,000 meters above sea level. From its mountain heights the terrain slopes gradually east to the Pacific, carrying most of China's major rivers. Qinghai contains a large part of the country's three and half million Tibetans, spread over Gansu, Sichuan, Yunnan and, of course, Tibet.

We flew to Xining, capital of Qinghai Province, and received accommodations in a spacious, if rather seedy, government hostel. Xining means "Pacified West," originating from the conquest of large western ethnic regions by the powerful Han Chinese imperial armies. The dusty, dilapidated city was being brightened by much new construction. The fragrance of skewered mutton wafted from scattered street stalls, but our hosts warned us against the tidbits, if we valued our digestion.

This was my second visit to Qinghai. My first was in 1947, a few months after my arrival in China, and before I was married. I met a representative of UNNRA (UN Relief & Rehabilitation Administration) at a party in Shanghai, an Englishman, who wanted to check out a rumor of the presence of Russian refugees from the USSR in Qinghai. He asked if I would act as his interpreter, all expenses paid. I promptly agreed. It sounded like an exciting adventure. I neglected to mention that I could scarcely converse in standard Chinese, to say nothing of the gutteral northwest version.

We flew to Lanzhou in a converted US Army transport plane, and rested a day drinking hot chocolates made with yak milk. There was no train, or even a bus, to Xining, so we hitched a ride in the mail truck, which ran only twice a week. It took hours, fording streams suddenly formed by sporadic rain squalls, and nosing along hilly roads in the dark, but we finally reached Xining.

Qinghai was then ruled by Mohammaden warlord Ma Pufang, a potentate with an oriental-style harem, dozens of children, a crack modern army, and absolute control. He received us the day after we arrived. My Englishman was properly dressed in a conservative business suit, but I could wear only the riding breeches and high-laced boots I came in.

Ma Pufang had no interest in our attire. He assumed we could not have come without high Kuomintang approval, and he wanted us to convey his indignation to Chiang Kai-shek. The Generalissimo's flunkies in the mainland had the temerity to

257

break open the shoe boxes neatly packed with Qinghai opium and co-opt it without paying a penny, in flagrant violation of the understanding reached by both sides. Ma Pufang demanded that this dishonest practice be stopped immediately.

We promised to faithfully relay his message, and returned to our quarters, where we were instructed to wait. Before coming, people had told us the warlord gave his visitors valuable presents. To stimulate his generosity my English companion had sent him the excellent quality gold cufflinks he was wearing. We expected at least a pair of fine leopard skins. At last our gifts arrived, small but neatly wrapped. Eagerly we opened them. Autographed framed pictures of Ma Pufang!

It was some consolation the next day to be escorted to the Tibetan temple called Ta'er Monastery, or Kumbum, home of the Panchen Lama. Together with the Dalai Lama in Lhasa, he was the spiritual leader of the disciples of Lamaism, in other words, all of China's Tibetans. In 1947, he was still a little boy of nine or ten, guided and governed by a villainous looking regent. We were allowed to take pictures of him, sitting in an open courtyard in the sunlight with a small Pekinese dog at his feet. He became chief Lama for the whole country after the Dalai decamped in the 1950s with a band of disgruntled landlords and aristocrats.

I again visited Ta'er Monastery in 1985 with my CPPCC group. It was still lavishly decorated and ornamented with solid gold, paid for by the pennies of the impoverished believers. Year after year, these honest, ignorant tattered folk traveled miles to reach Kumbum, prostrating themselves every few steps, wrapped only in sheepskins which served both as their garments and their bedding, bringing their painfully accumulated precious coins to exchange for a perfunctory blessing.

It infuriated me and churned my stomach. I agreed in principle with the government's policy of freedom of religion. But it seemed to me not enough was being done to bring more enlightenment and intelligent application to the clergy and their followers. Even the insides of the temple depressed me. The monks carved exquisite little figures of colored yak butter, set in religious panoramas. Their artistry attracted many visitors. But the temple interior was dark and gloomy with dreary old hangings, and misty with incense smoke. I couldn't wait to get out into the fresh air again.

I celebrated my seventieth birthday in December. My office threw a big party for me in a hotel dining room. Friends and colleagues made speeches, graciously exaggerating my merits and accomplishments. I basked in the warm, family atmosphere, so typically Chinese. But it all seemed unreal. Seventy, that was old. I didn't see myself as old—except when I looked in the mirror. But it didn't worry me. I still had a lot of mileage left.

The Chinese have a phrase *Yi ren xiang qing*—"people in the arts despise each other" to describe worthies who back-bite anyone and everyone in the same field. The malady is unfortunately well-known among Chinese intellectuals. In

November 1986, they had an opportunity to see it demonstrated in the international arena.

The occasion was the International Conference on Contemporary Chinese Literature convened in Jinshan, a pretty suburb of Shanghai. I was one of the Chinese representatives. Over 50 delegates from some 20 countries attended, including authors, translators and critics. Their impressions of modern Chinese writings and translations ranged from favorable to enthusiastic. Several wondered why, in over 80 years of Nobel Peace prizes, not one Chinese creation was deemed worthy of an award.

Professor Malmquist, delegate from Sweden and a participant in the academy which chooses the literary award recipients, offered an "explanation." He admitted many of the Chinese works were of top quality, but claimed their translations were poor. He singled out novels translated and published by Beijing's Foreign Languages Press generally, including my rendition of Ba Jin's *Family*.

Modesty prohibited me from retorting with a squashing refutation, but a number of other delegates did it for me. They hailed my translation as one of my best, pointing out that it was used as text material for university English courses, and that an American publishing house did me the honor of reprinting it as their own property, although it did acknowledge me as the original translator. (Since China had not yet joined the international copyright convention I was unable to sue them.)

Another delegate noted that Malmquist was a professor in the Chinese Department of Stockholm University, and himself an active translator of Chinese literature. He wondered whether this might not have influenced the impartiality of the good professor's judgment.

In any event, wrathful delegates cried, this was just a flimsy excuse and beside the point. Prizes should be given for the original works, not for their translations. Previous awards showed that the Nobel Academy heavily favored European over third-world authors, that it opposed politically liberal writings, that it never gave a prize to a work from a "communist" country unless it attacked that country's system of government. Anyhow, several delegates insisted, it was wrong to overestimate the importance of the Nobel Prize for literature. The correct appraisal of a writer's talent comes from his own society, from his readers, not from some foreign official body.

Jews in Old China: Studies by Chinese Scholars was published in Tel Aviv in Hebrew under the title *Bnei Yisrael Besin Haatika* in 1987. The translator was Yakov Sharat, son of the famous Moishe Sharat who had served concurrently as Minister of Foreign Affairs and Prime Minister in the 1950s. Perhaps partly on the strength of this, plus the wide circulation of the English original, I was invited to attend the Second Asian-Jewish Colloquium in Hong Kong.

259

The conveners had approached the Chinese Academy of Social Sciences and said they would have representatives from all major Asian countries, but as yet no one from China. Could the academy recommend a Chinese scholar who could report on the history of the Chinese Jews? "We know just the man," the academy replied, and gave them my name. I had done a book on the subject, and I was a citizen of China.

Eyebrows rose when I walked into the conference hall in Hong Kong in March that year, and was introduced as "the participant from China." Inevitably, one of the delegates quipped, "You don't look very Chinese."

"And you don't look very Jewish!" I retorted. They came from such countries as Japan, Israel, the Southeast Asian nations, and Australia. We all laughed.

Sponsored by the World Jewish Congress, the conference was chaired by Malcolm Fraser, former Prime Minister of Australia, Sir Zelman Cowen, former Governor-General of Australia, Yoram Dinstein, Pro-Rector of Tel Aviv University, and Isi Leibler, President of the Asia Pacific Region of the WJC. I read my paper on the history of the Chinese Jews, and speakers reported on the situation and problems of the Jews in their respective countries. We also heard about anti-Semitism in Japan, which has almost no Jews at all. It was a good conference, lively and informative.

While in Hong Kong I was interviewed by the press, and on the radio and TV, almost entirely about China today, and very little about the Jews. That was fine with me. It gave me another opportunity to put in a few licks for the home team. Though Hong Kong was better informed, the Western media was still delivering reams of misinformation about China, as much out of ignorance as of malice. They kept trying to judge Chinese events on the basis of their own cultures, their own standards, their own preconceived notions of China. Sometimes they were hampered by Beijing's inaccurate translations of political terminology. I referred to this in an interview in March of 1987 on Hong Kong Today, Channel 3:

Q: Perhaps you can shed some light on the very recent happenings— the backlash against bourgeois liberalism, for instance. How do you see things changing in China?

S: First of all, as a professional translator I would like to say "bourgeois liberalism" is a terribly inept and misleading rendition of the sense and what it means in Chinese. Nobody is opposed to liberalism or liberalization in China. It seems to me what they are really worried about is the attempt of some persons to superimpose bourgeois political concepts on a socialist society. Certainly there are various other aspects of bourgeois society which are very welcome in China—bourgeois management and technology, etc. I don't myself, and I don't think the Chinese, particularly oppose what is bourgeois in an overall generic sense.

I felt, too, there were many things in the West well-worth being learned by the Chinese. One was a concept of law and legality. Matters which were blatantly illegal were often accepted with equanimity. Some were reported with only mild reproof in the press. I wrote a hot letter about one such situation to the English language *China Daily* in June 1987. It said:

> Your report on how legal knowledge was publicized in Huaiyuan County, Anhui Province, would be comic if it were not so disgraceful. Local officials and policemen, in the name of instructing petty offenders on observation of the law, arbitrarily imposed fines totaling 200,000 yuan for lateness or absence from "lectures." Their hapless victims were "handcuffed, trussed up, beaten, or prodded with electric police batons" until they paid in full. Two thousand yuan was pocketed by the "instructors," 60,000 yuan went to the "officials." The remaining sum—about 150,000 yuan—simply vanished.
>
> Although these mentors in legality are apparently guilty of extortion, fraud, assault and battery, malfeasance in office, and most likely grand larceny, judging by your report no legal action has been taken against them. A few have been dismissed from their posts, or required to write "self-criticisms"—mild slaps on the wrist for serious major offenses.
>
> Under the circumstances the poor beneficiaries of this course on law observance will probably come away with the impression that in Huaiyuan County, at least, it doesn't matter what crimes you commit; what counts is having the right connections.
>
> A nationwide campaign to acquaint the public with the law and concepts of legality is certainly necessary. But the authorities should make very sure that the teachers are exemplary citizens who are themselves completely law-abiding, and that those who commit crimes are prosecuted, regardless of their position or status.

China Daily published my letter, deleting my third paragraph about the convenience of having the right connections. I hope the delicacy of the editors was not due to vestigial feudal etiquette which frowns on saying anything unpleasant about persons in authority, even those who tolerate violations of the law.

This reluctance is the flip side of the feudal coin which teaches respect for parents, teachers, elders, and those generally of higher rank. Such respect is still fundamental in China today, and makes for a pleasant well-ordered society, but it is in danger of being eroded by individualistic, selfish impulses arising from an increasingly materialistic environment.

261

Phoenix went with me in the autumn of 1987 on a home leave to the States. We covered more territory and met more people than at any other time before or since. I had agreed to speak at a dozen or so chapters across the country of the US-China People's Friendship Association. During the months of September and October we covered Los Angeles, Denver, Minneapolis, Madison, Milwaukee, Chicago, New York, Washington DC, Dallas, Tucson, San Francisco, Portland, Seattle, and back to LA. In each place we stayed at homes of members of the association I think we learned more about our respective countries and each other chatting over coffee at their kitchen tables than in the more formal meetings held by the chapters. Our hosts also took us around and showed us the local sights. It was very homey and satisfying.

In a side-trip from New York we went up to Canada as the guests of impresario Moses Znaimer and attorney Michael Levine. We had met them in Beijing a few years before when they came to China as members of a motion picture delegation. Moses had a TV station (which interviewed me), a simulated rocket trip into space, and a play being performed on all three floors of a house through which the audience was free to wander.

Michael was a prominent entertainment lawyer, and the nephew of Sadye Bronfman, a grand old lady extremely active in Jewish affairs. I spoke about the Chinese Jews at the Sadye Bronfman Centre in Montreal. Sadye, then over 90, gamely sat through it all and, when it was over, came up and kissed me. Eldest son, Edgar, is today president of the World Jewish Congress and, I would imagine, a large stockholder in the family-run Seagram Company, brewer of the famous whiskey.

The Royal Ontario Museum in Toronto asked me to give a talk on the 2,000-year-old terra-cotta warriors unearthed from an imperial tomb in Xian. I had written the preface to a pictorial album about them we had published in Beijing. Fu Tianchou, prominent sculptor and close friend, did an excellent job on the text, providing a detailed exposition not only on the artistry but on the technical methods employed as well. We planned the book and put it together. It sells in three or four language editions.

The first clue to the existence of the relics was revealed in the 1920s, when a man digging a well struck water and, beside it, a life-size figure of a terra-cotta warrior. When he exposed the entire figure the water suddenly drained away. Sure that the warrior was "evil," the man hastily reburied it. He said nothing about it, until 1974 when other farmers, digging another well about a kilometer and a half away, unearthed fragments of terra-cotta warriors and horses, which experts identified as dating from the Qin Dynasty (221-206 BC). They were from the tomb of Qin Shihuang, the first emperor and the founder of the first feudal empire known as Qin, from which foreigners derived the name "China."

A man of remarkable talents, he created a centralized autocratic government which was maintained in virtually the same form until the fall of the last imperial dynasty in the early 20th century. He promulgated a code of law, and standardized the written language, currency, weights and measures—even the axle lengths of wagons and chariots.

He built a vast network of tree-lined roads, 50 paces wide, radiating from the Qin capital Xianyang, 20 kilometers north of Xian. He joined into a single 3,000-kilometer Great Wall (extended to 6,000 kilometers in later dynasties) the separate walls previously erected by the northern states to deter raiding nomadic tribes.

For his personal glorification he built a number of elaborate palaces, the largest of which, E Pang, was said to have had a reception hall capable of holding 10,000 people. The only other colossal undertaking that matches this magnificent palace was his mausoleum. Covered by a huge mound on the slopes of the Lishan Mountain south of the Weihe River, it was originally enclosed by rectangular inner and outer walls, four and six kilometers respectively in perimeter.

Although the mausoleum is yet to be excavated and explored, we know from written records that it was an underground palace complex. According to Sima Qian, who wrote his *Records of the Historian (Shiji)* some 100 years after the First Emperor's death, the ceiling of the tomb chamber is a model of the heavens, and its floor a map of the empire. Jewels and other treasures buried within are guarded by devices triggered to release arrows at any intruder. The workmen who installed the finishing touches were buried alive to ensure that the secret of the entranceway died with them.

Archaeologists had long suspected there must be more to the imperial interment than what Sima Qian described. In earlier times members of the aristocracy were buried with retinues of sculptured figures to accompany them on their journey to the nether world, instead of the humans and animals once ritually sacrificed and entombed together in the still more distant past. Where was the First Emperor's entourage? Now, after two millennia of silence the archaeologists had the answer.

Painstakingly, they set to work and unearthed a veritable terra-cotta army of warriors and horses standing in formation in corridors between rows of rammed earth in three pits. Wooden pillars and beams supported roofs of woven mats covered by alternate layers of plaster and earth up to ground level. Many of the figures were in fragments and had to be reconstructed piece by piece. Today, on exhibition are some 1,000 warriors and 24 horses, a small fraction of the 6,000 figures the pits are estimated to contain.

One of the most amazing features of the terra-cotta warriors is not only their difference in dress, armor, weaponry, headgear and hairstyle, but in their physiognomy and facial expression. Monotony is a common failing of group sculpture. But here we have about 1,000 figures, each with his own distinctive personality. We see men of different ages, temperament and ethnic origin. This was achieved by creating ten different head shapes and faces. Eyes, eyebrows, noses, lips and ears also vary widely.

The warriors' heads were made from several dozen different molds in a semi-finished state, then embellished by hand. Even heads from the same molds often differed. Ears were pressed out in separate molds and affixed later. So were moustaches. Hair, headgear, lips and eyes also show traces of being added separately.

The horses are vivid recreations of a large vigorous breed which could gallop long distances at high speed. With strong, well-shaped bodies, full nostrils, small ears cocked forward alertly, they look ready to spring into motion. Their saddles, covered with rows of studs and decorated with tassels, originally were painted red, white, brown and blue, and designed to look like leather. The quality of the workmanship is extremely high. The saddles have no stirrups, which did not come into China until around the fifth century.

All the figures were modeled from a finely textured gray clay which when fired produced a delicate finish. The figures were painted in colors after firing. Only traces of this paint remain today.

The variety of bronze weapons, still sharp and shining despite 2,000 years underground, demonstrate the advanced level of Qin metallurgy. Chemical analysis has revealed that the swords and arrowheads are primarily of bronze and tin with traces of rare metals, and that their surfaces were treated with chromium. It must have taken many years of experimentation to create the Qin crossbow with its intricate trigger mechanism. Similar weapons did not appear in Europe until centuries later. The Qin crossbows were small enough to be wielded by mounted archers. Their darts easily pierced the shields of the well-armed Roman legionnaires in the battle of Sogdiana (Samarkand, in present-day Uzbekistan) in 36 BC.

The finds are enclosed in a large hangar-like exhibition hall with an area of 16,000 square meters, now open to the general public. Although only a fraction of the tomb has been exposed so far, it is already hailed by many as "the Eighth Wonder of the World."

When I finished speaking at the Royal Ontario Museum there were many questions about this archaeological wonder, and only a few about the Jews in old China, and even less about China today. Perhaps, like me, my listeners were over-awed by the reminder of what an ancient and highly cultured past modern China springs from. You never know what an audience is going to ask when you are a Jewish-American-Chinese who has lived for years in what to them seems an exotic land.

Questions in America ran more true to form, but they were penetrating, and made me think carefully. On the "Midday with Sandra Gair" program in Chicago on WBEZ in September, this is how I was quizzed:

Q: Do you feel over the years that you have changed in any significant way?

S: Yes, very much so. When I first arrived I was, I believe, a typical brash young New Yorker, ex-lawyer —

Q: Oh, ex-lawyer?

S: Yes, I'd been a theatrical lawyer in the Paramount Building before World War II for a couple of years. I came from a background where I was taught to believe that the world is out to get you, and you'd better hit first and scramble as hard as you can to get to the top, and not be too fussy about stepping on other people's necks in order to get up there. I don't claim to have been all that villainous, but I certainly was influenced by that type of society.

When I got to China I found that here were people—I'm not talking just about the Communists or the political people—who were very kindly and considerate, very family-oriented people who, if you were their friend, there was absolutely nothing they wouldn't do for you, to an embarrassing extent.

You couldn't help having some of it rub off on you. I became ashamed of my crasser and less virtuous qualities and, I hope, changed a bit.

I found that no matter how brilliant and hard-pushing and upwardly mobile you were, in that society at that time you could not accomplish much. You simply had to work with your group in some form of collective or cooperative endeavor.

Studs Terkel interviewed me that same afternoon for his program on WFMT. We had met a few years earlier in Beijing in the home of Dr. George Hatem, whom Studs greatly admired. He had the warmest feeling for China, and we had a very good chat. On only one point I felt called on to contradict him. He said:

Q: China is a very conservative country, its history, its legacies. . . .

S: I don't know I would agree with that entirely, Studs. Up to the 16th or 17th century, China was the most advanced country in the world, not only culturally but scientifically and technologically. You don't get that way without taking chances and experimenting. I think it was only later that they became ingrown and developed a "Middle Kingdom" kind of mentality and grew partly defensive because they were already feeling the beginnings of incursions of the colonial countries. That was when they drew back.

Q: You're right, you're right, of course. I remember George Hatem telling me there were scores and scores of revolts and rebellions through all the centuries that were put down. So that the upheavals and wanting another way were always there.

S: Yes, the upheavals were very bold, courageous and outgoing. But what they wanted to do was put new wine in old bottles. Of course, historical conditions were not such that they could conceive of having a social and political system other than feudalism. They weren't even ready for capitalism, to say nothing of socialism. All they wanted was the clean honest man on a white horse, the good official who would be a good emperor.

I was pleased, intellectually sated, by the time we returned to Beijing in November. It was a pleasure exchanging ideas with bright, probing minds. I was able to give them something and, at the same time, it sharpened my own thinking and showed up the gaps and flaws in my own knowledge.

The death of Rewi Alley saddened me at the end of 1987. We were quite close. It became routine for me to visit him every Sunday morning in his park-like compound that had housed the Italian Embassy before liberation and was now the headquarters of the Chinese People's Association for Friendship with Foreign Countries.

Rewi, a New Zealand engineer and poet, had come to China in the 1920s, and was hired as a factory inspector in the International Settlement in Shanghai. The workers were children whose average age was 14. They were severely undernourished. Their ulcerated hands were being eaten away by the chemicals used in the chromium-plating process. The kids worked long hours, and lived on the premises in miserable quarters. Their pay was a pittance. They were sickly, disease-ridden. The death rate was high.

Daily exposure to these horrors, and the prevailing miseries all around him in Kuomintang China, quickly pushed Rewi Alley over to the side of the revolution. He worked diligently for the Communist underground, concealing a secret transmitter in his flat, helping those on the politically "wanted" list escape, delivering guns, and staying in close contact with Madame Soong Ching Ling. Not a Communist herself, Soong was the chief liaison of the Party in Shanghai. Luckily, as the widow of the revered Sun Yat-sen, she was beyond harassment by Chiang Kai-shek's gestapo.

I met Rewi in 1947, when he came down to Shanghai for a meeting of the China Industrial Cooperatives (CIC), where I was serving as legal adviser. Rewi was then organizing rural handicraftsmen into cooperative workshops and factories that were producing much-needed consumer goods and military supplies. During the nominal truce period between the Kuomintang and the Communists, to the rage of the Chiang Kai-shek clique Rewi had seen to it that the Liberated Areas got their share. Subsequently, he became the head of the Baillie School in the wilds of Gansu Province, where he taught famine refugee children literacy and mechanical technology. This further irritated the Kuomintang,

266

since their creed was to keep poor peasant kids ignorant and poor. Only the timely arrival of the PLA saved Rewi and the Baillie School from an all-out attack by Nationalist troops.

After liberation he moved to Beijing. He continued to act as a guiding force for the CIC, and wrote several books about his experience, translated Chinese Tang poetry and created scores of poems of his own. Mainly, he was a source of wisdom and enlightenment for innumerable callers from all over the globe who had questions about China. They ranged from scholars to diplomats, to curious ordinary folk. He was on first-name terms with princes and prime ministers. George Bush, then the US Ambassador to China, always hailed him with a cheery "Hi, Rewi!"

My regular Sunday morning visits were something we both looked forward to. If for any reason I couldn't show up, Rewi would phone and want to know why. He was forever trying out his latest poems on me. (I said I was the equivalent of the illiterate peasants to whom Tang poet Bai Juyi used to read his verses to test whether they were comprehensible to the uneducated.) I wrote a preface to one of his volumes, and a few book reviews. I, of course, sought his opinions on some of my own scribbling.

What we enjoyed most was just chatting about the latest news and gossip. We talked freely, and sometimes scathingly analyzed events and personalities, domestic and international. Rewi's experience, his vast store of knowledge of how things worked in China, were invaluable. Occasionally I could supplement with a bit of information and a few personal observations.

I loved and respected Rewi. When he died in December 1987, three weeks after his ninetieth birthday, my sense of loss was profound.

si Leibler, one of the sponsors of the Asian-Jewish colloquium I had attended in Hong Kong, invited Phoenix and me to Australia in April 1988, to talk about Jewish affairs in China. I spoke at a few places and was interviewed by the press. As usual, at least half the questions were about present-day China. Isi was very hospitable. We traveled to the shore and saw silly penguins waddling out of the sea at dusk. In Melbourne we watched a play about miscegenation in pure colloquial Australian which we couldn't understand. We were enchanted by Australia, with its manicured parks and splendid beaches—at least those parts we were able to visit around Melbourne and Sydney.

On the way back to Beijing we stopped for three days in Singapore, and were simply staggered by the cleanliness and order. Laws against spitting, drunkenness and jaywalking were strictly enforced. Locals boasted you could eat off the floors of their numerous little restaurants. After visiting a few we were ready to believe them. Standards of education were high and there was little unemployment. It gave me, as a former New Yorker and a present Beijinger, an enormous boost to see that with an honest government and unrelenting effort it was indeed possible to create a

267

clean livable city. True, the big metropolises are much more complicated but, nevertheless, the principle is there.

During our visit to the States in 1987, we had spent a few days in Los Angeles with Jerry Mann and his wife Marian in their spacious home in Pacific Palisades. We had introduced Marian to Jerry some years before, and the fruit of their happy marriage was their little daughter Sarah, then about six years old. Sarah had fallen in love with Guo Xin (Fragrance) when we showed a picture of our granddaughter, and pleaded that we send Xin to live with her and be her big sister. We had all laughed indulgently. Phoenix and I assumed our daughter Yamei would never allow her ten-year-old child to move so far from home.

Marian again made the proposal in the summer of 1988, To our surprise Yamei was all for it. Xin would be able to start school in September. Hurried preparations were made. Xin wanted a foreign name, and she chose Stella because Xin sounds something like Xing, another ideograph which means star.

We got her a Chinese passport, a US visa, a plane ticket, and put her on an Air China flight to San Francisco, where Marian would meet her. We asked a couple of Chinese diplomats who were taking the same flight to look after her, and deliver her to Marian. Marian wasn't there when the plane arrived, so they turned her over to the airport attendants. Marian's flight from LA had been delayed. When she rushed in half an hour later, out of breath, Stella was sitting quietly on a bench, waiting. After Stella conveyed by sign language that she was not too tired, they took the next plane back to LA, and Pacific Palisades.

Stella and Sarah shared the same bedroom. Closets overflowing with a profusion of toys, their own video and TV, clothes galore added to the Chinese child's confusion. Gradually, she was able to converse with Sarah—kids can always clear language barriers much better than adults. Marian drove them to school every morning, and picked them up late each afternoon. It was a very good LA municipal primary school which conducted special classes for children just arrived from foreign lands. There were several.

For a few months Stella wept softly into her pillow every night. She was very homesick, and everything was so new and alien. It also infuriated her not being able to talk—a painful situation for a talkative little girl. But by the end of the year, Stella was sitting in the same classes with the other American kids and arguing with Sarah over the merits of various candies and junk foods. We spoke to her by phone every few weeks, and were convinced she really meant it when she said she was doing fine.

In October, George Hatem died. He was my best friend in China. An American doctor, fresh out of med school, he had come to Shanghai in 1933 to pick up experience in tropical and venereal diseases before returning home to North Carolina. Except for a few visits he never left.

George went to Yanan in response to Mao Zedong's request for an American doctor in 1936 and gave medical treatment to everyone from simple peasants to the highest Communist Party leaders. He set up the first real hospital in the Liberated Areas, traveled with the troops to the front, and became a "diplomat without portfolio" extraordinary, meeting with scores of visiting foreign dignitaries and journalists, and explaining to them in idioms they could understand what these Chinese "Reds" were all about.

He was appointed advisor to the Institute of Skin and Venereal Diseases, and later the Ministry of Public Health, after the People's Republic of China was established. He became a world authority on leprosy and public health, and won several international awards. But his activities as unofficial foreign liaison never stopped. He was jokingly admired as the "best PR man China ever had."

George was also guide and mentor to the whole British and American expatriate community. We came to him with our medical problems and with all the questions about the many political developments we could only imperfectly understand. George was always there, and sometimes ahead of us in helping set things right. If there hadn't been the phrase "Let George do it," someone would have had to invent it. Relaxed, jocular, unpretentious, like many Americans, he was at the same time a soft-spoken Southern gentleman, invariably patient and considerate.

Perhaps because we understood each other so well, I learned more about China from George than from any other source. Particularly with the advent of the "cultural revolution," Rewi Alley and I were constantly grilling him, demanding that he explain the failings of Mao Zedong, and the decline in the moral atmosphere. A loyal member of the Chinese Communist Party, George was at the same time a completely honest man. His answers, though occasionally distressing, made sense to me.

He said, to oversimplify, that Mao had "stopped listening to Mao Zedong," in other words had stopped adhering to the precepts he himself had advocated. To a lesser extent, this was also true of the Communist Party generally, said George. The Party had failed to come forward with a new clearly defined ethical program to replace the faulty concepts it had destroyed.

In the end, though everyone tried to slow him down, George worked himself to death. He had been suffering from a number of ailments for years, and eventually, in October 1988, Dr. George Hatem, known to millions as Ma Haide, died of cancer and other complications.

As the saying goes, "They don't make many like him any more."

The absence of guiding standards was markedly manifest in the kind of television programs being aired. I complained about this in a letter to *China Daily* which they published in November. It said:

In view of the quantities demanded to fill the ever-increasing viewing time, a small proportion of mediocrity can be forgiven. What is to be hoped, however, is that the really bad items can be kept out.

For example, in a mini-series called *Hunter*, we have our hero arriving at the flat of his girlfriend late at night, marching off with her to the bedroom and, after being served breakfast in bed by the young lady the next morning, leaping happily out, naked, to join her, at her invitation, in a shower. One can hardly complain about the deterioration in the morals of some of China's young if this is the kind of "cultural" items we are presenting.

The same gentleman, who is a plain-clothes policeman in a major US city, later calls on a man he "questions" by punching him to the ground, thrusting him toward an open window and threatening to push him out. This is illegal and in violation of police department regulations in America, China and every civilized country in the world. Surely the television network is not suggesting that this is a procedure worth copying?

About the same time my instincts as a lawyer were outraged by something I learned from a report in an American periodical. This is the letter I dashed off for the Minister of Justice:

The late comrade Ma Haide told me that the cruel exploitation of child labor which he saw in foreign-owned factories in pre-liberation Shanghai aroused his deep hatred of the oppressors, and was one of the main spurs which caused him to take the revolutionary road.

I was shocked to read in the enclosed copy of an article in the October 31 issue of the US magazine *Business Week* that, 50 years later in the People's Republic of China under the leadership of the Chinese Communist Party, exploitation of child labor is again occurring in four of the special economic zones. Moreover, although such activity is illegal, the factory bosses insolently flaunt their contempt for Chinese sovereignty and law, and callously disregard the welfare of the children. I was surprised to note the local authorities seem unable to prevent this.

I hope the Ministry of Justice will take immediate steps to implement the following measures:

1) Remove all children under 17 from the factories and return them to their families and schools.

2) Bring criminal prosecutions against the factory bosses and their underlings for their violations of the law, and impose sentences of fines and/or imprisonment.

3) Publicize these proceedings in the press, and encourage local people's organizations to educate the parents of children and the general public in the legal and moral issues involved.

4) Urge the local press and both the Communist and non-Communist Party organizations to play a more active role in observing and reporting any abuses of children in the future.

I never had any reply, nor did I expect one. The Chinese, among the most courteous people in the world, rarely answer mail if they are officials, or even acknowledge receipt. All I was hoping was that my letter might attract attention, and perhaps stir up some action. I'm not sure that it did. Exploitation of child labor continues in south China, though not as much as before.

Israel, Tiananmen, and
Chinese Law
1989-1990

The biennial Jerusalem International Book Fair notified me in March, 1989 that they would be exhibiting *Bnei Yisrael Besin Haatika*, Yakov Sharat's Hebrew translation of my *Jews in Old China: Studies by Chinese Scholars*, and invited Phoenix and me to attend as their guests. We were excited by the prospect, but were sure the Chinese authorities would not agree, since there were no diplomatic relations between China and Israel.

We applied for passports anyhow. They were granted promptly, on approval, we heard later, at a very high level. The Israelis mailed in visas from their Consulate in Hong Kong.

We flew from Beijing to Frankfurt, where we were able to board an El Al plane. After only a few hours we arrived at the Tel Aviv Airport. Security was tight. Everyone's luggage was carefully searched. The man who met us drove us to Jerusalem, pointing out on the way scenes of Arab ambuscades during the last war. He delivered us to Mishkenot Sha'ananim, the guest house of Teddy Kollek, mayor of Jerusalem, an honor usually reserved for world famous figures in literature and art. The apartment we occupied bore the brass nameplate "Artur Rubenstein." Though pleased, we were mystified by this red-carpet treatment.

It all became clear the next day. Ruthi Kahanoff, then First Secretary of the Asia Division of the Ministry of Foreign Affairs, came to call for us in her rather beat-up sedan. We were in fact guests of the Ministry. Ruthi was to help us arrange our program and be our escort for the next two weeks. She had studied Chinese language and culture in Beijing, and was completely in love with China. She was also charming, beautiful, and very competent.

All our expenses, including air fares, were paid by the Israelis. In answer to questions by a reporter, a ministry spokesman, who refused to be identified, said we were tourists, "but not ordinary tourists." No one believed us when we denied having been sent to probe the possibilities of establishing diplomatic relations. We were the first Chinese citizens to visit Israel on Chinese passports with official permission. That seemed a good enough reason for the Israeli Ministry of Foreign Affairs to make sure we heard their side of the story.

Joseph Hadass, Assistant Director-General of the Ministry, invited us to lunch at a *glat* (strictly) kosher Chinese restaurant. The food may have been kosher, but it certainly wasn't Chinese. The owner and the staff came from Thailand. Anyhow, we appreciated the Director-General's good intentions, and were very interested in what he had to say.

China, he alleged, did not thoroughly understand the difficulties of the state of Israel. Ever since its creation by a UN mandate in 1948, its right to exist had been denied by the Arab countries. They persistently attacked, year after year. Israel gained considerable territory in 1967, after driving back invaders from Egypt, Syria and Jordan, and again in 1973. Israel offered to return most of this land, but the Arabs refused to talk with them. The PLO slogan was "no ceasefire, no negotiations, no peace." Their avowed aim was to destroy Israel. Only very recently, under world pressure, had the Arab stand softened somewhat, though Arafat still refused face-to-face talks, demanding instead an international conference.

According to Hadass, Israel would willingly return to the Palestinians most of the "West Bank" land captured in 1967 if Israel's security could be guaranteed. Since this "West Bank" ran to within 15 miles of Tel Aviv on the Mediterranean and other cities along the coast and cut the city of Jerusalem in half, Israel would reject any changes in the present status of these cities. All the rest of the "West Bank" could be given over to a Palestinian state—independent or autonomous. Although Hadass didn't spell it out, I got the impression that Israel would insist on retaining military control of the state which would be formed by the Palestinians. He and several other Israelis to whom I spoke said repeatedly they could not entrust their security to any other military forces than their own.

That, as I understood it, was the Israeli government position at that time.

A similar attitude seemed to prevail among most segments of the Israeli population. They didn't trust Arafat, and said even if he was sincere—which they doubted—he could not control the factions which still wanted to kill all the Jews. A public opinion poll showed that 90 percent of the Jewish public favored the establishment of an independent Palestinian state, but only if they felt absolutely sure of a peaceful coexistence.

Prices were high, but the people seemed prosperous. Young couples bought, rather than rented, their flats. Cars were so numerous as to present serious traffic problems. Arabs in Israel were better off financially than they had ever been before. But Arab discontent and nationalist sentiment was growing stronger every day, exacerbated by brutal suppression by the Israeli army. Everyone agreed that a negotiated settlement was the only solution, but opinions varied widely, both among the Arabs and among the Jews, on how it should be conducted.

I was interviewed on Israeli TV and by the local and international press. Much stress was placed in their coverage on the fact that we were from the People's Republic of China. This was mentioned at the opening ceremony of the Book Fair, where Premier Shamir came over and shook hands.

At another ceremony Phoenix and I were introduced to President Hertzog. He told us he had been invited by the parents of an American Jewish boy who would be Bar Mitzvahed in Kaifeng that summer, and hoped that he, Hertzog, would be permitted to attend. (Of course, the Chinese could not permit the president of a country with whom China had no diplomatic relations to visit even in a "private" capacity.)

At the invitation of the Hebrew University of Jerusalem, I spoke at the Faculty Club on Mount Scopus before a large audience crammed into a small room. Questions were trenchant but friendly. Afterwards I had lunch with the faculty of the Chinese department. They had translated a few early-twentieth-century novels, but nothing created since the establishment of the People's Republic. One or two of them were perhaps surprised to find that I had neither horns nor a tail.

Phoenix and I had a talk with Vice-Premier Peres lasting almost an hour in his office. We were struck by its simple, almost scruffy appearance—a carry-over, perhaps, from Israel's difficult, not too distant, revolutionary past. Peres was warm and friendly, saying he had heard about me from American Jewish intellectual Noam Chomsky. He asked many questions about China, and urged us to send his regards to Madame Deng Yingchao, widow of Zhou Enlai. He indicated a great respect for the Chinese premier whom he had met some years previous at an international conference.

Like China, Israel is immersed in antiquity. Ruthi Kahanoff and other friends showed us a few of the hundreds of ancient sites. Famous Jewish and Christian biblical relics. Remains of old Greek and Roman and Crusader structures. Masada, a steep-sided clifftop, where a few hundred stubborn Jews finally committed suicide rather than surrender to thousands of besieging Roman legionnaires. "Tels," great mounds of man-made earthen plateaus where centuries of succeeding civilizations were built one on top of the other, reflecting the cultures of the numerous nations which at one time or another invaded and conquered the country. Only a few hundred have been excavated so far. A crossroads between Asia, Europe and Africa, Israel has always been a mixture of races and religions. This adds to the complexity of their problems today.

For me, it was a shaking experience to be confronted by my roots, face to face. My earliest ancestors could have been the Jews of Abraham and Joseph, or Phoenicians or people of the dozens of neighboring tribes and nations who converted, or still later converts in Africa and Europe. I could not claim any clearly identifiable blood line, or color of skin, or particular body or facial features. I was any and all of these. But here was where it started, the primary essence of me as a Jew began here. I found an origin.

This did not make me a Zionist, or a believer in Judaism. I felt it was good for Jews who wanted it to have a country of their own. At the same time I thought it

274

was reasonable for Jews in other lands to continue to be part of other cultures. Nor did Judaism, or any other religion of the supernatural, have any appeal for me.

What made me most conscious of being a Jew, and of the absolute necessity of Jews fighting together for their common interests, was the Jewish history I learned in the Memorial Hall of the Apocalypse in Jerusalem and the Museum of the Diaspora in Tel Aviv. Jews are no longer of the same ethnic origin, many do not believe in the Hebrew religion, not all favor the establishment of a Jewish state. But all are descendants of persons who had been driven from one country to another, who were slandered, discriminated against, tortured, persecuted, massacred, for 2,000 years right up to and including the Nazi obscenity. They had been the perennial victims, the convenient excuse for plunder and inhumanity.

I had experienced little anti-Semitism in America, and none at all in China. But in Israel I was confronted with appalling histories of its persistence. In various parts of the world it was again spewing to the surface. Jews could disagree on many things, I felt, but unless they aggressively united against anti-Semitism they were risking a repetition of its most virulent forms.

Not everything in Israel attracted me. Religious intervention in the law seemed backward. I thought the Hassidic costumes ludicrous and limiting their women to being breeding machines insulting.

What I did admire without any reservations were the kibbutzim. We visited the socialist one near Ein Gev. It was much more successful than the Chinese communes. Primarily agricultural, it also had a few small workshops that did everything from silkscreen printing on T-shirts to making intricate trigger mechanisms for sophisticated American weapons.

Education up to college level was free. There was no charge for eating in the large, bright community dining halls, where all members, including the highest officials, were on the roster for cleaning the dishes and mopping the floors. Policies and rules were reached by democratic discussion, but once they were decided, everyone had to obey.

When I asked the kibbutz members how it was that they were able to do better than the Chinese communes, they said, "Our people joined voluntarily." A telling dig. Unfortunately, today, these utopian organizations are no longer able to survive in what is fundamentally a capitalist society.

Phoenix and I were impressed by the idealism and creativity of most Israelis. They were also practical, and urged China to take a realistic view regarding diplomatic relations with Israel. They said not only would recognition enhance Israel's international prestige and strengthen their bargaining position with the Palestinians, it also would assuage domestic fears that Israel was entirely too dependent on US support. The year before, 1988, the United States had given three billion dollars in "aid" under an agreement requiring Israel to spend half on American military hardware, and the rest on American commercial products. They argued that recognition would not injure China's economic relations with Muslim countries, pointing out that several countries were able to trade freely with Muslim nations while still maintaining diplomatic relations with Israel.

I promised to relay their views when we returned to Beijing. I also arranged contacts between publishers of literary translations and persons in the film industry and their Chinese counterparts.

The most dramatic event in China in 1989 was the so-called Tiananmen Incident. What sparked it was a sit-down demonstration in May by college students on the huge square in front of the "Gate of Heavenly Peace"—the main entrance to the old imperial Forbidden City. The square is flanked on the east by the Museum of Chinese History and the Revolution, and on the west by the Great Hall of the People.

They were protesting against administrative abuses and failures in the schools, and corruption and inefficiency in the government, and demanding more freedom and democracy. Some Beijing local residents supported them, adding their own demand for a curb to the rising inflation. No one voiced any attack on either the Communist Party or the socialist system.

The demonstration was peaceful at first, almost festive. Whole families turned out on Sundays, carrying children or pushing baby carriages, to offer the students words of encouragement. I rode down on my scooter to have a look. The streets were so jammed with spectators I had to get off and walk along with my vehicle to move with the crowds. Bumping and jostling were impossible to avoid, yet everyone was cheerful and courteous, even the most brash and ordinarily prickly young pedestrians. A workers' group from the municipal steel mill also joined the protesters.

Leaders of the government admitted their faults and promised to rectify them. They had several formal discussions with student deputies, broadcast live on the national television network. The students remained camped on the square on and off for about six weeks, although they were urged to go back to school, since it was graduation examination time. The municipal authorities provided them with food, running water, mobile toilets, pup tents, and daily collected their garbage. Teams of doctors and nurses working shifts attended to their medical needs.

The students kept upping their demands and refused to leave. At last it was determined to move them out. Most people, although sympathizing with the students and supporting their protest, felt the demonstration had been allowed to go on too long. I could not conceive of a demo on the Mall before the Washington Monument being permitted to last six days, to say nothing of six weeks. The officials had been bending over backwards to prove how "democratic" they were, and now they were stuck.

276

But when it was learned that troops were to be sent in, many people were opposed. Old mamas stopped army trucks at entrances to the city and urged the soldiers not to go on, while at the same time in the old tradition plying them with tasty snacks. In the city, road blocks were set up at every major intersection. Any vehicle resembling an army conveyance was stopped and the driver questioned. I saw that happening at the Dianmen intersection a few blocks from where we live. In one or two places long-distance buses were emptied of passengers and burned. We had the feeling of being under siege.

Unarmed troops finally arrived and were driven away. Then came more troops, carrying weapons. Demonstrators in a number of parts of the city attacked them with stones and clubs, and seized some of the weapons and army vehicles. A few soldiers were killed. One or two of their bodies were mutilated. I saw a boy hanging from the pedestrian overhead Dongdan crossover. The corpse had been doused with gasoline and burned.

The troops opened fire. It is still not known who gave the order. Casualties were heavy. Original Western estimates of "tens of thousands" were later scaled down to "thousands," and then "hundreds." The average Chinese said there shouldn't have been any casualties at all, that there had been an excessive use of force, that shooting was unnecessary. They pointed to the example of Shanghai where Jiang Zemin, then the secretary of the municipal Party committee, where the mayor had negotiated the protests to a peaceful conclusion with the assistance of the trade unions and the youth associations. Not a single soldier had been involved.

The day after the clash I rode my scooter to Changan Boulevard, the wide avenue which runs between Tiananmen Rostrum and the square, and parked in the large yard in front of the Beijing Hotel. It was filled with cars and waiting drivers. They told me two of their number had been killed by stray bullets from the Square a few blocks away.

I took the elevator to the restaurant on the eighth floor of the hotel annex. There were no diners. The restaurant had a balcony offering a good view of the square. When I went out waiters pulled me back. They pointed to holes pitting the building wall, and said there was still danger from stray shots. Tanks were massed in front of the square, their guns trained on a row of demonstrators sitting athwart the avenue quite near the hotel.

I went back down into the yard. Warning shots were fired into the air, and the sit-downers fled in our direction. I flopped down behind one of the cars. A very frightened girl leaped the low perimeter fence and crouched beside me.

"Do you think it's alright if I take shelter in the hotel lobby?" she asked.

I cursed under my breath. This was still the time when no Chinese without formal identification was allowed to enter hotels catering to foreign guests. I assured her it was absolutely alright. She ran inside. I got up and brushed myself off.

Fortunately, nobody had been killed that day. But the events of the day before shocked the world. Many Beijing residents were angry, coupled with a profound sense of shock that the beloved People's Liberation Army should have been used against the people. Some of the blame was placed on Premier Zhao Ziyang who, it was felt, vacillated badly. He was removed from office. Other sections of the leadership seemed to have erred at the opposite extreme. An editorial carried in the *People's Daily* labeled the demonstration "counter-revolutionary," a charge which the students indignantly denied, and only strengthened their intransigence.

The explanation of the leadership apparently was that they were frightened by the possibility of a return to the chaos of the "cultural revolution." They insisted that above all China needed peace and stability. There was a crack-down on dissent, and some badly needed intellectuals and specialists fled the country.

Even more horror and indignation were expressed outside China. Most of it was genuine, but analyses were often confused, and occasionally distorted. The media tended to pick up the wrong end of the stick, sorrowing that China failed to conduct its society in accordance with the First Ten Amendments of the US Constitution, instead of probing the root causes of China's problems.

Internal stability, which was indeed essential, was maintained, but at a severe cost. Although the Communist Party was still believed to be the best and only possible leader of China, people were disturbed by the inefficiency and clear lack of unity among its commanders.

A large memorial meeting honoring Dr. George Hatem originally scheduled for June had to be postponed until September. Because of the demonstrators on the square the reception for visiting Soviet president Mikhail Gorbachov had to be shifted to the airport. China lost face. It was a blow to Chinese prestige.

What worried China more were the signs of political disintegration within the Soviet Union and other communist-dominated countries in Europe. They had proclaimed socialism a failure, disbanded their Communist parties, and announced they were switching over to capitalism. This speeded a drop in their economies and a deterioration in their social order. Nationalist separatism was on the rise. Religious intolerance and enmity increased.

The Chinese said they could understand why these countries should want to get rid of autocratic, overcentralized rule, but thought they were making a mistake to abruptly discard their existing economic machinery and adopt wholesale a Western capitalist structure in the name of embracing a market economy. The results showed a severe worsening of conditions in the Soviet Union and Eastern Europe.

Everyone agreed that some reforms were needed in China. The question was what reforms, and how intensive? Opinions centered around four schools of thought:

1) Admit that socialism had failed and also embrace the capitalist system. Very few people took this position.

2) Abandon the present economic reform policy and revert to central control of all aspects of the economy and society. This, the opposite extreme, also did not have many followers.

3) Proceed with the reforms, but more cautiously and at a slower pace, with the main emphasis on the ideological remoulding of the top leadership, and expunge noxious bourgeois influences from abroad.

4) Recognize the necessity of enhancing the political sensitivity of government and Communist Party leaders, and implement their political education as indispensable adjuncts to improving China's social and political climate. But under no circumstances use these, or any other activities, as an excuse to oppose, hinder, or downplay the central goals—economic reforms and opening to the outside world.

Advocates of the fourth approach, which was predominant at that time (and is still predominant today) said there was no indication socialism had failed in China. On the contrary, since the reforms and opening to the West were introduced in the late 1970s there had been a striking improvement in China's economy. Most felt this was due to a sharing of control between the central and the local government bodies, combining both a market and a planned economy, and learning technological and managerial methods from the West—but all within the parameters of a socialist economic system. China had been cautious in her handling of the reforms, and moved ahead slowly, devoting ten years to the steps taken thus far. As she gained experience, she would advance more quickly.

Proponents of this concept admitted that undesirable influences had indeed crept in from the outside, and that some of the high leaders had shown themselves sadly deficient in their understanding of Marxism and in the practical application of political principles. But, they said, these failings could and would be corrected through education. As the economy and the people's well-being continued to improve over the next five decades even the most skeptical would be convinced that Chinese-style socialism was eminently suitable to China.

"What are you going to do for an encore?" a Chinese friend asked me after Beijing had settled down again. *Jews in Old China: Studies by Chinese Scholars* had been well received, and a writer was supposed to write. When I protested weakly that I couldn't think of a suitable theme, he brushed my objection aside.

"You were once a lawyer, weren't you?" he said. "And you've been translating Chinese literature. Why not do something that encompasses literature and law?"

I liked the idea. There were many operas and stories centering around legal controversies. I checked with colleagues of Phoenix in the theater. They helped me select and find dramas with feudal criminal law themes. Two episodes on the miscarriage of justice were ready-made in the Ming Dynasty classic novel *Outlaws of the Marsh* which I had already translated.

A fascinating source was annals of old criminal cases such as *Cases Solved by Good Officials*, compiled in the Song Dynasty (960-1279). These were not official records, but semifictional accounts set down for general reading by gentlemen of literary bent.

To give the book a solid foundation I started with treatises by two Chinese legal experts, one contemporary and one ancient—Zhou Mi, professor of criminal law and procedure in the School of Law of Beijing University, and Song Ci, a 13th-century high judicial official and medical examiner.

Zhou Mi had just published a book *History of Chinese Criminal Law*. From it I extracted the evolution of criminal law from the very beginning. Song Ci's *A Manual for the Prevention of Injustice* was actually a text for forensic medical examiners. I borrowed liberally from that as well.

I called my book *The Law and Lore of Chinese Criminal Justice*, a title suggested to me by Martin Levin, a former executive of the Book Division of Times Mirror and later a prominent lawyer in the publishing field. We had met in Beijing some years before and had become good friends.

The nature of Chinese feudalism is not well known in the West. I hoped to throw some light on its judicial system, which was one of its main bulwarks, and which embraced laws and a legal philosophy. Despite occasional slight modifications, these remained fundamentally the same for over two millennia—something of a record in world judicial history.

Zhou Mi traces the growth of Chinese law from primitive society, when there was no law. He says:

> In primitive society everyone was free and equal. Disputes were solved by the persons involved. Custom was able to settle most problems. Because people had to cooperate to contend against the dangers of nature, the strong did not oppress the weak, and there was no crime. The efforts of every individual were needed to sustain common survival. No one could be spared to form a special governing body, and none was needed.

Not until the 23rd and 22nd centuries BC, when private property had come into being and life was more complex, did the concepts of crime and punishment emerge. But there was still no concept of law. The pattern of social evolution in China up to this point was essentially the same as that of other peoples in other parts of the world.

But then, says Zhou Mi, distinctly Chinese characteristics began to appear. The punishments imposed, for example, ranged from fines to tattooing, to beatings, to amputation of ears, noses, and feet, to castration, to execution. A curious feature was that certain dress was prescribed as part of the penalties. A person tattooed with the mark of a wrong-doer could only wear a cloth head covering but not a hat—which could shield his face from view. A man sentenced to having a foot amputated could only wear hemp, but not silk, sandals. A castrated culprit could not wear a full-length gown but only a knee-length one, to indicate that he, like the garment, had been "cut off." A man about to be decapitated could only wear a cloth tunic without a collar.

Punishments, while creative, were aimed to bring about the reform of wrong-doers, and they were sparingly applied, says Zhou Mi. Wherever possible the culprit was exiled rather than given physical punishment. Those who harmed society unintentionally were treated leniently. Only those whose acts were deliberate and remained unrepentant were punished.

Primitive society began drawing to a close. Already patriarchal, its growing flocks and expanding farms were proving too much for the male heads of families to handle alone. Clan and tribal leaders, instead of killing their war captives as before, enslaved them to help with their labors, and the practice soon spread to other property holders.

A tribal confederation in the 22nd century BC formed the Xia Dynasty, a slave nation inhabiting the fertile Yellow River Valley. The enormous changes which ensued were colorfully described in *The Book of Rites (Li Ji)*, many cen-turies later:

> The old social order disintegrated, and there was private ownership. People cared only for their own children and relatives, and worked only for themselves. The post of Great One [leader of the tribal confederation] be-came an inherited [rather than an elected] one. Cities and towns were fortified. Rules of conduct and laws were written down, fixing relations between monarchs and ministers, fathers and sons, older and younger brothers, husbands and wives. A social [class] system was established. Boundary lines were drawn, setting up private fields. The strong kept retinues of warriors and advisors, and strived for their own advancement. Robbery, pillage and warfare were the result.

While there had been punishments in China's primitive society they had been enforced by the community for violations of the interests of the people as a whole. The laws and punishments of the slave state imposed the will of the ruling nobles and slave owners upon the commoners and slaves. Slaves were outside the law. They were chattel, not people. They could be beaten, sold or killed by their masters with impunity. It was not uncommon for them to be slaughtered, some-times in large numbers, and buried with their deceased masters so as to serve them in their afterlife.

Since the laws were deemed of divine origin, they could not be questioned, says Zhou Mi. The theory was that the king, as the "son of Heaven," transmitted Heaven's mandates to the nobles and slave owners, who of course interpreted them as they saw fit, to their own benefit. The prisoner did not know what he was accused of, or why he was being punished, only that he had violated an edict from Heaven.

So cruel and ruthless were the punishments that the slaves staged slow-downs and mass desertions. Gradually they were replaced by peasants who worked the land under grants or leases from the growing landlord class in return for a share in the yield. But these people had to be assured of a certain degree of legal security if they were to remain on the land. For this reason they, and the landlords, to say nothing of the slaves, strongly favored a clear definition of the law.

Over the years the nobles and slave owners were compelled to capitulate, says Zhou Mi. Two of the states, Zheng and Jin, publicly proclaimed their laws around 500 BC. This was bitterly attacked by Confucius (hailed by some Western scholars for his "benevolent" views).

"Is Jin seeking its own destruction, throwing away its authority, making no distinction between the aristocrats and the lowly?" he cried. "If the commoners have inscribed laws how will they respect the nobles? How can the nobles rule if they are put on a par with the lowly?"

But the tide was too strong. Feudal economic relationships and feudal social concepts were sweeping the country, slave society was sliding into its final decline. In 221 BC the State of Qin conquered the other six states and unified them into a single kingdom, to be known to the outside world as "China." Although pockets of slavery remained for centuries, Chinese society was essentially feudal.

The laws of the states were revised and consolidated into a single national code. There was no distinction between civil and criminal law. During the Three Kingdoms period (220-280) its great statesman and lawmaker Zhuge Liang stressed a fair and equitable application of the law, regardless of rank or personal connections. This became a stated principle of subsequent dynasties, though more often honored in its breach. Throughout the entire feudal era, from the third century BC to the twentieth century, the laws were employed to guarantee the authority of the rulers and to suppress the people.

Zhou Mi describes the methods of courtroom interrogation, and the types of beatings and tortures employed to induce confessions of the accused and the testimony of witnesses. Only a few persons were exempt: The high-ranking and specially privileged, people over 70 and under 15, those who were ill, and pregnant women—until 100 days after childbirth. The aristocrats, the officials and the big landlords were granted leniency and special consideration when they committed crimes. If they were tried at all, they were treated with the utmost courtesy. No judge would have dared to have them beaten.

China's judicial system appears far more civilized compared with that of feudal Europe. The ecclesiastic courts in Europe, run by the Catholic church, could try non-Catholics as well as Catholics. In the name of suppressing heresy it created an investigative unit called the Inquisition, which diligently sought to expunge liberal thought and discussion. It cruelly persecuted enlightened philosophers, natural scientists, and anyone who exposed the dark side of church practices or opposed feudal authority. After being beaten and tortured by secret tribunals, victims of the Inquisition were imprisoned, exiled, or burned at the stake, their property confiscated.

No religious body in feudal China ever performed judicial functions or joined the ranks of the big landlords. Buddhism and Taoism, the main religions, were influential only indirectly, in that their precepts were called upon, or distorted, by various monarchs and members of the elite to justify their methods of control.

Europe was more backward. In some countries duels were permitted to settle disputes between litigants. Duels between nobles were fought with swords. Commoners fought with cudgels. All duels were fought to the death.

Proof by "divination" was also popular in medieval Europe. The accused, the complainant, or a witness, would be thrown into a pond, or have his hand immersed in scalding water or boiling oil, or placed on a red-hot iron, or stabbed with an animal horn. If he didn't drown, or could withstand the pain, or was not pierced by the horn, he would be credited with telling the truth. Very few passed these tests successfully.

The Chinese courts were mercifully free of such absurdities, and some efforts were made to provide fairness in feudal criminal proceedings. Tang Dynasty (618-907) law stated that whoever gave false testimony, either for the defense or for the prosecution, should be punished himself as if guilty of the crime charged, but in two degrees less of severity.

There was even a rule of privileged communications. Except in cases of conspiracy to revolt against the emperor, or kill one's own senior relative, or to murder an important official, no one could be prosecuted for covering up the crime of a close relative, nor could an underling be charged for concealing the guilt of his master.

These rules were designed to protect the feudal hierarchy, the clans, and the patriarchal family structure. The man in the street was the victim, not the beneficiary, of the law in feudal China, Zhou Mi concludes.

Song Ci, born in 1186, was something or a rarity in China's feudal bureaucracy—an able, conscientious official. He held a number of important administrative and judicial posts until his death in 1249, and had years of experience in personally conducting inquiries into cases of suspected mayhem and murder. With this as a basis, he wrote his famous *A Manual for the Prevention of Injustice* as an aid to crime investigators, with special emphasis on forensic medical examinations. It proved a valuable guide for hundreds of years. After recommending measures for coping with venality, bribery, corruption and incompetence, Song Ci sets rules for determining causes of death under suspicious circumstances.

"Most of the deceased have been stabbed or battered to death or killed in fights," he says, "or they have hung or drowned themselves, or have been strangled or drowned by others, or died of illness. But," he cautions, "sometimes it is difficult to distinguish between suicide and murder. The causes and complications in such cases are many, and the medical examinations must be conducted with the utmost care. Going off by a hair," says Song Ci, "can make you miss by 1,000 *li*."

His advice deals with even especially difficult cases, such as a woman or an elderly husband with no visible injuries, death after a drunken brawl, a traveling victim who had not been robbed. How can an examiner distinguish between suicide-hanging or murder-strangulation, suicide or murder by a bladed instrument? How can he tell whether a body was decapitated, or burned, before or after death? Was the victim poisoned, did he fall to his death? Was he killed by a tiger? Did eating or drinking to excess finish him off? Was too much sex the cause?

(For the last, Song Ci's tip is: "If a man overindulges in sexual intercourse his vital energies will be depleted and he will die on the body of the woman. Such cases must be examined carefully. If he did indeed expire from this cause, his penis will still be erect. If not, it will be flaccid.")

These few items, considerably condensed, demonstrate Song Ci's broad knowledge of crime and human anatomy, and his unusual ability as an investigator. Talents such as his were frequently in vain in feudal China. Competent investigators were constantly being hamstrung by venal underlings, corrupt gentry, and money-hungry officials. Song Ci was well aware of what he was up against, and the likely consequences. Nevertheless, he did his best, and left behind a practical scientific textbook for forensic examiners.

The literary section of *The Law and Lore of Chinese Criminal Justice* is comprised, first, of "mysteries," actual cases which were passed down verbally as short popular folktales. I include 15 of them bearing such titles as: "The Headless Wife," "When Is a Mother Not a Mother?," "Delayed Sentence," "In Pursuit of Paper," and "The Ploy That Failed."

This is followed by three more "folktale mysteries" taken from the compilation *Cases Over the Centuries Where Justice Triumphed*, and then "Four Crime Dramas," extremely popular operettas in which the clever magistrate finds the truth through a maze of confusing clues.

I conclude with two favorites of mine, extracts from the classical novel *Outlaws of the Marsh*, a source of operas and folk forms in China and Japan and parts of Southeast Asia. While in Chinese operas justice usually triumphs, in the classical

Chinese novel, more in keeping with reality, it usually fails. The hero wins retribution only by going outside the law.

The two examples chosen are strikingly presented in this 14th century novel about twelfth century brigands. Men from every walk of life, and a few women, most of them quite respectable by the standards of their day, take to the hills to escape persecution by corrupt officials. The first is Lin Chong, the second is Wu Song, both minor civil servants. In each case, downfall is linked to a beautiful woman—Lin Chong falls because the son of a high official lusts after his wife, Wu Song because his sexy sister-in-law, Golden Lotus, lusts after him.

Both are wrongfully convicted, and both are compelled to take the law into their own hands.

Chinese criminal law was founded on moral and ethical concepts affirming the righteousness of a paternalistic authoritarian society. These concepts governed Chinese life for two millennia, and were accepted as right and proper not only by the rulers but by the ruled in their millions, as well. They were part of a rigid structure which ensured social cohesiveness to a vast empire for centuries, whether in times of unity or strife. As legal standards they obviously were well suited to China and the Chinese, or they would not have lasted so long. Judging by the accounts presented in *The Law and Lore of Chinese Criminal Justice*, whether true or imaginative, few Chinese questioned China's approach to law and order.

What was questioned, and reviled in bitter complaint, was the distortion or complete by-passing of the judicial system by cruel and corrupt officials, the ease with which the rich and powerful could escape punishment or buy favorable judgments, and the immense practical difficulties confronting persons of lower social status seeking redress of grievances. This was the prevailing characteristic of criminal law in feudal China.

Although in Chinese folk tales, opera and fiction we frequently encounter the selfless dedicated investigator, he should be taken with several grains of salt. He was the "clean" official so longed for by the ordinary man. He was also yet another manifestation of feudal Chinese worship of authority, of accord with patriarchal dominance of human relations. While this made for an orderly law-abiding society, it also provided a salubrious environment for bureaucratic and autocratic rule.

Law was a means by which the officials kept the people in their place. It was something the people tried to avoid as much as possible. There was no conception of it being an instrument whereby the people could run their own society and when, if necessary, rule their rulers.

At a time when the Chinese people are attempting to attain an ideal of legality and legal rights I thought it would be useful to present the historical background from which these developments are emerging. The book aroused quite a bit of interest among foreign readers. After being published by New World Press in

Beijing in 1990, it was also produced in Singapore later the same year under the aegis of Times Academic Press.

That summer I went to the States on another home leave, stopping first in LA. I stayed in the Pacific Palisades home of Jerry Mann and wife Marian where my Chinese granddaughter Stella had been living. She had shared a bedroom and attended the same primary school with their daughter Sarah since 1988. Stella had progressed so rapidly once she learned how to speak that by the time I arrived to attend her graduation she was at the same level as her American classmates in school, had become a Girl Scout, was friends with neighborhood kids and their dogs, and was learning piano and karate. Taller and prettier, she was wearing casual but expensive clothes.

Marian threw a big Fourth of July party that overflowed from the house into the garden and the swimming pool. Stella chatted easily with the other children in quite acceptable English. But I found, when she and I talked together, that she was stumbling a little with her Chinese.

The question was what to do with her now that she had finished primary school. Marian thought the public high schools in LA would be too rough, and per-haps even a little dangerous, for a well–brought up Chinese girl child. Breck, an excellent prep school in Minneapolis, had said they would accept her, but after she was a bit older. And she missed her parents, and her Chinese was slipping. We all agreed, including Stella, that it would be best for her to go back to school again for a couple of years in China, and then decide what to do next. After an exchange of tearful farewells with Sarah and Marian, I put Stella on a plane to Beijing.

I went on to St. Louis, where I had an appointment for a cataract examination. My near-sighted eyes had been getting worse and worse since childhood. By 1990, at the age of 75, my glasses were of bottle-bottom proportions. I had tried contact lenses in Beijing, but they seemed too much of a nuisance, or I was too clumsy—anyhow, they didn't work very well for me. Dr. Hu Tiansheng, the head ophthal-mologist in Beijing's Capital Hospital had put me in touch with Dr. James Bobrow, an American cataract specialist who had visited China a number of times to demon-strate the surgical procedure. Jim had agreed to examine me to determine whether my eyes were operable.

He decided they were, and did both eyes ten days apart. Such operations are very expensive in America, and I would have had to borrow in order to be able to pay. But it seemed that his mother and my mother, although they didn't know each other, lived only a few blocks apart in the same neighborhood in Flatbush, and Jim generously waived his fee. God bless Jewish mothers.

The result was a miracle. Not only could I see clearly, but all the colors were rich and beautiful. For months I kept reaching for glasses I no longer wore to take them off before I washed my face. I didn't need them in the theater, or to watch movies or television. I did have to use a special pair for reading—because I had become a bit too far-sighted.

Opinions in China were divided as to whether the change enhanced or detracted from my beauty. Phoenix had a hard time getting used to me without glasses. She said I had lost my "soul glow"—a theater term for what actors and actresses are supposed to have shining through their eyes to project their inner feelings. Other Chinese critics said no one without glasses could look like a scholar. I said I was happy to return to the ranks of the masses. I think now everyone accepts the new me.

While in New York I called on friend Martin Levin in his high-rise law office to discuss a project I had in mind. I wanted to write the biography of Dr. George Hatem, who had died in 1988. He had been my best foreign friend in China. I admired and respected George very much, feelings matched by hundreds of thousands of Chinese.

Martin Levin encouraged me to do the book and helped me along the way. Because my Chinese is pretty good I was able to interview Chinese doctors and colleagues who had worked with George in hospitals and on the grasslands, and read written materials and reports. I had long talks with his Chinese family, with some of his American relatives, and with many of the foreigners who knew him well. I listened to tapes of talks and interviews for radio and TV in China and America. And I remembered the many things we discussed and did together in long years of friendship.

I was finally able to shape it all into a biography entitled *Ma Haide: The Saga of American Doctor George Hatem in China*. It was published by Cypress in San Francisco in 1993. A Chinese translation is now being prepared.

From New York I flew to Amsterdam to spend a week with Paul Van Hessen and his wife Nina in their home in the Hague. I had met Paul in Beijing not long before, and his story thrilled me. He came from a middle-class Dutch Jewish family. When the Nazis invaded Holland he escaped and fled to England. He joined the RAF where it was discovered that he was a natural flyer. They trained him as a pilot of a Mitchell. He flew several missions over Germany, bombing the hated Nazis with grim satisfaction. After the war he returned to Holland and married Nina, who had been doing dangerous work in the underground. Now he was a prosperous manufacturer of sausages, helping the Chinese organize their own business.

The Van Hessens were very hospitable. Nina showed me art galleries and museums. Paul took me to see the inner machinery of Holland's magnificent system of dams and canals that drove back the sea and created fertile fields. We also visited the Chinese department in Leyden University and the oldest Jewish synagogue in Holland. Holland has a large Jewish population, descendants of people expelled from Portugal centuries before. A lucky thing for Holland, for they produced geniuses ranging from Spinoza and Manasseh ben Israel to descendants like Cardozo and Bernard Baruch.

I was amused when, after a fine dinner in the Royal Netherlands Hotel where I was scheduled to give a talk about China, Paul led me to the Mata Hari Room. For some reason I could not understand the lady, who was shot as a spy for the Germans during World War I, was something of a heroine in Holland. Hanging on the wall was a full length oil portrait of the beautiful actress who played her in a popular drama.

A charming country, Holland.

Media Encounters and
Treks to the Interior
1991-1994

Since childhood in New York, and all the time I was growing up, and as a student in law school, and in my few years as a practicing attorney, and while I was overseas in the US Army during World War II, I was assured that America was the standard bearer of democracy and freedom of speech and the press, enjoyed by Americans to an extent known by no other people of the world. I more or less accepted this as a truism, but gradually came to realize that while these were indispensable first steps, they really weren't worth much unless you could follow through.

The press could expose crime and corruption, but that didn't seem to lessen them. You could stage *MacBird*, a play satirizing President Johnson and his First Lady, but the barbs just rolled off their backs. You could march in mass demonstrations against the war in Vietnam, but Washington continued to send American boys to kill and be killed. US armies went from Vietnam to Panama, Somalia, Kuwait. . . .

Although Americans have the wherewithal, their "freedom" is often simply a safety valve for blowing off steam. They can talk and write and demonstrate, but on important issues nothing much happens. There are savings and loan rip-offs, with the tax-payers footing the bill. Public buildings are blown up. Para-military private training camps are permitted. Hate groups send nasty letters, make threatening phone calls, to persons demanding reforms. Crime, drugs, vice, violence. Is that what American freedom and democracy are designed to defend?

The land of my birth has a very special place in my heart. I am stricken by what America has become. It was not that way when I was young.

China had been an autocratic feudal country for centuries. You couldn't criticize the emperor, or attack the social system. I was pleased after liberation to see some signs of democracy beginning to sprout. You still couldn't publicly attack the higher leaders, or question the social system, but you could, at least, write petitions, demonstrate against grievances, and criticize in the press without risking your neck.

As a member of the CPPCC I was not only permitted, but indeed urged, to criticize freely in *ti an* (proposals) sent directly to the offending unit or person involved. I submitted several such proposals, and they were duly forwarded. I also became something of an inveterate letters-to-the-editor writer, addressing my missives mainly to the English language *China Daily*, which almost always carried them. I'm afraid I was not much more effective than my fellow grousers in the United States.

Still, I felt I had to keep trying. One of the things that distressed me was to find that the Chinese TV industry was not only broadcasting Chinese bilge, but was importing and showing quite a lot of Western bilge as well. In a letter to *China Daily* in February 1991 I noted that some of the American imports were particularly bad. I said:

> First we had *Garrison's Guerrillas* in which convicted American murderers and criminals are recruited to stage attacks on the German Nazi forces in France during World War II. They are depicted as innovative, daring and effective. This is pure fiction, and an insult to the French Resistance Movement, whose members were the real heroes who fought courageously against the Nazis, and were a major contributor to their defeat.
>
> Then came *Rambo*, a veteran of the war in Vietnam, where he spent his time in dirty commando tactics against the Vietnamese people striving desperately to hold off the invaders. Crazed by his experience, he uses the same tactics after returning home, and single-handed confounds thousands of soldiers and police. Rambo infuriated GI veterans and the general American public, who bitterly resented any attempt to justify the rare maniacs who enjoyed the slaughter, and to glorify the war they so thoroughly detested.
>
> On January 6 at 9 p.m., on prime time, Chinese TV viewers nationwide were presented with a gem by Twentieth Century Fox. It was skillfully dubbed in Chinese, and its title rendered as *Comanche Bandits*. The film tells how a stereotyped Western sheriff, played by John Wayne, aided by only a few other bold warriors, defended innocent white settlers against hordes of howling red savages.
>
> As American historians have reported in sickening detail, during the 19th century the native American Indians were driven from their land to make way for white settlers, and ruthlessly slaughtered by army troops when they tried to resist. In a few decades their population was cut in half.
>
> It is very unfortunate that hundreds of millions of Chinese TV viewers should be exposed to historical falsehoods and ethnic slurs. Such films slander races of other lands, and are a mockery of China's consistent policy of friendship and respect for all peoples.

Ever since the successful Asian-Jewish Colloquium in Hong Kong in 1987, its sponsor, the World Jewish Congress, in the person of Isi Leibler, had been keen on strengthening cultural ties between China and Israel. The times seemed suitable. Diplomatic relations had been established, and there already were some commercial contacts. Isi began discussing, by correspondence and occasional visits, the prospects for a conference on Chinese and Jewish histories and philosophies, and the relations between them, with the International Cultural Exchange Center of China, a nongovernment organization.

I was asked to act as intermediary. In the ensuing months I was on the phone a lot, relaying proposals and counterproposals between Melbourne and Beijing. It was decided to convene a conference in Beijing early in 1992, to be entitled "Cultures Old and New: A Chinese and Jewish Dialogue," and a list of participants was agreed upon.

The Chinese scholars included six professors of philosophy, four specialists in world religions, a director of the Institute of Nationality Studies, two historians, a dean of Studies in the Jinling Union Theological Seminary, and a researcher on the history of the Chinese Jews (me).

Among the nine foreign scholars three were from Tel Aviv University, one from Hebrew University in Jerusalem, the former President Yitzhak Navon of Israel, President Norman Lamm of Yeshiva University, and American writer Chaim Potok. A few of them brought their wives, and a group of tourists latched on to combine auditing the conference with an opportunity to see something of China.

We met in April 1992, in the garden estate known as the State Guest House. Formerly you had to be a king or a prime minister to get in, but later special visiting foreign groups were also accommodated, at stiff prices. We lived in large frame houses, each with its own dining room, surrounded by trees and spacious lawns. There was also an enclosure of peacocks, beautiful birds with ugly raucous voices.

The conference lasted three days. Some very good dissertations were read, and several interesting matters were raised in the free discussion periods. Similarities were noted in Jewish and Chinese family relationships and in traditional social concepts. One Jewish scholar wondered how the Chinese could have had a moral code without an established religion and a belief in a Supreme Being. I thought that was an important question, and was disappointed it was not explored further.

Most of the participants were satisfied with the conference, and enjoyed chatting informally with scholars from other countries, and for that matter with colleagues from their own country who, what with everyone being so busy and living far apart, they seldom have a chance to meet. The conference turned out to be the beginning of an exchange of visiting scholars between China and Israel.

While I was pleased with the main directions in which China was moving, I met with frequent irritants in everyday life, things which I felt should have, and could have been prevented. Safety precautions were blatantly ignored everywhere—on

291

work sites, in factories, on the road. People were injured, killed, but compensation was rarely paid, and those responsible were rarely punished. Sometimes the legal machinery did not exist, or if it did the victims didn't know about it, or even if they did they didn't understand how to utilize it. In a country of over a billion individuals there was only a handful of lawyers who could help them enforce their rights.

Actually, the problem was more in the prevention than in the cure. Most local governments had safety regulations, but they were not enforced. Inspectors were lax, or bribed, a phenomenon not unknown in other countries. But other countries had compulsory insurance, and the insurance companies kept a close eye on the insured to make sure they would not have to pay out damages. This kept safety violations down to a minimum much more effectively than the supposed diligence of the government inspectors.

But this was not how things were done in China. I was frustrated. All I could do was write letters to newspaper editors. Here is one I sent to the *China Daily* in December 1992:

A recent item reports the death of 11 workers killed on a building site in Wuhan, Hubei Province, and the death of another 11 plus the injury of six others earlier in the month, also in Wuhan.

Although the amount of economic losses is stated, there is not a word of sympathy for the men killed and maimed and their economic loss, to say nothing of the misery inflicted on their families. The construction companies are merely "urged" to take out accident insurance in the future.

This is like urging the weasel to be more considerate of the the hens. The construction companies are unprincipled scoundrels who will stop at nothing to make money. Of course the workers and their families can sue the owners of the property, and the construction companies, whether they have taken out insurance or not. But even under the best of circumstances seeking redress in the courts requires more time and money than the ordinary person can afford.

The key to the prevention of the repetition of such tragedies lies with the local governments. They should pass ordinances decreeing: a) No construction is allowed without a government permit; b) No permit will be issued unless the construction company produces an insurance policy providing full compensation for death, personal injury and damage to property; and c) Stringent civil and criminal penalties for any violation of these provisions.

I recommend that such ordinances be enacted by local governments all over China.

I sent the same recommendation to the Chinese People's Political Consultative Council, as a member, to be forwarded to the appropriate government agency. The CPPCC relayed it to the National Insurance Company, which has no power to pass government ordinances. That is the last I heard of the matter. China will gradually have to learn the concept of legal rights for the individual, and how to enforce them.

In the summer of 1993 we received word that Stella had been accepted in the Breck School in Minneapolis as a second year senior high student, on full scholarship. What's more, Margaret Wong, dean of foreign students, had arranged for her to live in the home of one of the American girl students, hosted by the girl's family. We were overjoyed. Otherwise, we could not have afforded the costs. Breck was one of the finest prep schools, with an excellent record of getting its graduates into universities. I was already scheduled to go to America on home leave, and prepared to take Stella with me and deliver her to Breck.

About two weeks before our departure date, Augustine Zycher, an Israeli television producer, telephoned me from Jerusalem, saying Keshet Broadcasting wanted to do a Yaron London program in which he would interview three long-time Jewish residents of China. These would be David Crook from London, Ruth Weiss, a Viennese, and Sidney Shapiro, a New Yorker. Would I take part? I tried to beg off, explaining that I was about to leave for the States, that I was still making preparations, that I didn't have the time. But Augustine swore they would do my scenes first, I would be all finished in three days.

I let myself be persuaded. Yaron London arrived with complete crew, and we went to work. He was affable, and had a sense of humor. I liked him—that is, until I realized he was out to discredit China by discrediting me, a Jewish expatriate who admired and supported the People's Republic of China.

He started by saying that I was a journalist who played an important role in propaganda. "Tell me, honestly, how many times you lied." he demanded.

When I replied that I was not a journalist, and that my field was not propaganda but literary translation, he switched to another line of attack.

Q: During the Cold War, the Korean War, and the Vietnamese War you were in the enemy's camp.

A: Which enemy?

Q: Well, you were an American. The Chinese fought against America. How did you feel?

A: I didn't fight against America. The Americans said they weren't in it. The Americans said it was a United Nations war. The Americans never declared war. They never got permission from Congress to send boys to be killed and kill other boys. How could I be in the enemy's camp?

293

Over the years, I had happily consented to play in three Chinese motion pictures, part-time, strictly as an amateur. London hinted that this showed my anti-American bias. I hinted that the Chinese took a jaundiced view of US military operations abroad.

Q: You played in two or three Chinese films, as an American villain?

A: I was an honest-to-God villain in one as an intellectual, a professor in a university. And then in my next venture I was a real villain. I became the commander-in-chief of the US Army Air Force in Korea. You couldn't be any worse than that, could you, shooting down Chinese planes? I vowed I would never play in any more movies. First, because I didn't like to be the villain—the kids in the lane were saying "Heil Hitler" to me. And my wife, who was a real actress, was very scornful of my talents.

London fastened on this opportunity to question me about Phoenix's four years' house arrest in a camp for cadres during the "cultural revolution." He claimed that I "accepted" it with equanimity. I said I didn't accept it at all, that I hated it, and was very much opposed. London sneered.

Q: No doubt you saw yourself, and the fate of your wife, as blood on the axis of the revolutionary wheel?

A: That's your term, not mine. That's pejorative argumentation.

Q: I admit that.

A: Oh, you admit it.

I had heard from Israeli friends that he was abrasive. I was prepared for hardball, but not for dirty pool. London tried another tack.

Q: In 1963 you decided to renounce your American citizenship and become a Chinese citizen. Why did you do that?

A: It took me a little while to make up my mind. I came in 1947. But in 1963 my mother came. And she was well satisfied that I had a happy home, a good wife, I was enjoying life, my work was satisfactory, I had good neighbors, and so on.

Q: And you needed the accord of your mammy?

A: Yes, I wanted that, I wanted that very much.

Scoffing at a son who hoped his mother would be satisfied with his life abroad was hard going even for London. He made his final attempt.

Q: Do you find it difficult being a Jew in China?

A: I'm not a good Jew, but I'm certainly a Jew. I feel, as a Jew, that I have a responsibility to my fellowman. That it's not enough to be well-fed and have a pleasant life, that I should do something in return. And this is what the Chinese people, and their government, and their Party, have professed to do. So there is no contradiction.

I doubt whether London was pleased with my answers. Nanguanfang, the lane I live in, is famed for its old traditional architecture. Tourist agencies bring foreign visitors to see it. But London showed none of that in his production. Although there were three new automobiles in front of the house, he filmed men pushing an old car which had run out of gas. He did a shot of me emptying the garbage into a simple collection cart. We walked quickly through the front garden, and into the house. The garden was lush with summer roses, and there were fine Chinese paintings on the living room walls. None of that was shown either.

He asked nothing about the sort of work I had been doing in China during the past 40 years, the many books I had translated and written. Not even about *Jews In Old China: Studies by Chinese Scholars*, which had been translated into Hebrew and published in Tel Aviv, and was the reason Phoenix and I had been invited to Israel in 1989. Nor about my other activities in China and in international Jewish cultural affairs. Things which one would imagine would be of interest to his Israel, TV audience.

He did film and record one lively sequence in which I said his approach was marred by bias and preconceived notions about China. London did not have the courage, or the honesty, to include it in his final product. The film was a colorful, technically proficient job, but superficial, one-sided, and therefore ultimately misguiding.

London sent copies of it to David Crook and Ruth Weiss, his other two subjects, but not to me. I hope it was because he had the grace to be ashamed.

Stella and I flew from Beijing to San Francisco in the middle of August, 1993. She had to report to Breck by the twentieth. After spending a few days in a hotel and wandering around, I put her on a plane to Minneapolis, arranging to follow a week or so later. My friends the Bernies, had been away, but now they were back, and I moved into their fine home in Hillsborough. With this as a base of operations, I visited Cypress Press a few times. They had just published *Ma Haide: The Saga of American Doctor George Hatem in China*, and we discussed promotion.

Staying with Barbara and Norman Bernie was always a treat. In her seventies, Barbara was vital, intelligent. Among other things as a young woman, she had been a model. She was still beautiful, active with her American Foundation of Traditional Chinese Medicine.

Norman was also very bright. A jobber in textiles, he could easily have afforded to retire, but he could not bear being idle. He swam in their pool, and played golf farther out in the hills at a club he proudly took me to see.

I flew from San Francisco to Minneapolis, where Stella had already started classes at the Breck School. Kathleen Barlage, who was one of the trustees and who had two daughters at Breck, was hosting Stella that year, and she kindly offered to put me up during my visit. A competent, charming person, Kathleen and her husband were separated, and she ran the large house alone, with some help from the girls. They had a big Persian cat with one green eye and one blue, and a tough little terrier named Skippy. He bit anyone he didn't trust, which was most people. Luckily, he formed an immediate affection for me. I like dogs, and they can sense it.

Breck is an attractive school. One-story buildings spread over a large countrified campus, well-lit airy classrooms, lively teachers. Coming from rigid overdisciplined China, I was struck by the way the students were stimulated to think for themselves, to speak up, to argue. I sat in on Stella's American History class, and spoke to Margaret Wong's Advanced Chinese students, and enjoyed both experiences.

Kathleen and a friend and the girls took Stella and me to the State Fair. Stuffed with hamburgers, hot dogs and soft ice cream, I waddled among prize pigs and goats and horses, and watched crazy people leaping to their death from high towers, only to be snapped back from destruction at the last second by long elastic ropes to which they were attached. We walked miles. I was so dazed and weary by then that the whole thing seemed completely reasonable.

Though Stella had to struggle a bit at first with some of her subjects, not having had the background and specialized vocabulary of the American students, she caught up with them by the end of the term. She had a flair for writing. In her compositions she jumped into free expression with both feet. She defended Bill Sykes, the wife-beater in *David Copperfield*, and thought there was something to be said for *Macbeth*. Later, using material I facsimiled her from Beijing, she strongly supported Beijing's role in Tibet. Her teacher, an Irishman, gave her an "A" for that.

We were fortunate in the loving care Stella got from Margaret Wong, head of the Chinese Department and dean of the foreign students. Margaret had come to America when she was very young, and had suffered from discrimination as a foreigner and as a woman. She felt a particular empathy for Stella, and was an indefatigable advisor and a warm friend. I was able to leave Minneapolis confident that Stella would get along fine. And she did.

On the East Coast I stayed with sister Ruth and brother-in-law Jack in their home in Marlboro, NJ. They were sorry Phoenix hadn't come, but could understand she might be bored. They were pretty bored themselves with their placid existence in the Jersey countryside and were thinking of moving—maybe to Chicago

296

where their daughter Joan was, or to Cleveland where son David lived. For me it was a chance to relax in the familiar surroundings of snacks I used to eat and dreamy nostalgic music, and reminisce about family history.

I went into "the city"—meaning New York, of course—several times. From Marlboro, in what we native New Yorkers, who snobbishly imagined ourselves sophisticates, used to call "the wilds of Jersey," it was a whole day's adventure. Ruth had to drive me to the village center, where I boarded a bus which needed 40 minutes to reach the Lincoln Terminal on Ninth Avenue and 42nd Street in Manhattan, and then take a crosstown bus to get to the centers of the publishing business on the eastern side of the city. At the end of the day I had to do the whole thing in reverse to return to the house in Marlboro.

Martin Levin took me to a jammed delicatessen for lunch. We dined on half-inch thick pastrami sandwiches garnished with French fried potatoes and fat garlicky pickles. Martin congratulated me on the publication of *Ma Haide* and said it was time for me to go on from where I left off in *An American in China*. A lot had happened in China, and to me, since 1979. On second thought, he said, it would be better if I told my story from childhood and carried it right through my years in China to date. People would be interested to learn why a fairly typical American should want to spend his life in China And they were curious about this country once called the "Sick Man of Asia." What had brought it to the throes of an economic boom? My book might be able to tell them, or at least provide some substantial clues. Martin urged me to write my autobiography. He said he would help me get it published.

I was easily persuaded. Although fully retired, I had been busy with a variety of activities, had been to a lot of places, talked with a lot of people, accumulated a lot of impressions. Rightly or wrongly, I had my own ideas on a number of things in China and the world, and I felt like talking about them. All I had to do was to put them down on paper in a brilliant and fascinating manner!

Of course I could never do it that well, but once I started I was glad I had begun. Not only did I have to dredge my memory for people and events, I had to re-examine and re-appraise them. At times I also had to pass judgment on myself in my relations to them. The results, while not always flattering, were always edifying. I recommend that everyone who has the time, and the brass, should write his or her autobiography. You are reading mine right now.

In Los Angeles, I stayed with Sally and Jon Quinn in Long Beach. We had met in Beijing, where they had been the year before. They had invited me to be their guest on my next visit to America, and I was glad to accept their hospitality. Jon was "Papa Jon" who ran a couple of vegetarian stores. He and Sally practiced what they preached, and I never had a shred of meat during the week I spent in the Quinn home. To my surprise, their food was very tasty, though I was not ready to forego steaks and chops permanently.

297

They lived in a comfortable rambling house in a leafy lane near a large park. We talked a lot about China, which they liked very much. Jon took me shopping at a discount center in a huge warehouse. They had all kinds of merchandise selling at bargain prices. I bought a packet of a dozen pairs of heavy wool socks, ridiculously cheap, enough to last me a lifetime.

The Chinese Consul General invited us to dinner, along with a few leaders of the Los Angeles branch of the US-China People's Friendship Association. I was horrified to hear the association was planning to ask Sidney Rittenberg to be a guest speaker at their forthcoming national convention in Seattle. I protested and strongly urged them against it, reminding them of the man's reprehensible conduct.

Rittenberg had written an autobiography called *The Man Who Stayed Behind*, which had been published in the States some years after his return from China. In it he attacked the Chinese Communist Party and viciously slandered Mao Zedong, whose aphorisms he was so fond of ardently quoting. Rittenberg called Mao, the guiding spirit of the Chinese revolution, "the biggest slave master of all, the master of all slave masters!" The very mention of Mao had Rittenberg frothing at the mouth. "Mao was Satan, the evil genius, the cruel monster," he cried. "When the name ran through my head it seemed the most obscene, horrible. Mao, Mao, Mao!"

Nor did Deng Xiaoping, respected leader of the post-Mao period, escape his venom. In 1980 Deng had called for the repeal of a provision which the Gang of Four had inserted into the Constitution legalizing the "right" to post unsigned and unsubstantiated libels against anyone and everyone, a practice which had caused serious damage to many innocent people. According to Rittenberg, Deng's proposal proved that "dictatorship was back in force."

His one attempt to show that he was not entirely devoid of decency came in the form of his alleged "love" for Premier Zhou Enlai. In the book he created a scenario with himself in prison, stricken to learn of Zhou's death. "I tore the cuff off a pair of my black cotton prison pants and made myself a mourning band," Rittenberg solemnly asserted.

The story would have been more impressive were it not for the fact that Chinese prison pants are not black and they have no cuffs!

Rittenberg paints a very unlovely picture of himself in the book. He says that during the "cultural revolution" he thought himself a "kingmaker" who had attained "a hard-won position of power and influence." He admits that he "had supported factional violence [and] that meant Jiang Qing"—leader of the fanatic Gang of Four. [So much for Rittenberg's "love" of Zhou Enlai, who Jiang qing considered her arch enemy.] He confesses to "selfishness . . . weakness . . . opportunism . . . fear . . . self-interest."

Reviewers in America were quick to spot Rittenberg's character deficiencies. The *LA Times* and *Newsweek* called attention to the fact that during the "cultural revolution" he denounced old colleagues "left and right." The *Washington Post* says: "He turn[ed] away from persecuted friends [and] rationalized violence. The story confirms his reputation as a doctrinaire political climber."

The man was a slippery liar. As John Fraser, Canadian journalist, noted in his book *The Chinese* some years before, "No two people get exactly the same story from Rittenberg." When talking with Rittenberg, says Fraser, "you do have to keep your wits about you."

How in the world could the US-China People's Friendship Association invite a person of this kind of moral fiber, someone so scurrilously unfriendly, to speak at a Friendship Association convention?

My words fell on deaf ears. Rittenberg did speak at the convention in September. Not only was the USCPFA remiss. The Chinese Ambassador, who should have known better, was obviously very ill-informed. He too appeared at the convention, in a real blooper of Foreign Office bureaucratic inefficiency.

I had some media coverage while in Los Angeles, a TV interview in Long Beach, and an occasion to send a letter to the *LA Times*. They had carried a news item about a proposed rebuilding of the Kaifeng synagogue. The *Times* published my reply which said this:

> I am visiting here from my home in Beijing, and a news item in the *Times* (August 14) concerning the Jewish community in Kaifeng, China, a millennium ago, recently came to my attention. It says that "few are able to explain how the group made its way from ancient Judea to central China."
>
> The fact is that over the past 300 years several Western and Chinese historians, based in part on records inscribed in stone by the Jews themselves, have described their route.
>
> To those interested in learning the details, I immodestly recommend a book I edited and compiled, *Jews in Old China: Studies by Chinese Scholars* (Hippocrene, New York, 1984). A Hebrew edition was published in Israel in 1987.
>
> I am not a Chinese Jew, but as a Chinese citizen who celebrated his bar mitzvah in Flatbush in 1928, I believe I may confidently lay claim to being a Jewish Chinese!

In September, I again was inspired to send another letter to the editor, this one to the *New York Times*. The *Times* had published a long, and generally quite good, article in two parts by Nicholas Kristof, who had been their correspondent in Beijing, summing up his observations over a two-year period. In replying to one of his comments, I wrote:

Although you present many facts, you are unable to explain how it is that an allegedly repressive regime can create a soaring economy and provide its people with many social amenities. You say this is "annoying to democrats," and wonder whether repression of the citizenry might not be the best way for emerging nations to go.

I am married to a Chinese actress and writer. Most of our friends are in the arts. I obtained Chinese citizenship in 1963. Since 1983 I have been a member of the Chinese People's Political Consultative Conference, a nongovernmental appointive body whose function is to criticize proposed legislation and policy and set forth counterproposals. These friends and colleagues are part of the limited number of well-educated Chinese from which the relatively tiny segment of "dissidents" spring. We are just as outspoken as they, but advocate reform rather than overthrow of the government.

Our argument is that the main impediment to China's advance is not repression, or bourgeois influences, or insufficient democracy, but a recrudescence of feudal attitudes and practices, and a deterioration of moral values.

After returning to Beijing in December, I encountered another instance of bureaucratic handling of the Rittenberg scandal. Reviewing his book, *The Man Who Stayed Behind*, *China Daily* praised it to the skies. I sent a letter to the editor, saying their review had "evoked ironic and bitter laughter among those of us who knew him." I said it was preposterous to call him a "self-denying revolutionary" replete with "heroic human spirit," adding that "in fairness to the many who suffered as a result of his deeds, it is necessary to keep the record straight."

My letter was published. Rittenberg was furious. He threatened to sue *China Daily*. Of course he never did. The chief editor apologized to me for the review, asserted he didn't know about it, that he was away at the time. I said the apology should have gone not to me, but to *China Daily*'s readers. Could it be the editorial staff all stopped thinking any time the chief editor wasn't around?

To add insult to injury, Rittenberg featured prominently as a commentator in a BBC television smear of Mao entitled *Chairman Mao the Last Emperor*, aired in December 1993, to coincide with the 100th anniversary of Mao's birth.

Yet he was allowed to open and maintain an office in Beijing as a "consultant." Rittenberg claimed in an interview by Seattle journalist Nick Gallo that his clients included Levi Strauss, ARCO, Digital Equipment, Polaroid, Campbell, Mike Wallace, and Billy Graham. He boasted about a list he had retained of telephone numbers giving him access to Chinese executives.

"The home numbers of officials are considered a state secret," he said. "Yulin [his wife] has a whole book of them."

He admitted to being concerned at first that his autobiography might "anger the Chinese" and cause his company to "lose our contacts."

"But," he said, "we're prepared for that risk. We won't starve."

In view of the unprincipled mentality of some Chinese officials, it appears that Rittenberg's confidence was fully justified.

The mentality of policymakers in Washington regarding China was not so much unprincipled as rigid, hypocritical and impractical. They were trying to ride roughshod over the Chinese and force concessions, as they had decades ago. The new method was a gimmick called "human rights," and it simply was not working. I sent a letter to the *New York Times* suggesting how the situation might be improved. Published in March 1994, it read:

> In August 1944, John S. Service, career diplomat, then acting as political officer to the US Army's observer group in Yanan, had a lengthy conversation with Mao Zedong. The defeat of the axis powers was in sight, and Mao was already thinking of how to build a new China once the war ended. He told Service he would be willing to go to Washington and discuss Sino-US future relations with President Roosevelt. He never received a reply.
>
> Coolness became overt hostility after the People's Republic of China was formally proclaimed in 1949. In 1951 the US Seventh Fleet plied the Strait separating Taiwan from the mainland. America imposed an economic embargo against China, and pressured its major trading partners into doing the same. Guns were fired in anger just on the other side of Chinese borders, first in Korea, then in Vietnam. China felt threatened. At one point during the Korean War, General MacArthur boasted his troops would be "over the Yalu by Christmas."
>
> The effect of all this was to thrust China into the arms of the Soviet Union—which proved to be very bad for China, and created serious consequences for the United States. The lesson was not lost on Washington. It was obvious that friendly relations with China were in America's best interests. The climate rapidly improved, starting with the visit by Nixon and Kissinger in 1972, and followed by extensive commercial activities fueled by China's economic boom.
>
> But Cold War warriors die hard. Though small in number, they are noisily vociferous. Their favorite weapon is alleged violations of "human" rights. This, as against Asian nations, has turned out to be not a spear but a boomerang.
>
> The Chinese have a strong sense of dignity and propriety. They think it presumptuous for a mere infant of a country, historically speaking, to tell a sovereign state ten times its age and possessed of a highly cultured civilization,

how to live. China has its own Constitution and a body of laws guaranteeing internationally recognized civil rights, including the right to a decent livelihood. The Chinese consider specious the argument that economic well-being is only a "social," not a "human," right. They feel that democracy cannot survive on an empty stomach, any more than a full stomach can supplant democracy. They want both, simultaneously.

While most Chinese will admit to some failings in the protection of their civil rights, they insist that interference in the internal affairs of a sovereign nation is a violation of international law. Moreover, they claim to be quite competent to deal with such problems themselves.

In any event, the Chinese are well aware of America's military incursions into little countries abroad, and its miserable civil rights record at home. They witnessed the beating of Rodney King on their TV news, they read in their newspapers about American jails overflowing with prisoners—mostly Black. Their daily press gives wide coverage to US crime, drugs, poverty, homelessness, graft and corruption. Such a country, the Chinese maintain, is not fit to talk about violations of citizens' rights in other lands. America is completely lacking in moral authority.

And now, to heap absurdity on cant, it has become apparent from the statements of visiting US politicos and trade negotiators that these gentlemen care nothing about Chinese rights, whether labeled "human" or "civil." They promise to tone down their slanders immediately, if only the Chinese will grant them more economic concessions. That is actually the name of the game.

America's human rights razzle-dazzle has brought a loss of face and a lessening of respect for American policy-makers in China, and in Asia generally. It is time to quit the flummery and get on with genuine, mutually beneficial, business.

Anyone who knows anything about Asia—scholars, students, diplomats, businessmen—will tell you the absolutely worst way to attempt to accomplish anything in this area of the world is to strike an arrogant, hectoring pose. It only arouses angry resentment or, still worse, contempt. My letter was just one of a storm of similar reactions expressed throughout Asia. In spite of the obduracy of Washington's more obtuse bigots, they caused some superficial modifications in America's Far East policy, mostly verbal. The real changes would not come until compelled by realities such as Japanese and European competition for Chinese trade, and China's own growing economic strength.

Phoenix and I visited Shenzhen again in March of 1994. We had been there before—first, when we met my mother coming over the bridge from Hong Kong in 1963, and then once or twice while passing through from other places. Shenzhen was an attraction as one of China's four special economic zones, places where foreign companies had been encouraged to invest.

It had enjoyed some success, and the city of Shenzhen had changed from a fishing village to a modern metropolis with broad streets and shiny office buildings. Most of its outside financing came from Hong Kong, the great seaport and commercial center only a few miles south of the border.

But progress was slow until Deng Xiaoping arrived in 1993 and called for major reforms. Chinese companies could be government owned, semi-private or private. Foreign investors could join them in partnerships or corporate joint ventures, or wholly own and manage their own companies. They could lease property for 50-year terms at attractively low prices. The policy of tax-exemption for joint ventures with foreigners during their first three years of operation was continued.

We had heard in Beijing about the boom which resulted, and wanted to see for ourselves. A small group of foreign old-timers and their wives flew down, shepherded by the Foreign Experts Bureau, which facilitated access to officials and enterprises. The companies we visited made good quality consumer goods, household commodities, and electrical appliances. Hundreds of trucks plied between Hong Kong and Shenzhen every day, bringing in raw materials and returning with finished or semi-finished merchandise. At that time there were only two entry-exit points, and long lines of trucks were backed up, waiting to pass Customs inspection. We were told more were being built.

Everywhere we went we had to detour because of highway construction, or crawl along behind trucks laden with building materials for the blocks of new housing mushrooming on both sides. We were deafened by the noise and smothered by the dust. Shenzhen was clearly bursting at the seams, and prosperity was just around the corner.

That was how it appeared. Friends who lived there told us a different story. They said while there was a lot of activity in the spin-offs—shipping, banking, insurance, infrastructure, entertainment, tourism, etc., there was not much production bringing profit to China. The big money was earned by the foreigners. They built factories, hiring mainly uneducated Chinese girls fresh from the farms, paid cheap wages, and provided slapdash dormitories. Safety regulations were ignored. Girls were burned to death in one fire because exits were blocked with packing cases. Many local officials were crooked and bribable.

Deng's ideas were sensible, very good, said our friends. The problem was they were being perverted to serve the needs of dishonest Chinese businessmen, frequently in cahoots with officials. For example, a company would form a partnership with some Hong Kong or foreign corporation, obtain a bank loan on the strength of the foreigner's credit, and open an office tax exempt for three years.

If his company didn't do well—and most of them didn't—he would form a new company under a different name, find another foreign partner, and start again, tax free for another three years.

Shenzhen did have a number of honest, efficient Chinese enterprises, but they were in the minority. Local residents were afraid foreign investors might pull out if they could find cheaper labor and even more favorable inducements in other parts of China, or elsewhere in Southeast Asia. It might not happen soon, since the proximity to Hong Kong was a powerful inducement, but it was worrying.

Below Shenzhen, the southernmost border of Guangdong Province extends down into a bulgy peninsula comprising the territory of Hong Kong. Zhuhai and the Portugese colony of Macao are west across the bay formed by the estuary of the Pearl River. Only about 40 miles of water separates Zhuhai from the western shore of Hong Kong's Northern Territories. A railway connects it to the city of Guangzhou to the north, and it ties in with a network of rivers. Because of its ideal conditions, Zhuhai was also chosen to be one of China's first four special economic zones.

We crossed over from the Shenzhen port of Shekou (Snake Mouth) on one of those propeller driven ferries that rides on a cushion of air. Our passage was only slightly bumpy, skimming across small waves, but very noisy, rock music from loud speakers adding to the din of the engines. Our hosts put us up in a good hotel with a view of the distant sea. It also had bungalows for tourists who wanted them, and Mongolian-style felt tents, although we were well over 1,000 miles from the Mongolian grasslands.

The western part of Zhuhai would be devoted to electronic, biological, energy and environmental protection enterprises, business, trade, real estate and tourism. To avoid the mess which Shenzhen had created by building its infrastructure and expanding its physical plant at the same time, Zhuhai had done all of its layout and infrastructure first. Its streets were wide and clean, the public utilities were installed, offices and residences built. In a word, everything was in order and ready to go into operation.

The plan was to build a steel-rolling mill, chemical plants, and a large warehouse and storage area near the coast. Zhuhai has an excellent deep water natural harbor with a port area larger than Rotterdam's. They were building a huge oil depot and wharves capable of handling tankers of up to 250,000 tons in capacity. Zhuhai would be able to supply oil to Hong Kong, Southeast Asia, Japan, Korea, and Taiwan. In five years' time it would be a major international transfer and storage point for petroleum products, gas, and chemical derivatives. Forming a vital corner in the triangle with Guangzhou and Hong Kong, it would affect the economic development of the whole of southeast and southwest China.

In Zhuhai, as in Shenzhen, a wide variety of organizational structures was permitted, with only loose overall control from Beijing at the top. It was very close to free enterprise. We heard no tales of government corruption, thus far, at any rate. Everyone seemed very young, very confident, very eager. Whether this situation will prevail after the money starts rolling in remains to be seen.

I set out in August for the Ningxia Hui Autonomous Region as a member of a CPPCC inspection team. There were about 100 of us, plus another 16 persons consisting of staff, doctors, nurses, security men, secretaries, drivers and reporters. Forty-two of the CPPCC members were Communists. The remainder were affiliated with various other parties, or independents. Eight of the 42 were women.

This was another of the several CPPCC junkets organized each year to investigate almost every form of endeavor in China and report back to the top government authorities, along with recommendations for reform. I had been on half a dozen of these tours since joining the CPPCC in 1983, and had always found it fascinating, and very revealing, to get down to grass roots and see the actual situation and talk with people face-to-face. I was interested in Ningxia because it has a large Hui, that is Muslim, population. Many CPPCC members apply to join these annual tours, but the numbers are necessarily limited. Only persons who appear to be the most useful to the particular investigation are accepted.

The ones in this group came from a wide variety of professions. We had a researcher in the Academy of Traditional Chinese Medicine, a secretary of the Writers Union, an official of the Ministry of Foreign Trade and Economic Cooperation, a person in the Department of Geology and Mining, someone from the Academy of Chinese Folk Theater, an economic researcher in the Academy of Social Sciences, and the chairman of the Institute of Psychology.

I was in Section Four. We included a doctor of neurology, the director of the Children's Development Center, the head of the Motion Picture Academy, a professor in the Academy of Agricultural Sciences, a professor in the Institute of Nationalities, the vice-director of the Chinese Committee for Economic Cooperation in the Pacific Rim, and the dean of the Institute of Vocal Music.

We left Beijing about 10 a.m. from an Air Force base now offering civilian commercial flights, and arrived in Yinchuan (Silver Valley), capital of Ningxia Hui Autonomous Region at noon. We were settled in a city government compound containing several guest houses amid flower garden surroundings. Most members were two in a room. Being over 75 I was entitled, all to myself, to a large parlor and bedroom, a good bathroom, radio, TV, endless supplies of hot tea and fruit, including delicious Ningxia honeydew melon.

In this Hui autonomous region, one-third of the 4.8 million population are Muslims, descendants of Arab and Persian traders who came to China in the Tang and Song, in the seventh to twelfth centuries. Some say their ancestors were captured by Genghis Khan in the 13th century when his armies were returning from conquests in Europe.

Ningxia is a long strip of land sticking down with the upper half in Inner Mongolia and the lower half surrounded by Gansu to the east, west and south. A pleasant plateau, about 3,000 feet in altitude, with generally good weather, it is on the Yellow River. It has railroad connections in four directions, lots of coal, some agriculture, and is ideal for development—so the locals say.

But it is plagued by economic problems. We visited a tire factory, a chemical fertilizer plant, and a coal-washing plant which exports five types of washed coal in plastic bags to ten different countries. The quality of their output was good and they should have been making a profit, but they weren't. They complained they couldn't get enough credit, or that their taxes were too high, or that their customers—mainly large government enterprises—didn't pay their bills—mainly because the things the enterprises were producing, such as steel and cars, were selling poorly.

Ningxia, as an autonomous minority region, gets special government allotments and tax exemptions. Some of the money has gone into an over-optimistic economic expansion of buildings and shops and glittering gas stations. But the prevailing shortage of funds and investments makes Ningxia's economic future doubtful. Foreigners are willing to invest, but demand exorbitant terms.

We visited the remains of the Xixia (Western Xia) Kingdom. It lasted from 1038 till 1227, when it was wiped out by the Mongols of Genghis Khan. Ningxia means "the Pacified Xia." Stone tombs of the emperors in what is now the desert look like large muffins. Mainly local Tibetan tribes, the Xias evolved their own sophisticated form of writing. Not much is known about them.

Our hosts took us to an unusual new amusement park called Sha Hu, meaning "Sand [dunes] and Lake," about a one-hour drive north from Yinchuan. You ferry south across a reedy lake to where the ceaseless northwest winds have stopped the high marching sand dunes right at the edge of the lake.

For a small fee you could hire a two-humped Bactrian camel for a short ride. You mounted when it was kneeling. It rose rear-end first, and nearly dumped me over the front hump, then rose on its front legs, nearly tossing me off backwards. It walked with a more swaying gait than a horse, comfortable enough if you relaxed and swung with it. I imagine it would be wearying if you had to do it for an hour or more. To dismount, you had to wait till the camel knelt first on its front legs, then on its rear.

The dunes provided a high steep slope down which brave souls slid on rented toboggans. I sat on one and grasped handles on either side. The descent was breathtaking and very fast. It was over in about five seconds. Climbing back in the deep soft sand, dragging the toboggan, was hard work. It took three healthy young men to haul me to the top.

Not as much fun but more important was Shapotou, an area of vast sands a few miles away. Here Chinese experts were creating miracles in desertification in a

306

UN Environmental Protection Program. By weaving webs of grasses and planting shrubs which could survive with almost no rainfall, they had stopped encroaching dunes in their tracks, and went on to turn them into cultivated fields. The Chinese agency lectured and demonstrated in other desert-stricken countries, and trained foreign specialists who came for short courses. Shapotou also claimed it was short of funds, and pleaded that our CPPCC urge the Beijing authorities for more financial support.

I was constantly moved by the hard-working technicians and agronomists and scientists and engineers we met all over China on our CPPCC tours, men and women working for low pay under grueling conditions, cheerfully going about their jobs with virtually no thought for themselves. Every time I worried about the backwardness and graft and corruption, these modest heroic folk quickly restored my confidence in China's future.

A five-hour drive south from Yinchuan took us to Haiyuan. On a high loess plateau of poor soil, it was populated by a large, ancient Muslim community. When it rains they have some wheat, and grass for their sheep, but there had been no rain for the past two years. Their beautiful children, who clearly showed their Arab and Persian ancestry, depended on charitable donations for their clothing. One little boy of about eight was wearing as his sole garment a business suit jacket that came down to his ankles. In spite of their extreme poverty the community was reluctant to leave the land they have lived on for centuries and move down to a lower area which had been offered to them where there were good irrigation conditions.

Water was the key, and the mighty Yellow River ran along a large stretch of Ningxia's north-eastern border. It was providing some irrigation and power, but only a fraction of its full potential. The officials were pleading for more funding from Beijing. Our CPPCC group promised to put in a word for them, but warned the prospects were dim. China had a host of projects all in urgent need of financing. We asked whether they might expect help from the Arab countries. They said they were setting up a development bank and were trying to tap some of the rich Muslim business conglomerates in the Middle East. There had been a few promising responses, but the terms were unacceptable—the right to control Chinese Muslim religious leaders.

Further north in Ningxia there were a few prosperous Muslim communities where they raised beef cattle. Relatively enlightened, they provided a general education for their children. Even the girls went to school. One lovely 16-year-old I talked to had finished four years of primary—the usual amount of schooling for most kids. She liked rock music, and had pictures of pop stars on the walls of her room. She wanted no more school, and was not interested in finding a job. All she had to do was pick a husband from the dozens of wealthy suitors who would surely be pounding on her door.

In Ningxia about a third of the girls were Mohammedans. Theirs was a more rugged type of beauty, almost Western, with highly colored complexions. Those who have been liberated from the strictly orthodox strictures of Muslim homes no longer wore the headcovering formerly demanded of women, and were open and direct in manner.

The Han Chinese girls who constitute the majority nationwide, always very attractive, were now blossoming out in better cut clothes. Many went tooling about on flashy ten-speed bikes.

Zhongwei in the western section of Ningxia was an industrial city on the railway, just above the middle section of the upper reaches of the Yellow River, which here was not yellow but blue. However, an aluminum-smelting plant, one of China's four biggest, was poisoning its workers with deadly fumes, and dumping its polluted waste water into the river, killing the fish. This plant and others, by excessively tapping the underground water, had dangerously lowered its level. The plant had a showy reception and dining hall for impressing visitors. They had just built a new extension with the same lack of pollution control.

The city had a Buddhist Temple, the *Gaomiao*, built in the 15th century. It contained a Heaven and Hell, the latter including 18 torture rooms for the punishment of sinners—those who in life committed the feudal crimes of being "disloyal, unfilial, undutiful, unfaithful or shameless." The demons and their victims were all enacted by gruesome mechanical figures, who moved in dim green light to the accompaniment of awesome sounds and screams. A guide was stationed at the doorway of each of the rooms. I asked one of them—a sweet young girl—whether she wasn't frightened to stand all day so close to such horrors.

"Oh, no," she replied with complete seriousness. "If you haven't done anything wrong, you have nothing to worry about."

There were no placards, or any other material, in this Hell explaining to visitors that they were viewing a demonstration of superstitions used to terrorize people into submission to autocratic feudal rule. Male chauvinism, for example, was touted in the Sawing Room. A woman was shown being sawed in half down from the top of her head, separating her front from her back. Her sin was that she remarried after her first husband died, instead of remaining a "chaste" widow according to feudal morality. Half of her therefore was awarded to her first husband, half to her second.

The only indications of moral and ethical guidance I saw in Ningxia was offered not by the government or the Communist Party but by the imams, that is, the religious leaders of the followers of Islam. As the most respected members of the Muslim communities, they were the logical bridges between the officials and the Muslim masses. Unfortunately, the authorities seemed to be making little effort to win them over. Few of them held any grass-roots official positions. Only one or two were represented in the higher echelons.

Even less seemed to be being done for the rank and file Muslims. Ningxia had no newspaper devoted to their affairs. None of the Han Chinese papers had even a single column concerning them. I came away with the impression that the government leaders did not realize sufficiently the importance of the Hui Muslim population in a Hui autonomous region.

I said as much in a report I submitted, on returning to Beijing, to national government leaders.

After striking a blow for the Muslims in Ningxia, I felt constrained, in December, to defend the Jews in America. I did this in a letter to the *China Daily* which read:

> In your November 28 issue an article entitled "Magazine Has a Recipe for Success" included what it described as a "witty remark in the United States" as follows: "Americans' money is in the hands of the Jews and the Jews' appetite is in the control of the Chinese."
>
> The remark is false on both counts. The bulk of Americans' wealth is in the hands of non-Jews. Further, while some Jews occasionally go to Chinese restaurants, their appetites are drawn less by the quality of the food, which in America generally is not very high, than by its cost. The average American Jew has to watch his pennies.

I fully agree with the adage: "The price of liberty is constant vigilance," particularly when we include in our understanding of "liberty" freedom from prejudice and bigotry.

309

Summing Up Half a Century
1996

January, 1995, started with an announcement that the Chinese Literature Foundation had awarded prizes to six Chinese literary translators, four for renditions from English into Chinese, two for translations from Chinese into English. I was one of the two, for *Outlaws of the Marsh*. The other was Yang Xianyi who, together with his British wife Gladys Tayler, had produced a very readable version of *A Dream of Red Mansions*.

The literary community was pleased. While we liked to joke that *traduttore e traditore*—the Italian quip "the translator is a traitor," everyone felt it was time to recognize that literary translation is a commendable form of creative writing.

Instead of a silver loving cup, each received a beautiful cloisonne vase mounted on a wooden pedestal with an inscribed brass plaque. Very Chinese. Mine stands on a Ming Dynasty end table in an obscure corner of our living room. Also very modestly Chinese.

Washington's disinformation gnomes continued to invent wild stories designed to show how naughtily abusive China was of "human rights," hoping these unrelenting attacks would somehow soften Beijing up in trade negotiations. They had no effect at all. In February, the Information Office of the State Council of China finally got around to replying to the "Human Rights Report" issued by the US State Department the year before.

Step by step, it refuted each of the current lies, providing the true facts in detail. It also pointed out some of the wretched inhuman conditions in the United States, as compared with China's social record.

At the same time, leaders of Third World countries subjected to "human rights" slanders poured torrents of anathema down on Washington heads. Delegates to a human rights conference in Malaysia said the problem in their countries was not human rights, but poverty, imposed and compounded by Western economic domination.

A Kenyan professor teaching in the United States said people in his country were very conscious of how "human rights" were applied to Blacks. He noted that approximately 40 percent of the prisoners on death row were African-Americans. "In the United States today," he said, "there are more male descendants of African slaves in prison than in college."

One might suppose such reactions would evoke a certain amount of rethinking of American Third World policy. But the gentlemen with the Bill of Rights in one hand and a fistful of trade concession demands in the other are nothing if not staunch. We can only hope more intelligent, and more practical, minds will eventually prevail.

Stella came home in May on her first vacation after entering the Breck prep school in Minneapolis. Part of a group of students who would receive credits for touring China, she remained on after the others went back. Taller and huskier, she complained it was really hard to stay slim on an American diet. She was popular, had friends, went to dances, and had done well in her courses. Stella had matured, and she had made up her mind—she didn't want to spend her life in America. China was her home, and she would return after she finished college.

That was fine with us, parents and grandparents. Although naturally we hoped she would be with us because we loved her, we had been mentally prepared for her to remain in America, and come home only for occasional visits. China was backward, there were better job opportunities abroad.

Now, that was changing. China was riding a rising economic wave. Many foreign companies were looking for young people who were bilingual, and who knew a little about business, or science, or technology, or a dozen other things. The job market for girls like Stella was wide open. To live in her own country, and be with her family and her friends, and be able to earn a good living—that was perfect. We all felt happy with the prospects.

She had scored high on her PSAT (Preliminary Student Aptitude Test), taken at Breck, and a dozen colleges had written to her, inviting her to apply. When she returned to Breck at the end of the summer she still didn't know which college would take her, or what precisely she wanted to major in. But there seemed little doubt she would be accepted into a good school, and obtain at least a partial scholarship.

Fifty thousand women from every corner of the globe gathered in Beijing in late August and early September 1995, for the Fourth World Conference on Women. The numbers were so enormous that the conference had to be divided in two sections. The Non-Government Organization, or NGO, embracing about 35,000 delegates, met in Huairou, a beautiful suburb some 20 miles from the city proper. The municipal authorities had done a marvel of organization, and the congregating ladies expressed great satisfaction with the food, the accommodations, the transport, the shopping, and service facilities. There were even day care centers for the kids some of the women had brought along.

Dozens of tents were set up, in which different topics were discussed and argued. Delegates could wander from one to another and participate in whatever was going on. It was very fresh and spontaneous. The ladies were delighted to be able to exchange views with women from other lands, and with their Chinese hosts. Generally, they all got along fine, except when a couple of ringers from an alleged

311

"human rights" group handed out phony material on Tibet. At that point, a few Tibetan women delegates refuted them so overwhelmingly they shamefacedly slipped away.

A UN-sponsored women's conference was proceeding at the same time in Beijing in the city proper, attended by a mere 15,000. This was more official and more formal. Dignitaries and heads of state from various countries addressed the meeting. Hillary Clinton also spoke, straddling the fence in a speech designed to please everyone and which ended, as such talks usually do, pleasing no one. I don't think it earned her husband any support, since she vacillated as he often did on important issues.

It was a miracle that when the conferences ended, the delegates from both meetings were able to hammer out a joint declaration of principles on which all agreed. The women vowed they would return to their respective lands and fight to have these principles implemented. It wasn't going to be easy, but they said it gave them courage to know they had sisters in so many countries struggling for the same goals, women they could depend on for support.

Almost universally they came away in love with China, charmed by the warm and easy and caring Chinese. All the slanders they had been deluged with in their hometown press simply vanished in the face of reality. They became good friends and strong allies in the battle for women's rights.

One of the most astonishing (to me) articles which emerged as a result of the conference appeared in *Beijing Review*, China's weekly news magazine. It compared the difference in rights between women in America and women in China. Here, in essence, is a sample of some of the items:

> The US Constitution contains not a single article providing equal rights for men and women. A constitutional amendment to that effect, submitted to the US Congress in 1923, was not passed until 1972. Ten years later, in 1982, it was invalidated because it failed to receive ratification by the required number of state legislatures.
>
> China's Constitution, adopted in 1954, stipulates: "Women in the People's Republic of China enjoy equal rights with men in all spheres of life, including political, economic, cultural, social and family life." On the basis of this, China has enacted more than ten laws, such as the Law on the Protection of Rights and Interests of Women, Marriage Law, Electoral Law, Criminal Law, Civil Law, Inheritance Law, and Labor Law, all containing specific provisions protecting women's rights.
>
> American women did not obtain the right to vote until 144 years after the founding of the United States. Chinese women were granted such rights immediately on the establishment of the People's Republic in 1949.

Only about 1 percent of the members in the US Congress are women. In China's Congress, women constitute 19.6 percent.

Three percent of senior management jobs are held by women in the United States. In China, it's 10 percent.

In the United States women have 32 percent fewer job opportunities than men. In China's urban areas, the figure for women is 16 percent.

Women university engineering graduates: America, 15 percent; China, 27 percent.

Skilled industrial women workers: In the United States they receive 59 percent of men's pay. In China, the pay is equal.

Crimes against women, such as rape, murder, robbery and assault, in America are 18 times the figure in China, which has a population five times that of the United States.

Divorce rate: about 50 percent in America, about 10 percent in China.

This is the sort of thing that makes Chinese skeptical when Washington tries to address them in a high moral tone. That is not to say China is without fault. Male chauvinism remains strong. But it's changing now that women are proving increasingly competent as money earners on the farms, in light industry, and in business.

The US-China People's Friendship Association was planning to hold its 20th anniversary convention in Indianapolis in October 1995, and they invited me to attend as a guest speaker. I gladly agreed, and started to prepare to answer some of the questions I knew I surely would be asked about human rights. Not a few Americans had been brain washed by the distortions appearing in books and articles written by "China experts."

To get some first-hand information I visited Beijing Prison, about 50 miles outside the city. It held some 900 inmates, all men, of an average age of around 30. Eighty percent were in for economic crimes, 7 percent were violent offenders. Their sentences averaged ten years, or less. Only 3 or 4 percent were recidivists, as against the national average of 6 to 8 percent. (In America it was over 40 percent.) About 80 percent had a middle-school education.

The whole area was enclosed by a high wall and was guarded. But there were trees and flowers on the grounds, and no bars on the doors and windows of the dormitories. Each of the rooms contained two or three double-decker bunks, and a few chairs and tables. The men kept their belongings in lockers in another room, and they had keys to the lockers. There was a TV room where they could watch programs chosen by the guards. They could read newspapers and discuss the news.

Classes were held in political and social morality, and in literacy. Special emphasis was placed on an appreciation of labor—every person must work for a living to be a useful member of society. We visited a large garage where the inmates learned to repair cars. They received pay. Most kept a net of around 100 yuan a month, after the cost of their meals was deducted. That varied because there were three price levels from which they could choose. The food I saw looked pretty good.

Discipline was maintained by a merit and demerit system. General behavior and conduct on the job were regularly appraised. Very good performance could result in lessening of sentences by up to five years. Periodic family visits were allowed. A few exceptionally well-behaved prisoners could go home for weekends. Each prisoner was taught one or two technical skills. They were given certificates of ability on release. Most of them were able to get jobs.

According to the warden the aim was not punishment but reform. "The old society turned men into devils," he said. "The new turns devils into men. We want to make them useful members of their communities." To this end, not only were the individual prisoners carefully observed, but the guards discussed among themselves their own methods and behavior.

The warden told us this was one of nine prisons in Beijing. Only one was used for women, and that was half empty. For the whole country there were 1.2 million prison inmates out of a population of 1.2 billion, that is, one in 1,000. Violent crimes were decreasing, but economic crimes were on the rise. There was a lot more money around, and more schemes to get hold of it.

At the last minute I had to call off my trip to the States and my appearance at the USCPFA conference. Phoenix had been suffering from failing kidney function for several years, and the ailment took a turn for the worse. She spent ten days in the hospital until her condition improved. We brought her home, but she required care. Since I worked at home, I could help look after her. Moreover, by not spending a month abroad I would be able to use the time to finish the first draft of this book by the end of the year.

One of the most important functions and duties of a member of the Chinese People's Political Consultative Conference is to submit in writing formal proposals regarding the work of the government. I had been rather lax, and had excused myself with the knowledge that few of these proposals produced any substantial change. But I was approaching 80. I didn't know how much longer I could remain in the CPPCC. If there was anything I felt strongly about, this was the time to speak up. Though I had little hope it would be acted upon, I submitted a proposal entitled, *Nicotine Is a Deadly Poison of Enormous Harm to the People; Therefore the Raising of Tobacco and the Production and Sale of Cigarettes Must Be Prohibited*. I addressed it to the Standing Committee of the Political Bureau of the Central Committee of the Chinese Communist Party. It read as follows:

China has more cigarette smokers than any other country in the world. No one questions that cigarettes are a dangerous health hazard, which is now spreading among women and children. The argument most often put forward against the prohibition of cigarettes is that doing so would cause heavy financial loss to the tobacco farmers, to the cigarette factory workers, and to government tax revenues.

These are not insoluble problems. The farmers can be subsidized to plant other crops. Tobacco factories can be converted to the manufacture of other products, and the workers subsidized during the conversion or transferred to other industries.

Admittedly, large tax revenues would be lost. But the losses to national income caused by cigarette smoking are much greater. This is clearly evident when we add up the medical costs to victims who are ill or dying from smoking cigarettes, plus the medical costs to persons around them (including their wives, children, fellow workers, etc.) whom they indirectly pollute, plus the drop in efficiency of millions of people in many fields of endeavor because their health is sapped by cigarette smoking, plus the high costs of patrolling land and sea borders against smugglers. . . . No doubt many more items could be added to this list.

While the monetary aspects of the problem are important, from the standpoint of socialist morality they are beside the point. Nicotine in cigarettes is a deadly poison. It kills more slowly than the so-called hard drugs, but it is a lethal drug and it affects a much greater number of people. To permit the continued use of nicotine-bearing cigarettes, for any excuse or "explanation" whatsoever, is a gross violation of the fundamental Communist Party principle of serving and defending the people.

A large part of the cigarettes manufactured in China is exported, resulting in harm to people in other countries as well. This violates the Party principle of socialist internationalism.

Whether we view the matter from a purely monetary viewpoint, or from how it affects the welfare of the people of China and the world, cigarette smoking is very harmful and should be stopped. Few people here disagree with this argument.

The problem is complicated by the financial concerns of the special interest groups involved. It would be difficult to overcome their objections to possible legislation or administrative orders unless the Party first takes a firm stand as a matter of principle and policy.

I therefore address this plea to the Standing Committee of the Political Bureau.

In a letter with similar content which I subsequently sent to *China Daily*, and which they published in December, I added the following information:

> Medical experts from 30 countries attending an international conference recently in Thailand presented shocking evidence of the devastating damage cigarettes are inflicting on people in Asia-Pacific areas.
>
> China, whose 300 million smokers consume 30 percent of the world's cigarettes, has the world's highest annual death rate from cigarette-induced diseases—500,000. That figure is expected to reach 2 million annually by 2020.
>
> Over 70 percent of China's middle-aged men smoke. Some 50 million children and adolescents probably will die from cigarette smoking when they reach maturity.

There is mounting concern in China over the dangers of cigarette smoking. Ads for cigarettes are prohibited in the press, on TV, on billboards. Cigarette companies can no long sponsor athletic events as an excuse to prominently display their names. Schools conduct educational campaigns against cigarette smoking by children and teenagers (but not by their parents).

These peripheral assaults have had little effect, in fact the number of cigarette smokers in China has increased, and the number of smoking-induced illnesses is mounting rapidly. Foreign manufacturers, whose sales in their own countries have fallen due to fears of lung cancer and heart disease, move heaven and earth to get their products into China, with considerable success. Although their sale is illegal, you can buy them openly at any of the thousands of street stands.

It is unfortunate that the authorities, while encouraging a number of measures to limit cigarette smoking, are failing to extirpate the evil at its root, as they did with opium.

Opium was a terrible scourge in old China, ruinous to the health and a drain on personal income. Millions smoked, whether they could afford it or not. Coolies who carried sedan chairs up mountain slopes could get one puff from an opium pipe for two coppers at rest stations along the way. Everywhere you saw bleary-eyed, runny-nosed addicts, yawning uncontrollably, their lungs starved for lack of oxygen.

After liberation, the new government acted promptly. Except for limited amounts used for controlled medical purposes, raising of the opium poppy was prohibited, as was the manufacture of the drug, and its sale. The measures were extremely effective. Penalties for violations were severe. Within a year opium smoking as a drug habit was gone.

To me it is beyond comprehension that the Chinese authorities should fail to take decisive action against the raising of tobacco and the manufacture and sale of cigarettes. The damage they do is more widespread than opium, and is clearly criminal.

While crimes were always punishable by law in old China, the concept of legality in the civil sense is something new. The Chinese are vague about their civil rights. In the old society, for example, businessmen rarely entered into contracts. Their word was their bond. Nowadays people do sign contracts. But in the event of what we would consider a breach, they seldom take the case to court. Instead they try to work things out through an intermediary, or by direct discussion. This is hardly a course I can object to. What troubles me is that they don't seem to realize they have enforceable legal rights.

Nor are there many actions for injuries to persons or property. Those which are brought are strictly for pecuniary damage. If you are knocked down and injured by a negligent driver of a car (or more often, a bike rider) he is expected to pay your doctor's bills and make up for the pay lost on your job. I have never heard of recompense being sought for pain and suffering. It doesn't mean such a claim could not succeed, only that so far it has not occurred to any plaintiff to make this demand.

Why not? Because of the concept that the individual's inner feelings are secondary to the influence on society as a whole. This was the accepted norm under 2000 years of feudalism, and it has been continued under socialism. In fact, it jibes perfectly with the socialist stress on collective effort and social stability. Unpleasantness is better swept under the rug. One can get damages for humiliation as a result of libel or slander, for loss of "face," but this is not so much for individual affront as for the fact that libel and slander are deemed upsetting to social propriety and community equanimity.

In any well-ordered society it is necessary to subordinate the wishes of the individual to the public good. But that is quite different from the continuation under socialism of the autocratic traditions of China's deposed feudal society, from the taking for granted that all persons in authority—in every division of society—are unquestionably correct and should be unquestioningly respected and obeyed. The distinction is not always borne in mind.

Autocracy and paternalism were the linchpins of feudal rule. At the top was the emperor, who floated in an ethereal atmosphere of semidivinity. Down the line of awesome officials you came to the county magistrate, modestly known as "the father and mother of the people." He was the investigator, the judge, the jury, the ultimate determiner of the fate of all persons and all property. While there was a right of appeal, in most cases the decision of the magistrate was accepted as final.

In the rural areas, where 80 to 90 percent of the population lived, the heads of clans exercised almost complete control. They could confiscate property, fine, arrest, have the accused beaten, or put to death, for violations of the clan's moral

317

code, which was itself authoritarian and paternalistic. Their powers were on a par with those of the local authorities, and often had a more immediate impact.

The father was the absolute head of the family. He owned all the property. His wife's property became his when they married. She had no right of inheritance. He could beat her and the children with impunity, and even kill them for particularly heinous violations of feudal morality. While most fathers were kindly, decent beings, the menacing aura surrounding them was always there.

Highly regarded—though miserably paid—in feudal society was the teacher. He inculcated the sons of better-off families with the feudal tenets replete in every text. Learning was by rote. No questions were asked, or expected.

Today, while these tyrannies have been officially discarded, the echoes are still audible. Training in the traditional attitudes starts in childhood. The highest praise one can offer of a little boy is that he *ting hua*—he is "obedient." Grade school children when not reading or writing must sit with their hands behind their backs, or clasped firmly together on their desks, "to keep them out of mischief." Although it is better now, right up through university questions are rarely asked in class, and memorization is stronger in the learning process than rationalization.

The father is still very much the head of the family. Most children would not dream of entering into a marriage, for instance, of which he did not approve. He decides all family disputes and controls the finances.

Young people in the workplace are generally obedient, and careful not to give offense to their superiors. Government directives and government agencies receive immediate initial respect, although complaint and protest are more frequent than in the old days. The worst breach a citizen can commit is to endanger "stability." When the interpretation is taken to its extreme it can mean simply failing to be obedient to authority.

The student protests at Tiananmen were labeled "counter-revolutionary," in other words, "treason." Any questioning of the correctness of the behavior of the paternalistic leadership simply could not be countenanced. The students were quashed, and with them a lot of their enthusiastic and creative contributions to progressive change. They became noticeably more quiet, as did a large part of the intellectual community. The loss to China went beyond the infringement of student rights to free speech.

No doubt there were a few villains and scoundrels among them who sought to take advantage of the confused situation for purposes of their own. It would have been surprising if there were not. But a few rumbles do not make a thunderstorm. The reaction of the leadership shook the Chinese because it was needlessly harsh, and demonstrated a lack of confidence in the people and an inability to deal democratically with a crisis.

318

According to their Constitution the Chinese have the same democratic rights as anyone else. The reason they don't speak up so often, so loudly and so clearly as Americans is not that they have no right to. During the "cultural revolution" China suffered from a frenzied insanity, and people didn't speak for fear of the fanatics then in control. But that was a temporary aberration, and China soon returned to an era of relatively frank expression of opinion.

What inhibits open indignant blasts at wrong-doing, with pointing of fingers and naming of names, in China today is a Chinese reluctance to wash dirty linen in public. They try to save embarrassment not to the culprit but to his family, his associates, the community, and to the authorities—who should not have allowed such a thing to happen in the first place. It is not the Chinese way to drag shameful matters out into the open. They proceed against the culprits forcefully, but quietly, "through channels." This was traditional in China, and it has not changed.

A corollary to an oversensitivity to the sanctity of the authorities is an undersensitivity to the well-being of the millions of individuals who collectively constitute the people. This violates the primary duty of the leadership who, according to Mao Zedong, must preserve the interests of the masses. Meaning not just their economic comfort, but also their physical and mental health, their psychological ease.

Recent newspaper reports reveal serious deficiencies in all these areas. More importance is attached to "economic" crimes than to crimes against human dignity. Members of a gang which specialized in kidnaping little boys for sale to families in other provinces who wanted sons were sentenced to only a few years in prison. Men who forged receipt books and sold them to stores, enabling the managers to conceal actual sales and cheat the government out of taxes, were sentenced to death and executed.

There has been a marked slackening in concern for the people's health. Endemic diseases are a worrying problem for more than 80 percent of Chinese cities. Nationally, a large part of the population is again at risk from endemic diseases which had earlier been eradicated. Lax public health work and insufficient medical care are blamed. Snail fever still prevails in 123 counties in the lake areas of south China, which are home to 66 million people. Animal plague is the most serious and widespread it has been for two decades.

Some middle school teachers apparently have not lost the old feudal attitude of being the stern disciplinarian whose job is to brutalize the pupils into getting good grades. Instead of boosting the students' self-esteem and easing feelings of inferiority, they bludgeon them with comments like: "I'm ashamed of having a student like you," or "Get out," or "You're retarded!" Some teenagers have to quit school. A Beijing schoolgirl attempted suicide.

Feudal hangovers are the devil of the piece in almost every aspect of Chinese life. Although there have been several major educational campaigns, in the 40-odd

319

years since the establishment of the People's Republic, not one has been directed against the evils of the feudal mentality.

The most important event of 1995 was the promulgating of China's blueprint for economic and social development during the last five years of the 20th century and the first decade of the 21st century. Audaciously it proposed to quadruple the 1980 per capita gross national product by the year 2000, and within the following ten years double the 2000 GNP. If successful, the standard of living of the average Chinese will be vastly improved.

The obstacles are formidable. Not everyone is sure China can do it, to put it mildly. At a full meeting of the Central Committee of the Communist Party, the problems were dispassionately set out in the form of 12 inharmonious relationships. To paraphrase, they were stated thus:

1. Between reform, development and stability. Development is the key to the solution to all of China's problems, and reform the guarantee of the effectiveness of development. Neither can be implemented without a stable political and social environment.

2. Between speed and efficiency. There is a tendency to push for a high growth rate at the expense of quality, to start new projects on too large a scale, to neglect scientific and technological improvement and the upgrading of labor efficiency. Needed is a socialist market economic structure, implemented by appropriate administrative and legal measures.

3. Between economic growth and population, resources and environment. Family planning is essential to control both the size and the quality of the population. China should expect an increase of 200 million more people in the next 15 years. They will have to be fed, and provided with good living conditions and opportunities for employment. Rural township enterprises and small businesses should be able to employ much of the surplus labor from the farms. China's limited arable land, water and mineral resources must be environmentally protected to meet the demands of an expanded population. Industries and the public must guard against waste and pollution.

The true measure of economic growth is not simply gross national product but GNP per capita. To quadruple this by the year 2000 China must increase her output by at least 8.7 percent annually. At present 43 percent of production is eaten away by population increase. China has to keep population growth to a much lower rate than production output in order to attain the per capita target.

Healthy young men and women are leaving the farms in large numbers because government prices for agricultural products, particularly grain, are too low. Rural township enterprises seem an excellent practical way of employing much of the surplus rural labor. Some members of a farm family work in a newly established workshop or small factory, while the rest remain on the land. Or they go only in slack agricultural seasons.

But greedy local officials quickly ruin many of the more successful enterprises with fees and taxes as soon as they start to grow, or simply take them over. The young people then gravitate to the already overcrowded cities, increasing problems of crime, pollution, housing and supply.

The township enterprises in some places are themselves proving a problem. They tend to duplicate each other's products, turning out more than the market can bear, and quality is often poor. They heavily burden sources of supply and transport facilities, and dump their wastes into the nearest stream or field. Arable land is spoiled, water rendered undrinkable. Local officials are persuaded to turn a blind eye. Pollution is worse in heavily industrial regions, but public pressure has forced more restraint.

Today the policy is to encourage the development of efficient township enterprises, and at the same time enlarge existing small towns and cities, or create new ones, where modern planning and management can be implemented to absorb redundant labor from the farms.

Commentators have expressed concern over the cultural effects of consumerism. They say urban youths especially identify more with consumer goods than with traditional values. The meaning of life is tied to money and luxury items. They fear this will widen the gap between rich and poor, and cause social unrest.

4. Between agriculture, industry, and the tertiary sector. (The tertiary sector includes banking, finance, insurance, transport, shipping, real estate, the service trades and so on.)

Agriculture is of the utmost importance. It not only has to feed and supply sideline products to over one billion people, it also must provide raw materials for industry. It is a huge market for industry and the tertiary sector. Basic government policies must be improved, and more government funds provided. Science and technology must be brought into full play.

China's per capita consumption of major manufactured products is relatively low. All sectors of the economy are dependent on the manufacturing industry for large amounts of advanced technology and equipment. Its enormous potential has yet to be tapped.

Development of the tertiary sector reduces the strains on capital and resources, provides large employment opportunities, and optimizes the product mix. It needs to be standardized and management improved. Top priority must be given to serving the daily needs of the majority of the people. Financing and real estate operations should be guided into healthy channels.

About 80 percent of China's 1.2 billion people live in the countryside. The government has been underpaying the farmers for crops and decreasing its investment in agriculture. Meanwhile, the costs of farming have been rising, and taxes have increased. The prices farm families have to pay for consumer goods have also risen. With lower incomes farmers are buying less, thus adversely affecting China's industry whose main market is in the rural areas. Improving the income of the farmers—the vast majority of the Chinese people—is fundamental, and urgent.

Beggars have appeared again on the streets of Beijing. I hadn't seen any in years. They are few in numbers, professionals, not persons really in need, but it is a disturbing sign of the times.

5. Between the eastern and the central-western regions. Under the Ninth Five-Year Plan, starting in 1996, China will intensify its efforts to narrow the widening gap. The farther regions should speed up reform, make full use of their abundant resources, and develop appropriate industries. The eastern region should update their modes of operation, raise quality and efficiency, and provide help to the more backward regions.

The remote regions are rich in everything from oil, minerals, and cotton to delicious perishable fruits. Bringing the railways in and spreading the infrastructure will increase income and lure more foreign investment. This in turn will attract engineers and specialists, expand the population, and create a boom comparable to the opening of the American West in the 19th century. Some of the investors presently concentrated along the east coast will try to get a piece of the action in the hinterlands as well.

6. Between a market economy and macro control. Chinese socialism stresses the importance of both immediate economic efficiency and long-range planning. There should be a freer hand in all market regulated economic activities, particularly those of the competitive and infrastructural industries.

At the same time the central government should continue to give guidance and exercise control over market activities. China is in the process of transforming its economic system, upgrading its industrial structure, and speeding its economic development. This makes an improved macro-control system, supplemented by economic, legal and administrative measures, all the more necessary.

Government functions must be transformed, and government administration separated from enterprise management. The existing setup of government organizations is not compatible with the development of a socialist market economy.

322

How free the free market should be is a question faced by every country, regardless of political system, according to its own circumstances. China has leaped over the capitalist stage and moved from feudalism directly into a form of socialism, in a world dominated by capitalist superpowers. It is cautiously feeling its way, unprecedented and unique, surprisingly well thus far. The result will depend, in part, on how successfully China can juxtapose the structural and organizational mix.

7. Between the public and collective enterprises as compared with the individual, private and foreign-funded enterprises. The predominance of the public (that is, the government at various levels) sector is a cardinal principle of socialism, and is basic to a socialist market economy. The bulk of the country's assets should be owned by the public or by collective enterprises. The public enterprises should continuously develop and expand. At the same time the non-public enterprises should be encouraged and guided as necessary supplements to the socialist economy.

Public enterprises are owned by the people as a whole and are operated either by the national government or local governments on behalf of the national government. The large public enterprises are directly controlled by the national government and run China's fundamental industries and build the infrastructure. They produce half the gross domestic product, and contribute 90 percent of the output value of minerals, processed petroleum, electricity and water. To a large extent they control market supply and influence prices. They employ hundreds of thousands, and provide cheap commodities for lower-income families.

On the minus side, more than one-third of the public enterprises are in the red, burdened by huge debts, heavy taxes, and the obligation to support thousands of retired workers and employees. Most of these are small enterprises operated by local governments under agreement with the central authorities. More than 90 percent of their working capital comes from bank loans. Their problems are compounded by bad management, an abundance of redundant employees, and interference in their internal operations by government administrators. Ironically, their failings have proved a boon to township and private enterprises. Their more talented personnel resign and join the better-paying nonpublic companies. At the same time these people retain their rights to the housing and social security provided by the public enterprises which formerly employed them.

Some of the smaller public companies are encouraged to merge or go into bankruptcy. This measure is adopted with caution. Putting too many unemployed on the streets could cause unrest.

8. Between the rich and the poor. In place of the former egalitarian distribution of income, present policy allows some localities and individuals to become rich ahead of others, if their earnings are legal. The income gaps between some of them are too large. Polarization must be prevented. The tradition of frugality and hard work should be maintained and splurging discouraged. A common prosperity will be attained by gradually increasing the income of all.

American economist Thorstein Veblen would surely have been startled had he lived to learn of "conspicuous consumption"—which he excoriated as an evil of capitalism—in a socialist society. We see it everywhere among the *nouveau riche* in China's business world. (It must be noted that the big spenders are conspicuous because they are a very small segment of a very large nonaffluent society.) Not all ofthese gents are private entrepreneurs. Some are officials in government commercial organizations. One can't help wondering where they get their money.

A few of the larger public enterprises have found a convenient way to increase their earnings without increasing production. Because of their size and status they have easy access to bank loans. They relend the money at higher rates to smaller firms which have difficulty in obtaining credit. Or they play the real estate market, or engage in other speculative activity. They spend more time in the money game than in developing new products, despite the fact that the demand for good durable merchandise in China far exceeds supply. Getting rich is now respectable, and certain firms and some individuals are not too fussy about how they get there.

Bringing prosperity to the average person is a lot more difficult. His income has risen a bit, but so have inflationary costs and expenses. He is not thinking about becoming wealthy. He will be satisfied if he can stay where he is financially.

9. Between opening wider to the outside world and self-reliance. The first must be based on the second. China should develop its own technologies at the same time it introduces advanced technologies from abroad. While utilizing foreign funds, China should be accumulating funds of her own.

This is a difficult policy to implement. China has to offer sufficient returns to induce foreign entrepreneurs to invest, and yet not give so much away that she loses more than she gains. Excessive tax breaks and real estate bargains have been all too common, as have overly generous terms on income sharing and control. The Chinese are often inexperienced and naive, and are easily deluded by foreign parties to a deal. Big foreign corporations are generally honest, though tough. But the smaller ones frequently engage in sharp practices and deliver shoddy products. Big or small, all the foreign enterprises play their cards close to their vests and reveal as little as possible of valuable technology and managerial expertise.

The Chinese authorities are aware of this, but say privately they can accept being taken advantage of—until they have learned enough and are strong enough to act more independently. They call this "paying their tuition."

Foreign enterprises know that in providing funding and technological and managerial skills they are creating potential Chinese competitors. But the Chinese market is so large and luscious they are willing to give away more than they would like in order to grab a maximum of big profits now, and let the future take care of itself. They also put up with outrageous rentals and other charges and the occasional need to pay bribes and kick-backs. The advantages are not all on the foreign side.

Opinions vary among Chinese economists, not on the desirability of "opening the door," but on how wide and how quickly it should be opened, and how Chinese enterprises should respond to its opening. Some feel China should not rush into becoming a member of the World Trade Organization. They say it would expose tens of thousands of Chinese firms to competition from foreign goods, which are mainly of better quality and more attractively presented than domestic products. Many workers could lose their jobs.

Others contend that foreign competition should be welcomed. They say it stimulates Chinese factories to improve the quality of similar merchandise. In practice, this is often not the case. The Chinese manufacturer is quickly driven from the relatively affluent and demanding urban market. But, instead of improving its products, the factory takes them to the rural areas, where the market is infinitely larger and people are willing to buy somewhat inferior goods if they are cheaper. The result is two markets—one for foreign imports, and one for domestic goods, and little improvement in domestic quality.

Prevailing opinion is that the policy of opening and reform is theoretically sound. Foreign input and foreign competition are a stimulus—provided Chinese management, methodology, worker skills, equipment, incentives, and government assistance and guidance are intelligently employed.

10. Between the central and local authorities. China is a large country with a big population, complicated conditions and uneven economic development. Local authorities are best suited to deal flexibly with local conditions. At the same time, since the nation's economy is organically integrated the central authorities must ensure an overall balance and co-ordinated development.

The results of delegating power to the local authorities have generally been good, but some have paid undue attention to their own interests, and have failed to do what they should in implementing central government principles and policies. Some have even disobeyed orders and defied prohibitions. The power belonging to the central authorities has not been completely centralized and, in some aspects, it is over-decentralized.

The division of economic management rights between the central and local authorities must be clearly defined, with local power subject to centralized guidance.

The large enterprises are operated by the national authorities. These are important. 800 of them own 63 percent of China's total industrial assets, account for 70 percent of national industrial sales, and contribute 74 percent of China's industrial taxes.

A tentative program is shaping up whereby public enterprises operated by the local governments on the provincial level and below will have the power to reorganize, merge, lease, or sell them. In the past few years local governments' powers have expanded and their financial income has increased. They now get over 70 percent of China's total revenue. The local governments claim their income is not excessive since they are burdened with all the costs of local development, economy, education, culture, and civil and judicial affairs. The central government has been able to limit their ballooning power somewhat by introducing a system of dividing taxes and exercising overall control of the economy.

The duel goes on. "You have your *zheng ce* (measures), we have our *dui ce* (counter-measures)," is a popular local saying. The local governments do everything they can to vitiate national orders which they consider to their disadvantage. Some falsify reports to Beijing. It is an extremely serious problem, with no solution immediately in sight.

11. Between financing national defense and financing the national economy. While a strong defense guarantees national security and economic development, it can only be built on the foundation of a solid national economy. More high technology and scientific research should go into defense, and the equipment of the armed forces should be further modernized. At the same time, the defense establishment should engage in both civilian and military production and make them interoperational.

One of the plagues in emerging nations is the incessant jockeying for power between the military and the civil authorities. Failures of the economy are usually the excuse for takeovers by the military, who don't as a rule do any better but have the hardware to prevent being unseated once they are in.

326

The Beijing government wants to ensure there are no coups in China, but it is more concerned about building a strong defense against outside aggression. China has a long history of being attacked and invaded by foreign powers, with each incursion setting the country back by decades. Her rapid growth and rising prosperity have aroused envy and fears in certain other countries, all of whom have a record of unscrupulous assaults, military as well as civil, on targets they consider weakly defended.

The Chinese armed forces are the fire brigades who rush into disaster areas, give timely aid on the farms, build roads, railways, and help with scores of dirty and difficult jobs. They also teach valuable skills to thousands of young men and women recruits every year and instill in them a sense of morality and social responsibility.

12. Between material and cultural-ideological progress. There should be no conflict between them. These are mutually dependent goals. Under no circumstances should temporary economic growth be achieved at the expense of cultural and ideological advance.

The policy of reform and opening to the outside world has brought China good political and economic results, and internally there has been considerable progress in the cultural and ideological fields. But ideological and political education has been weak. There is more money worship and pleasure-seeking. In some places public security is poor. Corrupt and ugly phenomena have reappeared.

It is imperative to carry on the fine traditions of the Chinese Communist Party and of China's cultural heritage, nurture moral integrity, absorb all the achievements of world civilization, and upgrade China's ideology, morality, science and culture. They must keep pace with, and be included in, the overall plan for national economic and social development.

When the reforms and opening to the outside world began in the 1980s, morality was said to be as important as material gains. But then Deng Xiaoping was quoted as saying that it was not wrong for persons who had made special accomplishments to get rich before the general public, and the tone of newspaper articles and editorials began to change. Some insisted the economy had to be improved first. Once there was money around and more economic activity it would be time to start worrying about morality and ethics. In fact material gains would themselves help raise moral standards.

Reality didn't work that way at all. Many interpreted the dictum that getting rich was not bad as meaning that any way you got rich was good, that you didn't have to be too fussy about how. Crime, graft and corruption grew. There was a flourishing of the old vices, and a few new ones invented.

To antiquated, fusty concepts left over from feudal society, the "advanced civilizations" of the outside world were able to contribute twists made more interesting by their advanced technologies. We were deluged with toothpastes, hamburgers, movies and TV programs stressing the torments of frustrated neurotics, lots of sex and violence, fashion shows with skinny, voguish models, and other blessings of the Free World.

When concern was voiced about this new foreign invasion, nonchalant free-wheelers quoted Deng Xiaoping. Hadn't he said: "When you open the window it doesn't matter if a few flies get in."

True enough, but he hadn't said you needn't swat the flies that did get in.

In the blueprint for China's advance into the 21st century, the 12th item on the agenda regarding "cultural-ideological progress" is, in my opinion, fundamental. None of the other goals can be attained without a moral rearmament.

Immorality as manifested in crime, vice, and corruption is obvious and serious. But its greatest danger to China's social stability lies in the immorality fostered and perpetuated by certain pernicious elements in China's feudal heritage that have persisted to this day. Despite frequent lip service to the need to expunge them, the damage they continue to wreak has been underestimated. Little action is taken against them. It's rather like Mark Twain's remark about the weather: "Everybody talks about it, but nobody ever does anything about it."

Using "connections," paying bribes, putting private loyalties above public good, blind worship of authority—practices like these are considered to be almost required behavior for advancement and survival in such an environment. It is difficult to implement lasting reforms, however good the plans put forward, however honest and well-intended the leadership. China has won her political revolution, but the revolution against feudalism is still unfinished.

During the Mao era China had a moral code. There were clearly defined standards—for the average citizen as well as for the Chinese Communist. People knew what was admirable, what was despicable, and most Chinese behaved accordingly. When the fanatic faults of the Mao era were discarded, the code was discarded with them. No new code has replaced it. Inevitably, greed and corruption rushed in to fill the vacuum.

There is a vague call to "carry forward the fine traditions of the Party as well as the fine ideas and culture of the Chinese nation." The leadership has to do better than that. It must state specifically what these fine Communist traditions are, what the fine ideas and culture of China's feudal heritage are. It must tell why they are worthy of respect, and explain how essential it is for everyone to implement them in their daily lives. The whole population must talk about them, analyze them, appreciate them. And the highest leadership must first lead by example. There is a Chinese saying: "The roots start at the top."

328

In addition to a firm moral foundation, a key requirement to a successful future is leadership by central authorities of the highest quality. That is, the heads of the Communist Party and government organizations in Beijing. (Most of the major government leaders are at the same time Communists.) The Party creates the policies and oversees their implementation. The government makes the laws and puts them into effect.

The role of the Communist Party is crucial. Can it impel government leaders on the provincial level and below to adhere to Party policies and fully implement government laws? Can it inspire the Chinese people to continue their enthusiastic drive to a new socialist China? Can they, together, create a society which has plan and purpose, and affords the freedom and personal incentive conducive to maximum creativity?

I find both Communist and government leaders in Beijing quite impressive. With few exceptions they are efficient, talented, and sincere.

Provincial party and government leaders are generally of equal caliber, but they are faced by a perplexing dilemma. They are responsible for the livelihood of millions of people. Local requirements frequently conflict with those of the country as a whole. There is constant pressure to first look after those closest to home. How well or badly local leaders do their jobs, how honest and intelligent they are, their ability to think in national terms, determine how quickly or slowly China moves forward.

What then are China's prospects, in view of her many problems? Will she collapse under their weight as did the former Soviet Union and the communist countries of Eastern Europe? Can China really win out?

Historically, in the 2000 years since China came into being as a unified country, she has suffered from some of the worst vicissitudes any nation could experience—famines, floods, droughts, natural calamities, foreign invasions, internal revolts and insurrections. But she survived them all, blessed by the possession of a cultured civilization and a humane philosophy, an absence of the religious mania and bigotry that tore nations apart in the West, and virtual freedom from the racial persecution and strife long plaguing Europe.

Chinese feudalism, when it became outmoded by the developments in the material world, began evolving into a Maoist Marxism suited to China's particular circumstances. Tacking politically and economically between too much to the Left and too much to the Right, and although saturated culturally with remnant feudal influences, it hewed to a generally forward course.

The severest threat to the People's Republic of China from the outside since its inception has always been the United States. America has persistently menaced China with armed might pressing close to the country's borders, surrogate sabotage, embargoes, trade sanctions, and an unrelenting smear campaign. There are some who point to US commercial activity in China as proof of a fundamental change in American attitudes. They claim Ike Eisenhower's statement that Washington's policies are dictated by what he called "the military-industrial complex" is no longer applicable.

Such an approach is unlikely, however, with regard to China. For one thing the People's Republic is much stronger militarily than some banana republic or oil sheikdom. Moreover, not only are US business interests not put at risk in China, they are afforded the rare opportunity to invest in a country with a large low-wage labor force, rich natural resources, a stable government and society, and a huge expanding market. China's inexpensive products are a boon to American merchants and consumers. It would not make sense for America to be hostile to China. This seems to be the opinion of China's political analysts and knowledgeable Americans, as well.

America has indeed toned down its military bluster with regard to China. However, the Chinese are by no means putting all of their eggs in an American basket. The Hate-China crowd is very strong in Washington. Most virulent are not the lily-white religious nuts but the adherents of the "domino theory." A financially successful, politically secure, diplomatically independent socialist Asian country might set a tempting example to other Far Eastern nations where American interests are much larger. Beijing is warily widening her world diplomatic and economic ties, and has entered once again into a closer rapport with Moscow. Increased attention is given to stability and the strengthening of China's military machine.

The USSR was another adversary, starting from the Khrushchov era. Moscow reneged on promised military aid and cooperation, and staged a number of border incidents. With the collapse of the Soviet Union the military problem vanished. Now several of the nations of the disintegrated, formerly mighty country are trading with China and maintaining friendly relations, and Beijing is on good terms with the Russians.

Some friction exists with the Philippines and a few of the Southeast Asian neighbors over claims to various islands, but not of any particular intensity. China's suggestion that disagreements be shelved temporarily and all cooperate to develop the disputed territories has been accepted as sensible and mutually beneficial. Although there is still room for improvement, relations with China's 50-odd ethnic groups are harmonious and getting better. No serious dissatisfaction exists within the remote border regions, including Tibet, despite the attempts of foreign "humanitarians" to stir it up.

Taiwanese wreckers and CIA agents have ceased landing on Chinese soil, at least for now. Occasional visiting provocateurs are picked up, but they are so obvious and clumsy they are simply laughed out of the country.

All in all, China's security is sound. There is no immediate physical danger from the outside. Internally, while inequities sometimes arouse local resentment, it has not been strong enough to result in serious antagonism. Even the Tiananmen demonstrations were not against the government, but against corruption within the accepted establishment.

The country is domestically stable, the Communist Party is supported by the majority of the people. Certainly there is no viable alternative, and no one is suggesting any. Broad structural and operational reforms have begun within the government and within the economy. Enormous engineering projects are under way. Chinese science is quietly making significant contributions. Education is being intensified. There is more democracy and freedom of the press, some new creations in the arts, more exchange of scientific and cultural knowledge, internally and internationally, and a large increase in trade. All of this is highly visible to even the most casual visitor.

Today, an inextricable connection between the material and the ethical is recognized as indispensable by the Chinese Communist Party leadership. The very influential though small political parties and social groupings concur. "Ethical" for China, it seems to me, means a marriage of the most enlightened feudal concepts with Chinese socialist moral values.

In response to an exhortation by Jiang Zemin, Chairman of the Chinese Communist Party, fascinating pillar experiments have begun in a number of places to turn all of China into a land of "spiritual culture."

Take Zhangjiagang, for example. A river port city on the Yangtze, about 80 miles west of Shanghai, it is a large industrial center. While its output has been increasing nearly 30 percent annually, it is virtually pollution free. Its streets, homes and building are spotlessly clean and sanitary. Carefully maintained public flush toilets are numerous, and conveniently located. The city abounds in lawns and trees and flowers. Its sidewalks are paved with red tile.

Every resident carries a little booklet reminding him of strict injunctions against such evils as smoking in public places, gambling, jaywalking, littering, misbehaving. Out of a population of one million there are less than 200 arrests per year for criminal and misdemeanor offenses. Zhangjiagang is governed by a combination of ethical education and specific legal rules. The family is the foundation, social good the primary responsibility.

While elsewhere some skepticism remains, several cities have caught the fire. Shanghai has instituted "three no's" for public conduct, and the city of Kunshan in Jiangsu is boasting it will be even cleaner than Zhangjiagang. The reason for the growing optimism is that Zhangjiagang is proving it is not only possible to combine culture with material gain—it is also very profitable on both counts.

The ability to discover and expand upon the innovations of the masses, the people at the grass roots, has always been one of the great virtues of the Chinese Communist Party, as demonstrated by every major political and economic advance from land reform onward. It seems to me that once again the Party is using this approach to knife through the bugaboo of ethical and cultural sloth. Initial results are excellent, public response is enthusiastic. I am confident that on the basis of the Party's record this difficult and complicated roadblock will be swept away. And that will make all the difference.

The People's Republic of China has entered a vital lap in its race toward socialist goals. At 80, after nearly 50 years in China, I am starting what may very well be the last lap for me. What have I learned, what has my life here meant to me?

First and foremost I feel privileged to have been able to witness and take part in one of the boldest revolutions in world history. Thanks to the vision of a small group of individuals, and the hearty response of hundreds of millions of mostly uneducated, impoverished, modest, hard-working men and women, it was possible not only to put a sick and feeble China back on its feet, but to make it an important force not just in Asia but in the whole world. Whirling along in the storm, I have been alternately moved, shocked, frightened, confused, frustrated, irritated, angered, thrilled, but always exhilarated, convinced that this enormous drive had a conscious goal, and was definitely getting there.

As the years went by, though I never lost my strong streak of Americanism, I felt more and more that China was my country, my home, my family. There is an easy comfortable warmth and kindliness about Chinese society, things I hope will never change. They certainly haven't changed in what people feared would be a new alien atmosphere of a Communist-led society. I have found the Chinese Communists to be communists alright, but they are very Chinese communists, with all of the best qualities of the traditional Chinese.

Admittedly, there are aspects of life here I didn't, and still don't, like—some of the feudal hangovers, as already indicated. On the other hand I admire the Chinese disapproval of the "Me" cult, their scorn of the self-seeking individual who shamelessly boasts and postures.

By the same token, their ideal citizen is one who seeks justice and freedom and democracy strictly within the parameters of what they call "serving the people" and what the West calls "the greatest good to the greatest number." No real difference in concept, but I believe the Chinese come closer to implementing it in practice. In the West it is frequently watered down by personal considerations.

The same goes for standards of decency, proper behavior, human relations. Again, in both societies they are more or less the same. Here too I feel the Chinese are able to maintain them better. It's not that they are born better, or because of something they inherit with their genes. People of all races start life with the same fine potentials. It's the terrible pressure of the rat race in "freely competitive" societies that inhibits the best in people. In a fair and decent environment the human spirit flourishes.

Today, in China, the proper dialectic is being reiterated, the traditional Golden Mean is favored once again, the scramble for prosperity is being counterbalanced by a striving for a civilized, cultured humanity.

The opportunity to participate in this magnificent endeavor and the conviction that its lofty aims can be achieved are what make my life in China so eminently satisfying.

I said this at a testimonial luncheon my office gave me on the occasion of my 80th birthday. It was on December 23, 1995, two days before the celebration of the coming of Jesus, and three days before the anniversary of the birth of Mao. (Obviously, these dates are not listed in order of their importance!) Many of my old Chinese and foreign friends and colleagues were there, and several high officials. A few speakers courteously exaggerated my accomplishments.

I also spoke, in Chinese. I said what little I had achieved, I could not have done without the help and encouragement of those present. "You are all my teachers," I declared, "and I thank you."

I briefly reviewed my years in China, and paid tribute to two close friends who had passed away—Seto Waiman and American doctor Ma Haide, George Hatem.

"The person to whom I am most grateful," I said, "is not here today, because she is in the hospital recovering from an operation. I'm talking of my wife Phoenix."

(She was very ill, suffering from kidney failure and uremia. An abdominal dialysis device had been installed in the hope it would prolong her life for a year or two. We were not sure it would. I was very worried, and went to the hospital every day.)

I told how I had met her when I first arrived in Shanghai in 1947, of the dangerous underground revolutionary work she was doing, of how I became involved, of our attempt to reach the Liberated Areas, of the careers we pursued after the People's Republic was established.

"Phoenix was of enormous help to me in my literary translations, in my writing, and in my international activities," I said. "She deepened my love of the Chinese people and my appreciation of Chinese culture. I am profoundly grateful."

I did not know it, but she was never to come home. She died in the hospital at the age of 83, peacefully, on January 21, 1996.

Among her papers I found the memoir I have been quoting from here and there in my story. It had been written in October 1993, a cheerfully positive summation. She called it *Recollections of Eighty Years—Looking Forward to Our Golden Wedding Anniversary*. It said, in conclusion:

During the past 15 years we have both retired but we continue to write. Sha Boli has done one book after another. His latest is a biography of Ma

Haide. I have scribbled many short essays, and am still working on my *Recollections of Eighty Years*.

Decades of enduring together, relying on each other, have welded us in heart and mind.

We have loved, quarreled. Only today do we seem to know each other, only now do we understand each other's character, temperament, loves, hates, sorrows, joys. Long years of wars, "movements," first one then another, threatened at times to distort our personalities. Today, at last, we seem to have discovered each other's merits and weaknesses.

"I've lived longer in China than I have in America!" Sha Boli says. "I'm more deeply attached to China than to the land where I was born and raised. Every three years, when I visit America on home leave, I come hurrying back before my leave is up. Why is it that I can't bear to be away from China? I don't understand it myself!" he laughs.

We used to lose our tempers easily when we were younger. We've got over that now. We've learned to respect each other's opinions, and not always demand acceptance of our own.

And we seem to have avoided the stubbornness and prejudices of the elderly.

Of course we both suffer the ills of old age—bad hearts, high blood pressure. But medicines control them. They are not serious.

We live in an old house in a small compound. Both of us are fond of flowers. I like roses. He likes all sorts, and potted plants. We each have our favorites. Gardening requires care and hard work. Every spring when the first roses bud we keep going into the garden to admire them. When they blossom, old friends come and share our pleasure.

Our home is in a scenic area in the northern part of the city, near Shisha Lake. We stroll around it mornings and evenings, enjoying its charm as it changes with the four seasons.

How beautiful is Beijing in golden autumn, how beautiful is the golden autumn of our lives!

The winds and rains of the past are over. The hair at our temples is gray. Smiles grace our wrinkled faces.

We treasure our remaining years—our peaceful, happy, quiet, harmonious remaining years! Much was valuable in our past, which has gone so quickly. I don't know how we traversed that bumpy road. Will future generations be able to learn anything from our experience?

To think that we, coming from opposite sides of thousands of miles of the Pacific Ocean, have been able to share a life of 45 years! Five more and it will be our Golden Wedding Anniversary!

I have told only a little of our time together, hoping to reflect a trace in the history of China and the world, and perhaps increase a bit the understanding of our friends of the period in which we lived.

Our lives were far from the idyllic picture Phoenix painted in 1993 during the short period that remained before her death early in 1996. She suffered discomfort and pain as her illness deteriorated. I agonized helplessly watching the approach of the inevitable.

Essentially her summary of our not quite half a century of marriage was accurate and true. I might have put a few of the details differently, but she captured perfectly the complexity of the strong love between us and the turbulence of our times.

It struck me that in all our years of marriage she had never once written about me in any of her articles until this memoir. When she described some of the many things we did together, I was often barely mentioned. I wish I had noticed earlier, and had been able to ask her why. Whatever the reason, she seemed to have opened the floodgates in the memoir. Her love and admiration came pouring out. I was very moved.

Phoenix was more than a wife to me. She was an integral part of China, a continual stream that flowed between China and me, the essence of a people, a culture, a society. It was thanks to her that I was able to adapt and live contentedly in a China which became my China. To love a Phoenix was to love a Dragon. Understanding and loving the Chinese Dragon made me love and appreciate my Chinese Phoenix all the more.

Only now that she is gone are her many diversified accomplishments being fully recognized. In addition to having been a fine essayist, she was an actress on stage and screen, an author, an editor, a play doctor, a supporter of local theater, a film and drama critic, a developer of budding talents, an able administrator. . . .

At a "Remembering Phoenix" meeting, friends and colleagues praised her unswerving devotion to China's cause, her outspoken fury at dishonesty and corruption, her concern for others, her complete disinterest in fame or personal gain.

People abroad who knew her sent faxes and letters commiserating the departure of this "beautiful person" who was so "delightful," "charming," "intelligent," so "warm." I don't know whether they made me feel better, or worse.

Fortunately she left thousands of words in stories and essays in which I can hear her voice, savor her flair, sense her lively mind. I pored over them, seeking consolation—and found that they are finely crafted impressions of people, places and events which together form an intimate mosaic of Chinese history during the

335

past 50 years. Phoenix's poetic prose, besides being beautiful, is highly informative. She will endure as long as people can read.

I was both pleased and saddened to learn that several things she had been looking forward to were coming to fruition, all in 1996. Literature and Art Books, in Shanghai, announced it would produce her latest collection of essays, *Mirages*. A translation of my biography of American doctor George Hatem (called Ma Haide in China), would be published in Chinese. My favorite translations *A Sampler of Chinese Literature From the Ming Dynasty to Mao Zedong* would appear under the aegis of Panda Books, a subsidiary of the Foreign Languages Publication Administration Bureau. And New World Press, another division, decided to publish *My China: The Metamorphosis of a Country and a Man*, the story you are holding in your hands.

Life goes on. In our garden the tulips have pushed through, their pods are turning yellow. Pointy red buds sprout miraculously on the dark gnarled bark at the bases of Phoenix's rose bushes.

And, of course, China goes on, driving courageously along a new uncharted course, beset by twists and turns in an unstable universe.

I have tried in these pages to tell something of what it was like to be a particle in the centrifuge that created one of the most momentous changes in Chinese history. Can my miniscule presence have had even a shade of impact? I would like to think it has. Certainly the influence of the Chinese revolution on China and the world is beyond question. It has brought a better life for the Chinese people, a better chance for peace and prosperity for people in other lands.

I hope, in the time that remains, to continue doing my bit. I consider myself lucky to have the opportunity.

Index

Illustrated Histories from Hippocrene Books

England: An Illustrated History
Henry Weisser
English history is a rich and complex subject that has had a major influence upon the development of the language, laws, institutions, practices and ideas of the United States and many other countries throughout the world. Just how did all of this originate over the centuries in this pleasant, green kingdom? This concise, illustrated volume traces the story from the most distant past to the England of the present day. It highlights the most important political and social developments as well as the greatest cultural achievements. Along the way, it includes brief accounts of the most striking persons and events that have helped to make England's history so rich and colorful. This is a book for students, travelers, or anyone interested in England's vast heritage.
150 pages • 5 x 7 • 50 b/w illustrations • 0-7818-0751-4 • W • $11.95hc • (446)

Ireland: An Illustrated History
Henry Weisser
Erin go bragh! While it is easy to appreciate the natural beauty of Ireland, the Emerald Isle's history is also a rich and complex subject of study. Spanning prehistoric and Celtic Ireland to modern times, this volume examines the people, religion, social changes, and politics that have evolved into the tradition of modern Ireland. Henry Weisser takes the reader on a journey through Ireland's past to show how historic events have left an indelible mark on everything from architecture and economy to the spirit and lifestyle of the Irish people.
166 pages • 5 x 7 • 50 illustrations • 0-7818-0693-3 • W • $11.95hc • (782)

The Celtic World: An Illustrated History
700 B.C. to the Present
Patrick Lavin
From the valleys of Bronze Age Urnfielders to the works of twentieth century Irish-American literary greats Mary Higgins Clark and Seamus Heaney, Patrick Lavin leads the reader on an entertaining and informative journey through 150 captivating pages of Celtic history, culture, and tradition, including 50 illustrations.
191 pages • 5 x 7 • 50 illustrations • 0-7818-0731-X • W • $14.95hc • (582)

Poland in World War II: An Illustrated Military History
Andrew Hempel
Poland's participation in World War II is generally little known in the West and is often reduced to stereotypes advanced by the media: of German planes attacking the civilian population in 1939 and of Polish cavalry charging German tanks. In actuality, it was not an easy victory for the Germans in 1939, and after the conquest of Poland, the Poles continued to fight in their homeland, on all European fronts, and in North Africa (Tobruk). This illustrated history is a concise presentation of the Polish military war effort in World War II, intermingled with factual human interest stories and 50 illustrations and maps.
150 pages • 5 x 7 • 50 b/w illustrations/maps • 0-7818-0758-1 • W • $11.95hc • (541)

Russia: An Illustrated History
Joel Carmichael
Encompassing one-sixth of the earth's land surface—the equivalent of the whole North American continent—Russia is the largest country in the world. Renowned historian Joel Carmichael presents Russia's rich and expansive past—upheaval, reform, social

change, growth—in an easily accessible and concentrated volume. From the Tatar's reign to modern-day Russia, the book spans seven centuries of cultural, social and political events. This is a book to be enjoyed by a diversified audience. From young scholars to those simply interested in Russian history, here is the perfect gift idea, a handy guide for travelers, and a wonderfully concise yet insightful survey of Russian history.
255 pages • 5 x 7 • 50 illustrations • 0-7818-0689-5 • W • $14.95hc • (781)

Israel: An Illustrated History
David C. Gross
Despite its physical size, Israel from earliest times to the present, has always been a major player on the world stage. The birthplace of Judaism, which in turn became the mother religion of Christianity and Islam, Israel holds a very special place in the minds and hearts of hundreds of millions of people, particularly in the western world. This concise, illustrated volume offers the reader an informative, panoramic view of this remarkable land, from biblical days to the twenty-first century. Since its foundation a scant 50 years ago, Israel has emerged as a veritable magnet and spiritual resource for Jews and Gentiles alike. With topics exploring art, literature, sculpture, music, science, politics, religion and more, here is a wonderful gift book for travelers, students, or anyone seeking to expand their knowledge of Israeli history, culture, and heritage.
150 pages • 5 x 7 • 50 b/w illustrations • 0-7818-0756-5 • W • $11.95hc • (24)

Korea: An Illustrated History
David Rees
Koreans call their country Choson, literally "morning freshness" or more familiarly, "The Land of the Morning Calm." Although

its climate has been a peaceful one, the storms weathered by this turbulent, strife-torn country also account for a well-balanced, historical survey of Korea to the present.

Early chapters succinctly depict a rich Korean heritage. In resisting absorption by their powerful neighbor, China, Koreans successfully established their own state and distinctive culture, language and traditions. The latter chapters deal with events after 1945, examining how the communists took control of the northern half of the country occupied by the USSR. The Korean War was a watershed in the country's volatile history, leading to ever-increasing isolation and industrial stagnation in the north, and an economic boom and fiery politics in the south. Illustrations and maps throughout.

150 pages • 5 x 7 • 50 b/w illustrations/maps • 0-7818-0785-9 • W • $11.95hc • (152)

Mexico: An Illustrated History
Michael E. Burke
This handy historical guide traces Mexico from the peasant days of the Olmecs to the late twentieth century. With over 150 pages and 50 illustrations, the reader discovers how events of Mexico's past have left an indelible mark on the politics, economy, culture, spirit, and growth of this country and its people. Tragedies and triumphs, dependency and conquest, social class and power—all are explored in depth, and are the result of the author's own extensive experience in and research of Mexico.

This wonderfully concise, yet extensive and insightful survey of Mexican history is a valuable resource for students, travelers, and anyone interested in the history of this fascinating country.

183 pages • 5 x 7 • 50 illustrations • 0-7818-0690-9 • W • $11.95hc • (585)

Asian Language Dictionaries and Learning Guides from Hippocrene

English-Bengali Dictionary
38,000 entries • 1,354 pages • 5½ x 8½ • $28.95 hardcover
• ISBN 0-7818-0373-X • W except India • (166)

Bengali-English Dictionary
30,000 entries • 1,074 pages • 5½ x 8½ • $28.95 hardcover
• ISBN 0-7818-0372-1 • W except India • (177)

Learn Bengali
160 pages • 5 x 7 • $7.95 paperback • ISBN 0-7818-0224-5
• NA • (190)

Bogutu-English/English-Bogutu Concise Dictionary
4,700 entries • 98 pages • 5½ x 9 • $9.95 paperback
• ISBN 0-7818-0660-7 • W • (747)

**Cambodian-English/English-Cambodian
Standard Dictionary**
15,000 entries • 355 pages • 5½ x 8¼ • $16.95 paperback
• ISBN 0-87052-818-1 • W • (143)

Cantonese Basic Course
416 pages • 5½ x 8½ • $19.95 paperback • ISBN 0-7818-0289-X
• W • (117)

Dictionary of 1,000 Chinese Proverbs
200 pages • 5½ x 8½ • $11.95 paperback • ISBN 0-7818-0682-8
• W • (773)

Chinese Handy Dictionary
2,000 entries • 120 pages • 5 x 7¾ • $8.95 paperback
• ISBN 0-87052-050-4 • USA • (347)

English-Chinese Pinyin Dictionary
10,000 entries • 500 pages • 4 x 6 • $19.95 paperback
• ISBN 0-7818-0427-2 • USA • (509)

Beginner's Chinese
150 pages • 5½ x 8 • $14.95 paperback
• ISBN 0-7818-0566-X • W • (690)

Hindi-English/English-Hindi Standard Dictionary
30,000 entries • 800 pages • 6 x 9 • $37.50 hardcover
• ISBN 0-7818-0387-X • W except India • (280)
30,000 entries • 800 pages • 6 x 9 • $27.50 paperback
• ISBN 0-7818-0470-1 • W except India • (559)

Hindi-English/English-Hindi Practical Dictionary
25,000 entries • 745 pages • 4⅜ x 7 • $19.95 paperback
• ISBN 0-7818-0064-6 • W • (442)

English-Hindi Practical Dictionary
15,000 entries • 399 pages • 4⅜ x 7 • $11.95 paperback
• ISBN 0-87052-978-1 • NA • (362)

Teach Yourself Hindi
207 pages • 4⅜ x 7 • $8.95 paperback
• ISBN 0-87052-831-9 • NA • (170)

Indonesian-English/English-Indonesian Practical Dictionary
17,000 entries • 289 pages • 4¼ x 7 • $11.95 paperback
• ISBN 0-87052-810-6 • NA • (127)

Japanese-English/English-Japanese Concise Dictionary, Romanized
8,000 entries • 235 pages • 4 x 6 • $11.95 paperback
• ISBN 0-7818-0162-1 • W • (474)

Mastering Japanese
368 pages • 5½ x 8½ • $14.95 paperback
• ISBN 0-87052-983 • USA • (523)
2 Cassettes: ISBN 0-87052-983-8 • $12.95 • USA • (524)

Korean-English/English-Korean Practical Dictionary
8,500 entries • 365 pages • 4 x 7¼ • $14.95 paperback
• ISBN 0-87052-092-X • Asia and NA • (399)

Malay-English/English-Malay Standard Dictionary
21,000 entries • 631 pages • 7¼ x 5 • $16.95 paperback
• ISBN 0-7818-0103-6 • NA • (428)

Nepali-English/English-Nepali Concise Dictionary
6,000 entries • 286 pages • 4 x 6 • $8.95 paperback
• ISBN 0-87052-106-3 • W except India and Nepal • (398)

Concise Sanskrit-English Dictionary
18,000 entries • 366 pages • 5 x 7 • $14.95 paperback
• ISBN 0-7818-0203-2 • NA • (605)

English-Telugu Pocket Dictionary
12,000 entries • 386 pages • 5 x 7⅓ • $17.50 hardcover
• ISBN 0-7818-0747-6 • W • (952)

Thai-English/English-Thai Dictionary and Phrasebook
1,800 entries • 200 pages • 3¾ x 7 • $12.95 paperback
• 0-7818-0774-3 • W • (330)

Beginner's Vietnamese
517 pages • 7 x 10 • $19.95 paperback
• ISBN 0-7818-0411-6 • W • (253)

All prices subject to change without prior notice. To purchase Hippocrene Books contact your local bookstore, call (718) 454-2366, or write to: HIPPOCRENE BOOKS, 171 Madison Avenue, New York, NY 10016. Please enclose check or money order, adding $5.00 shipping (UPS) for the first book and $.50 for each additional book.